BAD LIEUTENANTS

BAD LIEUTENANTS

THE KHMER ROUGE, UNITED FRONT, AND CLASS STRUGGLE, 1970–1997

ANDREW MERTHA

CORNELL UNIVERSITY PRESS
Ithaca and London

Thanks to generous funding from Johns Hopkins University, the ebook editions of this book are available as open access volumes through the Cornell Open initiative.

Copyright © 2025 by Andrew Mertha

The text of this book is licensed under a Creative Commons Attribution-NonCommercial-NoDerivatives 4.0 International License: https://creativecommons.org/licenses/by-nc-nd/4.0/.
To use this book, or parts of this book, in any way not covered by the license, please contact Cornell University Press, Sage House, 512 East State Street, Ithaca, New York 14850. Visit our website at cornellpress.cornell.edu.

First published 2025 by Cornell University Press

Librarians: A CIP catalog record for this book is available from the Library of Congress.

ISBN 9781501781001 (hardcover)
ISBN 9781501780998 (paperback)
ISBN 9781501781025 (epub)
ISBN 9781501781018 (pdf)

To Steve Heder, mentor, colleague, friend

Turning and turning in the widening gyre
The falcon cannot hear the falconer;
Things fall apart; the centre cannot hold;
Mere anarchy is loosed upon the world,
The blood-dimmed tide is loosed, and everywhere
The ceremony of innocence is drowned;
The best lack all conviction, while the worst
Are full of passionate intensity.

—William Butler Yeats, "The Second Coming"

Contents

List of Illustrations ix
Preface xi
Abbreviations xv
Chronology xvii
Key Individuals xxi
A Note on Sources xxv

Introduction: Political Cycles: United Front and Class Struggle   1

1. The First United Front: Colonizing the Movement from Within, 1970–1972   27
2. Before and After Year Zero: A World of Class Struggle, 1973–1978   46
3. Dusting Off United Front Doctrine, 1979–1984   79
4. Command and Control in the Shadows and on the Periphery, 1985–1989   104
5. An Unattainable Political Space, 1990–1993   135
6. Back to Basics: Scorched-Earth Class Struggle, 1994–1997   152

Conclusion: "Pure Socialism"   179

Selected Glossary 193
Notes 197
Bibliography 227
Index 241

Illustrations

0.1. Caricature of Khmer Rouge leaders — 10
0.2. Ieng Sary — 13
0.3. Son Sen (left, with glasses) — 17
0.4. *Ta* Mok — 22
1.1. Khmer Rouge leaders in the *maquis*, 1979 — 28
1.2. Field notes from 1970 US incursion into Cambodia — 34
2.1. Administrative map of Democratic Kampuchea from mid-1977 — 68
2.2. Annotations ("1, 2, 3") by Son Sen (aka Khiev) on confession of Long Muy (aka Chuon) — 69
3.1. Khmer Rouge troops carrying supplies inside Cambodia — 81
3.2. Individual united front members' publications — 95
3.3. Layout of Pol Pot's headquarters 87/870, 1990 — 100
4.1. Khmer Rouge soldier with hill tribesman and his family — 107
4.2. Troop movements, 1985–1988 — 108
4.3. Khmer Rouge troops inside Cambodia, 1983 — 109
4.4. Female Khmer Rouge porters inside Cambodia, 1983 — 111
4.5. Principal NADK military corridors, 1985–1993 — 113
4.6. Khmer Rouge soldiers interacting with villager inside Cambodia, 1983 — 114
4.7. Consolidation of refugee camps by coalition partner — 120
4.8. Khmer Rouge cadre lining up recruits, Phnom Malai, 1979 — 127
5.1. "What Is the Virtue, the Quality, the Reality, and the Responsibility of Democratic Kampuchea in the Past, Present, and Future?" 1986 — 138
5.2. NADK order of battle, early 1990s — 142
6.1. "Draft Plan," 1994 — 155
6.2. Khmer Rouge banknotes, ca. 1993 — 158
6.3. Pol Pot's bunker, Kbal Tonsaong — 169
6.4. Final resting places of *Ta* Mok and Pol Pot — 177
7.1. Khmer Rouge leaders meet with Mao Zedong, June 1975 — 182

Preface

This book has a somewhat rambling origin story. I was visiting the Chinese revolutionary site of Yan'an, engaging in a bit of Red tourism in the fall of 2016, when, billeted in a cadre convention hotel, I decided that what would eventually become this book (at that point a study of the command and control/bureaucracy of the post-1979 Khmer Rouge) would best be abandoned. Data were difficult to come by, and I found myself, by this time, increasingly uninspired by my work on the project.

I rounded out that trip with a few days in Cambodia following a forty-eight-hour layover in Hong Kong. After spending the day hiking the trails on Hong Kong Island, I had dinner with the irrepressible Stéphanie Giry, who suggested that before ditching the project altogether, I reach out to Steve Heder once I got to Cambodia. Although I had had some previous contact with Steve—he had generously brokered a consultancy at the Extraordinary Chambers in the Courts of Cambodia some five years prior—I countered that he was extremely busy, but also (something I knew from direct experience) that he did not suffer fools gladly. And I didn't want to present him with what was at best a half-baked research agenda. Stéphanie, however, can be extremely persuasive, and I agreed to email Steve.

A few days later, I was on the Thai-Cambodian border in and around Anlong Veng, trying to reconstruct the command and control order of battle during the 1980s with ex-Khmer Rouge soldiers. That night I contacted Steve and told him about the project. The next morning, I awoke to an email attachment—precisely the order of battle I was trying to reconstruct, which would have taken me years at the rate I was going. He suggested we meet, so I flew down to Phnom Penh. Over coffee, he told me that as he was retiring, he had "three or four more books in" him, but if I was going to write this one, that would save him from having to do so himself. But, he said, I would have to do it *right*. To help me accomplish this, he offered access to his by then mythical private archives, suggesting that I visit him in London that December. I did, and we began the arduous task of going through tens of thousands of materials in a Hackney storage space, transporting them to the London School of Oriental and African Studies, where I spent three vending-machine-food-fueled days of up to fourteen hours scanning/digitalizing as much as I could physically carry. (I followed up with subsequent trips in April 2017, December 2017—exhuming some 1980s-era original Khieu Samphân documents—and December 2022, digitalizing photos Steve had taken along the Thai-Cambodian border in 1979–80.)

Even with such an auspicious first step, it took a lot longer than I had ever thought it would to finally come up with this book. During those intervening seven or so years—extended because of a move from Cornell to Johns Hopkins/SAIS (School of Advanced International Studies) and by a stint as vice dean at the latter—I was aided by the kindness of scores of people. David Ashley, Elizabeth Becker, Cole DeVoy, Michael Eiland, Carla Freeman, Sos Kem, David McCracken, Maria Repnikova, and John Yasuda read early drafts and gave extraordinarily helpful comments. Elizabeth and Sos in particular took a great deal of time out of their schedules, and I remain deeply indebted to them. Denny Lane enthusiastically provided key materials and the initial motivation for this project. Ambassador Kenneth Quinn generously recounted his time along the Vietnamese-Cambodian border. Neil Loughlin, a fellow recipient of Steve's largesse, helped manage the reams of material we had to work through. Peter Bartu graciously shared his first-person interactions with Son Sen. My good friend the late ambassador Benny Widyono spent hours with me recounting his time in Cambodia in the UNTAC (United Nations Transitional Authority in Cambodia) period and thereafter.

There are many individuals whose dedication and hard work resulted in the documentary sources without which this project could not have succeeded. Although my interactions with the authors of these materials are, unfortunately, only at best indirect—through the texts themselves—I owe them an enormous debt of gratitude.

I was ably assisted by a number of Khmer-language journalists at Radio Free Asia, Vanrith Chrea, Boramey Phal, and Seila Polham. My in-country research assistants—Keo Duong, Kuong Keany, Jocelyn Vega, and the tireless Chanta Lach—were integral to the project. Kunthea Chhom and Hannah Phan graciously proofread the Khmer text. My research assistants at Cornell and at SAIS—Wendy Leutert, Deboleena

Rakshit, Jeb Benkowski, Zoe Liu, Hasta Colman, and Zhuoran ("Z") Li—were of the highest caliber. The Center for Khmer Studies (CKS) research library in Siem Reap was another helpful resource. Colin Grafton and Keiko Kitamura somehow managed to continue working with me despite all the best attempts of the SAIS bureaucracy. It is thanks to them and Rithy Panh's Bophana Center that I am able to include the astonishing photographs by Naoki Mabuchi. Gamze Zeytinci and Mark Bailey allowed me to roll over research funds, making it possible to underwrite a not insubstantial amount of the research, subvention, and other costs associated with the project.

I also thank Lucy Rhymer and two anonymous reviewers at Cambridge University Press. Their reviews were extremely thoughtful and encouraging, but they would have pushed me in the direction of a book I didn't really want to write. Lucy graciously allowed me to take the manuscript to Cornell University Press, where I have been beyond delighted to work with the extraordinary Jacqulyn Teoh as editor par excellence.

My immediate family—Isabelle and Sophie—made working at home a pleasure and gave me the time and space necessary to work on this book on every chair, chaise, couch, stoop, and hammock between Washington, DC, and Ithaca, New York.

All of which brings me back to that initial reconnection with Steve Heder. More than anything else—the archival materials, insights, introductions, reading of unpolished drafts—Steve gave me back something that I had somehow lost along the way: a genuine love for the magic of scholarship. This includes the chance opportunities and dumb luck, the physical strain, and the shoe leather interviewing. Most of all, however, it is the art of sitting back and privileging the *thinking* process. Although I am not religious, I can appreciate the power that Christians call "the mystery of faith" as a deep, driving force. Steve reacquainted me with the equally compelling and seductive "mystery of scholarship." That is a gift for which my dedication of this book to him is, comparatively speaking, a modest token of gratitude.

Despite all the guidance, advice, and support of these individuals and others, the inevitable errors that remain are mine.

Abbreviations

AEK/KSA:	Khmer Students' Association
ANKI (កងទ័ពជាតិដើម្បីខ្មែរឯករាជ្យ):	Armées Nationale pour Khmer Indépendant (the successor of the ANS), military wing of FUNCINPEC
ANS (កងទ័ពជាតិសីហនុនិយម):	Armée Nationale Sihanoukiste
CGDK (រដ្ឋាភិបាលចម្រុះកម្ពុជាប្រជាធិបតេយ្យ):	Coalition Government of Democratic Kampuchea
CPAF (កងកម្លាំងប្រដាប់អាវុធប្រជាជនបដិវត្តន៍កម្ពុជា/ កងកម្លាំងប្រដាប់អាវុធប្រជាជនបដិវត្តន៍ខ្មែរ):	Cambodian People's Armed Forces (under the PRK)
CPK (បក្សកុម្មុយនីស្តកម្ពុជា):	Communist Party of Kampuchea (formal title of the Khmer Rouge)
CPP (គណបក្សប្រជាជនកម្ពុជា):	Cambodian People's Party
DK (កម្ពុជាប្រជាធិបតេយ្យ):	Democratic Kampuchea
DNUM (ចលនាសហភាពជាតិប្រជាធិបតេយ្យ):	Democratic National Union Movement (founded by Ieng Sary)
ECCC:	the Extraordinary Chambers in the Courts of Cambodia
FANK (កងយោធពលខេមរជាតិ):	Forces Armées Nationales Khmères, the Khmer Republic military, 1970–1975
FUNCINPEC (រណសិរ្សរួបរួមជាតិដើម្បីកម្ពុជាឯករាជ្យ អព្យាក្រឹតសន្តិភាព និងសហប្រតិបត្តិការ):	the post-1979 Royalist party, Front Uni National pour un Cambodge Indépendant, Neutre, Pacifique et Coopératif
FUNK (រណសិរ្សរួបរួមជាតិកម្ពុជា):	Front Uni National du Kampuchéa or Front Uni National Khmer, the military wing of GRUNK
GRUNK (រាជរដ្ឋាភិបាលរួបរួមជាតិកម្ពុជា):	Gouvernement Royal d'Union Nationale du Kampuchéa, the first united front government, formed May 1970
ICP:	Indochinese Communist Party (precursor of the CPK)

ABBREVIATIONS

KPNLF (រណសិរ្សរំដោះជាតិប្រជាជនខ្មែរ):	Khmer People's National Liberation Front, post-1979 PDK united front partner
MOULINAKA (ម៉ូលីណាកា):	Movement for the National Liberation of Kampuchea (Mouvement pour la Libération Nationale du Kampuchéa)
NADK (កងទ័ពជាតិកម្ពុជាប្រជាធិបតេយ្យ):	National Army of Democratic Kampuchea, successor of the Revolutionary Army of Democratic Kampuchea; formed 1979; disbanded late 1990s
NCR:	non-communist resistance
PAVN:	People's Army of Vietnam
PDK (គណបក្សកម្ពុជាប្រជាធិបតេយ្យ):	Party of Democratic Kampuchea (electoral arm of the Communist Party of Kampuchea)
PRK (សាធារណរដ្ឋប្រជាមានិតកម្ពុជា):	People's Republic of Kampuchea
RAK (កងទ័ពរំដោះកម្ពុជា):	Revolutionary Army of Kampuchea (armed forces of Democratic Kampuchea, 1977–1979)
RGC (រាជរដ្ឋាភិបាលកម្ពុជា):	Royal Government of Cambodia
RTA:	Royal Thai Army
SoC (រដ្ឋកម្ពុជា):	State of Cambodia
UNBRO:	the United Nations Border Relief Operation
UNHCR:	the United Nations High Commission for Refugees
UNTAC:	the United Nations Transitional Authority in Cambodia
VWP:	Vietnamese Workers' Party

Chronology

1949–1957: Pol Pot, Ieng Sary, and Son Sen pursue studies in Paris and establish the Cercle Marxiste there; they return to Cambodia in the latter half of the 1950s and join the Kampuchean People's Revolutionary Party.

1950: *Ta* Mok joins the Indochinese Communist Party, operating in his home province of Takeo.

1953: Cambodia secures its independence from the French. Norodom Sihanouk returns from France to lead the Kingdom of Cambodia.

1954: Geneva Accords end hostilities in Indochina.

1955: Sihanouk abdicates in favor of his father to take a more active role in politics and founds his political party, the Sangkum Reastr Niyum.

1963–1964: Pol Pot assumes leadership of the Workers' Party of Kampuchea (formerly Kampuchean People's Revolutionary Party); Sihanouk's regime cracks down on leftists; Pol Pot, Ieng Sary, Son Sen, and others escape to the *maquis*.

1965: Pol Pot visits China.

1967: Samlaut Rebellion occurs in Battambang province. CPK movement gains initial momentum.

1970: Sihanouk ousted from power in March; Lon Nol assumes leadership of the new Khmer Republic. United front organizations GRUNK and FUNK established with Sihanouk as titular head. Most of the Cambodian countryside comes under GRUNK control by the end of the year.

CHRONOLOGY

1971–1975: Workers' Party of Kampuchea renamed the Communist Party of Kampuchea (CPK). Ieng Sary in Beijing as representative of the CPK in China. Son Sen becomes chief of staff of the CPK and takes command of the Central Military. *Ta* Mok solidifies control as Southwest Zone secretary.

1973–1975: Launch of first class struggle by the CPK, including purges of Vietnamese and Khmer Hanoi from GRUNK, occurs in the countryside. Consolidation of CPK control over GRUNK, sidelining of Royalist elements, full-scale agricultural collectivization.

1975: "Liberation" of Phnom Penh and other cities by the CPK; forced exodus of urban residents to the countryside. Pol Pot and Ieng Sary meet Mao Zedong.

1976–1978: CPK establishes Democratic Kampuchea; intra-CPK purges intensify. Ieng Sary sets up Foreign Ministry, assumes role of foreign minister. Son Sen assumes oversight of Ministry of Defense and nationwide prison network, notably Tuol Sleng (S21). *Ta* Mok's control over the Southwest is entrenched and extended to other zones. All three politically vulnerable.

1979: Vietnamese invasion and collapse of Democratic Kampuchea. Hanoi-backed People's Republic of Kampuchea (PRK) established; renamed the State of Cambodia (SoC) in April 1989. US recognition of the People's Republic of China at Hanoi's expense. Chinese invasion of Vietnam. Soviet invasion of Afghanistan further isolates Moscow and by extension Hanoi. Sary, Son Sen, and Mok scatter into the Cambodian countryside.

1979–1980: Refugee crisis along the Thai-Cambodian border.

1981: Establishment of FUNCINPEC Site B refugee camp.

1982: Establishment of the second united front between CPK (now PDK), KPNLF, and FUNCINPEC.

1984: Ieng Sary begins to lose power within the PDK elite.

1985:	Vietnamese dry season offensive and rollout of K5 plan. Hun Sen elected prime minister of the Hanoi-backed People's Republic of Kampuchea. Establishment of Potemkin village–style camp run by Ieng Sary at Site 8.
1985–1986:	Creation/consolidation of KPNLF Site 2 refugee camp.
1986:	Issuance of document "What Is the Virtue, the Quality, the Reality, and the Responsibility of Democratic Kampuchea in the Past, Present, and Future?" signaling an end to the second united front. Reduction in Soviet aid to Vietnam while Hanoi seeks a way to disentangle forces from Cambodia.
1989:	Withdrawal of Vietnamese troops from Cambodia.
1991:	Paris Peace Agreement signed. Mok put in charge of Corridors 1001 and 1003 (combined into Corridor 1008). Khieu Samphân attacked and forced to leave Phnom Penh—along with Son Sen. The latter begins to slowly lose influence as prospects for PDK victory at the ballot box diminish.
1993:	UNTAC elections in Cambodia, boycotted by the PDK. Victory by Royalist FUNCINPEC, but Hun Sen made co–prime minister along with first prime minister Norodom Ranariddh. Rise of the hard-line faction within PDK, led by Mok.
1994:	Issuance of "draft plan" for the future of the PDK, leading to return of scorched-earth policy and launch of second class struggle, which largely benefits Mok. Son Sen takes over control of Division/Front 450 but fails to consolidate his position.
1996:	Hun Sen and Ranariddh mount competitive campaigns to encourage PDK troops to defect. Defection of Ieng Sary.
1997:	Pol Pot orders the execution of Son Sen, Mok, and Nuon Chea. Son Sen killed. Pol Pot arrested and tried in Anlong Veng by Mok.

1998:	Death of Pol Pot under Khmer Rouge imprisonment.
1999:	Arrest of Mok.
2006:	Death of Mok while awaiting trial.
2007:	Arrest of Ieng Sary, Ieng Thirith, and Nuon Chea by ECCC authorities.
2010:	Ieng Sary indicted by ECCC.
2013:	Death of Ieng Sary while in ECCC custody.

Key Individuals

The CPK/PDK was a clandestine organization during its rise to power, for reasons made clear in the pages to follow. The movement did not shed this approach to governance and communication even after 1975. As a result, there is a dizzying array of code numbers, *noms de guerre*, and function-specific aliases that were established during wartime and carried over into civilian governance. Some are far better known by their aliases (Pol Pot) than by their birth names (Saloth Sâr). I have tried to err on the side of completism (even though what I have listed here remains frustratingly *in*complete). For example, as shown in the list that follows, Son Sen (សុន សេន) was known as "Brother 89" (បងៃ៨៩), "Khiev" (ខៀវ), "Khim" (ឃឹម, used as his signature for *laissez-passers*), "47" (៤៧, when referred to as chief of staff), "Brother 62" (បង៦២, when conducting S21 business), and so on.

There is no standard romanization for the Khmer language. Vorn Vet can be written Vorn Veth or Von Vet; So Phim has been written as Sao Phim or Sao Pheum. I have sought to privilege common forms of romanization as well as consistency in the text.

Chan (ចាន់), born Mam Nay (ម៉មណៃ): Deputy to Duch at S21/Tuol Sleng, distinguished by his extreme cruelty.

Duch (ឌុច), born Kaing Guek-Eav (កាំង ហ្គេកអ៊ាវ): Commandant of S21/Tuol Sleng directly under Son Sen.

Hou Youn/Hou Yuon (ហ៊ូ យន់): CPK leader whose views often conflicted with the vision of his more radical colleagues during the civil war, when he was minister of the interior with authority over communal reforms and cooperatives, over collectivization, and in 1975 over the abolition of currency. Executed 1975.

Hu Nim (ហ៊ូ នឹម), aka Phoas (ភាស់): GRUNK minister of information and Democratic Kampuchea minister of propaganda, succeeded in that post by Yun Yat. Executed 1977.

KEY INDIVIDUALS

Hun Sen (ហ៊ុន សែន): Ex–Khmer Rouge regimental commander of Region (តំបន់) 21 in the Eastern Zone, defected to Vietnam in June 1977; foreign minister, chairman of the Council of Ministers, and prime minister under the Hanoi-backed People's Republic of Kampuchea; prime minister from 1993 (co–prime minister 1993–1997) until 2023.

Ieng Sary (អៀង សារី), born Kim Trang, aka Van (វ៉ាន់), aka Nên (នែន, after the Vietnamese invasion as he was leading Chinese diplomats to safety): Democratic Kampuchea foreign minister and chief international envoy for the CPK/PDK. Defected 1996; arrested 2007. Died 2013.

Ieng Thirith (អៀង ធីរិទ្ធ), born Khieu (ខៀវ) Thirith, aka Pheaa (ភា): Wife of Ieng Sary; former Democratic Kampuchea minister of social affairs. Died 2015.

Kè Pauk/Kè Pork (កែ ពក), born Kè Vin (កែ វិន), aka Brother Number 13: "At-large" zone commander during Democratic Kampuchea period (acting secretary of the Northern Zone after purge of Koy Thuon) and mobilized (with *Ta* Mok) to cleanse the Eastern Zone in 1977. Sidelined in 1986 after coming under suspicion of border smuggling. Defected 1998. Died 2002.

Khieu Samphân (ខៀវ សំផន), aka Hæm (ហែម): Loyal and long-serving "service intellectual" for, and outward (moderate) face of, the Khmer Rouge leadership, holding several key formal positions throughout the history of the movement, but with no independent power base.

Koy Thuon (កុយ ធន), aka Thuch (ធុច): Northern Zone secretary from 1970 until 1976; reassigned as Democratic Kampuchea minister of commerce (succeeded by Vorn Vet). Executed 1977.

Meas Muth/Meas Mut (មាស មុត), aka Khe Muth (ខេមុត): Commander of the Democratic Kampuchea navy and CPK chair of Kampong Som; son-in-law of *Ta* Mok.

Ney Saran (ណៃ សារ៉ន់), aka Ya (យ៉ា): Northeast Zone secretary. Executed 1976.

Nhim Ros/Nhem Ros (ញឹម រស់), aka Muol Sàmbăt (មូល សម្បត្តិ): Northwest Zone commander during Democratic Kampuchea who disagreed with Pol Pot over agriculture policy. Executed 1978.

Norn Suon/Nuon Suon (នន់ សួន): Southwest Sector 25 secretary and later tasked with finance and setting up a Ministry of Agriculture in 1975; his S21 confession implicated and anticipated the future political exposure of Ieng Sary, Son Sen, and *Ta* Mok. Executed 1976.

Norodom Ranariddh (នរោត្តម រណឫទ្ធិ): Son of Norodom Sihanouk, party leader of FUNCINPEC and winner of the 1993 UNTAC elections. Died 2021.

Norodom Sihanouk (នរោត្តម សីហនុ): King and prince of Cambodia; titular head of FUNK; father of Ranariddh. Died 2012.

Nuon Chea (នួន ជា), aka Brother Number 2: Second-in-command of CPK/PDK. Died 2019.

Ny Kân/Ni Kan/Ni Korn (នី កន), born Son Nhan: Youngest brother of Son Sen. Longtime aide to Ieng Sary; key military commander during the last years of NADK unraveling whose defection likely increased Pol Pot's suspicion of Son Sen.

Pol Pot (ប៉ុល ពត), born Saloth Sâr (សាឡុត ស), aka *Om* 87 (អ៊ំ ៨៧), aka 870 (៨៧០), aka Brother Number 1 (បងទីមួយ), aka 101: Leader of the CPK/PDK from 1962 to 1997. Died 1998.

So Phim/Sao Pheum/Sao Phim (សោ ភឹម), born So Vanna (ស៊ូ វណ្ណា), aka Sao Yan, aka Phim (ភឹម): Eastern Zone commander. Accused by Pol Pot of being a Vietnamese spy in 1978, he committed suicide to avoid torture and execution.

So Saroeun (ស៊ូ សារឿន): NADK general and part of the "next generation leadership," who directed the execution of Son Sen in 1997.

Sok Pheap (សុខ ភាព): Commander of NADK Division 450. Refused to take part in the post-1994 PDK scorched-earth policies and was instrumental in negotiating his and Ieng Sary's defection in 1996.

Son Sann (សឺន សាន): KPNLF leader instrumental in forming the second united front in 1982. Not to be confused with Son Sen.

Son Sen (សុន សេន), aka Khiev (ខៀវ), aka Khim (ឃឹម, used as his signature for *laissez-passers*), aka Brother 89 (បង៨៩), aka 47 (៤៧, when referred to as chief of staff), aka Brother 62 (បង៦២, when conducting S21 business): Minister of defense and chief of internal security during the Democratic Kampuchea period; subsequently commander of Corridor 1001. Executed 1997.

Ta **Mok** (តា ម៉ុក), born Chhit Choeun (ឈិត ជឿន), aka *Ta* 15 (តា ១៥): Former Khmer Issarak, commander of the Democratic Kampuchea Southwest Zone and Corridors 1003 and 1008. Surrendered 1999. Died 2006.

Vorn Vet/Von Veth (វន វេត), born Sok Thuok (សុក ធួក), aka Von (វន), aka Vet/Veth (វេត), aka Sok (សុក): Former Southwest Zone commander; subsequently Democratic Kampuchea minister of commerce. Executed 1978.

Y Chhean (អ៊ី ឈាន): Longtime associate of Ieng Sary. Commander of NADK Division 415. Along with Sok Pheap, refused to take part in the post-1994 PDK scorched-earth policies and was instrumental in negotiating his and Ieng Sary's defection in 1996.

Yun Yat (យុន យ៉ាត់), aka At (អាត់): Wife of Son Sen; former Democratic Kampuchea minister of propaganda. Executed 1997.

A Note on Sources

This book draws from a wide range of source materials. Perhaps the most important of these come from the private archives of Steve Heder. The documents made available to me were mostly from the UNTAC period and contained both official and unofficial communications and analyses, but also a robust set of interviews with refugees on the Thai-Cambodian border conducted by UNTAC officials and other adjacent Cambodia hands from 1979 to the early 1980s. Scattered among these were other interviews, news reports, glossy magazines, force structure designations, inspired musings, and other materials that Steve had collected over several decades as a Cambodia watcher.

Another set of materials came from Colonel Dennison "Denny" Lane, whose enviably colorful career included monitoring the Khmer Rouge camps in the early 1980s and then again at the end of the decade. His notes are extensive, descriptive, and analytical, and written in the rich voice of the increasingly rare "soldier-scholar." I include them with the reference the Cambodia Border File.

I also drew from some two dozen field interviews that go back as far as 2009, when I first started conducting research in Cambodia. A few are interviews that informed an earlier book, *Brothers in Arms*, but most of them date from after that book was published. Over the years—really beginning around 2014—hitherto open and engaging interviewees began holding back, eventually self-censoring because (they told me) of prior de-anonymization by (mostly) journalists who had guaranteed confidentiality, as well as changes in the overall political climate. In some cases I relied on research assistants to conduct these interviews, and during the 2020 summer of COVID, Chantha Lach not only interviewed but also provided sound and visual documentation that proved to be extremely helpful. Other Cambodia watchers, many of them in Washington, DC, where I am now based, also provided important recollections, observations, and additional materials.

A NOTE ON SOURCES

As in previous work, I anonymize the interviewees unless they already appear in the title of the transcripts and have been published elsewhere.

Files from the Extraordinary Chambers in the Courts of Cambodia, where I served as consultant in 2010-11, were extremely helpful in fleshing out the details of the Democratic Kampuchea period as well as the 1970-1975 civil war era, offering first-person accounts, observations, and vignettes that, I hope, give the figures somewhat of a three-dimensional character.

I include noncommercial photographs by myself, Steve Heder, and Naoki Mabuchi (courtesy of Colin Grafton and Keiko Kitamura). The Mabuchi photos were taken behind enemy lines in 1983, when he—somehow—was allowed to follow alongside NADK troops. I have relied on all these photos to give a sense of what the refugee camps and Khmer Rouge activity in Cambodia during the 1980s looked and felt like. Some are published here for the first time.

Introduction
Political Cycles: United Front and Class Struggle

> We are not about to share power with anyone....
> If we are to stop halfway, then it wouldn't be a
> revolution, it would be an abortion.
>
> —Leon Trotsky, *Sochineniia*

On April 17, 1975, just after the Cambodian New Year, black-clad soldiers of the Communist Party of Kampuchea (CPK), commonly referred to as the Khmer Rouge, entered Phnom Penh, "liberating" the Cambodian capital after five years of civil war. Within a matter of hours, they began emptying entire city blocks of their residents, forcing them into the countryside with little more than the clothes on their backs. This was part of a deliberate effort to destroy class distinctions, one that became punctuated by bursts of unimaginable violence and was sustained by a cruel cold-bloodedness. For this was a revolution that, as Cambodia's new leaders boasted, would far surpass all those that had come before: the Russian, the Chinese, the French. From the very first hours of its existence, the new state, eventually known as Democratic Kampuchea, pitilessly eradicated all societal class distinctions, eliminated all private property, ended all means of capitalistic exchange, including money, and expunged, with laser-like focus, all remaining enemies of the regime, real or imagined—and all in the name of a hitherto unseen form of radical Marxism. This was Year Zero (ឆ្នាំសូន្យ).

Not surprisingly to anyone but the Khmer Rouge elite, this literalistic embrace of Marxist tenets was unsustainable folly. It was thus perhaps inevitable that three years, eight months, and twenty days later, on January 7, 1979, Phnom Penh was liberated again, this time by the

Vietnamese. By the next day, the leader of the Khmer Rouge, Pol Pot, had retreated by helicopter to the provincial city of Battambang, where he met with his foreign minister and brother-in-law by marriage, Ieng Sary. Sary had arrived by train earlier, escaping just hours before Vietnamese troops entered the capital.[1] He immediately proposed that to fight a guerrilla counterinsurgency against the Vietnamese, it would be necessary to issue guns to the people. Pol Pot ridiculed him: even if they had possessed adequate weapons stocks, distributing them was riskier than not doing so. As Ieng Sary recalled, Pol Pot pointedly said, "Hand them out and see if they don't shoot you in the head, comrade."[2] Pol Pot may have been responsible for mass murder on a grand scale, but he wasn't stupid. He had an inkling of how unpopular the Khmer Rouge had become after nearly four years of mass executions, starvation, disease, and misrule, during which an estimated quarter of the Cambodian population had perished.

This is why what happened next is so baffling. Following one of the bloodiest political experiments in modern history under a leadership described by David Ashley as "not only astoundingly ruthless but also fractious, unrealistic and strikingly incompetent,"[3] the Khmer Rouge rebounded after 1979 to rule over vast swaths of Cambodian territory for another *two decades*—more than *five times* as long as it had officially ruled Cambodia as Democratic Kampuchea. Throughout this time, it enjoyed a significant measure of public support against its adversaries in the countryside, pockets of which continue to the present day. What accounts for this durability, particularly given that Khmer Rouge crimes against humanity had been directly or indirectly experienced by most Cambodians who were alive in 1979 and had become a matter of public record?

The dominant narrative of the Khmer Rouge describes how it rose to power in the early 1970s, ruled the country with millions perishing under its watch, and fell from power when its members fled to the hills in the face of the invading Vietnamese army in 1979. The story of what happened afterwards is often an afterthought, a postscript, or remains starkly incomplete.[4] If one were to stop here, as most people do, the only noteworthy conclusion to draw from the ludicrously unsuccessful Democratic Kampuchea regime was the number of people it killed or otherwise brutalized. And it would tell us nothing about the "second life" of the CPK. Getting a handle on the puzzling longevity of the movement thus requires a loosening of the timeframes to which it is typically tethered.

As it turns out, Sary's suggestion to remobilize was not completely off base, only slightly premature. Within a few years, he would reestablish the outward face of the CPK as the legitimate rulers of Cambodia from his well-appointed compound along the Thai-Cambodian border. Other fleeing Khmer Rouge leaders like Son Sen, who mysteriously disappeared into the forests for almost two years following his escape from Vietnamese-occupied Phnom Penh, would emerge, reborn, to lead a new insurgency embedded throughout the Cambodian countryside. Still others, like *Ta* Mok, would retreat to their territorial power bases to restart the struggle that they had been waging for more than a generation. They were able to do so because—surprisingly—their new strategy amounted to almost exactly what they had done a decade before, both in terms of their rise to power and, ultimately, in their approach to governance.

But what *had* they done previously?

A barroom quip from a respected colleague provides a starting point. In conversations with myself and others, David Chandler, doyen of Cambodia studies, has maintained that the Khmer Rouge were capable of doing exactly—and *only*—two things: participating in *united front* and engaging in *class struggle*. "United front" can be defined here as the mobilization of the maximum number of possible allies, interested parties, and fellow travelers in pursuit of the overthrow of a common enemy with the ultimate goal of fully dominating this political coalition. "Class struggle" refers to the notion that the class-based capitalist system of production is unfixable and thus it, and any of its adherents, can *only*—indeed, *must*—be destroyed.

In this book I present these two distinct practices as akin to scope conditions, the universe of possible Khmer Rouge approaches to securing and maintaining power. They function both as an empirical description of the movement leaders' mindsets and as an explanatory framework. To fully appreciate this binary approach, however, we cannot simply focus on the 1975–1979 and the post-1979 eras as distinct and separate from each other, as the literature does. Rather, we need to extend the study of the Khmer Rouge to encompass this entire period—from the first united front established in 1970 to the final gasp of the second class struggle in 1997—and within this singular framework so as to better analyze both the weaknesses and the durability of the Khmer Rouge. In doing so, we can acknowledge what is possibly the one genuine, albeit dubious, conceptual innovation bequeathed to us by the CPK: Pol Pot and his movement were able to transform a linear relationship between the Marxist concepts of united front and class struggle into a *cyclical* one.

Seen in this light, the twin "liberations" of Phnom Penh take on a very different significance. In most accounts, April 17, 1975, signals the start of a new regime, defined by violent class struggle. But in fact it was a *continuation* of class struggle that had been going on in the countryside since 1973. January 7, 1979, in the framework I propose, signals not a new era but a pivot to the past, a shift away from class struggle and back to the rubric of united front.

If this seems a bit bewildering, it is for good reason. The fact that, by 1982, the Khmer Rouge returned to its 1970–1972 united front policy, allying with some of the very same actors it had collaborated with prior to the Democratic Kampuchea period in order to now expel Vietnamese forces from Cambodia, is in fact remarkably counterintuitive. That is because, while the path to power in which a united front morphs into class struggle makes an innate sort of sense and is replete with historical examples, the reverse—that is, the reestablishment of a united front after an extended period of class struggle, particularly of the eliminationist variant carried out by the Khmer Rouge—is distinctly *not*. As Ashley, to quote him again, puts it, "The trouble with 'united front' tactics, which involve deceptively disguising the real goals of a revolution in order to gain the short-term support of long-term enemies, is that they can only really be used once."[5] The Khmer Rouge did it *twice*.

The Duality of United Front and Class Struggle

As history shows, the CPK was singularly unable to move from an insurgency to a successful governing organization, both in the mid-1970s and again in the early 1990s. The movement's own comfort zone was the foxhole, not the statehouse. This was because the CPK was adept at organizing and mobilizing itself alongside (or, more accurately, at the expense of) its united front allies. But it was far less so at parlaying or consolidating its gains once these allies were no longer necessary, useful, or desirable. Any agency suggesting otherwise that was exhibited by CPK elites, with the possible exception of Pol Pot himself, was constrained and shaped by the ideological imperatives and real-world consequences of this relationship between united front and class struggle.

This delimitation to either united front or class struggle was due to two mutually reinforcing strands in the political DNA of the Khmer Rouge movement which were themselves a product of an unsophisticated, literalist understanding of Marxist politics that sucked any of the complicating "gray area" out of the room. The first was an acknowledgment as accepted fact among its top leaders that they would surpass (and evade the shortcomings of) other countries' experiments in Marxist rule by studiously avoiding any dilution of, or deviation from, the radical leftist political line held by its leaders. The second was a conviction that they were surrounded by hostile forces who sought not just to dilute the line but, by doing so, bring down the movement. It was a conviction reinforced by policy failures that, given this rigid orthodoxy, could only to their minds be explained by treasonous enemies not yet eliminated. Former allies had not simply outlived their usefulness; they threatened the purity and thus the continuation of the movement. In such a way, the universe of political imperatives for the Khmer Rouge was defined by the duality of united front and class struggle.

United Front

The term "united front" was articulated in December 1921 by the Communist International ("Comintern") Executive Committee as a call for the "greatest possible unity of all workers' organizations in every practical action against the united capitalists," while assuring revolutionary socialists and other participating currents "absolute autonomy" and "freedom in presenting their point of view."[6] Although its casual usage describes any form of joint action between revolutionaries and non-revolutionaries, the goal is to bring the latter into the revolutionary camp or eliminate them from positions of power if they refuse (and hold them in suspicion regardless). The notion of the united front was conceived as a practical response to the downturn in mobilization and recruitment in the wake of the Russian Revolution when, ironically, socialist revolutionary organizations were flanked by other movements (compromise-inclined reformists as well as those who vacillated between reformers and revolutionaries, even those in favor of maintaining aspects of the status quo) vying for popular support and, with it, political power. As Leon Trotsky put it: "If we were able simply to unite the working masses around our own banner or around our practical immediate slogans, and skip over reformist organizations, whether party or trade union, that would of course be the best thing in the world. But then the very question of the united front would not exist in its present form."[7]

United front strategy accomplished several goals at once. First, it served as an organizational vehicle to maintain unity amidst the fog of revolutionary struggle. Second, it put non-revolutionary alliance partners on the defensive in competing for the mantle of the political struggle in question. Third, it provided a setting within which the revolutionary forces could demonstrate the superior organizational, political, and tactical skills of communist workers in championing the united defense of working-class interests. Finally, it allowed an intimacy of contact that provided the revolutionaries with "actionable" information on their erstwhile allies that could be useful in purging them at some future date.

In the cases of the CPK's rise and return to power, united front was a necessary means by which the Khmer Rouge could leverage what little legitimacy it had—if not to seek the minimum of legitimacy in the first place. By the end of the 1960s, the CPK was little more than a ragtag group of insurgents with nary a rifle among them. Even though Cambodia's leader, Prince Norodom Sihanouk, was tilting to the right from around 1968 onward, he—and not the CPK—was on the receiving end of China's largesse and support; Beijing had viewed him, a leftist-leaning royal, as a "unicorn" in a world otherwise populated by "black swans" and "gray rhinos" and thus as a model in China's desire to cultivate followers in the nonaligned movement. Sihanouk was also widely popular throughout the Cambodian countryside. The only chance for the CPK to move beyond occupying a pathetic footnote to history would be to somehow supplant Sihanouk or, short of that, ride the prince's coattails. When the opportunity arose, it was Pol Pot and not Sihanouk who immediately and enthusiastically embraced a united front. And when the united front came to encompass a somewhat less desirable (from Pol Pot's perspective, at least) alliance with North Vietnam and the Vietnamese communist insurgents in the South, the CPK found itself in the position to leapfrog into leadership of the front. From 1970 to 1973, the CPK expertly and ruthlessly expanded its control within, ultimately dominating the united front just as the doctrine prescribed.

Similarly, ten years later, at the dawn of the 1980s, the Khmer Rouge used the negative legitimacy of the Vietnamese-backed government in Phnom Penh, the People's Republic of Kampuchea (PRK), as a springboard to ally with both Royalist (Sihanouk again) and other non-communist resistance groups. As internal CPK documents reveal, the aim was to cobble together a broad-based united front aimed at expelling the Vietnamese and, beyond that, to dominate the post-PRK domestic political landscape. Ultimately, whether in 1973 or 1993, when united front doctrine was no longer viable or necessary, the CPK (and its successor, the Party of Democratic Kampuchea, or PDK) would pivot to the only alternative it was constitutionally capable of embracing: class struggle.

Class Struggle

The term "class struggle" also occupies a long and distinguished place within the Marxist universe even as it has been kneaded and twisted over time and across space. At its root is the notion that the capitalist system of production is unfixable and thus can *only* be destroyed. As Marx and Engels put it, "The issue cannot be the alteration of private property but only its abolition, not the smoothing over of class antagonisms but the abolition of classes, not the improvement of existing society but the foundation of a new one."[8]

Although used by moderates as a criticism of Marx and Engels, the phrase "the worse, the better," commonly attributed to Lenin, aptly describes the process of class struggle itself. The intensity of class conflict was only to be fully resolved by the sheer force of historical materialism: "In the class-consciousness of the proletariat, historical necessity coincides with freedom of action; the opposition of human will and the 'objective' course of events ceases to exist, the . . . will and initiative [of the working class] are themselves part of the necessary course of history."[9] Those holding ideas or political prescriptions sympathetic either to capitalism or to moderation in managing or mitigating its negative effects were taken to deny historical inevitability and could therefore had to be pulverized into oblivion—or, as Pol Pot was fond of saying (quite literally)[10] into fertilizer—by the tectonic plates of history's inexorable progress. By the late 1920s, Lenin's successor, Joseph Stalin, argued that as communism continued to advance, class struggle "would become more and more violent."[11]

This, in fact, turned out to be the case in the Soviet Union, then in China, and then—in its purest, most literal form—even more so in Cambodia. When Khmer Rouge soldiers began their final march on Phnom Penh in April 1975, they were not simply saying the quiet part out loud; they were shouting it from megaphones as they took over areas of the city. CPK theoreticians appear to have followed Chinese and Vietnamese examples of identifying the poor and lower-middle-class peasants as the only revolutionary classes. To eliminate the objective material disparities between what they termed the revolutionary "old people" (ប្រជាជនចាស់) or "base people" (ប្រជាជនមូលដ្ឋាន) and the bourgeoisie, the latter were emptied out of the cities and forced into peasant life in the unforgiving countryside. Many others were simply liquidated.

Yet class struggle, for the CPK, did not stop with the exile of the bourgeoisie and the purging of the ancien régime. The ever-present threat of subversion and thus reversion back to pre-revolutionary conditions meant that revolutionary efforts had to be carried on in perpetuity—so long as the CPK had the power to do so. As a CPK intellectual described it: "Their [the bourgeoisie's] economic foundation has already collapsed, *but their views still remain, their aspirations still remain.* Therefore, they continue to contradict . . . the revolution. Whether they can carry out activities against us is the concrete condition which prompts us to continue the revolution."[12] No deviation from this line of permanent revolution was thus possible. And in fact, the elimination of such deviation, as long as there was a state apparatus that could do so, remained a self-perpetuating reality. The logic was immutable: the legitimacy of this repressive mechanism was guaranteed by the inevitability that the regime (like *any* regime) would fall short of achieving the totality of its political vision.

The "correctness" of this approach was reinforced in a meeting between Mao Zedong and newly victorious Pol Pot and Ieng Sary on June 21, 1975.[13] Mao had warned them not to "copy China's example wholesale." The CPK delegation interpreted this (likely accurately) not as a call to moderation but as the exact opposite: an encouragement to reject Chinese-style bureaucratization and thus keep Cambodia's revolutionary fire alive and unadulterated. For the CPK, this approach bore the apparent benefit of avoiding the complication of trying to resolve the contradictions presented by the transformation of an insurgency into a ruling power. The easier way out, it would seem, was to simply use instead scorched-earth tactics, both figurative and literal, to destroy them altogether. And so there would be no "unity of opposites" for the CPK, or Yang Xianchen's notion of "one divides into two" (一分之二), but instead a brutal turbocharging of Mao's understanding of dialectical synthesis as "the completed development of one side, the elimination of one side, and the resolution of the contradiction."[14] As the Chairman put it elsewhere, using vivid Pol Potist imagery, "to synthesize is simply to consume the enemy" (综合就是吃掉敌人).[15]

Thus was the CPK determined to out-radicalize Mao's China. One CPK cadre said that while China had wound down its Cultural Revolution, Democratic Kampuchea was "making a Cultural Revolution every day."[16] The Khmer Rouge sought to succeed where even Mao had failed, even if this meant the complete subordination of formal and informal institutions, from ministries to marriage to ideology. This was what Pol Pot called "socialism in every aspect" and "the task of building socialism once and for all"[17]—in other words, "pure socialism."

To Study a Singularity

How does one begin to tell the story of this peculiar mode of political being that the CPK willfully, dogmatically embraced? How does one capture, let alone analyze, the odd admixture of unexpected cunning and mind-boggling ineptitude that led to the CPK's stunning durability as much as their downfall? After utilizing and abandoning several approaches—historical institutionalism, path dependency, civil conflict, insurgency, and so on[18]—I found myself returning time and again to focus on individual leaders and how they shaped, and were shaped by, events and institutions throughout the life of this movement. The story of the CPK, after all, is a story of human aspiration and folly.

These men, these "bad lieutenants" whose lives and career trajectories I embed in this study, are three of Pol Pot's top colleagues: Ieng Sary, Son Sen, and *Ta* Mok. I have chosen them because they are integral to the CPK's creation and dissolution as well as all the points in between. Through following their narratives over the course of the Khmer Rouge's history, I can thus disaggregate the movement into something vastly more complex than the predictable residue, the *bave d'escargot*, left from a mere focus on Pol Pot's seemingly ironclad leadership.

The discerning reader may have several questions about the approach this book takes. First, *why eschew a broader, comparative analysis?* Since I am a political scientist by training, this would have been my default approach. But while it is possible to compare the CPK with other Marxist insurgencies and governing regimes, such a comparison inevitably ends up being intellectually uninteresting. That is because of what we will come to see as the pervasive mediocrity of CPK leaders. Who actually enjoys reading about mediocrity *qua* mediocrity? Using Zhou Enlai or Andrei Gromyko to tease out an understanding of Ieng Sary is something of an intellectual letdown, as is using Lin Biao or Gyorgi Zhukov to gain insight into Mok's infinitely more modest achievements. China's Great Leap Forward is a multifaceted tragedy that can act equally as a metaphor and as a measuring stick for the evolution of Chinese

FIGURE 0.1. Caricature of Khmer Rouge leaders. CPA Media Pte Ltd / Alamy Stock Photo.

communism, while the widespread, brutal starvation from Democratic Kampuchea's 1975 Phenomenally (បាតអស្ចារ្យ) Great Leap Forward or its 1977 Four-Year Plan in All Fields was simply the result of overextraction of resources from the mouths and bellies of those who produced it.[19] Indeed, the short life of Democratic Kampuchea does not provide the minimum necessary for comparison between cases on just about any aspect of governance. I could go on, but such a book would practically be begging to be put back on the shelf after only a few pages.

Second, *what about other Khmer Rouge leaders through which to explore this topic?* Some might suggest another potential candidate, Khieu Samphân, one of Pol Pot's earliest compatriots. But he is not an appropriate figure for this book's purposes: despite his consistently high profile throughout almost the entirety of the movement, he was ultimately a secondary player among Khmer Rouge elites—a kind of "service intellectual" to his political masters rather than a field commander or decision-maker. One former Party of Democratic Kampuchea (PDK) cadre didn't mince words: "In the secret structure, Khieu Samph[â]n has no seat."[20] He was, in Steve Heder's memorable phrase, "Moloch's poodle," someone "whom [Pol Pot] can completely control."[21] His value was ruthless loyalty based on his *proximity* to power. In practice, Khieu Samphân did not actually decide people's fates or implement CPK decisions to purge its ranks; rather, he ensured that "intended victims were relaxed and did not suspect the imminence of their death."[22] Indeed, when Khieu Samphân suggested that he take on some of Brother Number 1's workload, Pol Pot responded, "You can't even control your children, how can I entrust you with work?"[23] Even Mok would ridicule him, telling a bodyguard that Khieu Samphân's feet "don't touch the ground" (that is, he doesn't know anything).[24]

Finally, *why not just focus on Pol Pot and Nuon Chea?* This book is an analysis of a movement, not a biography of its top leader or his second-in-command. There are already several excellent biographies of Pol Pot and his political vision.[25] This book instead looks at practice, not theory; at the enforcement of the Khmer Rouge program rather than the construction of it. As one Khmer Rouge cadre put it: "When speaking about an issue, Pol Pot was very good at explaining it in a very lucid, clear way which convinced you that he'd found a complete solution to the problem. But when it came to implementation, his solution would fail. Then he'd put forward another idea which . . . would again seem very convincing and yet the same thing would happen again. And, so, after a time, I no longer believed in him."[26] This strongly suggests that one must look beyond Pol Pot and Nuon Chea to understand how the Khmer Rouge functioned (or didn't) and evolved (or devolved) as a movement. Both these figures floated above direct governance and control, remaining at the apex of the movement rather than as the people in the weeds charged with operationalizing CPK policy. To tell the story of the *movement*, one must focus on the policy implementers rather than on the policymakers. Teasing out variations in their approaches to united front and class struggle strategies provides historical precision, analytical dynamism, and empirical richness otherwise lost by privileging the very top of the Khmer Rouge pantheon.

The three "lieutenants"—Sary, Son Sen, and Mok—have some analytical purchase as well. These three individuals' approach to governance and their responses to the political changes during the period under review here place each of them distinctly on different points on the spectrum between united front on one end and class struggle on the other. The political lives of these three individuals—much more than that of the rather two-dimensional Pol Pot—better explain the totality of the CPK from its harried beginnings to its brutal approach toward governance to its remarkable rebirth and, ultimately, to its ignoble, violent demise.

Dramatis Personae

Ieng Sary, Son Sen, and *Ta* Mok were key implementers of Pol Pot's vision from the very beginning of the Khmer Rouge movement all the way to the very end. Their political and social backgrounds show that each of them had an inclination to occupy a particular space along the spectrum between united front and class struggle. Sary, although no saint, was most comfortable with pursuing policies of united front. Mok had little patience for anything that deviated from violent struggle, whether class-based or not (he rarely bothered to make such a distinction). And Son Sen demonstrated an initial comfort with managing the tangible machinery of class struggle while subsequently failing utterly to move toward a nonviolent politically competitive framework, ultimately epitomizing, it can be said, the CPK/PDK's being itself. It was the impossibility of occupying the spaces in between united front and class struggle that also led, quite directly, to his own demise.

Man Without a Mountaintop: Ieng Sary

Ieng Sary died in 2013, but his political career ended in pathos six years before, when the arresting party representing the ECCC (Extraordinary Chambers in the Courts of Cambodia, the international war crimes tribunal charged with bringing Khmer Rouge leaders to justice), arrived at his flat in Phnom Penh. He was informed, somewhat awkwardly, that despite a guarantee of amnesty made by Hun Sen a decade before, he was now being arrested for crimes against humanity and was to be taken into custody. The same was true for his wife, Ieng Thirith, who served as minister of social affairs during the Democratic Kampuchea period and was a sister-in-law of Pol Pot.[27]

While the ECCC officers were all ensconced in the waiting room, Sary slumped in his chair, with the seat next to his—Thirith's—remaining conspicuously empty. When asked where she was, Sary said that she was in the bathroom "getting ready"—putting on makeup, fixing her hair, and so on. In a comedy of errors illustrative of much of the ECCC's activities, nobody had thought to include a female arresting officer. There was little the party could do but wait for Thirith to emerge on her own.

After what seemed like an interminable back-and-forth, the officers decided to gingerly check on the former minister and bring her out to the waiting area. Taking the seat next to her husband, Thirith began babbling incoherently: something about a bicycle, how she and Sary had lived in Japan after 1975, when they first met. Finally, she asked what *she* was doing there. As she was holding forth, Ieng Sary buried his head in his hands. At first, a member of the arresting party thought that Sary was hiding his head in shame and embarrassment over Thirith's bizarre display. But it turned out that Sary was silently, even tenderly, acknowledging what was slowly dawning on everyone else in the room: that Ieng Thirith had lost her mind.[28]

Ieng Sary has been described with an unenviable set of negative personality traits—careless arrogance, exceptional indifference to others' suffering, an abundance of opportunism, even greed—but it is difficult to imagine the other Khmer Rouge leaders discussed in this book expressing even this small hint of humanity over a personal tragedy. Indeed, it is not inaccurate to see Sary in some ways as a rather sad, even pathetic figure, while fully acknowledging his complicity in one of the most bloodthirsty political experiments of the twentieth century. This

FIGURE 0.2. Ieng Sary. CPA Media Pte Ltd / Alamy Stock Photo.

observation provides an apt personal and professional description of Sary from the waning days of Democratic Kampuchea through his arrest and eventual demise while on trial for crimes against humanity—one that complicates his reputation as a chief architect of the bloody Khmer Rouge movement.[29]

Ieng Sary (ឥៀង សារី), aka Van (វ៉ាន់), was born Kim Trang in 1929 to a relatively well-to-do ethnic Khmer family living in Vietnam. He studied in Prey Veng[30] and subsequently attended the Lycée Sisowath in Phnom Penh on a scholarship. It was there that Sary organized the 1949 student strike against colonialism. It appears that Sary was not overly popular, however, as he garnered the nicknames "cat" (ឆ្មា) and "crooked teapot" (ប៉ាន់ទេរៀង).[31] Sary then won another scholarship, this time to Paris, for his secondary baccalaureate. Though he never completed this degree, it was in Paris that he deepened his association and friendship with Pol Pot, whom he had met in 1947.[32] His expatriate experience reflects a cosmopolitanism that seems to have been unique among his surviving elite colleagues and that served him well in his roles as chief liaison with his united front colleagues in Beijing and eventually as foreign minister after 1975.

While in Paris, Sary had, in 1951, co-founded the Cercle Marxiste,[33] and by the following year he had become a member of the French Communist Party, claiming the support of FCP secretary Maurice Thorez himself. Just before setting off for Paris, he became engaged to Khieu Thirith, whom he had met at the Lycée Sisowath. She eventually joined him in the French capital, where they were married in 1953. The epicenter for these radicalized Cambodian expatriates was 28 rue Saint-André-des-Arts, where Sary lived with Thirith. She went on to study English literature at the Sorbonne. Her sister Khieu Ponnary married Pol Pot not long thereafter, joining the two men as relatives through marriage.[34]

Sary's years in Paris provided him with doctrinal knowledge that reinforced his already demonstrated commitment to leftist politics in Cambodia as well as his ability to mobilize disparate groups toward the realization of these political goals. But he lacked a real power base. The Khmer Rouge leadership boasted a pantheon of military commanders—Son Sen, So Phim, Nhim Ros, Kè Pauk, *Ta* Mok, Koy Thuon, Vorn Vet, and Cheng An—whose value to the movement, and eventual place in its hierarchy, was determined on the battlefield. The same could not be said of Ieng Sary. His distinctive position is perhaps best described using the internal political vocabulary of China's communist leaders: if, as, Mao Zedong said, "China's revolution was made by many mountaintops,"[35] where "mountaintop" (山头) refers to power bases and factionalism, often born out of military achievements, then Sary—to the extent that Cambodia's revolution was also made by many mountaintops—was a man who did not occupy any of them.[36] This left his position particularly vulnerable relative to those of most of his colleagues, to the point where it took him out of the equation by the 1990s.

What he did have, however, was control over a key institution in Democratic Kampuchea: the Foreign Ministry, B1. This did not make Ieng Sary powerful so much as it made him *relevant* to Pol Pot and Nuon Chea. The ministry was the part of the Khmer Rouge government that liaised with other countries, particularly the Chinese and North Koreans. It hosted and housed foreign delegations and employed a battery of translators and interpreters who monitored foreign radio broadcasts and provided foreign-language versions of Khmer Rouge propaganda.

B1 also housed an inordinate number of "intellectuals," or individuals largely though not exclusively culled from the ranks of the united front. Not an insignificant number of them were taken away to be tortured and executed with Sary's knowledge, if not at his initiative, but many were also held in "reeducation" centers instead, forced to grow vegetables and other crops to feed B1 employees and even for export. And although former Foreign Ministry staff remembered Sary as being cold and aloof, many B1 personnel survived, even as their class backgrounds would otherwise have made them far more vulnerable to the regime. Indeed, several key Foreign Ministry officials would continue to work with, under, and alongside Sary until well into the 1980s and beyond.

As this suggests, Sary, although a true believer in the cause of the CPK, simply did not possess the ultra-orthodox Manichean worldview that so many of his elite colleagues held with infallible conviction. In other words, he was able to appreciate, and participate in, what we might recognize as the subtleties and foibles of normal human interaction. A seemingly throwaway story recounted by Steve Heder about an encounter he had with Sary illustrates the point:

> We were supposed to meet in this hotel in Chanthaburi, so I was holed up in the hotel, waiting for him to come, and he didn't arrive at the appointed time, which was like 9:00 a.m. or something like that and the clock kept ticking and then he doesn't show up until 10:30–11:00. He knocks on the door and he's dressed in this kind of golfer's outfit and he says, "I'm Ieng Sary." I said, "I know, I recognize you." And he says, "I'm sorry I'm late,

I apologize for being late." We do the interview and then we go to lunch. We're off tape [and] then I suddenly recalled that there was this thing in the CPK doctrine that if they did harm to people they had to apologize to the people, so I said, "You know, given the fact that you had this doctrine and given the fact that we now know that a lot of the harm was being done and you seem to indicate that harm *was* being done, was there ever any thought of apologizing either at the time or after the fact?" And he said no because "we didn't intend for that to happen." So then I said, "But you didn't intend to be late, and you apologized for being late" [Laughs]. And he got what I was saying. He was the kind of person who could take that kind of thing, you know—*whoops!* [Laughs]. Whatever else you might say, he *was* capable of irony, not like the [other leaders]. He understood irony, could appreciate irony.[37]

Would Son Sen or Mok (or Khieu Samphân, Nuon Chea, or Pol Pot, for that matter) react this way to a jibe from a foreigner? Unlikely. As we will see, the others at the very top of the movement bore very little resemblance character-wise, in public or in private, to Sary as revealed by this anecdote. Indeed, as Peter Bartu recalls: "No one [in the leadership] raised their voices, [demonstrating] a natural taciturn style that they learned along the way, in which very little is revealed about the individual. . . . [I]t's all business." Leaders like Khieu Samphân, Chen Youran, Mak Ben, and Tep Kennal, who seemed to have "come out of the same apparatchik school," each embodied this approach. But perhaps nobody more so than Son Sen.[38]

A Tamarind Growing from a Turd: Son Sen

Cheung Phnom (ជើងភ្នំ), a village not far from the Khmer Rouge's erstwhile headquarters at Anlong Veng (អន្លង់វែង), lies on a trail that snakes its way through a ridge in the Dângrêk Mountains (ភ្នំដងរែក) and winds with seeming aimlessness for miles before eventually terminating at Pol Pot's bunker at Kbal Tonsaong (ក្បាលទន្សោង). There is a grim, pitiless, postapocalyptic feel to it.[39] The occasional peasant dwelling, swidden field, or young soldier peering out from the underbrush only serves to underscore the isolation of what feels like the last place on earth. The village is not particularly exotic or picturesque, although in rare spots nature punctuates the landscape with an impossibly still pool of water or an unexpectedly breathtaking explosion of local flora.

For the most part it is hot, dusty, and, until recently, littered with unexploded ordnance and land mines, pockets of which have yet to be cleared. The townspeople—even today made up of a not insignificant number of ex–Khmer Rouge and their extended families—exhibit an almost palpable sense of suspicion of, even loathing for, outsiders.

It was here in the early morning hours of June 10, 1997, that farmers realized something was amiss. One of them recalled: "I heard shooting near *Ta* Mok's house, the Kandal house [also called the "mango farm house"].... [W]hen I went out from my house to make a fire to scare the mosquitoes from biting my buffalos . . . I heard a lot of shooting."⁴⁰ What they were hearing were the very sounds of class struggle playing out as sixty-seven-year-old veteran Khmer Rouge leader Son Sen was gunned down, along with his wife, Yun Yat, and three generations of his family members. Some three hundred soldiers, under the command of So Saroeun and Nhem San, had been dispatched from their regular duties guarding Pol Pot's bunker and descended on Son Sen's compound, surrounding the area. As soon as their car headlights

Figure 0.3. Son Sen (left, with glasses). CPA Media Pte Ltd / Alamy Stock Photo.

illuminated the compound—two separate houses, one for the adults and the other for the children—the soldiers began firing.

Son Sen's son-in-law and nephew were the first to be shot. Yun Yat caught the next spray of bullets, just as she exited the house. Although Son Sen had a Chinese-made K-59 pistol and two bullet clips on his belt, he was unable to get off any rounds before the soldiers opened fire on him as he ran toward his wife's lifeless body. He was shot in the right temple and right cheek, she in the left ear and lower back.⁴¹ The soldiers gathered another six members of Son Sen's family—the couple's two daughters, two nieces, a nephew, and Yun Yat's younger sister—and marched them along the path toward Kbal Tonsaong. After they had walked a kilometer or so, the women were made to undress, after which all six of the captured family members were either beaten to death or burned alive.⁴²

By the mid-1990s, as we will see, Khmer Rouge policy—from burning villages to killing foreign backpackers to forced collectivization—had defaulted back to that of 1973–1978. No Khmer Rouge leader (with the possible exception of *Ta* Mok) was more devoted to this revival of class struggle than Son Sen, who performed a whiplash-inducing about-face from his attempt at securing legitimacy through the political process following the 1991 Paris Agreements. In doing so, Son Sen unwittingly provided the perfect distillation of the binary Khmer Rouge universe of united front and class struggle, if in a concentrated, volatile form.

Ironically, however, that same embodiment of the CPK's own orthodoxy was what led to his execution, as Pol Pot suspected Son Sen of abandoning the movement in order to enter the political process in the same way that Ieng Sary had defected from the CPK's successor, the Party of Democratic Kampuchea (PDK), just the year before. If Ieng Sary found himself leaning into the united front and *Ta* Mok into class struggle in the churn between the two endpoints, Son Sen tried to occupy the impossible space in between. While Sary's relevance in maintaining the external optics of the united front throughout the 1980s gave him a second lease on life—allowing him to die peacefully (although in state custody) some two decades later—Son Sen's commitment, born out of a combination of opportunism, desperation, and ideological conviction (but above all through his tendency toward intemperance), led to his seemingly inevitable, violent demise. His death, one might say, was but a foretelling of that of the movement itself.

Like Sary, Son Sen (សុន សេន), also known as "Brother 89" or "Khiev" (ខៀវ), was a Khmer Krom, a Vietnam-born "downriver Khmer." He was born in 1930, and when he was a young boy, his family moved to Phnom Penh. Son Sen also followed the trajectory of others among the future Khmer Rouge intelligentsia by studying abroad, receiving a scholarship in 1950 that he used to take up history and philosophy in Paris, subsequently taking up academic positions in Cambodia. (He was highly respected by his students at the École Normale for being an excellent teacher.) And like Sary, he retreated into the jungle, known as the *maquis*, in the 1960s, when Sihanouk began his crackdown against leftists.

By 1975, Brother Number 89 had become a national military leader. Son Sen belonged to the Central Committee Military Committee alongside Pol Pot, Nuon Chea, and zone commanders So Phim and *Ta* Mok. He also served as minister of defense and chairman of the General Staff, the central commanding unit of the Revolutionary Army of Kampuchea (RAK). The General Staff communicated with all RAK division commanders and their divisions as well as independent units on everything from data collection to political education to field command.[43] Following the establishment of the new revolutionary regime in April of that year, Son Sen was at the top of the CPK's effectively combined military and the state security bureaucracy (សន្តិសុខ), which extended via successive levels in some places all the way down to the villages.[44]

If Democratic Kampuchea is known above all as the place where class struggle knew no bounds—where uncountable tortures, confessions, and executions took place, both at the infamous security prison S21 (better known as Tuol Sleng) as well as at thousands of undocumented killing sites—the person who oversaw the apparatus by which such killings happened, Son Sen himself, remained distant from much of the scrutiny. Although Kaing Guek-Eav (aka Duch) has gone down in history as S21's prison chief, his immediate supervisor was Son Sen. The latter micromanaged the goings-on at S21, carrying out daily hours-long phone conversations with Duch and often annotating drafts of confessions induced under unimaginable torture. In this regard, Son Sen was outranked only by Nuon Chea and Pol Pot, and he gave over this responsibility to Nuon only in late 1978, when he was called upon to purge the Eastern Zone and take over command of it in the face of an escalating series of battles with Vietnam.

Son Sen's extremely powerful position within the ranks of the CPK was, however, belied by his lack of popularity. Unlike Ieng Sary, whose diplomatic savoir faire earned him at least a degree of admiration, however begrudging, from those around him, and unlike *Ta* Mok, whose munificence left him beloved among his constituents despite his renowned brutality, Son Sen was respected but never really liked. There was a certain unsettledness or insecurity as well as a healthy amount of arrogance in his character which perhaps accounts for this easy pivoting between united front and class struggle, but which also translated into a standoffishness that endeared him to no one. Pol Pot's aide-de-camp Phi Phuon described him—evidently not without bias—as "tall but of rather frail construction, he looked like a climbing vine," and as "an anxious, nervous man who worried about trifles and easily lost his self-control."[45] Peter Bartu recalls "never [seeing] the guy spontaneously laugh.... [H]e never used a Cambodian aphorism, [not like] some of the Cambodian interlocutors—they weren't short of characters, commanders in the field—they were hilarious, natural leaders, outgoing and gregarious." Rather, he appeared to Bartu as "a very professional individual who is also playing a tough game of 'Texas Hold 'Em' at the same time,"[46] meticulously examining all the minutiae of any given aspect of politics and governance with the cold precision of a mathematician.

That standoffishness sometimes veered into a contemptuousness which ultimately left Son Sen with no friends. None other than Nuon Chea recalled an exchange in which Son Sen criticized him for being devoted to Pol Pot rather than to the communist movement. Publicly berating Nuon and his subordinates, he told them, "All of you are something like a tamarind growing out of a piece of shit." When Nuon was asked if it was because of remarks like this that the people and his own comrades generally hated Son Sen, his reply was an unhesitant "yes." In the end, Son Sen's charge was as much an accusation against his comrades as it was an unintended confession, suggesting a mean-spirited man, out of the morass, for whom in the end there was no saving grace.

The Technician of Force: *Ta* Mok

Of the three "bad lieutenants" in this book, *Ta* Mok (តាម៉ុក) seems to have had the flattest political and military career arc. He was a consummate survivor whose prowess on the battlefield was barely affected when he lost an eye or when his leg was obliterated by a land mine. The one thing that stopped him in his tracks was the CPK shifting from a military strategy to a political one. Class struggle, particularly when exercised with a martial flair, was Mok's safe space; united front was his Kryptonite.

Ta ("Grandfather") Mok (also known as "*Ta* 15") was a walking contradiction. Like Ieng Sary and Son Sen, Mok possessed a brutal reputation (one oft-cited nickname for him was "the Butcher") that, while certainly well earned, belies the complex nature of his personality and approach to leadership and governance. Absurd rumors often swirled around him; for instance, he apparently hired bare-breasted ethnic minority female bodyguards and kept attack dogs "as big as horses."[47] His ruthlessness and temper were legendary, yet he was uniquely beloved by the people under his command; an interviewee described him as having "bad words but a good heart."[48] Even his soldiers who defected in the 1990s said they would return to fight for him if he called them back. He built numerous schools and hospitals in the areas under his control, yet he is rumored to have had his troops put vanquished foes into ovens to roast them alive.[49] He was the most "secular" of the Khmer Rouge elite, always more of a warlord than an ideologue, and took pride in never preparing before giving a speech;[50] as he once declared: "I am not afraid of the leaders who have a lot of theories because they never practice them. I myself have no theory. . . . I only know practice."[51] But he was also a devout Buddhist (as apparently was Nuon Chea) in his later years, and his grave in Anlong Veng is as much a religious shrine as it is a final resting place. He was Pol Pot's protector, until he captured him and put him on trial. Finally, he was the most militarily adept among the CPK leaders; yet once the Khmer Rouge movement was on its last legs, he was the figure with the least value to the Thai and Cambodian People's Party forces brokering a final end to the insurgency. He was not folded into the Royal Cambodian Armed Forces' upper ranks, unlike many of his subordinates who were given plum jobs, but instead waited to stand trial, dying in custody in 2006.

Mok was born Chhit Choeun (ឈិតជឿន) around 1924 to a large rich peasant family in Prakiep (ប្រគៀប) village in the southwestern province of Takeo. He was one of eight children. His education differed significantly from those of Pol Pot, Ieng Sary, and Son Sen in that it was far more traditional; after attending primary school in Trapeang Thom (ត្រពាំងធំ), a sub-district of Tram Kak (ត្រាំកក់) district, Mok entered the Trapeang Thurn pagoda and studied at the higher Pali School in the capital, thus receiving a scholarly education in Theravada Buddhism's liturgical language. Initially Mok had no greater ambition than to manage his family's timber business (an entire industry he would, ironically, manage on a much larger scale in the 1980s and 1990s). With the outbreak of the Second World War and the upending of French colonial rule, Mok found what would become his true calling: militarized anti-colonial struggle. Roving Vietminh forces purchasing timber from the

FIGURE 0.4. *Ta* Mok. CPA Media Pte Ltd / Alamy Stock Photo.

family influenced him to join the Khmer Issarak anti-French resistance, and Mok went to southern Vietnam for political training.[52] Eventually he became the head of the Issarak movement in Tram Kak.[53] Like many other young Cambodian communists, however, Mok was disappointed with the outcome of the 1954 Geneva Conference and chose to remain in the *maquis*. There he organized anti-regime militias in the southwestern countryside for the remainder of the 1950s and 1960s.[54]

Mok's rise within the CPK occurred somewhat later than that of others who eventually rose to the top of the movement. Long after So Phim and Nhim Ros had become secretaries of the Eastern and Northeast Zone, respectively, and even after Ieng Sary had become secretary in the Northeast, Mok remained subordinate in the Southwest to the former schoolteacher Ma Mâng (aka Pang) until the latter succumbed to a fever in 1968 in his native Kampong Chhnang, which was a rival Southwest Zone base area to Mok's in Takeo province.[55] By contrast, his counterpart in the Eastern Zone, So Phim, had been a field commander since the Geneva Conference almost fifteen years prior.

Mok wasted no time establishing family-based inroads into some of the key corridors of power, ensuring that his children married figures who held important positions. As an interviewee recalled:

> Mok . . . had lots of children. I think all of them were girls. Many of his [sons]-in-law held important positions such as Division commanders. *Ta* Muth was one of his sons-in-law. . . . Another son-in-law named Ren was in the beginning a courier. Then during the war he became a brigade commander, then after 1975 a Regimental commander, then in the end of 1977 a Division commander. . . . Another son-in-law was named Boran. He was a Central Committee courier before 1975. . . . The daughter Khom was the Secretary of Tramkak [Tram Kak] district during the war.[56]

Although elevated to the CPK Standing Committee during the civil war, Mok remained their junior colleague at the time of the Khmer Rouge victory in 1975—this despite the frontline ferocity of his troops, who were "among the most zealous [of the Khmer Rouge forces] and suffered some of the worst defeats of the war—notably during its suicidal attack on Phnom Penh in 1973 at the height of the American air war."[57] His time in the inner circle, however, was still to come.

Mok's power base was in the Southwest. As zone secretary, he would become a key enforcer of class struggle throughout the Democratic Kampuchea period. As other zone leaders fell under the scrutiny of the Center, implicated by other colleagues' confessions at S21, Mok and fellow zone secretary Kè Pauk brought in their zone forces to disarm, purge, and replace the militaries and the political leadership in the targeted zones. The most dramatic example of this was the purge of the Eastern Zone in 1978, after which the majority of Democratic Kampuchean territory now fell under his (and Son Sen's) command (much as Nuon Chea had done with the DK administrative apparatus). Mok remained a force to be reckoned with even after his retreat in 1979 and continued to lead CPK troops well into the 1990s, and his entrenchment within the Khmer Rouge's inner circle eventually led to the marginalization of even a colossus like Son Sen.

Throughout his career, Mok benefited from the intense loyalty of those who worked under him. Upon his eventual arrest in 1998, Mok, who also had the distinction (or the reputation) of having accumulated more revenue than any other Khmer Rouge leader through the timber trade with Thailand,[58] saw to it that his spoils were distributed among his soldiers. An interviewee recalled that Mok ordered his "military commanders to share that money with each soldier's family so they at least could buy two oxen to pull an ox cart."[59] In the final analysis, Mok was a figure who neither financially exploited the citizens under his control nor got entangled in the ideological calisthenics that CPK doctrine had twisted itself into over an accumulated thirty years of struggle. He didn't have to: insofar as a flattening of class distinctions was a key tenet of CPK doctrine, Mok practiced what he preached, at least visibly. When the late journalist Nate Thayer asked Mok directly what his ideology was, Mok's response was "the nation."[60] He never wavered from this position, and for that he was as beloved by his supporters as he was feared by his victims, on whom he unleashed the full force of the basest, most primordial forms of violent class struggle.

On the Road to Perdition

The contours of the bifurcated strategy that the CPK would abide by over the course of its lifetime were already evident from its incipience. The Khmer Students' Association (Association des Étudiants Khmers, AEK), founded in 1946 and to which Ieng Sary and Pol Pot belonged while in Paris, functioned as a proving ground for the Khmer Rouge's united front strategy *avant la lettre*. Headquartered at the Pavilion de l'Indochine at the Cité Universitaire in Paris, the AEK was originally led by Ea Si Chau and Yem Sarong and was deeply nationalist rather than doctrinally political. This relative calm was disrupted by the introduction of communist elements spearheaded by Sary and, later, Pol Pot (still going by his birth name, Saloth Sâr). The two formed a communist cell within the AEK, largely abandoning their studies in the process. When the AEK elected its second president, Vann Molyvann (later to become Sihanouk's chief architect and urban planner), the communists made their move to take over the AEK, appointing Hou Youn instead. They were thus able to eventually dominate the AEK, holding all its key positions.[61] The lessons the future Khmer Rouge leaders learned there were clear: colonize the larger movement to expand their own power and influence, but do so behind the scenes.

But it was also during this time, also in Europe, that the first in a series of perceived betrayals of the nascent Cambodian communist movement occurred, as Sihanouk was able to out-negotiate his counterparts—including, crucially, the Indochinese Communist Party—with Chinese support during the talks that led to the 1954 Geneva Accords. This gave the movement's supporters in Paris and those already fighting in the Cambodian jungles the sense of distrust that would provide the emotional throughline toward destroying their enemies with the tool of class struggle. Sihanouk subsequently created such a threatening environment for the left in Phnom Penh and other urban areas in Cambodia that its leaders were radicalized, with Vietnamese advice and support, from left-leaning bourgeois professionals into revolutionary comrades in arms alongside Issarak insurgents deep in the primeval forests of Cambodia. It was there and then that Ieng Sary, Son Sen, and *Ta* Mok would work under and alongside Pol Pot to forge the movement that became known forever as the Khmer Rouge.

The chapters that follow use the conceptual lens of united front and class struggle to analyze the political lifetime of the CPK movement, which began in earnest in 1970 and ended dramatically in 1997-98. Chapter 1 continues the origin story of the Khmer Rouge, tracking these three figures over the 1970-1973 period as they fled into the *maquis* and recounting their roles in the movement's transformation from a ragtag group of rural revolutionaries tucked deep in the forest into a viable political force in Cambodia through successful united front activities. Chapter 2 picks up where the previous chapter leaves off in 1973, when the movement shifted abruptly from embracing united front to deploying class struggle in the countryside and, after 1975, in the urban areas. This was a process that continued until the very early days of 1979, when Cambodia was invaded by Vietnam. During this period, Ieng Sary shed his military garb for that of an international diplomat, Son Sen rose from being military commander in the *maquis* to the minister of defense and director of the security apparatus for the entire Cambodian state, and Mok consolidated his position as the most trusted zone commander, eventually taking on military control over most of Cambodia's territory.

The next two chapters, spanning 1980 to 1989, examine what this book identifies as the second united front through the evolution of the front itself—an evolution that enabled the Khmer Rouge to distinguish itself as a civilian (in the refugee camps along the Thai-Cambodian border) and as a military (inside Cambodia proper) organizing force. It was then that the career tracks of Ieng Sary, Son Sen, and *Ta* Mok began to diverge dramatically. While Sary undertook to craft a second united front at the beginning of the 1980s, Mok busied himself with military matters and gave united front nary a thought. Son Sen, for his part, tried his hand (but ultimately failed) at becoming a politician.

Chapter 5 traces the doomed attempt of the CPK (now PDK, or Party of Democratic Kampuchea) to navigate the political realm through the electoral process, a "soft test" of the ability of the PDK to transcend the duality of united front and class struggle. The failure to do so led to the defection of Ieng Sary from the movement and the doubling down on class struggle in PDK-controlled areas inside Cambodia. It was then that Son Sen fell out of favor with the party's inner circle, while Mok ascended in his stead. Chapter 6 recounts the movement's return, true to form, to another class struggle between 1994 and 1997. No less violent than the first, it would ultimately consume the movement itself, once and for all—an end that our three "lieutenants," plotting for power in the *maquis* almost three decades earlier, did not in their blind faith foresee. The conclusion places these events in a broader political and historical context.

Chapter 1

The First United Front
Colonizing the Movement from Within, 1970–1972

> FUNK [the National United Front of Kampuchea] was only a cover.... [It] did not know that it had the Communist Party of Cambodia behind it and inside it.
>
> —Kuong Lumphon, "Report on the Communist Party of Kampuchea"

One of the more widely circulated images of Pol Pot alongside other members of the Khmer Rouge shows them walking single file along a path in a forest clearing. Gazing beyond the photo's frame on the left, Pol Pot leads the way, *krama* tossed casually over his shoulders, walking stick grasped firmly in his right hand, water canteen slung across his left hip, a grin on his face—the very picture of a man walking with a spring in his step. Immediately behind him is a personal bodyguard, then Brother Number 2, Nuon Chea; farther down the line, almost at the edge of the right frame, is Ieng Sary. Like Pol Pot, the men all appear to be walking with conviction; their heads held high, they march looking ahead and to their leader.

This photo was taken in 1979, not long after the Khmer Rouge had been ousted from power by invading Vietnamese forces. The original caption tells us that it was staged as a message to Hanoi that the Khmer Rouge were still a viable political force. Yet if it were not for this description, one might easily assume that the photo was taken almost two decades earlier. And indeed, one could just as easily have been forgiven for thinking so. But it can also be interpreted as a reset. For toward the end of the 1970s, members of the Khmer Rouge were exactly where they had found themselves in the 1960s: in the thick malarial forests of the

FIGURE 1.1. Khmer Rouge leaders in the *maquis*, 1979. CPA Media Pte Ltd / Alamy Stock Photo.

Cambodian backcountry after a harrowing escape from Phnom Penh—not vanquished, but regrouping.

The Khmer Rouge's retreat to the jungle in 1979 thus did not signal a break with its own past; it was a repetition of it. As we will see, there were certain continuities as well as discontinuities between the movement's rise to power during the 1960s and its subsequent rebound during the 1980s. *Ta* Mok, for one, was on the field of battle rather than in political or policy meetings during both periods; yet Son Sen emerged from the jungle in late 1980 a babbling, semi-coherent wreck rather than the force he had come to be in the 1960s. To understand how the Khmer Rouge succeeded in resurrecting itself in the wake of the 1979 invasion, then, one must turn the clock back to the beginnings of the Khmer Rouge insurgency, when it coalesced from a loose configuration of French-educated leftist intellectuals into a political movement—a moment which, even though separated from that of this photo by more than fifteen years, a Marxist revolution, and a foreign invasion, was eerily akin to it.

The First Escape to the *Maquis*

By 1957, Ieng Sary had returned from France and was teaching history at his alma mater, the Lycée Sisowath, and, after 1959, at Kampuchea Both (Kambuboth).[1] It was around then that Prince Norodom Sihanouk, who ruled the country after abdicating the throne to pursue a more direct political role, began cracking down hard on leftists in the capital. In 1963 Sary fled to the Vietnamese base areas near the Cambodian border with Pol Pot and most of the other urban Cambodian Marxists after their clandestine activities in Phnom Penh became too dangerous for them to continue.[2]

Son Sen had returned to Cambodia in 1956, becoming a teacher by day at the University of Phnom Penh and an operative for the nascent Cambodian communist movement under cover of darkness.[3] In 1962 he lost his administrative position as the director of studies at the university's Pedagogical Institute because of his "anti-Sihanouk views," though he was able to continue teaching as the principal at a government high school in Takeo province.[4] The following year, once Saloth Sâr had secured the secretaryship of the Communist Party of Kampuchea, Son Sen was appointed to the Central Committee. A year later, like Pol Pot and Ieng Sary, Son Sen fled Phnom Penh, reportedly in the back of a truck, hidden among the cargo, through the arrangements of Ngèt You, an undercover operative in the capital.[5]

It was a staggered and splintered exodus. As Son Sen recalled: "It was clear that if we remained in the city, we would be wiped out. So we had to go to the countryside to defend ourselves. We went . . . gradually, one or two at a time. That's why we ended up in separate places. We couldn't concentrate ourselves. A few of us went here and a few there. At that time there was no such thing as a liberated zone. We split up and went to different zones. But we were in contact with one another."[6] Some escapees joined up with Khmer Rouge elite like Ma Mâng and Ta Mok in the Southwest, Nhim Ros in the Northeast, and Koy Thuon and Kè Pauk in the North. Having never left Cambodia for France, these elites had spent much or all of the previous decade establishing themselves as military leaders in their respective zones. Other escapees, including Ieng Sary and Son Sen, fled across the border to Vietnam, where they received a modicum of protection provided by their Vietnamese comrades.

Despite the relative safety it offered, this isolation from urban areas—and, for some, a comfortable bourgeois existence—brought with it its own hardships. Apart from the looming threat of complete extinction by Sihanouk's forces, living conditions for the escapees were basic at best. If the food to which they were accustomed was scarce, the threats of disease and attacks by local wildlife were omnipresent. In the words of a former guerrilla: "Life there was very difficult. There [were] many sick and many died. We got rice from people and from foraging. People around the mountains were poor. They loved us but did not have any food to give us."[7]

Yet this period of the first escape to the *maquis*, which lasted until the end of the 1960s, proved to be formative for the Khmer Rouge. On one level, the absence of any viable political alternative for the revolutionaries—given Sihanouk's crackdown and China's preference for the prince's stable Sangkum-led[8] regime over the fledgling communist movement—compelled them to deepen their commitment to the revolution. On another, being displaced from the center of political action bestowed on the movement an independence and a relative freedom that until then had proven elusive.[9] This newfound room to maneuver enabled the Khmer Rouge to solidify their worldview and sharpen their organizing ability, laying the foundations for their eventual triumph in 1975 and hardwiring in them the lessons to which they would return in their second escape to the *maquis* in 1979.

A pivotal point in the organizational evolution of the Cambodian communist movement occurred in mid-September 1966, when, bristling under Vietnamese control, Pol Pot convened a meeting with other Khmer Rouge elites. This meeting resulted in three key outcomes: First, the eventual changing of the organization's name from what had been a "workers' party" to the Communist Party of Kampuchea (CPK)—a move that would theoretically distance the group from Vietnam (and the Indochinese Communist Party, ICP) and symbolically make it equal with other parties in East and Southeast Asia (and beyond) using "communist" in their name. (This change, however, was not made official for another five years, until 1971.) Second, the adoption of a program of armed struggle in the countryside, drawing from the Chinese experience. Third, the move of their headquarters back *into* Cambodia, to the northeastern uplands of Ratanakiri, among the Tampuan, Jaraï, Kreung, Lao, Brou, Kachok, and other hill tribes.

In the northeastern uplands, the Khmer Rouge put into practice what effectively became a key component of their organizational and political strategy: the exploitation of local grievances as a means of recruiting the support of local populations and augmenting their ranks. The uplands population, as Philip Short observes, had long been "a prey to the exactions of rapacious officials sent from faraway Phnom Penh, and to what one diplomat called the 'overweening superiority complex' of lowland Cambodians." As a result, they "had no love of Sihanouk's regime" and proved receptive to the CPK's cause.[10] For instance, the Bunong (ᠷᠦᠩ) of Mondulkiri province had established "their own network of independent villages, governed by their own inhabitants," rejecting the legitimacy of the Vietnamese and the

Khmer.¹¹ Indeed, one of the texts Pol Pot gave new recruits to read was the handwritten "Solidarity of the Minorities under the Revolutionary Flag" (សាមគ្គីជនជាតិក្រោមទង់បដិវត្តន៍).¹²

One tribe the CPK came to depend on particularly for protection was the Jaraï (ចារ៉ាយ)—not least because they "knew best how to enlist nature itself as a key component of guerrilla warfare." There was also a certain trustworthiness that the CPK found in them; as Sary put it: "With a Khmer soldier you never knew how he'd react. But a Jaraï would make sure I was safe no matter what it cost."¹³ The Jaraï, in turn, responded favorably to the opportunities presented by this burgeoning revolutionary organization, whose members they referred to as "forest soldiers." Pol Pot's longtime Jaraï bodyguard Phi Phuon, for instance, recounts how the people of Ratanakiri "respected and loved [Pol Pot] very much. . . . [T]hey were filled with the spirit of responsibility. . . . He inspired a lot of confidence. We could lay our lives in his hands . . . entrust our lives to him. He had nice words for us."¹⁴ And until the end of his life, Pol Pot himself had among his close protection forces combatants who were recruited as adolescents from upland Khmer families who had long served as Khmer Rouge forces, and who were raised in a special, isolated group. These children were provided with a basic education in "literature and history" that came, eventually, to revolve around the theme of the Vietnamese as aggressors bent on annexing Cambodian territory as they had done for centuries.¹⁵

As part of the effort to swell their ranks, the Khmer Rouge also mobilized three-person teams to recruit peasants in the northeast to join the movement. The meetings these teams held would take place outside the villages, in the forests, or somewhere discreet. The propaganda was simple: Marxist discourse that argued the peasants were the victims of economic policies favoring the bourgeoisie. Peasants who had been "brought over" to the revolution were subsequently encouraged to identify others to be educated by these teams (even as the teams had already identified among themselves who should be brought to future meetings).¹⁶

Working among and across these different groups in the northeast arguably honed the organizational and political skills that the Khmer Rouge needed in order to succeed in—and believe in—the strategy of a united front and as a political force. Yet the fact remained that in the mid-1960s, the communist leadership had yet to establish the kind of well- and fast-functioning courier service necessary to effectively coordinate among its party members scattered in various cells around the flatlands or uplands across the country. This lack of a nationwide command

and control network was to have tragic—and triggering—consequences. In the spring of 1967, Nhim Ros, Northwest Zone commander, and his deputy Kung Sophàl had successfully agitated the peasantry around Battambang to rebel against sometimes forced requisitions of rice. But this event, the Samlaut (សំឡូត) Rebellion, remained a fairly localized incident that was eventually violently repressed by Sihanouk's government. Without a network that would have allowed for better synchronization and reinforcements from members elsewhere, the rest of the Khmer Rouge were unable to do much to support it.[17]

Ostensibly animated by the Samlaut Rebellion, the Khmer Rouge appear to have evolved into something more than the ragtag group they had been up to that point. Their first acts of rebellion the following year were, however, rather trivial in scope, being mostly raids on police posts for whatever arms they could find. Kenneth Conboy, for instance, describes how, in early 1968, "a youthful CPK member borrowed a hunting rifle from a police acquaintance, then went to the latter's house and demanded bullets and a grenade before fleeing into the jungle with this minimal haul."[18] Such incidents evidenced a persistent lack of coordination, even direction, among the Khmer Rouge.

Admittedly, the unfolding of the rebellion over the next several months can be understood as, in Ben Kiernan's words, "a sign of the political maturity of the Cambodian revolutionary movement," demonstrating that it was "able and willing to actively begin, even if only in response to a severe threat to themselves from the right-wing government and the military after 1966, a Cambodian revolution in its own right."[19] But in truth, the idea of the Khmer Rouge becoming in 1968 a political force to be reckoned with was as yet laughable. It remained an underground movement and, from an organizational standpoint, could not even fill its ranks with peasant recruits. To use Maoist language, it was unclear whether it had the *spark*, let alone the *prairie*, to start a "prairie fire."[20] Though the CPK did enjoy a degree of support among local upland tribes who had traditionally been at odds with the political center in Phnom Penh, the CPK program of radical change was unpopular among most of the lowland peasantry, who remained largely supportive of Sihanouk despite the events in Samlaut and their increasing economic difficulties. As a result, the Khmer Rouge remained top-heavy, with a leadership whose strategy and vision objective conditions simply did not support.

Had things continued along this trajectory, the Khmer Rouge would have been little more than an obscure footnote in history, resembling

THE FIRST UNITED FRONT   33

Life of Brian's Judean People's Front more than the Chinese Red Army during the early stages of the Chinese communists' rise to power. But their fate would be upended just a little over two years later, when the effects of major geopolitical machinations thousands of miles away would trickle down into the forests of Cambodia, lead to a refining of the Khmer Rouge's organizational structure, and create an opportunity for the CPK—which they did not hesitate to exploit—to become a bona fide political movement. It began with the ouster of Sihanouk.

The 1970 Ouster of Sihanouk and the First United Front

While the Khmer Rouge exiles were finding their footing amid the upland forests of Cambodia, Sihanouk, in his position as head of state of Cambodia, was finding his own Overton window amid the political dynamics of the Vietnam War. Throughout the early 1960s, Sihanouk was convinced that Hanoi would eventually prevail over the United States and therefore endeavored to avoid agonizing the North Vietnamese while seeking to temper US influence through a policy of neutrality. Yet when it became apparent by the late 1960s that this policy could not keep either at bay, he reconsidered his position and began hedging his bets by accommodating both sides. Having previously permitted freedom of movement for Vietnamese communist troops and supplies along the sections of the Ho Chi Minh Trail that snaked through Cambodia, the establishment of Vietnamese communist bases in Cambodian frontier areas, and shipments to them of Chinese military supplies via the port of Sihanoukville (Kampong Som), he then effectively turned a blind eye when US Special Forces extended their operations into those areas and US Air Force B-52s began bombing them. Subsequently, during the May 1970 US incursion into Cambodia, it became clear that the Vietnamese were—at least for the time being—commanding the Cambodian communist forces.

It was in large part Sihanouk's attempt to accommodate both sides—or perhaps his failure to do so successfully enough—that eventually led Cambodia's National Assembly to vote for Sihanouk's removal from office on March 18, 1970. The overthrow of Sihanouk marked the beginning of the country's full engagement in the American war against communism in Indochina. The new leader, backed by military support from the Americans, was Lon Nol. In *Swimming to Cambodia*, Spalding Gray had joked that "the only thing we knew was that 'Lon Nol' spelled backwards was 'Lon Nol,'"[21] but in fact, Washington had a back

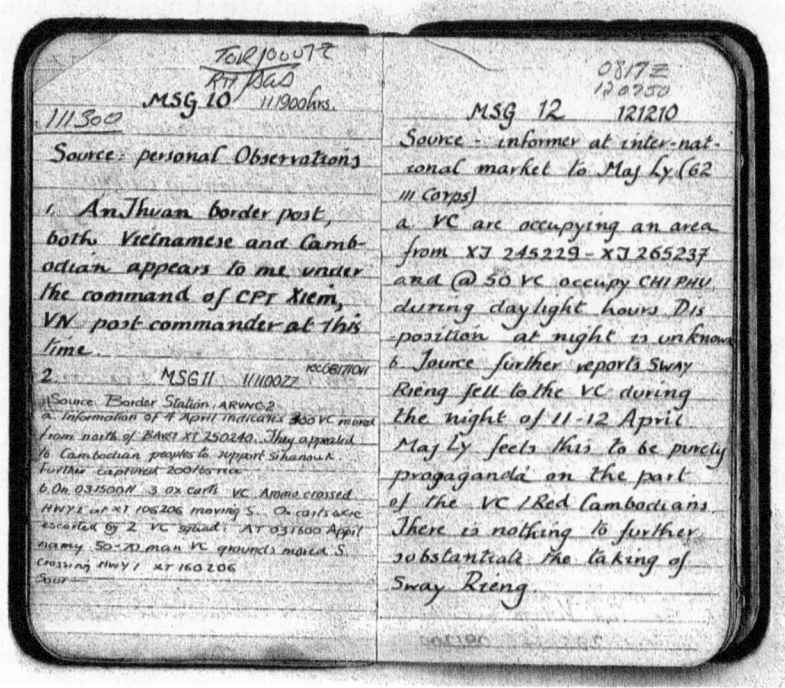

FIGURE 1.2. Field notes from 1970 US incursion into Cambodia. Denny Lane.

channel to Lon Nol throughout the 1960s, the CIA had written an extensive secret biography of him, and as early as 1966 the Cambodian press was warning that the United States supported Lon Nol replacing Sihanouk (about whom Lon Nol had had misgivings long before 1970).[22]

In one of his first acts after taking power, Lon Nol demanded that all Vietnamese communists leave Cambodia (and encouraged deadly anti-Vietnamese violence by Cambodians). The Vietnamese immediately responded by launching military operations to turn Cambodia into a communist country, suddenly seeing Cambodia as ripe for revolution. But as Steve Heder notes, "Despite the VWP's [Vietnam Workers' Party's] fawning re-evaluation of the Cambodian position after the [1970] coup, relations between the two Parties [the VWP and the CPK] did not improve."[23] The CPK's dislike for and suspicion of its powerful neighbor to the east was deeply rooted in the political DNA of Khmer culture. Notwithstanding a genuine attempt by the Vietnamese to win over the hearts and minds of Cambodian peasants,[24] the strength and battle-tested ability of the Vietnamese communist troops and the

Machiavellian politics of Le Duan, the head of the Vietnamese Communist Party, merely reinforced this traditional distrust of the contemptible Yuon (យួន).[25]

Sihanouk received news of his ouster on the tarmac of Moscow's airport as he was preparing to fly to Beijing at the tail end of a tour of France, Russia, and China. Once in Beijing, he was quickly persuaded to head a movement not only to topple those who had overthrown him and to drive out US imperialism but also to do so by armed revolutionary means and with Vietnamese military support. These deliberations resulted in the establishment under his auspices of the National United Front of Kampuchea (Front Uni National du Kampuchéa, or FUNK) in March 1970 and, later the same year, of the Royal Government of National Union of Kampuchea (Gouvernement Royal d'Union Nationale du Kampuchéa, or GRUNK).

The creation of FUNK was the opportunity for seizing political power that the Khmer Rouge had been waiting for. Certainly its alliance with FUNK's anti–Khmer Republic types, who included Royalist partisans (Khmer Rumdas, ខ្មែររំដោះ, or "Liberation Khmer," aka Khmer Sâr, ខ្មែរស, or "White Khmer") as well as Vietnamese-trained Marxists ("Khmer Hanoi"), can be viewed as rooted in a genuine desire to depose Lon Nol and throw off the yoke of US imperialism his regime represented. But for the Khmer Rouge, this strategy of a united front was precisely that—a *front* of being *united* as a *strategy* to attain political dominance. In the words of Kuong Lumphon, a primary school teacher who became disenchanted with the Khmer Republic and joined the CPK, "FUNK was only a cover [សំបកក្រៅ] . . . . [It] did not know that it had the Communist Party of Cambodia behind it and inside it."[26]

Under the generic, seemingly neutral (and eventually deeply sinister) name of Angkar (អង្គការ, literally "organization"), the CPK would use FUNK to attain its revolutionary ambitions. Even though the "runt of the litter" among other coalition members in terms of revolutionary pedigree and insurgency-based experience, the CPK would increasingly gain momentum as a political force in the early 1970s by converting, eliminating, or marginalizing pro-Sihanoukist elements. CPK members were placed in key positions of power, namely, at the district level or above. Where CPK cadres found themselves working at lower administrative levels, such as at the village or the commune, they were under strict orders to behave in ways that would gain the trust and support of the local population. In this way, the CPK slowly but surely colonized FUNK from below and within.

GRUNK was a government-in-exile based in Beijing and heavily populated by top officials from Sihanouk's time in power. It nominally represented the people residing in Cambodian territories controlled by FUNK. Over the course of the next five years, China provided GRUNK with an annual budget of $2 million as well as office space and living quarters at the Friendship Hotel in northwestern Beijing. These apartments, in Sophie Richardson's description, "housed approximately thirty staff members, several of whom were Cambodians with previous ties to the Cambodian communists or to the royal family," and the spaciousness of the quarters "facilitated a kind of physical and intellectual proximity between extreme ends of the Cambodian political spectrum previously unimaginable." Sihanouk, who had maintained often effusively cordial relations with the Chinese leadership since the 1950s, resided in the former French embassy, complete with swimming pool and ballroom. Even the *Chinese* embassy was physically relocated from the hostile Phnom Penh of Lon Nol's Khmer Republic to Beijing, where the Chinese ambassador to Cambodia, Kang Maozhao, carried out his functions as if he were on Cambodian soil.[27]

As already tense relations between the Cambodian and Vietnamese communists were reinforced by the ever-worsening Sino-Soviet divide, China's support for the CPK insurgency only increased. Indeed, China continued to provide arms, clothing, food, and even printed banknotes for use even after the CPK assumed complete power in 1975. This continuation of Chinese support was in no small part thanks to the diplomatic handiwork of Ieng Sary, the most fluent of our three "lieutenants" in the lingo of the united front.

Ieng Sary, "Special Emissary"

During the initial incubation period in the northeast, Pol Pot was joined by Ieng Sary and Son Sen and established mobile "Office 100," a base on the Vietnamese side of the border with Kampong Cham in Tay Nihn.[28] In 1966, Office 100 was moved inside Cambodia to Kântuy Neak (កន្ទុយនាគ, "Dragon's Tail") in Ratanakiri on the banks of the Toek Chrâp (ស្ទឹងទឹកក្រាប).[29] As described by Phi Phuon:

> Office 100 [was] located on the edge of a small stream with water in every season. The base was one kilometre wide by three kilometres in length.... All around, a fence made of half-timbered tree trunks was raised and surrounded by bamboo stakes and traps.

Behind was a large room that served as both meeting room and refectory, and a kitchen. In front of and facing a larger stream, named O'Kap, was built a sort of shed housing the office staff.... On the other side of the brook were the houses and fields of the village inhabitants.[30]

It was at this time that Sary was appointed Northeast Zone secretary and ran his operations overseeing Ratanakiri from Office 102 near Kang Lêng, some three kilometers from Office 100, until 1970. Sandwiched in between were a group of "thatched huts which served as a reception centre for couriers and visiting cadres from other parts of the country."[31] Zone 102 comprised Steung Trâng, Ratanakiri, and Mondulkiri (Region 105) provinces and was under the direction of Ieng Sary into 1970, when it was transferred to Son Sen.[32] In 1968, as Pol Pot moved to military compound K5 in the Kachâk tribal village of Nây (ណាយ), he took over Sary's duties as Northeast Zone secretary while the latter was dispatched to direct operations in Anduong Meas (អណ្ដូងមាស) and Bokeo (បរកែវ), where the CPK movement was at its strongest.[33]

Two years later, Pol Pot, his bodyguards and family, future Kratie CPK secretary Tiv Ol (ទិវ អុល), and about eighty soldiers embarked on a seven-month journey from Kântuy Neak to Steung Treng (ស្ទឹងត្រែង) and Office S17.[34] Sary did not accompany them, traveling instead to Hanoi to establish a clandestine radio station that broadcast missives from the liberated zones inside Cambodia via a special frequency. This station was run by Sary's wife, Ieng Thirith, who spent the 1970–1975 period managing the CPK radio station in Hanoi with the technical assistance and support of the Vietnamese.[35]

Following Sihanouk's establishment of FUNK and GRUNK on, respectively, March 23 and May 5, 1970,[36] Ieng Sary arrived in Beijing in mid-1970 and set up quarters in the capital's Dongdan district. He would reside there from 1971 to 1975 in a compound known as "la Maison des Khmèrs Rouges" (红色高棉家). From there he would have a direct telegraph link to Office 100 deep inside Cambodia.[37] Other GRUNK ministers stayed at the Friendship Hotel in Beijing's Haidian district, while their children were sent to study languages in the capital or medicine in Guangzhou (Canton).[38]

The following year, Sary was appointed "the official representative of the CPK to the CCP" with the title "Special Emissary of the Section of the Royal Government inside the Country." A representative Foreign Ministry office, B20, with attached offices B15–B18 in Steung Trâng,

Kampong Cham, operated on Cambodian soil in Sary's absence. Sary's appointment was a natural fit: although Ieng Sary was a true believer in the CPK's mission, he could also manage a broader set of actors and work with them (or, if the situation required, *against* them) to forge a broader coalition that would ultimately benefit the Khmer Rouge. As Pol Pot's special ambassador to China, Sary was charged with minding the titular head of the GRUNK coalition: none other than Norodom Sihanouk himself. But there was little love lost between the two. In Richardson's words, "Sihanouk and Ieng Sary detested each other, and ... [Sihanouk would] torment Ieng Sary by showing pornographic films in Beijing."[39]

GRUNK competed with the Khmer Republic missions abroad for the loyalties of those who had been posted overseas at the time of Sihanouk's ouster. Ouk Ket recalled being appointed to represent GRUNK in Senegal in 1971, seeking to expand support for the united front in Mali, Mauritania, Togo, Cameroon, and Niger, all the while articulating the united front, with Sihanouk as its leader, as the faction of resistance against the Khmer Republic.[40] Efforts by him and his colleagues around the world were successful: by the end of 1972, GRUNK had received recognition from some thirty countries and regimes, including North Vietnam, Sweden, France, the USSR, East Germany, Pakistan, the Palestine Liberation Organization, and North Korea.[41]

In practice, this meant that CPK sovereign authority existed in coordinated security operations that extended from the Cambodian forests into the Chinese capital and back. According to longtime Ieng Sary colleague Suong Sikoeun, China refused to bring charges against Ker Chhieng, one of Sihanouk's bodyguards and the son of the Cambodian ambassador to China, for leaking state secrets to the Italian embassy. Instead, the Chinese deferred to GRUNK in Beijing to deploy FUNK in Cambodia to arrest him, an action undertaken by a commando raid led by a Khmer Republic colonel who had defected to the Khmer Rouge. FUNK also directed the capture of Nouth Chhoeum, a pro-Sihanouk journalist who had been suspected of spying on behalf of Hong Kong intelligence. Ieng Sary was almost certainly aware of these operations and likely approved them.[42]

While in Beijing, Sary had visited Beijing's Number One Prison and may have drawn inspiration from how the Chinese worked to reform and reeducate their charges. Chinese prisoners were forced to continually read ideological materials and attend self-criticism sessions, and were placed in isolation and "brainwashed." One former Foreign

Ministry employee suggested that Sary would embrace these same methods for use in Democratic Kampuchea. This is, in fact, inaccurate.[43] Sary's exposure in Beijing was to a completely different approach from what the Khmer Rouge would eventually adopt: Chinese reeducation (however draconian) versus Khmer purges. As we will see, Sary employed the former throughout his term as foreign minister and sought to mitigate the latter when possible. He often acceded to the regime's embrace of eliminationist class struggle out of a combination of perceived necessity and self-preservation as distinct from conviction (Son Sen) or bloodlust (Mok). While one can only speculate as to *why*, it appears that Sary's focus on the movement prioritized legitimation and capitalizing on its successes and not obsessing about its failures.

In the spring of 1973, Sary somewhat reluctantly departed from China and navigated the Ho Chi Minh Trail all the way down to Phnom Kulen (ភ្នំគូលែន), the CPK's far more modest version of Yan'an. Sary's mission was to bring a long-insistent Sihanouk (who missed Cambodia terribly) to the CPK base area in order for him to be seen (and photographed) by and with the Khmer Rouge leaders, particularly GRUNK minister of information Hu Nim (ហ៊ូ និម), Hou Youn (ហ៊ូ យន, GRUNK minister of the interior, communal reforms, cooperatives),[44] Khieu Samphân, and Sary himself. (Pol Pot remained largely anonymous or in the background.) There, amid the pristine streams that animated the "Thousand Lingas" carved in the riverbed and sumptuous waterfalls, a beaming Sihanouk posed with his united front CPK partners. Newsreel footage accompanied these photographs in Chinese magazines and on Chinese television. The legitimacy that Sihanouk thus conferred on the Khmer Rouge on this trip was priceless for the CPK.

Apart from this and another trip in 1974 (when he accompanied a Chinese film crew from Kântuy to Kèp to film *The Heroic Kampuchean People in the Liberated Zone*), Sary stayed on the sidelines of the civil war, not returning to Cambodia full-time until a week after the Khmer Rouge victory on April 17, 1975.[45] In fact, Sary had his hands full in the Chinese capital, as the ideological cleavages within the GRUNK coalition were intensified, in part, by his own escalating rhetoric as he recruited more overseas Cambodians to join him in Beijing and eventually return to Cambodia. This was consistent with the hardening of the anti-Vietnamese political line by the CPK[46] and was emboldened by the late-stage Cultural Revolution factionalism between Chinese leftists and their pragmatist rivals. For his part, Sary grew close to such Chinese radicals as Kang Sheng and Yao Wenyuan, betraying his own biases in managing the "united front." This may have been done to deepen China-CPK relations as the Khmer Rouge in the *maquis* attempted to pull out of the Indochinese Communist Party's orbit, which would occur on the ground in 1972–73 by and largely through the efforts of our other two "lieutenants," Son Sen and *Ta* Mok.[47]

Son Sen: Lurking in the Shadows

Son Sen had originally bunked with Pol Pot at the Office 100 compound in Ratanakiri.[48] Around 1966, while zone secretary Ieng Sary was responsible for managing the movement in that province, Son Sen, as deputy secretary, oversaw Steung Trâng and Ney Saran in adjacent Mondulkiri. In mid-1968, Son Sen began training what would become the core of the Khmer Rouge military, the revolutionary guard units.[49] Later that year "he settled at Office K-1, located in the Jaraï village of Krachak" even though he reportedly "held the national minorities in contempt." The following year, Son Sen was appointed chief of staff and was given a new code name by Saloth Sâr (who used the occasion to rechristen himself Pol Pot, having hitherto operated under the alias Pouk [ពូក, "mattress"], ostensibly to "soften up" conflicts).[50] Previously known by the *nom de guerre* Kham (ឃំ, "one who bites"), Son Sen would henceforth be known as Khiev (ខៀវ, "blue").[51]

In addition to his role as chief of staff, Son Sen commanded the Central Military, an elite group that was deployed throughout the country during the civil war. It consisted of troops from throughout the CPK forces, including some thirteen divisions culled from the Northern, Eastern, and Southwest Zones, as well as troops from the West and Northwest Zones.[52] But he was also extending his portfolio to include internal security, the implementation agent in the operationalization of class struggle.

The security apparatus that would eventually be so closely associated with Son Sen evolved over time. Leadership of the Nôkôrôbal (នគរបាល) detention unit M13 in Sector 25 had passed from Chhay Kim Hor to Vorn Vet to, eventually, Son Sen. It was a facility that received prisoners sent down from the Center to be interrogated and executed, and was also responsible for the identification and liquidation of returnees from Vietnam.[53] In 1972, responding to appeals by M13 and with the approval of Son Sen, future Tuol Sleng/S21 commandant Kaing Guek-Eav, aka Duch, who found himself "in a situation of hating shit but having to step in shit," established M13B or M13Kh in Sdok Srat (ស្តុកស្រាត) village as a facility where prisoners could be released.[54]

The following year, concurrent with the shift to class struggle in the countryside and a hardening of CPK attitudes toward suspected threats to the movement, a secret office was established in Chrâk Sdech (ច្រកស្ដេច) village in Kampong Chhnang province. At this time Son Sen moved into the Damnak Smach (ដំណាក់ស្មាច់) railway station on the abandoned Phnom Penh–Battambang line,[55] after which discretionary treatment of prisoners (that is, releasing them) stopped almost entirely. (In fact, only one person was ever recorded as having been released from that facility.) Tellingly, in an exchange devoid of irony, Duch expressed gratitude to Vorn Vet—as he interrogated the latter before preparing him for his eventual execution in 1978—for having refused to punish him following a prison escape of detainees from M13B. This, of course, implied that sanctions would have been—and were—more brutal under Son Sen.[56] Indeed, while Vorn Vet (who had originally trained Duch in torture and interrogation techniques) would use the word "resolve" (ដោះស្រាយ) in handling such matters, Son Sen, tellingly, preferred the term "smash" (កម្ទេច).[57]

In addition, Son Sen and his wife, Yun Yat (aka At, អាត់, "tiny"), were in charge of social affairs, marking an interest in, if not quite an aptitude for, civilian administration. Although this portfolio would go to Ieng Sary's wife, Ieng Thirith, after 1975,[58] Son Sen's attention to this particular domain during this period of transition later paid off. At the time, there were three main youth organizations at the village level that Son Sen and his wife were ostensibly responsible for overseeing: the Patriotic Youth Organization, the Advanced Children's Organization, and the village *chhlôp* (ឈ្លប). The first two were charged with recruitment and ideological fashioning to motivate young people in the village to join the struggle. The *chhlôp* were responsible for security.[59] They were a kind of secret or "plainclothes" police, overwhelmingly children, who would spy on otherwise unsuspecting villagers. They would become Son Sen's foot soldiers in the countryside after 1975.

The period of the first united front thus saw Son Sen building up his power base within the military elite and within the security apparatus. He had an extensive military portfolio, but one that was also firmly within the political institutions that were emerging at the time, always remaining relevant and powerful within them. He seemed to be both comfortable and literate in the exercise of martial as well as political power. So was his battle-scarred subordinate, the equally brutal but far more colorful *Ta* Mok.

Ta Mok: An Army of One

Unlike Sary and Son Sen, Mok—the "skinny, bony ex-monk from Takeo"—had never quite left the *maquis*.[60] He had been waging a struggle against the French up to 1953 and against Sihanouk since the Geneva Conference of 1954, and his rejection of united front doctrine may have reflected his long-standing professional career goal to that point: the ouster of the prince. Not surprisingly, Mok had deep suspicion of, and little patience for, GRUNK. Instead, he concentrated on his regional power base in Cambodia's southwest, which at the time was a truly wretched place. As Philip Short quotes a soldier at the time:

> I had been told that Mok's base was very well-organised, just like the Chinese revolutionary bases during the civil war. . . . I couldn't wait to get there. . . . What did I find? Khieu Samphân, Hou [Youn], and Hu Nim were almost unrecognizable: Nim had lost most of his hair. . . . Hou [Youn], who used to be so well-built, was as thin as a nail. . . . Another comrade lay beside them, shivering and groaning with fever, and talking deliriously to himself in French. . . . The bodyguards were asleep on a bed nearby, under which were stocked provisions of elephant meat. They all had skin diseases and kept scratching themselves.[61]

After years of indeterminate struggle in these miserable conditions, Mok was thus predictably delighted that the Samlaut uprising and its residual effects were finally bearing fruit. As he once gleefully recalled in an interview, "I—not we, for once, but I [laughs]—. . . organized forces in the Southwest and mobilized an uprising to snatch arms from the police and militia in the provinces of Kampot, Takeo, Kampong Chhnang and Kampong Speu."[62]

Mok became acting Southwest Zone secretary when his immediate predecessor, Mâng, was felled by malaria in 1968.[63] After a three-year stint in Phnom Aural (ភ្នំឪរ៉ាល់), Cambodia's tallest mountain, in September 1970 Mok's forces crossed Tonlé Sap toward the Chinit River (ស្ទឹងជីនិត). There, Mok met up with Pol Pot and Nuon Chea, who had arrived from Ratanakiri.[64] But he didn't stay long. He was itching to get back to the battlefield and showed scant desire for engaging in the nonmilitary dimension of politics in general, and with revolutionary intellectuals in particular. Members of the intellectual class who had escaped to the *maquis* were seen as useful tools as the CPK laid the groundwork for an eventual CPK takeover of GRUNK,[65] but Mok had no patience for such subtleties. Intellectuals were such an anathema to Mok that in July 1971 none other than Pol Pot was eventually forced to establish a "special zone" to house them because Mok had "made so much trouble" for them, including issuing impossible ultimatums to leave the Southwest Zone.[66] Kè Kim Huot (aka Sot), Khèk Pèn (aka Sou), Chea Huon (aka Vanh), and Um Chhoeun (aka Mai) were all expelled from the Southwest and appointed sector secretaries far outside areas controlled by Mok.[67]

By 1973, the zones included the Southwest (Kampot, Koh Kong, Kampong Som, Kampong Seila, Takeo, Kampong Chhnang, Kampong Speu, Oudong, and Kandal provinces) under Mok; the Eastern (Kratie, Svay Rieng, Prey Veng, and Kampong Cham) under So Phim; the Northern (Kampong Thom, Siem Reap, Oddar Meanchey, and Banteay Chhmar) under Koy Thuon; the Northwest (Pursat-Battambang-Pailin) under Nhim Ros; and the provinces controlled directly by the Central Committee (Preah Vihear, Steung Trâng, Mondulkiri, and Ratanakiri). A "special zone" around Phnom Penh was also created in 1971 and administered from within Mok's Southwest Zone.[68] Mok was already establishing himself as a major regional player in CPK politics.

During this period Mok's combative reputation grew, as he went after those who fell within his expansive definition of class enemies. In 1973, Pol Pot again had to intervene to resolve this ongoing problem; in an attempt to affirm the position of the intellectual class in the movement, at least for the time being, and thus remove them from Mok's line of fire, he proclaimed—albeit somewhat cryptically—in the CPK journal *Revolutionary Flag* that "the political line of any class means the cadre is of that class." Mok also extended his suspicions to non-Khmer minorities. That same year, Hou Youn gave a speech in Koh Kong on the rights of Indigenous people in Cambodia. Mok forbade the broadcast of that speech in his area.[69]

Not only did Mok hold united front allies in suspicion, but also he even held his bona fide CPK colleagues in contempt. Mok was growing increasingly unpopular with other elites that were in regular contact with him within the Southwest Zone. Individuals like Chou Chet and particularly Thiounn Prasith as well as their staffers, spoke openly about the conflicts they had with Mok.[70] Eventually, in early 1974, Mok's constant prodding finally persuaded Pol Pot to liquidate *Ta* Chong on charges of spying for Thailand.[71] Mok oversaw his execution.[72]

Mok's predecessor as Southwest Zone secretary, Vorn Vet (ឫន វេត), had sought to mediate these conflicts as early as 1971.[73] But he met with uneven results[74] and earned Mok's undying enmity in the process. One such instance was the kidnapping of scholar François Bizot in 1970 (which eerily paralleled the PDK practice of kidnapping foreigners a quarter-century later). While Mok enthusiastically advocated for his execution, he was countermanded by Vorn Vet, then his superior, who thus saved the Frenchman's life. Years later, in 1978, Mok would scarcely conceal his delight following Vet's arrest, torture, and execution.[75] Bizot's musings provide insights about these two CPK leaders and their fundamentally different sets of personality traits that, juxtaposed, speak volumes about Mok: "The two men lived in different worlds.... They had nothing in common: the former [Vet] was a militant Communist from the fifties, passionate about ideals and justice; the latter [Mok] was purely a technician of force. A man of instinctive action, *Ta* Mok believed that doubts were best resolved by chopping everything short. In this respect he was less equivocal than [Vorn Vet] because he despised theory. [Vorn Vet's] weakness arose from his belief that power was expressed primarily through ideas."[76]

Mok attended key early 1970s meetings in which the CPK decided, once and for all, to separate from the Indochinese Communist Party and to take action to expel their erstwhile Vietnamese allies from Cambodian territory.[77] Previous negotiations aimed at securing a formal North Vietnamese withdrawal had led to Hanoi's acceptance in principle. But this was followed by their delaying or slow-walking the policy. One of Mok's subordinates in Takeo bitterly recalled that "the Vietnamese did not let us carry small arms, rather using Cambodian troops as porters for heavy ordnance.... Some Vietnamese ... had to be forced out ... [and] there was a lot of bloodshed in 1973 before all the Vietnamese finally left." Mok was more than willing to take the fight to the Vietnamese. He would tour areas under his control and personally instruct district and even village-level cadres to expel remnant Vietnamese contingents.[78]

Mok was thus one of the most enthusiastic and active CPK leaders when it came to marginalizing the Vietnamese as he had the intellectuals.[79] His abandonment of two key pillars of the united front strategy demonstrated how little he cared for it—and how little it suited his temperament. And as his bloodthirstiness indicates, his embrace of the CPK's only other viable option, class struggle, was unstinting. This would, as it turns out, carry him to the bitter end of the revolutionary path, further than either Son Sen or Ieng Sary would go.

On the Cusp of Two Worlds

By 1973, Phnom Penh had become the land of the lotus-eaters, wrapped in a narcotic cocoon of willful ignorance. Despite having lost huge swaths of the Cambodian countryside to the Vietnamese-assisted CPK from 1970 to 1973, the Khmer Republic appeared blissfully unaware of the severity of the problem and unwilling to face the reality on the ground. Foreign interlocutors, the United States included, were no better, as US diplomat William Harben recalled:

> [Lon Nol] issued a presidential decree ordering the arrest of anyone seen buying rabbits in the market. . . . [E]nemy agents, said the decree[,] . . . would tie timed explosives on the backs of the little beasts, which would hop into the army's entrenchments and blow them up! Since it had been broadcast on the state radio I knew that it would be circulated all over Washington by the FBIS [Foreign Broadcast Information Service] in unclassified form.
>
> Subsequently, an emergency high-level mission was dispatched to Phnom Penh, including a young National Security Council staffer who covered Cambodia.
>
> "Why is the situation so much worse than we thought it was?" he asked me at lunch in my villa. I told him that the ambassador had been discouraged from reporting the truth, "but anyway, there was enough material in the public print for any sensible person back there to realize that this place was going down the tube with its present leadership—like the rabbit bomb decree."
>
> "The _WHAT?_" He had never heard of it. Apparently, no one in Washington had dared send the item upstairs. The government concealed the truth from no one but itself.[80]

The anecdote underscores the casual but deadly lack of seriousness among those abroad—not to mention the ruling elite in Phnom Penh. The CPK, by contrast, could not have been *more* serious. In only a matter of months, a much darker but equally surreal reality would envelop the Cambodian countryside. This would be the turning point for the Khmer Rouge and for the country, as the wheel of history ground down all but the last vestiges of the united front and left in its place a vicious form of violent class struggle that would have few, if any, parallels in human history.

Chapter 2

Before and After Year Zero
A World of Class Struggle, 1973–1978

> The monster I kill every day is the monster of realism. The monster who attacks me every day is destruction. Out of the duel comes the transformation. I turn destruction into creation over and over again.
>
> —Anaïs Nin, *Henry and June*

In the late summer of 1994, the political prospects for the Khmer Rouge were looking increasingly grim, and their policies became correspondingly sinister. There was a dramatic uptick in the systematic killing of targeted local groups as well as a scheme of kidnapping foreigners, securing a ransom, and killing them anyway. *Ta* Mok, then commander of the military zone Corridor (ឡូម) 1008, had also ordered Khmer Rouge forces to murder Royal Government of Cambodia authorities on top of launching a scorched-earth policy in the countryside whereby residents of those areas were forcibly relocated and the entire landscape—quite literally—was set alight. If, for old Cambodia hands, the violence of this conjured up memories of widespread killings and burnings in the 1970s, that era appeared to be not too far from the minds of the Khmer Rouge either. Indeed, in a weeklong meeting with senior combatants in late summer 1994, Mok announced that "the situation had changed back to 1975 and so we have to use the tactics of 1975."[1]

In fact, Mok was off by two years. The "tactics" he described were the very same witnessed by Kenneth Quinn, then a young USAID official attached to the US consulate in Cần Thơ, Vietnam, not in 1975 but in 1973. On a Saturday in June that year, Quinn and his then fiancée had decided to hike up the crab-shaped Sam mountain, which sits atop the

Vietnamese-Cambodian border. When they reached the summit, where they could see perhaps ten to fifteen kilometers to the horizon, what greeted them was not, as they were expecting, pastoral scenes of farmers busy planting long-cycle rice for the December harvest. Rather, it was ominous columns of thick black smoke billowing into the air as far as they could see.

This apocalyptic scene was not a wildfire gone amok. Nor was it a group of farmers engaged in an overzealous round of swidden. An agronomist by training, Quinn knew what the controlled burning of a fallow field looked like. Quinn's suspicions that the smoke was a sign of something else entirely, something much darker, were confirmed over the next several weeks as scores of Khmer and ethnic Vietnamese fleeing Cambodia helped Cần Thơ consular officials piece together the scene Quinn had observed from the summit: the destruction of Cambodian peasant villages to force their residents into collectivized "liberated" areas under Khmer Rouge control.

As Quinn later affirmed, this destruction was "structured, planned, carefully thought-out, [and] not an aberration driven by enraged revolutionaries—as some people were hypothesizing at the time—who were driven mad by American bombing." The "compelling" evidence here, he explained, was that the burning was occurring in several provinces at the same time; as he put it, "If this was all haphazard, then maybe it could be happening in one of those regions but not the others, but it was all the same—villages burning—all on the same day in the region from the banks of the Mekong [River] going west and the region existing between the two branches of the Mekong, and the one to the east of the Mekong, which included Prey Veng province, and all of these, the villages were all burning at the same time."[2] Peasants were summarily forced to leave their lives behind and march to designated areas; as one of them recalled: "The landscape was very rough because of the bamboo stumps left from burning. We were beaten along the way as we walked, from 4:00 [in the morning] until 10:00 [at night]. They hit me with a gun, making me pass out. I saw white, then black, and then everything went dark. When I woke up, I saw yellow, then red. And I felt pain. After that, we were put in the deep forest in Koh Nhek [កោះញែក] district, called *Prey Chas* [ព្រៃចាស់], or 'Old Forest.' We were shackled. About thirty people guarded us."[3]

In forcing Cambodian villagers to resettle in CPK-controlled areas, the Khmer Rouge were ostensibly aiming to effectively mobilize them to produce and otherwise assist in the war effort against Lon Nol's

Khmer Republic troops (the Forces Armées Nationales Khmères, or FANK) and the anticommunist South Vietnamese forces. But this policy also had the political goal of locking in CPK domination over the united front. More than war effort mobilization, these actions also had the upshot of removing the population from the governing structures of the Khmer Rouge's allies in the fight against Lon Nol—the National United Front of Kampuchea (FUNK)—and placing them under direct Khmer Rouge control. They were, in other words, a prelude to the marginalizing of the CPK's FUNK allies through cooptation, exile, or outright killing.

Sidelining, Expelling, and Reorganizing

What Quinn saw was thus the beginnings of the Khmer Rouge's first large-scale engagement toward class struggle, their repression of what they believed to be residual elements of capitalistic society. Like the concept of the united front, class struggle for the Khmer Rouge must be understood as a strategy by which they attempted to obtain and maintain political power under particular circumstances even as its adoption reflected their adherence to ideological doctrine. In the 1990s, class struggle would take the form of scorched-earth policies, extrajudicial killings, and the targeting of in-party elites. But as *Ta* Mok's abovementioned order indicates, these measures were merely the revival of those carried out some two decades earlier.

Quinn was on the outside looking in. But it is also important to get a sense of being on the inside, *also* looking in. Although it is difficult to disentangle them in practice, there are at least three dimensions along which to trace the shift from united front to class struggle: economic, political, and martial. If the goal is a classless society free of exploitation, and class is an economic construct, it is necessary to shift to a program that eliminates these class differences. In the case of the Khmer Rouge, the economies in areas they held were increasingly collectivized, which eradicated class distinctions and punished those who resisted. Consolidating these gains required politically led class struggle against those who resisted, were *seen* to resist, or were otherwise impediments to this goal. Finally, all of this would be secured (and made increasingly difficult to reverse) through the military gains against FANK troops on the outside and united front allies from within.

The Economic Dimension

The burning of peasant villages Quinn saw from atop Sam Mountain was the implementation of a May 20, 1973, CPK leadership pronouncement on collectivization (សហករណ៍), a decision that, in Quinn's words, marked "a clear break with the Khmer Rouge's previous restrained policy of dealing with people."[4] Indeed, as a decidedly non-clandestine act, the burnings signaled a departure from the CPK's prior efforts to keep their intent of seizing control occluded. As Craig Etcheson notes: "Up until the May 20 decision, markets still existed in KR-controlled areas. Pol Pot and Nuon Chea had concluded that where markets existed, the merchants—rather than the CPK—were in control. This was a key impetus for the change to cooperatives: eliminate markets in a masterful stroke of class struggle, thereby totally transforming the economic infrastructure."[5] Thus, the summer of 1973 was also the exact moment when, as Quinn puts it, a new, radical phase of economic and social policy under the CPK began.

Economically, co-ops were seen as a mechanism by which to "rationalize" agriculture in order to maximize output to better feed the population and the military fighting on their behalf. A refugee described the setup this way: "The [regional] headquarters was self-reliant in terms of production [but] the army was completely supported by the co-ops.... For co-ops in which there was [sic] shortages, the upper echelon[,] which meant the district, arranged for a transfer of surplus from surplus co-ops. This system of transfers operated at all levels up to the Regional level and among Regions as well. [Region] 25 was rich in corn but poor in rice. So it sent corn to regions 13, 15, and 33. Meanwhile [R]egion 33 sent rice back in exchange."[6] This system eventually carried over—or was supposed to—into the Democratic Kampuchea era.

Initially, cooperatives were "lower-level co-ops," which conformed to the traditional Khmer villages; eventually they moved toward greater consolidation and CPK control. Within the village, peasants were organized into teams and brigades, as their counterparts in China and Vietnam had been during the communalization of the countryside. Administration consisted of a chairman, a vice chairman, and a committee member (appointed by the village chief); their responsibilities were upholding the general political line, security, and economics, respectively. These leaders could come only from the ranks of poor (those with no draft animals who could produce only a few months' worth of food) and lower-middle peasants (those who could produce enough crops for up to eight months of the year).[7] The co-op tended to organize around the inter-family group (of twelve to fifteen families), a key conduit for spreading CPK propaganda and policy. All land was collectivized, and production was managed at the co-op level, although peasants could have private plots of land near their homes.[8]

Other aspects of the economy were also collectivized. For fishing, this involved using central storehouses for fishing equipment and charging between five and ten individuals with providing the entire village with fish, which would be distributed equally. For cotton, a given village would collectively plant cotton and "cottage industry crops," and teams would be assigned to weave the cotton. Villages also had small medical units with staff of around five people, mostly poor peasants who had received one-month training courses in the use of traditional herbal medicines.[9]

Not surprisingly, there was some variation, particularly due to differences in economic conditions around the country's liberated zones. As one refugee recalled: "The people in [the] Northwest and East were relatively well off; the standard of living of the poor people in [the] Northwest and East was higher than [for] the middle [peasants] in [the] Southwest. The poor in the Southwest Region were really poor with no draft animals and land, but in other areas people were not so poor, especially along the riverbanks and fertile land."[10] This unevenness affected who would join a co-op, which was initially a voluntary matter. Those who could afford to opt out via, for example, mutual aid teams or by hiring out their draft animals often did so. In Region 13, some middle peasants joined, but not one of the rich peasants did (those who employed hired labor, whose land produced a surplus, or both). By 1974, the middle and rich peasants were placed under increasing pressure to join, and the CPK mobilized the entirety of the collectivized population to persuade the holdouts. The goal, after all, was to make class distinctions disappear. One resident pointed out that "the rich and middle peasants were dissatisfied but there was nothing they could do," and added, "In my [region, 13] we were successfully able to get everybody into the co-ops without bloodshed"—suggesting that this was not always the case.[11]

Although collectivization is at root an economic activity, it is also inherently a political undertaking. Politically, collectivization would serve to undercut traditional economic relations by sidelining the middle and rich peasants and making them ineligible for leadership positions. In some cases, these "class enemies" were treated with neglect, and their influence would dissipate with time. In other instances, a heavier hand was employed, whereby young CPK, who had been sent to the villages in the previous years as "sleepers," were now activated to employ "terror, violence and force."[12]

Relocations continued until December 1973 and were accompanied (and often preceded) by the purge and replacement of local officials by tougher new cadres brought in from elsewhere. Relocated persons were told to take the minimum number of possessions and were often ill-equipped to physically, let alone psychologically, undertake such a sudden move. There were many reports of people who died en route. Conditions in these new collectivized areas were crowded and dirty, with a lack of food and medical care, and focused on economic production and political indoctrination.[13]

Movement was also closely monitored. It was possible to travel from village to village, but crossing into a different commune, district, or sector required a pass from the corresponding administrative level. Village cadres had sticks and, in some fortunate cases, knives to enforce policy. Cooperative-level cadres made do with swords, bows and arrows, and lances, and traveled mostly on horseback.[14] One former cadre assigned to work as the deputy chief on the commune-level economics and commerce committee explained that trade outside that managed by his office was strictly forbidden. His comments capture the delimited nature of trade the CPK implemented:

> We had five people in the unit and used elephants to carry goods, mainly salt, from Kratie to sell to the people in the commune. The price was set by the district commerce committee. We just followed their orders. In addition, we traded clothing and other goods. My group was charged only with selling goods to the people and [remitting] the profits to the district level, which would take that money and give it to another group [within] the commerce unit responsible for buying rice, which would then be sent to troops at the front lines.... We would then request more money from Angkar [the CPK "Organization"] in order to buy more goods to sell to the people.[15]

These new policies did not always or necessarily make a great deal of local economic sense to the average peasant,[16] and were not universally embraced by the population. Even when output was no different from that of previous years, distribution *was*, as dictated by the type of "war communism" being practiced.[17] Any opposition was often met with retaliation, including imprisonment (given the filthy, malarial conditions, many prisoners died) or, in extreme cases, execution.[18] In the words of an interviewee, the CPK's efforts to implement and enforce these policies were driven by "raw emotion," that is, violence.[19]

The Political Dimension

The move from united front to class struggle also requires understanding the political cost-benefit calculations of the hitherto minority party—in this case, the CPK—as it sought enough momentum and political resources to gain control of the political superstructure. This was achieved by sidelining and expelling non-CPK elements through an insurgent overtaking of the alliance and a reorganization within, and eventually without.

In displacing rural Cambodians into Khmer Rouge–controlled areas, the CPK effectively robbed from its FUNK coalition allies the populations over which they might otherwise have held sway. This displacement, however, did not necessarily nor immediately translate into support for the Khmer Rouge. Sihanouk remained a popular figure in the countryside, and CPK efforts to dilute the prince's authority among coalition members were also challenging because of the preponderance of his elite followers in GRUNK and the large number of those sympathetic to him among the Khmer Rumdas in FUNK. As Quinn observes, "There were probably more Sihanouk followers than anything else among the ethnic Khmer."[20]

Thus, another tactic the CPK resorted to in their climb to power under cover of FUNK was the sidelining of Royalist united front allies. Even as they worked publicly with these Sihanoukists in the effort against Lon Nol's Khmer Republic, the CPK all the while burrowed into key leadership positions and mobilized party activists from the bottom up to squeeze non-communists out. They had to their advantage the non-communists' relative disorganization; in Quinn's words, Sihanouk's followers were "usually the least organized (and often not organized at all)."[21] As such, they were politically isolated and easily bested by the CPK because, as in the 1980s, the Khmer Rouge, in comparison to its coalition partners, tended to be better organized.

To soften the allegiance of Khmer peasants to Sihanouk, the CPK resorted to a time-tested political device, propaganda, the importance of which they had recognized early on in their march to power. One such propaganda unit in Steung Trâng in the Northern Zone was led by Hu Nim (who after 1975 became minister of information and propaganda). The unit ran printing houses and distributed *Front* magazine; there was also an art department and a department for scripting radio broadcasts. The CPK mobilized this propaganda infrastructure to blacken the prince's image. People would be let in on the various "schemes" Sihanouk had undertaken to hurt the Cambodian people. After encountering popular backlash, CPK cadres had to tone things down a bit, saying instead that he had "apologized" for "deserting the revolution" and for living the good life in Beijing while Cambodian soldiers faced death fighting on his behalf.[22]

Much as they had in purges going back as early as 1968 in Mondulkiri,[23] the CPK also sought to neutralize Sihanoukist supporters within FUNK, that is, the Khmer Rumdas. The transitional united front alliance with them was broken off in *Ta* Mok's Southwest Zone and several other areas as early as the beginning of 1972. By May 1973, the CPK began a wholesale purge of Sihanouk supporters, beginning in eastern Kampot province. The targets of this campaign included anyone who had served in the Sihanouk government before the March 1970 coup, "including village chiefs, minor functionaries, and even village guards."[24]

The Sihanoukists did not go quietly. On November 6, 1973, fighting erupted in two villages in Kampot province's Kampong Trach (កំពង់ត្រាច) district, when the Khmer Rumdas objected to the CPK policy of forcibly relocating the population in GRUNK-held territories. Tensions also rose two weeks later, when CPK officials, denouncing Sihanouk and imposing control over the harvest, became embroiled in an armed conflict. The Royalists obtained the support of five hundred villagers "armed with scythes, machetes, and hatchets" who killed nine CPK cadres, wounded twenty, and sent the rest retreating into the forests. Things escalated on December 6, when four hundred CPK troops clashed with five hundred Khmer Rumdas soldiers, resulting in about a hundred killed in battle.[25] A year later in Mondulkiri, one hundred Khmer Rumdas soldiers were sent to K11 prison in Koh Nhek, where almost all of them were executed.[26] So it was that the CPK began clearing from their path to power the impediments they once considered their allies.

The Martial Dimension

Managing the economic and political dimensions required a fierce amount of control, something that the CPK lacked so long as it was working alongside its erstwhile allies, the Vietnamese communists. This extended the purge of Sihanoukists to those with a close association with Vietnam. Following a series of crushing defeats of Khmer Republic FANK forces, and facilitated by the ease with which it could displace the Sihanoukists in FUNK and the rapport it enjoyed, to an extent, with the peasants, the CPK was able to rule wide swaths of Cambodian territory on its own by 1972. It no longer needed to rely on North Vietnamese forces and was eager to push them out of Cambodia altogether.

Ironically, the Vietnamese had trained the CPK so well that the former eventually were deemed to be no longer necessary and were expelled by the latter. There was no love lost between the CPK and the North Vietnamese despite apparent ideological affinities. Following a party congress in late 1971, Vietnam was designated an eventual "acute enemy" (សត្រូវស្រួច) of the movement. Khmer Rouge propaganda of the period asserted that North Vietnam had replaced the United States as the "number one enemy" of Cambodia: that Washington wanted to colonize Cambodia while Hanoi wanted to swallow it whole. The subsequent purge of Vietnamese military units and Khmer Hanoi members of the coalition was thus implemented "quite willingly and enthusiastically" by the zone and sector party committees.[27]

By the early 1970s, a fair number of Vietnamese military units had already been transferred back to Vietnam under their own high commands. Getting the remnants to leave took the form of negotiations between dependable CPK cadres and Vietnamese troop commanders. When those proved unsuccessful, the Khmer Rouge organized "popular demonstrations" (បាតុកម្មប្រជាជន) targeting the Vietnamese. When those, too, proved unsuccessful, the CPK launched military attacks against them, which extended into mid-1973.[28]

Steve Heder describes how the Vietnamese Khmer were "quietly liquidated by the simple method of calling them to meetings, study sessions or celebrations from which they never returned." The success of this method, according to a refugee, was due to the disparate locations of the Khmer Hanoi: "We called those Khmers from Hanoi to come study and someone led them away. So really we were expelling them. The majority of these Khmers were in the administrative positions[,] not military position[s]. These administrators were not concentrated. There were only one or two in each place separated from each other. So when we began pulling them out the others did not realize what was happening. And so we were able to get rid of almost all of them. Very few realized what was happening in time and escaped to Vietnam."[29]

With the Sihanoukists sidelined, Vietnamese elements expelled, and the countryside reorganized, the stage was set for the CPK to take power. And given the wartime context, the brutality on the battlefield between opposing sides, and merciless decisions about life and death, any threats from there on out to the CPK's political standing—that is, its utter domination (and thus obviation) of the united front—or failures in the economic program of collectivization would be countered with ruthless methods that the CPK had forged amid the horrors of wartime practices. In essence, and in such a way, the CPK obliterated Clausewitz's distinction between war and politics.

Democratic Kampuchea

The April 1975 victory over the Khmer Republic was accompanied by an immediate "screening" of class ranks among the larger population the CPK now governed, as well as any remnants of united front elements within it. Only hours after taking over Phnom Penh, Khmer Rouge forces began liquidating those classes that it deemed anathema to the revolution. These included leading politicians and top officials of the ancien régime, FANK officers, anticommunist political intellectuals, artists, ethnic Vietnamese, and even people who wore clothes that were fashionable in the 1970s (but not in the jungles of Cambodia). These were the top representatives of the class structure that the Khmer Rouge sought not simply to overthrow but to wipe off the face of the earth by eliminating its uppermost strata with extreme prejudice and making the rest transform, or else.

This search-and-destroy strategy continued for months, as people who had hidden their identities were uncovered and either "tempered" and "refashioned" (reeducated) or "smashed" (executed). The CPK's widespread and omnipresent intelligence network, honed for years in the *maquis*, was strengthened and expanded at every level, starting at the very top and extending to the very bottom, as children were separated from their families and incentivized to report on their parents' activities before and after the revolution. Borrowing liberally from the Vietnamese people's war approach but, again, in peacetime, the Khmer Rouge were completists ("better to kill ten innocent people than to let one guilty person go free"—សម្លាប់មនុស្សស្រុកត្រង់ដប់នាក់ជាជាងឲ្យ ដមនុស្សម្នាក់ដែលមានទោសឲ្យរួចខ្លួន—went a slogan of the time), and the butchering of Cambodian citizens on the basis of class expanded at an accelerating pace throughout the remainder of the regime.

Inevitably, the CPK began to consume its own. Once the exploiting classes had been destroyed through the violent dissolution of the united front, it was only a matter of time before the party's utopian vision—grounded in a degree of self-confidence that was as unbounded as it was unearned—would come to pass. By 1976, the most clearly identifiable class enemies had been eradicated, and, according to the merciless logic of the regime, this absence of the exploiting classes meant that the success of its economic program was assured. Yet this success was never to materialize, in no small part because it defied not only the Marxist laws of history but the equally immovable laws of science and political logic as well. To the Khmer Rouge leadership, however, there could be only one explanation: the revolution was being sabotaged. But since the counterrevolutionary classes had been eradicated, such disruption could only be coming from within. Onetime united front elements that now existed *within the CPK itself* (including anyone who argued for moderation or fact-based analysis that did not square with the "Upper Organization," អង្គការលើ) must be sabotaging the revolution.

On October 30, 1976, the CPK issued a document titled "Decision of the Central Committee on a Number of Problems: The Right to Decide on Extermination Inside and Outside the Ranks." For the remainder of 1976 until the fall of the regime, the key targets of the regime were the cadres (and their families and associates) *within* it. Some eighteen thousand people were tortured,[30] sometimes for months, at Tuol Sleng and—by strict design—dispatched at the killing grounds of Choeung Ek, while many thousands more were dispatched, no less brutally, in the other security facilities established throughout the country. An untold number were simply executed in the fields.[31]

In other words, the regime was going after those Khmer Rouge officials who were not sufficiently revolutionary—that is, they exhibited bourgeois tendencies and mindsets. This could be concluded from their behavior (anywhere from not meeting production targets to sexual promiscuity); through denunciations by colleagues, associates, or family; or because they demonstrated not having developed their "revolutionary consciousness" before the revolution (by not being dark-skinned enough, having "soft hands," or possessing a pre-revolutionary education). According to one Cambodian intellectual: "We lived under [the] French for almost 100 years. We wanted those nice things the French had at the time. And we wanted more. Who still wanted to sleep in the mud? We went to school because we wanted to have a better life. And the Khmer Rouge did not like that. . . . [Even] a person like Ieng

Sary ... during the Khmer Rouge era, from 1975 to 1979, he lived a bourgeois lifestyle."[32]

As Pol Pot told Nate Thayer in 1997, "These people were in the central leadership of Democratic Kampuchea, but they were not people *of* Democratic Kampuchea."[33] These people *not* of Democratic Kampuchea occupied much of the time and energy—in vastly different ways—of Ieng Sary, Son Sen, and *Ta* Mok.

Ieng Sary: United Front at Bay

Ieng Sary was singularly active and perhaps even uniquely skilled in his externally pitched united front activities, thus providing a degree of value to the regime. While this facet of his character can be understood as his being willing to do what was necessary to ensure his own survival, it nonetheless also led him to present as someone who was not at all in control of—or perceived by superiors and peers as being fully invested in—the world he was charged with managing. Indeed, in the parallel structures of Leninist systems, the Foreign Ministry (B1) party committee, consisting of Sau Hong, Phi Phuon, and Se Sè, reported directly to Pol Pot and not to Ieng Sary even as he occupied the post of minister of foreign affairs.[34] It was a complicated position for Sary to occupy.

Sary had essentially three tasks to accomplish when he arrived in Phnom Penh in April 1975. The first was setting up a foreign ministry; the second, having the ministry "organize the furniture and clean up the mess left in the homes of those who had been evacuated so that those living in Phnom Penh would have proper accommodation"; and third, figuring out how to "maintain the best possible relations with China with regard to aid and the like, because they [the Khmer Rouge leadership] did not want aid from anyone except the Chinese."[35] This was done through a warren of internal departments representing the diplomatic priorities of Democratic Kampuchea: the general political department, the secretariat, and the departments of protocol, information and propaganda, and production. The staff running these bureaus, which were little more than designated individual rooms or even simply designated desks, were appointed by Sary, who also determined their portfolios.

The general political department housed B1's core party organization and was staffed by second- and third-tier CPK personages such as Thiounn Prasith, Keat Chhon, Suong Sikoeun, Pech Bunret, Ok Sakun, So Se, So Phan, and Toch Kham Doeun. The secretariat supported the other offices in managing the inward and outward flow of documents, letters of congratulation, national ceremonies, the military days of friendly nations, as well as letters exchanged across all the embassies, to and from foreign governments, and preparations for international conferences. It was also responsible for coordinating communications between embassies inside and outside the country, including (and especially) in the realm of economic and commercial decision-making. Ny Kân, who would remain close to, if not quite inseparable from, Ieng Sary throughout his career, ran the protocol department. It oversaw training in the reception conventions of foreign diplomatic delegations, guests, and arranging cars and managing guesthouses as well as the gifts given in diplomatic exchanges (mostly goods stolen from private homes following the evacuation of Phnom Penh).[36] The information and propaganda department housed the Kampuchea Press Agency, which held the broad mandate of disseminating the "collective ideas of the new Kampuchean society" and the "guidelines and tasks to defend the nation and protect the interests of the revolution."[37]

In a country that reveled in its international isolation, Ieng Sary and his Foreign Ministry enjoyed a particularly high profile, if only because the office provided one of the few nodes of contact with the outside world. Unlike other Khmer Rouge leaders, who tended to speak in eerie whispers, Sary was capable of being gregarious, even charming. Perhaps this is why Sary was often identified as being largely on a par with Pol Pot at the very apex of the regime. Indeed, during the August 1979 show trial—universally referred to as the "People's Revolutionary Tribunal to Try the Pol Pot–Ieng Sary Clique for the Crime of Genocide"[38]—Sary was, along with Pol Pot, the only named defendant, underscoring the perception (but not the reality) of Sary's power within Democratic Kampuchea. In public perception outside Cambodia, it was Ieng Sary who was "Brother Number 2," rather than the actual occupant of that position, the far more ruthless Nuon Chea.[39]

A subordinate recalls that Sary was not prone to flattery, even though he did have his favorites and tended to give them preferential treatment. (When a colleague pointed this out, Sary responded, "'Comrade, they are all the same," and, upon that colleague's further reflection, "this was in fact true.") Sary seems to have been careful and measured in his pronouncements and advised his staff to exercise the same caution of thinking before speaking.[40] But he was more demonstrative than the serene, poker-faced Pol Pot.[41]

As would be expected, the Foreign Ministry had a much larger percentage of people—recovering Sihanoukists, professional diplomats, and intellectuals without previous portfolios—deemed politically unreliable and easily targeted by the regime. Indeed, Sary himself would run training sessions emphasizing "peaceful coexistence with non-revolutionaries."[42] It is frustratingly difficult to establish the precise relationship between Sary and those who were purged at the Foreign Ministry during the Democratic Kampuchea period. He was certainly complicit, but the circumstances that surround their dismissal, torture, and execution point to things that differentiate Sary from the CPK's other top leaders.

Thus, B1 attracted an inordinate number of members of the old elite—intellectuals and the bourgeoisie—who had linked up with the Khmer Rouge under the united front umbrella of GRUNK. Others had been abroad on April 17, 1975, and yearned to return home (and were encouraged to do so by the new regime, and Sary in particular). Many were sent to S21. Those spared torture and execution at the hands of Son Sen were taken for reeducation at a cooperative in Battambang, after which they were transferred to Chhrang Chamreh (ច្រាំងចម្រេះ, M1, later B60),[43] outside Phnom Penh, and eventually to Camp B30 (the "GRUNKist camp") and the adjacent B32 (the "FUNKist camp"). Although Nuon Chea was responsible for reeducation more broadly, progress reports from these camps were occasionally sent "directly to Ieng Sary," who, presumably, was waiting for detainees to be deemed sufficiently remolded to work at B1.[44] The proportion of intellectuals placed in or awaiting transfer to B1 put the Foreign Ministry under scrutiny among those in the leadership who espoused more orthodox, class-centric CPK views.

Not only were there a number of GRUNKists within B1, but also they appear to have clashed with Sary in ways that simply were not seen in the cases of the other Khmer Rouge leaders. For context, in 1976, grumbling among CPK troops stationed in Phnom Penh over their inability to marry or visit their families grew into actual unrest and talk of a second revolution to overthrow Pol Pot. Anti-regime sentiment continued, extending into the ranks of the intellectuals who "could not only see that Pol Pot's socialism was failing, but also articulate the reasons why." This seeped into the Foreign Ministry. Heng Pich (aka Chhân), a rumored Soviet-educated former GRUNK minister who joined the CPK in 1973 and was charged with supervising the construction of Foreign Ministry guesthouses, contradicted Sary's narrative of CPK successes in "ministry-wide study meetings" by quoting Lenin. He was taken to S21 on December 18, 1976. Sean An, a former fellow student in 1950s France, accused Sary simultaneously of dogmatism and favoritism. He too was arrested and disappeared.[45] This raises the question of whether the torture-induced confessions crafted at S21 were congealing into a narrative that placed Sary under a cloud of suspicion. If so, Sary would have been far from alone, but he seems to have been particularly vulnerable—and his Vietnamese accent didn't help.[46]

Many of B1's intellectuals were in fact managed by the production bureau, something that each ministry had in the regime's spirit of "self-reliance." B1's agricultural and animal husbandry facilities provided food for ministry personnel and for foreign guests in Democratic Kampuchea. There were robust reeducation facilities ("raising ducks and planting morning glory")[47] at Ta Khmau (តាខ្មៅ, B64), at Chhrang Chamreh,[48] and at Boeng Trabek (បឹងត្របែក), all of which were associated with the Foreign Ministry. An interviewee described his experience at Boeng Trabek as follows:

> Originally people at the Boeng Trabek [facility] were divided into 2 groups: (1) diplomats (2) students [and] those undergoing higher technical training abroad and others [returnees from] abroad. The 2 groups were completely separated. They were not allowed to have any contact with each other. We were in the same compound but there was a bamboo partition between us. Later the diplomatic group was said to be [at] B-32 while the other group was said to be [at] B-30. Those from [the] diplomatic group were assigned to keep Boeng Trabek clean. We noticed that those in ... B-30 continued to dress in foreign type clothes and we felt this was a sign that they were not considered "politically correct." In any case, all of us were considered by the cadre[s] to be united front people and not revolutionary.... [Boeng Trabek chairman Savon] was not older than 20 and was [of] Lao extraction and used to boast that he was illiterate. ... His language was very derogatory and he looked down on us, like we were dogs.[49]

Interestingly, Sary is recalled as having said that keeping "intellectuals planting vegetables contributed nothing and shortly after that, some intellectuals went to work in the Information and Foreign Ministry." But, the source added, "they were still on probation."[50]

The anti-intellectual purges throughout the party hierarchy in the first and second quarters of 1977 inordinately affected B1, peaking around March, when, notably, Sary was abroad on a tour of South and

Southeast Asian nations (though he endorsed the purge during a speech commemorating the second anniversary of the revolution).[51] While it is clear that Sary did not (dare) oppose the class struggle that had replaced the united front—in this case, the reeducation, purge, torture, and execution of the former GRUNKists within his ministry—he seems to have often been reactive rather than proactive when it came to arresting B1 cadres.[52] He even seems to have been able to run interference on behalf of some B1 officials. According to Steve Heder and Brian D. Tittemore, several department-level Foreign Ministry officials, who were named in the "confessions" of Tauch Kham Deuan and others arrested around this time as "traitors" for allegedly serving various foreign agencies such as the CIA, KGB, and Vietnamese, were never arrested, purportedly on account of Sary's intervention. "Almost all these individuals," Heder and Tittemore observe, "had worked closely with Sary in Beijing or elsewhere. Moreover, there are indications, again from the substance of confessions, that Sary may have attempted to assist other cadre[s] to avoid execution."[53]

In one instance, during a meeting, Mok told Sary that "he did not know how to use intellectuals," to which Sary responded, "If you don't know how to use them, give them to me."[54] Indeed, Thiounn Prasith, a B1 employee, said at one point that "without the intellectuals, the [Foreign Ministry] could not function."[55] While this placement did not guarantee their survival—far from it—it allowed these individuals to avoid almost certain death in Mok's Southwest Zone. In one extraordinary instance, when Prasith and another B1 employee, Keat Chhon, were targeted, Sary apparently told Pol Pot that if they were arrested, "the entire Foreign Ministry would have to be wiped out"—thereby saving them.[56]

Laurence Picq recalls that toward the end of 1978, not only had numerous employees of the Foreign Ministry "disappeared" in the steady stream of political purges, but also B1 had itself become a sort of holding cell for soon-to-be tortured and killed associates of Minister of Commerce Vorn Vet and even Son Sen himself (an "ante-chamber of death").[57] Picq's estranged husband, Suong Sikoeun, himself a former Foreign Ministry employee, does not dispute the existence of this prearrest "holding cell," but counters that the victims "in no way . . . [came] under *Bang* ["Brother"] Ieng Sary, but under the secret security committees of Pol Pot, Nuon Chea, Son Sen, and the latter's wife, Yun Yat. . . . [I]t was not *Bang* Ieng Sary who summoned them to the ministry, later to send them to their deaths." If even partially true (and it seems so, given Sary's portfolio), this also reinforces the somewhat reactive—even passive—role of Sary as a recipient of Pol Pot's, Nuon Chea's, and Son Sen's orders, rather than as a collaborator in formulating them. This is not to let Sary off the hook; he did, among other things, appeal to overseas Khmer to return to their homeland, many of whom were killed not long after disembarking at Pochentong Airport. All Standing Committee members, including Sary, knew about the existence and purpose of S21, even if they did not know the details;[58] Son Sen, after all, forbade prisoners' confessions to indicate that they had been tortured.[59] Rather, it is to place him in his proper, supporting location within the overall division of labor of the unstoppable statewide killing apparatus that Democratic Kampuchea had become by late 1978.[60] In fact, the received wisdom *within* pockets of the CPK apparatus appears to have been that there was a great deal Sary was *not* doing in service of the revolution.

Much has been made of the fact that Pol Pot and Ieng Sary were related by marriage to the Khieu sisters, Ponnary and Thirith. Although Pol Pot was not one to over-indulge his family members in the benefits accorded to him as the leader of the Khmer Rouge movement (unlike Mok or even Sary himself),[61] he appears to have made an exception in the case of his brother-in-law by marriage, as he would with his young protégés late in life. Simplistic as it may sound, Pol Pot's ties to Ieng Sary seem to have formed a not insignificant percentage of Sary's power base or, at the very least, his continued survival.[62]

All of this was provisional, however. If we pull back the veil of the Democratic Kampuchea era, and even the prior civil war period, it becomes difficult to identify an independent power base from which Ieng Sary could derive comfort or maintain personal and political security. In other words, although he ranked number six in the CPK hierarchy (after Pol Pot, Nuon Chea, *Ta* Mok, So Phim, and Vorn Vet) and continued to serve as a full member on the CPK Standing Committee,[63] Sary was far more vulnerable a figure than is often portrayed—certainly much more so than Mok or Son Sen.

Indeed, the seemingly halcyon days spent together in France did not provide any real sense of security for some of the other top leaders. Although individuals like Khieu Samphân[64] and Son Sen continued to serve the movement well into the 1990s, others such as Tauch Kham Deuan, Tauch Pheuan,[65] Hu Nim, and even Hou Youn[66] (who shared the same communist cell in Paris at the rue Lacepède as Pol Pot)[67] were unsentimentally liquidated as the regime began to consume itself in 1976.[68] It is impossible to know for sure, but it is certainly likely, as

Steve Heder argues, that the initial purges of the Khmer Rouge leadership reflected some degree of desperation among the people at the very top, that is, Pol Pot and Son Sen. These purges were meant to signal that these leaders were not beholden to such bourgeois intellectuals and to crack down on *precisely* those individuals who shared common formative experiences with them, somewhat contradicting Nayan Chanda's contention that "a tiny group of French-educated elite ... at the top dictat[ed] policy."[69] Thus, although the Cercle Marxiste provided a vital political association for expatriate Cambodians in France for some nineteen years,[70] membership within it was largely indeterminate when it came to predicting individual members' political futures in Democratic Kampuchea.

In a real sense, Sary's time in Beijing from 1971 to 1975 was probably more relevant than were his student days in Paris. As I argued earlier, his twofold job—monitoring Sihanouk to weaken the prince and help fracture the GRUNK coalition in favor of the Khmer Rouge while ostensibly supporting and maintaining the united front—was vital to the movement. This also meant, however, that Sary's work was purely political, with an absence of any meaningful experience on the battlefield as a political commissar, let alone commanding troops. In a revolutionary movement in which superhuman sacrifice was expected of everyone (as the death count of the 1973 offensive against Phnom Penh amply demonstrated), Sary's somewhat cozy tenure in Beijing, combined with his lack of a military portfolio, denied him the power and authority that could be taken for granted by many of those with whom he came into contact and against whom he was often compelled to compete. Put differently, while Sary tried to keep the embers of united front burning, on the other side of the ledger, Son Sen and Mok were ramping up class struggle as it consumed the revolution that begat it.

Son Sen and the Bureaucracy of Class Struggle

Son Sen, as indicated by his various code names and aliases—*noms de guerre* Khiev, Khim (ឃឹម, "zither," used as his signature for *laissez-passers*), Brother 89 (when contacted by military divisions), Number 47 (when referred to as army chief of staff), and Brother 62 (regarding S21 business)—wore a number of hats in Democratic Kampuchea.[71] The Ministry of Defense under Son Sen was an extensive command and control apparatus. Son Sen belonged to a Central Committee military (sub)committee, along with Pol Pot, Nuon Chea, So Phim, and *Ta* Mok, that went back to at least March 1972, sometimes with Son Sen's wife, Yun Yat, acting as an adviser. Son Sen also served as chairman of the General Staff of the Revolutionary Armed Forces of Kampuchea (RAK).[72] The General Staff was the central body of the RAK responsible for the command and administration of the armed forces and the coordination of various tasks, such as the establishment of Center-based military divisions.

Perhaps inevitably, the Ministry of Defense was in tension with the armies commanded by the zone secretaries. Son Sen spent the first two years of the new regime working hard to turn a patchwork of regionally defined (and self-identified) units into a national army.[73] This was challenging for three reasons. First, in large part Democratic Kampuchea's actual power dynamics were so deeply localized that the CPK's concept of an aggregate "zone" was only beginning to have a substantive meaning for many cadres and combatants. Their social and political universes were closer to home, at the region (ភូមិ) level or administrative units below that. Second, two of the zone commanders for much of the Democratic Kampuchea period, Southwest (និរតី) Zone commander *Ta* Mok and Eastern (បូព៌) Zone commander So Phim, were, along with Son Sen, on the CPK Standing Committee, making it particularly treacherous for Son Sen to try to pull their own power bases out from under them, at least without intervention from Pol Pot and Nuon Chea.

Third was the issue of class in a system defined by class struggle. Some of the tension between Son Sen and zone secretaries like Mok may have been due to—or were at the very least exacerbated by—the class differences between them. Son Sen's revolutionary zeal was beyond (ideological if not moral) reproach, but it was born out of a violent rejection of those with class backgrounds similar to his own, even as he continued to exhibit the very bourgeois tendencies he found to be fatal flaws in others. Mok's own Marxism, such as it was, simply ignored what was doctrinaire and instead was manifested in his inelegant behavior—something that would have made him a target of ridicule in Parisian cafés along the Left Bank, but which generated fierce loyalty from the troops he commanded on the battlefield.

Yet even Mok came from (rural) money, from the timber trade. The only truly high-level Khmer Rouge leader from a genuinely poor, even lumpen, background was Kè Pauk (កែ ប៉ៅក). Pauk never went to France like Son Sen, Ieng Sary, or Pol Pot; never went to Thailand or studied at a monastery like *Ta* Mok; and never served in the French army like So Phim. Pauk had never even lived in a town. As Steve Heder recalls: "I did go to [Pauk's] home village and talk to some old lady who knew him, who said, 'Oh, yeah, you know, he was from a poor family and couldn't make a living and got into cattle, oxen, and water buffalo, rustling, stealing. . . . Every once in a while, he would come back to the village and talk about making revolution, putting the poor in power, so that they wouldn't be under the rule of the intellectuals and the market people and townsfolk and all of that.'"[74] But rather than enjoy an elevated position because of his class background, Pauk was often deployed to enforce the dirty work formulated by Son Sen (work often solely attributed to Mok), such as the 1977-78 Eastern Zone purges. This repeated itself in the 1980s, when Kè Pauk was initially entrusted with the command of the short-lived Corridor 1002 but was sidelined in 1986 after being suspected by the inner circle of non-sanctioned border smuggling.[75]

Ironically, Pauk's very life story reminded some of the key leaders—subconsciously, at least—that they were from class backgrounds questionable from the perspective of the revolution. Some, as Heder argues, responded by doubling down on class struggle to demonstrate that they were true revolutionaries *despite* their own class backgrounds, all while going after those with similar ones. Nobody embodied this more than Son Sen. He seemed to think he could wash away any such class-related risks by throwing himself fully into the operation of the internal security apparatus. There was a precision to the approach Son Sen and his subordinate Duch took toward punishing subversives and maintaining the internal self-narrative of the regime—one that was an impossible forcing of the unforgiving sharpness of right angles and Cartesian uniformity onto the human condition, with special regard to class vulnerabilities. And given the politically turbocharged nature of the regime, even the most "secular" shortcomings of party leaders were necessarily assigned a political cause that betrayed these hapless individuals as de facto class enemies. This was very much a continuation of CPK practices in the *maquis* prior to 1975. As Heder puts it:

> The technique employed to carry out these purges was precisely the same as that used to purge the "outside the movement" "veterans" in the 1971-1973 period. There was no prior real intra-party debate, no mass-level mobilization for a "struggle between two lines," and no substantive post-purge criticism or analysis. Prospective victims were simply called in for "routine consultation," "advanced study," "emergency meetings," or "celebrations"

and, after a more or less prolonged and more or less brutal interrogation in which they were forced to admit their guilt . . . and name all their supporters, allies, friends, relatives, associates and colleagues as co-conspirators, they were killed. . . . [T]here was no warning that a purge was about to take place and afterwards often no admission that a purge had taken place. When the purge was eventually admitted, there was usually no other explanation except to say that the victim had been a "traitor."[76]

Son Sen approached this with an almost eerie calmness. While Nuon Chea would "shout and threaten" when he was dissatisfied, Son Sen, when he was unhappy with something, "would clean his glasses, taking time to explain [why]." It was possible to reason, even argue, with Son Sen. Not with Nuon Chea, who would simply assert that what he said was the "truth of the proletarian class," closing down any room to appeal.[77]

Much has been written about the torture and killing apparatus, the CPK state security organization (សន្តិបាល), which formed a key part of the governing infrastructure of Democratic Kampuchea.[78] As more and more execution sites are uncovered and witnesses come forward to share their experiences, we learn more about the centralized archipelago of reeducation camps and processing sites (quite apart from the makeshift killing fields) that dotted the countryside, like S24 at Prey Sâr (ព្រៃស), the District 105 Reeducation Office (aka the Kraing Ta Chan Security Center), the Au Kanseng Security Center, and Phnom Kraol, among many others.[79] Indeed, Mok's Southwest Zone boasted thirty-eight security centers, seventy-eight execution sites, and 6,032 mass grave sites scattered throughout it.[80] Most of the popular—and scholarly—focus, however, has been on S21,[81] commonly referred to as Tuol Sleng (ទួលស្លែង), after the school and neighborhood district on whose grounds it is located. This is because Tuol Sleng had national reach when it came to processing allegedly traitorous cadres in the party and army ranks, and this documentation remained, atypically for Khmer Rouge records, largely intact in the wake of the Vietnamese invasion.

These records confirm Son Sen's meticulous personal monitoring of torture-induced confessions, which he read and annotated.[82] Son Sen, unlike his immediate superior, Nuon Chea, was very much involved in the day-to-day operations of S21. He had daily telephone calls between 3:00 and 5:00 p.m. with Duch (Son Sen preferred to communicate verbally rather than in writing), as well as regular meetings.[83] He would follow up with the units of cadres implicated in S21 confessions before deciding to arrest them; he would often seek their opinions and, if the target was arrested, would consult their superior on the substance of the confession.[84] In other cases, as when the investigation would lead into the ranks of another Standing Committee member or senior leader, Son Sen would defer to Nuon Chea. Duch recalls, for instance, that when he forwarded the confession of Kung Kieng, aka Ing Vet (secretary of Battalion 631, 63rd Regiment, 164th Division), to Son Sen, the latter "annotated it on May 23, 1977, writing 'to the attention of brother Nuon personally, secret. (1) This document is very clear; (2) The majority of the persons implicated are in the unit of comrade Mut[h] another part is in 33 and 35.' Nuon Chea wrote in the margin, on a date which is not legible, in May 1977: 'already noted for the attention of Comrade Mok.'" These documents, according to Duch, "show that Son Sen requested the advice of Nuon Chea prior to making his decision."[85]

Son Sen would assign specific interrogators to particular torture victims,[86] as well as the methods to be used.[87] In certain high-profile cases, he "monitored the interrogation very closely, both by telephone and by demanding to take and read responses which were not yet final," as in the case of Northeast Zone leader Ya (Ney Saran), for which "he had successive corrections to make."[88] In Ya's case, Son Sen personally came up with the idea to use Ya's wife and children as leverage.[89] Son Sen would also determine what communications he would allow these victims to make to the Center (often denying them). He would even intervene in minutiae such as whether to address a particular high-ranking prisoner with the prefix "comrade" (សមមិត្ត or មិត្ត) or as "contemptible" (អា-).[90] Son Sen also directed the overall operations at the Choeung Ek killing fields, although not participating directly.[91]

All goods confiscated from Tuol Sleng prisoners were taken by Son Sen to be stored in the State Warehouse. In one bizarre instance, a break-in at Son Sen's quarters, ostensibly to steal watches that had been confiscated, raised Yun Yat's concerns that some S21 confessions could have been stolen—which implied, of course, that Son Sen took his work home with him.[92] As this also suggests, the couple worked closely together; as one B1 employee put it, "As they say, the husband was the captain, the wife was the major."[93] Phi Phuon goes even further: "Yun Yat exercised an undeniable influence over Son Sen. . . . When the latter was about to make a reasonable decision, she usually intervened to dissuade him and adopt an opposite measure. . . . She always wanted to have the last word over her husband."[94]

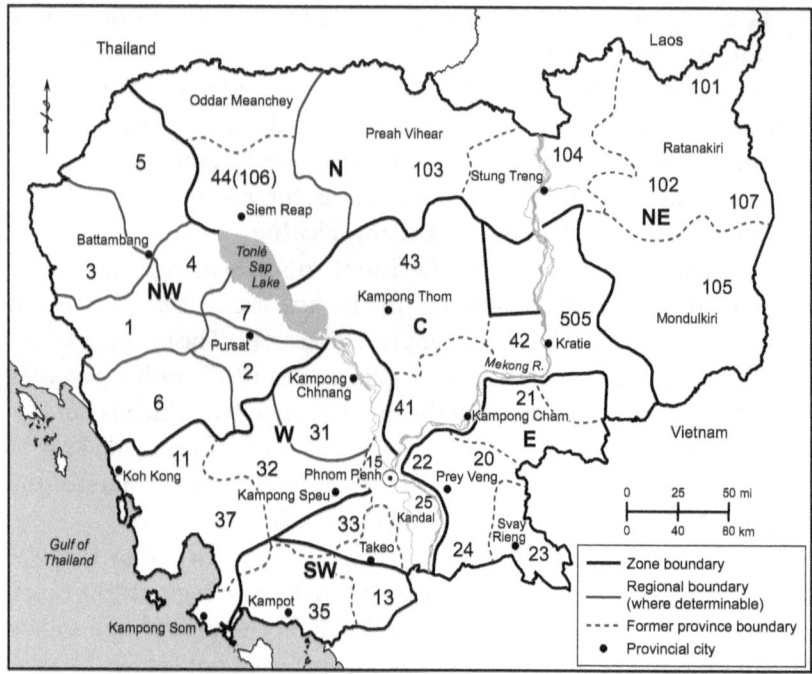

FIGURE 2.1. Administrative map of Democratic Kampuchea from mid-1977. Map by Gordon Thompson from Mertha, *Brothers in Arms*, 31.

Son Sen also managed the study sessions for S21 cadres, during which he laid out the goals of the institution and outlined the process of interrogating prisoners and the methods of torture. These included beatings, electrocution, waterboarding, forced consumption of human excrement, and other horrors, divided into three categories: "hot" (ក្តៅ, torture), "cold" (ត្រជាក់, interrogation), and "chewing" (ទំពាស់, alternating between the two). David Chandler writes that "many documents routed from S21 to the Party Center passed through Son Sen's hands, and dozens of memoranda addressed to him by top S21 cadre Duch have survived. So have many of his replies." Duch was so terrified of Son Sen that during one telephone call with him he soiled himself rather than ask for permission to go to the bathroom.[95] After all, Son Sen was particularly fond of using the phrase "no gain in keeping, no loss in weeding out" (ទុកមិនចំណេញអកចេញកំមិនខាត).[96]

Eventually, Nuon Chea took over the direct supervision of S21 while Son Sen was tasked with purging the Eastern Zone and, as the head of the military, fighting the Vietnamese on the shared border.

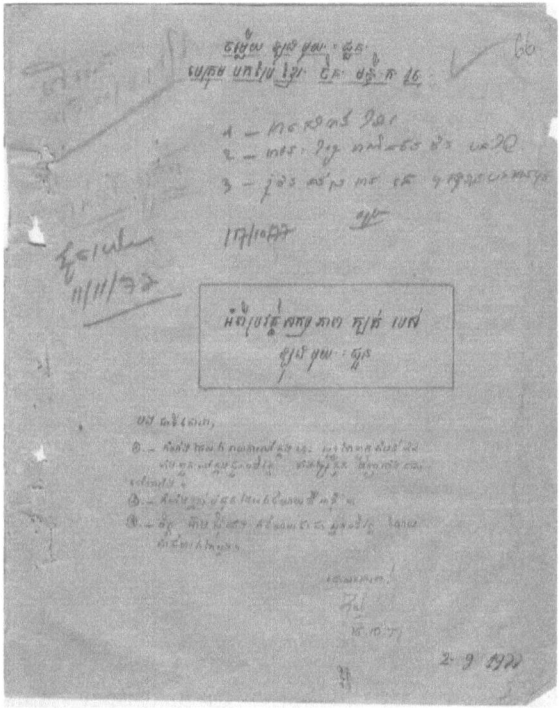

FIGURE 2.2. Annotations ("1, 2, 3") by Son Sen (aka Khiev) on confession of Long Muy (aka Chuon). Steve Heder.

Son Sen subsequently inherited the responsibilities of managing the Eastern Zone after the previous zone secretary, So Phim, shot himself rather than decide between excruciating torture and certain death in the capital or brutal execution on his own turf by *Ta* Mok.[97] But Son Sen's growing responsibilities were ultimately not enough, as we shall see, to save him from the very purges he himself was pursuing with such ardor.

Ta Mok: Flooding the Zone

There was no question that *Ta* Mok was a true believer, albeit not a particularly cerebral one. At a meeting to discuss what to do after the Khmer Rouge took over the country, Mok had said, "It is not necessary to have markets and cities. All people must be evacuated to the rural areas in order to build the rural economy."[98] But as Southwest Zone commander, Mok initially seemed to stand slightly apart from his comrades based in Phnom Penh, tied to his own physical space apart from the Center. Elizabeth Becker captures Mok's position this way:

> In many regards, Mok was the most provincial of the zone leaders, the least willing to see beyond himself and the Southwestern Zone. He slavishly protected his zone from interference by the Center or the other zones, to the annoyance of many. He was one of the newest members of the standing committee and at first he stayed out of the disputes and intrigues that broke out when the Center began doubting the loyalty of various zone leaders. Although his zone was powerful, his political profile was low, and the Center considered *Ta* Mok neither a threat nor a liability, not a problem that needed urgent attention nor a major figure who warranted a prize payoff.[99]

The specific space Mok occupied was significant as well.[100] The Southwest Zone "stretched from the flat central plains of Kandal and Kampong Speu provinces down to the white shores of the Gulf of Siam, and from the eastern delta border with Vietnam to the western maritime province of Koh Kong" after April 1975.[101] While the Southwest Zone was strategically important, it was also extremely poor. Heder notes how, by the late 1950s, the deteriorating economic situation in Southwest Zone provinces such as Takeo, Kampot, and Kampong Speu resulted in the Southwest possessing a higher percentage of landless poor and lower-middle peasants than anywhere else in the country, and because of relatively poor land and water conditions, even peasants who possessed land suffered.[102] This meant that the somewhat politically unsophisticated Mok was the ruler over the largest and most "politically correct" area in the country. And yet the Southwest Zone harvested more rice than any other zone in absolute (not in per hectare) terms. Moreover, unlike So Phim's Eastern Zone, which also bordered Vietnam, Mok's area remained largely at peace with its stronger neighbor. And, says Heder, the Center could always count on Mok's "ruthlessness and his military acumen," which in turn "gave him a major voice in Center politics."[103]

Mok's reliability existed in parallel with his geographically grounded independence. And yet the Southwest was also a challenge. There was, as mentioned, an influx of intellectuals from 1970 to 1975, which Mok handled by adopting an early propensity toward class struggle in his zone. And many of the denizens of the Southwest Zone were not, in fact, Mok's "people"; that is, sub-zone (sector, district, and sub-district) leaders' entourages were more parochially local than "zonal."

Indeed, Heder argues that the emphasis on the zone as a key organizational rubric may be overstated as far as the early days (and extending into the first *years*) of the regime were concerned. Because of purges within them that started in some places even before April 1975, and occurred on a significant scale thereafter, their political identity could not really congeal. Their overlords used them as mountaintops in their rivalries with one another and their machinations involving Brothers Number 1 and 2, but as those who were purged all too soon discovered, they were not guarantees of survival, political or corporeal. Part of the reason was that they were simply too big to be manageable. They were also a bit "unreal" as a tangible concept, echoing William Skinner's contention that China's early "people's communes" failed because they encompassed three times the area that had constituted peasants' natural social, economic, and cultural universe—what he labeled the "standard market area"—but on an even larger scale.¹⁰⁴ Local regionalism (កំបន់និយម) was deeply ingrained. The fact that the zones did not conform to natural borders or topography also did not help. The Southwest Zone, like the others, was thus not as unified as the conventional wisdom would have us believe. Therefore, already in 1975, "it had lost some of its strength and stature" and could not be made a genuine success both despite and because of being as "ardent" about "transforming its villages into cooperatives as it had been in fighting."¹⁰⁵ Rather than thinking about what has been essentialized as "the Southwest," it may be more accurate to think about this center of power as Mok's network of family and associates based in—and emanating out from—Sector 13, a network that, beginning in 1973-74, imposed its authority on other parts of the Southwest and then, in 1977-78, on other zones.

As he did during the civil war, after 1975 Mok continued to curtail whatever national ambitions he had—or at least the appearance of them—and instead focused on his extended network (ខ្សែ) of family and associates. This strategy was certainly meant in part to mitigate questions about the loyalty and reliability of Southwest Zone sector and district leaders. Mok had placed his son-in-law Khe Muth in a position to become secretary of Southwest Division 3 and enabled Muth's wife, Mok's daughter Khom, to become CPK secretary of Mok's home district of Tram Kak. Mok's daughter Ho ascended to the directorship of the Sector 13 (Takeo) hospital. His sons Cham and Chey served alongside their sister Khom on the CPK district committee. Their brothers Chong and Kol were made CPK secretary of Prey Kabbas (ព្រៃកប្បាស) and a ranking cadre in District 55/Prey Kabbas and a ranking cadre in

Sector 35 (Kampot), respectively. His brothers-in-law San and Tith also benefited: San became a ranking CPK cadre, while Tith became CPK secretary of Kirivong (គិរីវង់), District 109. Besides Muth, three other sons-in-law were similarly well placed. Boran had "begun his career as a courier for the CPK Center and then in 1975 took charge of a new factory in Tram Kak," while Soeun became a division commander and Ren a brigade commander. Mok's network also extended beyond the Southwest Zone and into the central state apparatus. Khe Muth advanced from being secretary of Southwest Division 3 to taking over the DK Centre Navy, which was built out of it, and to simultaneously taking the important position of CPK secretary of Kampong Som. Yin, the husband of Mok's daughter Ho, also became commander of Phnom Penh's Pochentong Airport. Yet others in Mok's family did not fare so well. Mok had another son-in-law, division commander Vinn, executed for adultery. And Mok's son-in-law Ren was a troublemaker into the 1980s: "a drunkard, [who] would siphon a full bottle of Mekong [whiskey] straight; when drunk [he] became brutal and [sometimes] happened to shoot his soldiers; [he] used to sleep with women and if they got pregnant would try to marry them to some of his regiment commanders."[106]

Family affairs notwithstanding, by mid-1978 Mok's political trustworthiness and ruthless efficiency in removing most of his fellow zone commanders had made him the most powerful among those who remained. As an interviewee recalls, "*Ta* Mok's troops swept everyone clean; everyone feared his troops."[107] In 1983 Mok crowed: "Why is it that only Southwesterners were used throughout Cambodia? [Laughs] The answer's clear."[108]

Wholesale Class Struggle

Zone leaders were extremely powerful until the exact moment they were not.[109] Indeed, it was precisely their power, Heder argues, that made them vulnerable. Over the course of long professional associations with the movement before and after 1975, inevitable articulated or implied minor doctrinal disagreements with Pol Pot's class-based orthodox policies that suggested the barest of cracks in the general line provided enough of a justification for Pol Pot to turn against them. It was "fortuitous" for Mok, therefore, that "the situation in the Southwest was relatively compatible with the general line formulated by Pol Pot in his position as Party leader," since "the Southwest was the poorhouse of

Kampuchea and thus the Region in Kampuchea where a line of all power to the poor and lower-middle peasants and rapid collectivization of economically irrational small holdings combined with a crash irrigation program . . . would be relatively tolerable and workable."[110]

But this was not the case elsewhere. The list of toppled zone leaders reads like a CPK who's who. The former Northern Zone (then 304)[111] commander made minister of commerce in 1975, Koy Thuon (កុយ ធន), was executed in 1977 because of his proximity to the leftist intellectual class now under suspicion; Northwest (ពាយ័ព្យ) Zone secretary Nhim Ros (ញឹម រស់) was killed after allegedly criticizing the strategy of excessive self-reliance; Northeast Zone[112] secretary Ney Saran (aka Ya, ណៃ សារ៉ន់ ហៅ យ៉ា) was executed in 1976 after having been accused of being too "soft" during border treaty negotiations with Vietnam; and Eastern Zone commander So Phim (accused of treason for "allowing" the Vietnamese to prevail over Khmer Rouge forces) committed suicide in the face of certain torture and execution in 1978.[113] The only original zone leaders who seem to have survived intact were *Ta* Mok and Kè Pauk, who together eventually inherited command of the Western, Northwest, Northern, and Central Zones.[114] As Heder wryly notes, "It seems that in the long run it was as dangerous to be a high-ranking Party member . . . from outside the Southwest Region as it was to be a big bourgeois evacuee from Phnom Penh."[115]

Mok and Pauk were the enforcers of class struggle in the zones. While Pauk remained at the top of the Central Zone, which included Sectors 41 (Prey Chhor, Cheung Prey, Kang Meas, and Kampong Siem districts), 42 (Tang Kok, Baray, Steung Trâng, Chamkar Leu, and Prek Prasap districts), and 43 (Santuk, Kampong Svay, and Stung districts), the Center then ordered some two hundred cadres from the Southwest Zone to take over the newly vacant positions throughout his zone administration and to eliminate some 20 to 30 percent of the officials who had not yet been carted off to S21. Mok's exuberance was consistent with his reputation as the "Butcher of Takeo," but his approach as a "technician of force" turned out to be counterproductive: Kè Pauk ended up complaining to Son Sen that the Southwest Zone secretary's methods "had destroyed our fundamental political foundation."[116]

Prior to 1975, Kè Pauk was the deputy secretary of the Northern Zone and secretary of the Siem Reap sector, and he replaced Koy Thuon at the top of the zone shortly after April 1975. At the beginning of 1977, he was called to Phnom Penh to conduct an "inspection tour," which turned out to be a euphemism for a meeting with Pol Pot and

Nuon Chea. He was also informed that the Northern Zone was rife with "traitors" associated with Koy Thuon, and that he should be ready to assist with their "processing." In February, Northern Zone cadres in charge of agriculture, industry, commerce, and public affairs were carted away in trucks. Some months later, more transport vehicles from Phnom Penh arrived to take away "5–6 chiefs of Region 41, 5–6 chiefs of Region 42, and 5–6 chiefs of Region 43."[117] Another wave of arrests zeroed in on functional region-level cadres, followed in May by a general purge of district (ស្រុក) and selected sub-district (ឃុំ) cadres. This "first stage" was completed by June.

Following this softening up of the political infrastructure, some two hundred of *Ta* Mok's cadres arrived to fill all these now vacant positions throughout the Eastern Zone.[118] A survivor from the region recalls that Southwest Zone soldiers "killed maybe 20 to 30 percent of the cadre[s], very secretly. . . . They made us work even harder, much, much harder. We worked twenty hours a day and slept four hours. We worked to find water, digging deep in the land for wells and to make canals. But we had a second rice harvest we didn't have before. And we ate good rice."[119] By then, Mok controlled the Northwest and Western Zones as well.[120]

In 1978, Mok and Pauk (along with Son Sen) were mobilized to clean up the ranks of the Eastern Zone (although one Eastern Zone resident recalls seeing Mok's troops milling about as early as November 1975).[121] The existing zone leader, So Phim (សូ ភីម), was extremely powerful. He was a colorful character whose drinking exploits "shocked even Mok, hardly the gentlest of men"; indeed, as Mok himself recalls, Phim "could really drink! [After drinking], we went to study [party documents] together. He didn't know his [ass from a hole in the ground]!"[122] So Phim was also an effective leader, but he could not escape the brutal reality of geography: his zone's shared border with Vietnam. As relations between the two countries deteriorated, defeats of Eastern Zone troops in border skirmishes mounted, and So Phim's political vulnerability skyrocketed.

Before the "purge mission" of So Phim's Eastern Zone, military commanders were summoned in mid-1978 to a meeting at *Ta* Mok's quarters in Takeo province. Those assembled were told that their mission was to "cleanse" those in the Eastern Zone "who had collaborated with the Vietnamese." This included actual Vietnamese as well as their Khmer collaborators. In all, seven hundred soldiers from Kampot province, a thousand from Takeo, and seven hundred to eight hundred from Kandal attended the one-day meeting. The next day they were sent to Phnom Penh, where they overnighted in Boeng Trabek, the location of Division 703 headquarters. The following day, Son Sen called another meeting, which Pol Pot and Nuon Chea also attended, to describe the purpose of the mission. Ordering all commanders to "prepare a comprehensive plan," he announced: "Our Southwest forces must be cautious with the forces in the East because they (the East) betrayed us. We must disarm and send those East forces to [the] rear line and arrange the front line to resist against the Vietnamese."[123] Those involved subsequently embarked for Svay Rieng, staying in Neak Loeung (អកលឿង) for a couple of weeks, during which time various meetings were held in preparation for the purge of the Eastern Zone.

It commenced with Pauk "returning to the Highway 7 Front HQ in Kampong Cham and summoning the commanders and political commissars of the Eastern Zone divisions and regional brigades to 'meetings,' where they were disarmed and detained."[124] Son Sen came down personally to supervise, accompanied by two tanks and two truckloads of some sixty security guards dressed in black uniforms.[125] Ieng Phan's Division 221, Dy's Division 703, Thy's Division 240, and even the naval division—in all, some ten thousand soldiers—were mobilized to make the arrests, led by Mok's Battalion 360.[126] Son Sen ordered Kè Pauk to summon forty-two Eastern Zone leaders—including sector committee heads Soth and Chan, as well as *Ta* Kim, the chairman of the Eastern Zone military division—to a meeting and arrested them all, along with their bodyguards. As Kè Pauk's son recalled:

> They killed those people in [*sic*] that same night. They ordered them to dig their own graves and take off all clothes except the[ir] underwear. They clubbed those people to the ground and then dragged the bodies into the graves (those graves were in the cassava farm). The distance from where Son Sen was staying to the grave sites was about 50 meters. Son Sen personally ordered the killing. I saw that killing with my own eyes, and because I felt pity to [*sic*] Uncle Kim, I sneaked [out] to look at the killing of those people. The killers were the soldiers in [the] black uniform[s] of Son Sen.[127]

Shortly thereafter, Pauk called the Eastern Zone secretary to a meeting. Outraged that a subordinate—Pauk was merely a deputy secretary—would summon him to a meeting, So Phim sent four different representatives in his stead, each of whom "disappeared." According to Philip Short, So Phim then attempted to seek a meeting with Pol Pot in

Phnom Penh to set matters straight, but he, along with his family and bodyguards, was attacked by Son Sen's forces just as they reached the capital. Wounded in the stomach, So Phim managed to escape and hide in the forest of Srey Santhor (ស្រីសន្ធរ). Six days later, however, his hideout was surrounded, and Phim shot himself; his wife and children were also captured and killed.[128]

Another account has Phim wrongly assuming the purge was a power grab by Pauk and escaping via Au Raing Ov (អូរាំងឪ) and Chihè (ជីហែ) to take his case directly to Pol Pot in Phnom Penh. Along the road, however, he picked up some leaflets that had been dropped by helicopter which read, "[So Phim] is a traitor selling territory to the Yuon, so, all brothers and sisters of the armed forces, please do not obey [So Phim's orders]."[129] They had Pol Pot's signature at the bottom. So Phim resigned himself to his fate and shot himself at Spean Veng (ស្ពានវែង).

In an obscene foreshadowing of what would befall him two decades later, Son Sen ordered that So Phim's corpse be transferred back to the capital on a captured US Army truck from which a loudspeaker broadcast to surrounding villages the message that had been printed on the leaflets. The corpse would be shown to onlookers as a warning. Son Sen then extended his control over the area, as indicated by the appearance of headless Cham minority corpses killed by Brother 89's "special intervention unit" and allowed to float down the river to a spot directly in front of Pol Pot's quarters.[130] Son Sen also went to Svay Rieng and held a meeting with commanders including Ieng Phan and Y Chhean, where he announced that "all soldiers removed from the East must be sent to build the airport in Kampong Chhnang, while their commanders must be arrested [sent to S-21]." Rank-and-file Eastern Zone troops—some nine brigades—were thus disarmed, herded together, and transported under guard by Southwest Zone troops to Kampong Chhnang province, where they were put to work on the Krang Leav (ក្រាំងលាវ) airfield under Chinese supervision.[131] These relocated Eastern Zone cadres were treated far, far worse than were the original workers on the project; a report notes that "workers were subject to execution at any time," whether they were summarily killed at the "forest just west of the airfield site" or "'sent away' for execution" in trucks to S21 or prisons such as the District 14 security office in Kbal Toek (ក្បាលទឹក).[132] Both Son Sen and Mok visited the site, the latter on regular occasions.[133]

The same sort of bloodlust was on display at the functional ministries, with Nuon Chea taking over almost all of them by the end of 1978. It is noteworthy that Ieng Sary's B1 was not among them. And yet, Ieng Sary was not beyond suspicion. Neither, as it turns out, was Son Sen or *Ta* Mok.

Foreshadowing

In a remarkable November 21, 1976, confession, extracted under months of torture at Tuol Sleng, CPK Southwest Sector 25 secretary Norn Suon (នន ស៊ុន, sometimes written នន់ ស៊ុន) lays out the personal characteristics of several of the top leaders—including Ieng Sary, Son Sen, and even *Ta* Mok—lucidly depicting their individual leadership styles while simultaneously providing evidence for why these individuals were ripe for targeting as class enemies by the end of 1978. Ieng Sary was seen as an intellectual who surrounded himself with people possessing an insufficient degree of revolutionary consciousness, whose "original class nature standpoint has nevertheless not yet been transformed into a solidly proletarian class standpoint." This was evidenced by a demonstrable bourgeois yearning for "their [former] residences and cars, moving around and sleeping freely, and profligately expending existing resources." Son Sen was someone who "still makes everybody recognize clearly that he is a high-level petty bourgeois intellectual, both by how he speaks and makes personal use of material things . . . [while also] tending towards transformation into a 'strongman'"; thus, in the eyes of Pol Pot and Nuon Chea, he was seen as someone adopting individualistic tendencies out of sync with the revolution, aided and abetted by his intellectual background, which put him in conflict with the proletarian consciousness sought by the regime and which he in turn worked to smooth out via his own ruthlessness. And finally, *Ta* Mok, although unassailable as a military commander and devoid of the softness of the former Paris students, was seen as unwilling to subordinate his individual interests and personality to the goals of the revolution; suffering from tendencies toward individualism—"he's quick-tempered, quick to scream and shout. . . . He displays a furious attitude, cursing thunderously"—and nepotism, Mok demonstrated his deviation from proper class behavior, which if "not headed off and fended off in time . . . could [also] become those of a 'strongman.'"[134]

Although too late for Norn Suon, the Vietnamese invasion in December 1978 provided a reprieve for the three individuals he so devastatingly described—particularly Son Sen, whose head was already on the chopping block and would likely have been separated from his body if not for the chaos that followed the lightning victory of the Vietnamese forces. The surviving Khmer Rouge leaders regrouped, but their previous individualistic shortcomings—presciently articulated by Norn Suon—would find their way back into shaping their strategies of governance over the territory they controlled two decades later. Reprisals would return with a vengeance, ending the movement and taking many more lives along with it. But rather than an unbroken continuation of class struggle, the CPK adapted to a prolonged shift backward to united front tactics, the subject of the next two chapters.

CHAPTER 3

Dusting Off United Front Doctrine, 1979–1984

> All you had to do was to let Pol Pot die! Pol Pot was dying and you brought him back to life.... Pol Pot had malaria... from the ashes the phoenix arises! [He] was reborn and sent to the battlefront to kill! To kill! To kill!
>
> —Norodom Sihanouk, quoted in T. D. Allman, "Sihanouk's Sideshow," *Vanity Fair*

In 1963, following student demonstrations in Siem Reap, Cambodia's leader, Norodom Sihanouk, had his minister Lon Nol compile a list of some thirty-four subversives, including Saloth Sâr (Pol Pot), Ieng Sary, and Son Sen. Coming on the heels of the disappearance (and presumed assassination) of previous CPK party secretary Tou Samouth (ទូ សាមុត) a few months prior, this was viewed as a credible enough threat to force remaining CPK operatives to flee the capital.[1] Those who stayed—like Khieu Samphân, Hou Youn, and Hu Nim—faced the real possibility of torture and execution. Indeed, upon their disappearance from public view in 1967, evidence suggested "that after having been seized and tortured the three men had been put to death in a particularly brutal fashion, one having been burnt to death by acid, the other two having been buried up to their necks in a field before being crushed to death under the tracks of a bulldozer.[2] As it turned out, these stories were as false as they were sensational. Instead, Khieu Samphân and Hou Youn had been hustled out of Phnom Penh "hidden in farmers' carts driven out ... in the dusk hour traffic," while Hu Nim vanished into the *maquis* that fall.[3] But the veracity of the rumors provides a sense of just how dangerous Phnom Penh had become for the CPK. Remaining in the capital meant death. They had a better chance of survival in the malaria-infested forests.

So it was a decade and a half later. On January 7, 1979, in an uncanny instance of déjà vu, CPK leaders were once again forced to leave the capital, this time without the luxury of darkness and shadows but in broad daylight. Invading Vietnamese forces had taken Phnom Penh, wresting political control from the rapidly scattering forces of the Democratic Kampuchea regime. As in the 1960s, the CPK found itself in a familiar vulnerable situation: a widely dispersed group of revolutionary irregulars wandering around the *maquis* in need of a central organizational apparatus that could broker an alliance with the non-communist resistance (NCR) to compensate for CPK weaknesses. In 1970, the catalyst had been the recently ousted Sihanouk's continued domestic and international legitimacy that underwrote a united resistance against the Khmer Republic. In 1979, it was the invasion of Cambodia by Vietnam, a country that—because of the invasion—became almost completely isolated diplomatically and condemned internationally, and that, more to the point, had now fully occupied its place in Cambodians' centuries-long consciousness as an adjacent existential threat.

The CPK (after 1980, the Party of Democratic Kampuchea, or PDK) was able to parlay these strengths and weaknesses into a three-pronged strategy: infiltrating and taking control over refugee border camps along the 817-kilometer-long Thai-Cambodian (and, to some degree, Lao) border, reconfiguring their fighting forces into regional strongholds, and seeking out a modus vivendi with the non-communist resistance under the rubric of a united front, forged in 1982. But a lot would happen in the three years leading up to the united front. Although the PDK looked back to its insurgent past, reanimating itself as a bona fide guerrilla movement, there were at the same time some differences on the ground, less in terms of strategy and tone, and more in terms of the external institutions and social organizations through which they were refracted.

During this period, Ieng Sary once again sought to forge a foreign ministry, also again in exile, but this time along Cambodia's northwest. Mok retreated to his traditional perch in the southwest to regroup. Meanwhile, Son Sen fell off the grid completely, presumably eking out an existence deep inside Cambodia's forests. All three were extremely vulnerable in the closing days of the Democratic Kampuchea regime. This vulnerability, combined with variations in the inclinations of each

FIGURE 3.1. Khmer Rouge troops carrying supplies inside Cambodia. Naoki Mabuchi.

of the three "lieutenants" to occupy distinct spaces on the united front–class struggle continuum, would shape their behavior and lead to varying political consequences for themselves and for the movement in the years to follow.

Ieng Sary, Barefoot Diplomat

In the extraordinary S21 confession by Norn Suon quoted at the end of chapter 2, we get a rare glimpse into how Sary was viewed by his comrades within the CPK:

> Older Brother Sary made important contributions with the Older Brother Secretary [Pol Pot], as he also did in the rural bases. He is solid as regards the political stance of the Party and has grasped the line and implemented the line well. In terms of attitudes and personality, [however,] he has yet to change his original nature. Everybody sees and recognizes that he is an important intellectual. And this is in accordance with his overt duties on the foreign affairs side of things. . . . None of the cadre[s] surrounding him who are his assistants as yet possess a solid standpoint in terms of a proletarian standpoint. Although it is true that he is popular, gracious and close with friends in general, making them very much warm to him . . . his *domestic work in the Party as a whole has not gone very deep.*

This is damning, deadly criticism for someone within a political movement that demanded political orthodoxy at the cost of all else. It extended to his subordinates in the Foreign Ministry; as Norn Suon continues: "Nowadays, all those who are his assistants are persons who have served the Sihanouk society, such as Keat Chhon, Chan Youran, Thiounn Prasith, etc., and who have still come to do foreign affairs work with him. Although it is indeed true that they are all loyal to the Party Organization, their *original class nature standpoint has nevertheless not yet been transformed into a solidly proletarian class standpoint.*"[4]

Sary's immediate family was also a target of criticism. The Sarys certainly weren't very popular. A former colleague of Sary's in Pailin recalls: "[Sary] and his wife were [a] tough couple and they cursed at me a lot when I made mistakes. . . . I dared not look straight at them."[5] Nuon Chea was even less forgiving. He had taken to referring to Thirith, Sary's wife, as "that bitch, Pheaa." ("Pheaa," ផា, was Thirith's revolutionary *nom de guerre*.)[6] When I worked at the ECCC, there was a rumor that the octogenarian Nuon allegedly even strong-armed and seduced Thirith's female nurse while they were all under quarantine for their trial, simply to annoy Thirith.⁷ As a self-identified bona fide intellectual, she certainly would not have cared for his earthy humor. A typical joke he made was about a bickering couple who went to court, where there was a sign that read, "Room where we decide disputes," but since there was a vowel missing, it became "Room where we cut off penises."⁸ Nor was Nuon Chea alone in his disdain for her. Defense minister Son Sen's wife, Yun Yat, who took over the Ministry of Information and Propaganda after the purge of Hu Nim, also had nothing but loathing for Ieng Thirith.⁹

To the extent that Ieng Sary was adjacent to the crosshairs of the regime's killing apparatus, the Vietnamese invasion provided an opportunity to delay what might have been inevitable just weeks, even days before. His place remained far from secure, however—and his (second) flight from Phnom Penh was somewhat ignominious. Sary took part in the CPK leadership's evacuation from Phnom Penh (January 3, 1979), its return from Battambang (January 4), its second evacuation to Battambang (January 6), and its entry into Thailand (January 9). He then trekked up to Poipet, on the Cambodian side of the Thai border, where a Thai military helicopter took him, Yun Yat, and a group of Khmer Rouge broadcasters to a little-used part of Bangkok's Don Muang airport under cover of darkness. He was given a Chinese passport under the name Su Hao (苏浩) to match his new *nom de guerre*, Nên (ឯៀន).¹⁰ According to Philip Short: "No Thai official was present. They were driven across the tarmac and hustled on to a commercial airliner for Hong Kong after all the other passengers had embarked."¹¹ Upon their arrival in Beijing the next day, Deng Xiaoping gave Sary a tongue-lashing and told him to wait for China to come up with a plan for expelling the Vietnamese from Cambodia.

That "plan" took the form of a military invasion of Vietnam by the People's Liberation Army in February, military aid to the CPK to fight the Vietnamese, and the establishment—with the participation of Ieng Sary—of a Chinese embassy-in-exile in the Cambodian jungle. When the United Nations Security Council passed a resolution condemning the Vietnamese invasion and recognizing Democratic Kampuchea as the legitimate state of Cambodia, Beijing decided it would send its representatives into Cambodian territory "to facilitate continuous normal interaction between the two countries while on the move." Rousing the troops, as it were, Vice Premier Geng Biao, himself a veteran of the Long

March, reminded the Chinese diplomats that foreign affairs cadres were "the People's Liberation Army without uniforms." Accordingly, during the night of February 10, eight Chinese diplomats, led by Ambassador Sun Hao, reached the jungles of Phnom Malai (ភ្នំម៉ាឡៃ), only half a kilometer from the Thai border. There they came across "three straw huts with pillars but no walls [which] could only block the rain and shade the sun. The beds and tables were made entirely of bamboo. Stools were blocks of wood." This, effectively, was the makeshift Chinese embassy to Cambodia.[12] Eight days later, Vietnamese activity forced them to retreat south, establishing another temporary headquarters in the forests just outside Pailin. This they celebrated by inviting Sary to a feast of "canned food . . . boiled with tree leaves to make a soup." They would abandon that location on February 23.[13]

Eventually, the group settled on the banks of Stung Kranhoung (ស្ទឹងក្រញូង) in the Cardamom Mountains,[14] where they planted the Chinese flag in what would be another makeshift PRC embassy for the next month. This location was only three kilometers south of the CPK leadership compound—where Pol Pot, Nuon Chea, Ieng Sary, and Khieu Samphân were billeted—but the walk took three hours because the forest was so dense with foliage. On March 27, they were forced to retreat again because of the proximity of Vietnamese troops, "[holding] diplomatic talks on the march." Around that time, the Khmer Rouge leaders decided that they should decentralize their authority in guerrilla fashion to better protect the movement from the Vietnamese. On March 29, Sary, who still held the foreign affairs portfolio, remained with the Chinese delegation as they bushwhacked their way through virgin forest for another two weeks. They reached the Thai border on April 11, where Sary saw them off.[15]

The Chinese had by then dropped the guerrilla-style embassy concept, but Sary was far from disabused of the idea of attempting a diplomatic approach to broker another united front. Phi Phuon, who had worked with Sary in the Foreign Ministry during the Democratic Kampuchea period, recounts that by April, "Ieng Sary had assigned So Hong and [Ny Kân] the responsibility of the Sisophon-Poipet-Bovel Front, while Thim and I were made responsible for a front extending from Ampil Pram Doem and Kampong Ley in the province of Battambang to Bœng Acheang (currently Stung Koy) in [Pailin]. Y Chhean and Théng (So Hong's younger brother) were to defend the [Pailin] region [while] Pol Pot settled at Pass 505 near the Thai border town of Trat."[16]

Sary would spend the next several years maintaining Democratic Kampuchea's seat in the United Nations while shuttling to Beijing, Pyongyang, and points in between to maintain support for the PDK, with no small amount of success. While in Cambodia, as we will see in the following chapter, Sary created a Potemkin village–style foreign affairs compound that did much to complicate the Khmer Rouge's image to outsiders, to the benefit of the PDK. So long as united front remained an ascendant strategy, Sary's vulnerabilities could be held at bay.

The Prodigal Son Sen

Objectively speaking, by 1978 Son Sen was in an extremely powerful position within the government of Democratic Kampuchea. Yet even with this formidable concentration of power, Son Sen had always been seen by his colleagues as "peremptory and his point of view 'bourgeois.'"[17] It is ironic, or perhaps a karmic inevitability, that some of the most damning testimony, precisely because of its accuracy, was provided by one of Son Sen's own victims while he was being tortured at Tuol Sleng—that of Norn Suon, as we saw previously. In his confession, Norn Suon also detailed that "Older Brother Son Sen is a native of Kampuchea Kraom and of a landlord family. . . . His spouse also had a high status as an intellectual, being a professor, too. Both the two, husband and wife, were experts and famous intellectuals in Cambodia and . . . in terms of their personal classness, they are higher-level petty bourgeois intellectual strata. Their standard of living was one of plenty enough. The family did not suffer from shortages." Then Norn Suon delivered an extraordinary proposition, one that was almost certainly relayed to Son Sen: that *Son Sen* himself "refashion[ed] the state of his personality and attitude into those of a worker-peasant in terms of both how he speaks and the way in which he lives his daily life," thereby placing them "in line with the requirements of the Party for advancing to leading [to] socialism and permanent Communism in Cambodia."[18] Being quite literally in the anteroom of death, Norn Suon likely went so far with this bold condemnation only because he knew he no longer had anything to lose. But for Son Sen, everything was at stake.

Son Sen was vulnerable on three points. The first was the inexorable need for the regime to sacrifice more and more senior cadres to feed the self-narrative it needed for its own legitimacy: that it was being destroyed from within by enemies of the revolution. Indeed, any organized group of people could be considered a traitorous cabal, even those who had earlier been considered immune. This came to include truckloads of prisoners from the factories, from regions hitherto considered "loyal," from the top management tier of Democratic Kampuchea's "ministries," and even among those defending the regime on the front with Vietnam. Kè Pauk describes the macabre atmospherics at the time in recounting how one of Pol Pot's favorite colleagues, deputy prime minister and minister of commerce Vorn Vet, was dispatched: Pol Pot asked Pauk if he had "enjoyed the film." Somewhat taken aback, Pauk remained in the Central Committee building when, at 1:00 a.m., Vet was arrested. It was then that Pauk understood that the "film" referred to Vorn Vet's arrest.[19] This was in November 1978. By December, Son Sen was himself under suspicion and, like Sary, only weeks, if not days, away from being sent to "his own remorseless institution."[20]

Second, and related to this, is the fact that an increasing number of people close to Son Sen were being named as traitors in their confessions, with each instance bringing him closer to processing at S21 himself. One of these was Ny Kân, Son Sen's younger brother, then the chief of protocol in Ieng Sary's Foreign Ministry. Although Ny Kân would rise to become the leader of Front 32 and a political and psychological adviser to Division 519 chief Saroeun,[21] he was quite vulnerable in late 1978 for his alleged role in the murder of leftist scholar Malcolm Caldwell—an event described in horrifying detail by Caldwell's trip mate, the journalist and author Elizabeth Becker.[22] Serge Thion writes that "it is not known if [Kân] was actually part of this plot or if this confession was fabricated in order to implicate Son Sen and bring about his removal . . . [but] Son Sen was the obvious target of the next high-level purge planned by the Security to purify the party and eliminate the 'traitors' hidden at the top."[23] More to the point, Son Sen had enjoyed close relations with Vorn Vet since the early 1970s, and the latter's liquidation only served to further destabilize Son Sen's position.

Third, having replaced So Phim as commander of the Eastern Zone, Son Sen did not fare any better militarily against the Vietnamese. This was a double liability, as Son Sen was responsible both for attaining victory in individual battles against the Vietnamese fought in his newly acquired Eastern Zone and, as minister of defense, for making a success of the nationwide war effort against Vietnam, both of which he was clearly failing to do. This came within a hair's breadth of sealing his fate; he was saved only by the Vietnamese invasion and the implosion of the regime.[24]

In the past, Son Sen had proven himself an adept tactical commander on the battlefield. But in taking over the responsibilities of So Phim (who was no military novice) in the Eastern Zone, he inherited a particularly challenging military command that was almost destined to fail. He fled, disappearing during the frantic collapse of the governing apparatus in early 1979. Son Sen vanished until almost two years later, when he emerged "from the mist" in late 1980. He appeared suddenly in Preah Vihear in the late fall of that year, "talking about Napoleon" and appearing to Steve Heder, who met him at that time, "dazed and confused."[25]

Never truly regaining the confidence of Pol Pot and Nuon Chea after 1978, Son Sen, like Ieng Sary, attempted to rehabilitate himself after the Vietnamese invasion. He was given a second chance, in no small part because the Khmer Rouge ranks had been decimated and the top leadership could not pick and choose (and, according to rumors at the time, at the behest of Thailand and China), by being placed in command of Corridor 1001.

Corridor 1001 was established when retreating Khmer Rouge divisions 801 and 920, after forming a political organization (the East Cambodia Committee), ran out of supplies and retreated to the Tonlé Ropov (ទន្លេរពៅ) area along Cambodia's border with Laos. It subsequently moved to Preah Pralay (ព្រះប្រឡាយ) in Oddar Meanchey province, to the east of Anlong Veng, in the Trapeang Prasat (ត្រពាំងប្រាសាទ) area. This was a strategically defensible area nestled between three borders (Preah Vihear, Ubon Ratchathani province in Thailand, and Ch'mpasak province in Laos). Its command post at this time was at the convergence of Thailand, Laos, and Cambodia, at Tonlé Ropov, opposite the Nam Yeun district of Ubon province (the site of a major clash between Vietnamese and National Army of Democratic Kampuchea (NADK) forces on Christmas Eve 1981). During the early years following the Vietnamese invasion, Corridor 1001 was a key point of contact among the military leaders who survived the DK period: *Ta* Mok, Kè Pauk, Meas Muth, Sou Met, So Hong, Ny Kân, So Saroeun, and Miech San.

Was Corridor 1001 a redemptive mountaintop, or was it a "shit brief"? The National Army of Democratic Kampuchea used Corridor 1001 as a launchpad to drive deep into Cambodian territory and organize resistance to the Vietnamese occupation forces.[26] But by 1981, Son Sen saw that he was being relieved of more and more field command duties. In response, he began to explore the political space between united front and class struggle. Unfortunately, he possessed little aptitude for coalition-building. In fact, as we will see, his failure in this capacity could not have been more complete (equal parts substantive and symbolic), as his ham-fisted efforts at united front were what made him the target of Pol Pot's final, and in a sense most dramatic and consequential, act of class struggle.

Ta Mok, Return to Tomorrow

Mok seemed to continue his upward trajectory during the Democratic Kampuchea era. Meng-Try Ea quotes Pol Pot issuing a rare compliment—"the Southwest [commanded by Mok] is the best"—to underscore this fact.[27] Michael Vickery concurs, calling the Southwest "the zone of 'Pol Pot-ism' *par excellence*."[28] It was the Southwest Zone that Kenneth Quinn observed amidst its radical CPK takeover in June 1973, with the burning of villages and the corralling of peasants into communal organizations under the close watch of Southwest cadres.[29] As one Southwesterner cryptically put it: "In November 1975 I went to [Ta Khmau].... This was in [Region] 25, part of the Southwest Region. In [Region] 25 there were a lot more rich and middle peasants, so there were a lot more *contradictions*."[30] Mok himself had little sentimentality for the fate of urban dwellers forcibly relocated to his region: "They came with empty hands."[31] In the Southwest Zone (unlike, say, the Eastern Zone), *everybody* wore black.[32]

In contrast to other top leaders, Mok remained in Phnom Penh as the Vietnamese invaded, joining forces with Sou Met (ស៊ូមិត), the commander of the air force, at General Staff headquarters, which Son Sen had abandoned that same day, January 7, 1979.[33] Mok's subsequent retreat to the border in the face of the invading Vietnamese army was conducted in a style befitting the way he approached his command. Recalls a former Khmer Rouge naval officer: "We walked for one month and [a] half from Roleak Kongchheung [រលាកកងជើង] in [Kampong] Speu all the way to the border. Some of us got sick but no one died. Once we got to the border, we received an order from *Ta* Mok via telegram that we need to send our men to meet him and take him to the border. We set up a base at the border, procured some rice to eat ... then we sent 20 men to meet him and bring him to the border."[34] In the meantime, Mok met up by chance with Phi Phuon's army in the forests of Kampong Speu and ordered them "to withdraw [their] forces from the battlefield to protect the leadership of the Party."[35]

Until December 1984, Khmer Rouge soldiers used Corridor 1001 as a base for maneuvers to organize anti-Vietnamese resistance deep inside Cambodian territory.[36] When it was overrun in 1984, the center of military and political gravity began a slow but steady shift, at the expense of Son Sen, to Mok, who was establishing a military force farther west along the Thai-Cambodian border just north of Anlong Veng. This would become the 1003 Military Battlefield Command, also known as Corridor 1003. It was, on balance, less vulnerable to Vietnamese "incursions" because it had far less of a common border with Vietnam (and Laos) than did Son Sen's 1001. Moreover, it appears that Mok spent far less time away from military activities than Son Sen. The evolving relative political weight of these two corridors was a harbinger of Mok's eventual rise and Son Sen's ultimate fall.

More than other PDK leaders, Mok invested much time and effort cultivating ties with the Thai military—even linking himself with General Chavalit Yongjaiyut, who held the positions of deputy commander in chief, chief of the General Staff, commander in chief of the army, and, eventually, commander in chief of the Armed Forces Supreme Command—through intermarriage and commercial ties.[37] Mok's network allowed him freer rein to hop across the border at will than was the case with his PDK leadership colleagues. Indeed, while Son Sen spent much time in Office/Zone 87/870 with Pol Pot and Nuon Chea, Mok's physical deployment elsewhere gave him a measure of independence and greater mobility into Thai territory. This seems to have made him the exception among PDK leaders, who were informed by the Thais that they could not pass through Thai territory too often because the Royal Thai Army (RTA) was under intense pressure to cease and desist aiding the Khmer Rouge.[38]

Initially Mok's deputy was his own son-in-law Meas Muth (មាស មុត), who also served as the committee chair of Kampong Som and head of the navy during the DK period, but after he was transferred to Sector 505, Mok installed Im Ngun (aka Khoem Ngun/Khem Ngun) as his deputy. From his base of operations in Anlong Veng, which bordered Sisaket province in Thailand, Mok established a set of frontline headquarters, designated "Anlong Veng," "40," "50," "800," "808," and "1002." These were located along strategic mountain passes that would make it easier for Khmer Rouge forces to enter Cambodian territory.[39] Corridor 1003's area of operations extended as far south as just to the north of Phnom Penh and comprised four divisions: 612, 616, 912, and

980 (and possibly a fifth, 925, operating around Siem Reap) directly under Mok.[40]

While Mok was building up military Corridor 1003, his colleagues were engaged in diplomatically brokering a united front. Although Mok remained a key part of the PDK leadership, his role was almost exclusively on the battlefield. He had little interest in a united front, which he considered abhorrent. But there was very little he could do besides bide his time, build up his army, and watch the second united front rise and fall again.

The Second United Front

The 1979-80 historical context forms the environment for the early incubation process of the second united front.[41] A combination of international events, including, inter alia, US establishment of diplomatic relations with China (very much at the expense of Vietnam), the increased closeness of Hanoi to Moscow, and, finally, Vietnam's invasion of Cambodia in 1979 greatly facilitated an environment whereby most of the international community, including the United States, Europe, China, and ASEAN (the Association of Southeast Asian Nations)—and in the absence of the Soviet Union and its allies—made it possible for the Khmer Rouge to maintain their seat in the United Nations and, indeed, to be viable at all. As one observer put it, "It is difficult to imagine how the Khmer Rouge with two weak Cambodian entities would have survived in the face of Vietnam"; indeed, "the powerful foreign backers could be considered essential members of the united front."[42] The first united front was also generously funded from outside, by Vietnam and China against US interests in the region. For the second united front, the roles of the United States and Vietnam were simply flipped.

US national security adviser Zbigniew Brzezinski (in)famously told Elizabeth Becker: "Pol Pot was an abomination. We could not support him, but China could."[43] It is widely believed, however, that the United States did in fact do so, albeit indirectly.[44] But while it is true that covert aid continued throughout the 1980s and into the early 1990s, it has also been demonstrated over and over again—from US support for the Republic of Vietnam to the Nicaraguan contras to Operation Enduring Freedom to the US war effort in Afghanistan[45]—that throwing money at a political entity lacking an actual program for action (in this case, effective governance) is far from sufficient to guarantee its success. The PDK were doing more than feeding at the trough. As in the period after 1970, for the Khmer Rouge, the establishment of a united front could create a multiplier effect in the scope and distribution of such aid.

Khieu Samphân remained the public face within the united front, but Ieng Sary brought the necessary gravitas behind the scenes and in front of the cameras. The two thus enjoyed a comparatively higher profile precisely because of the diplomatic deftness necessary in brokering a united front. Although he would regain a higher profile in the early 1990s as he attempted to enter the political fray in the lead-up to the United Nations–sponsored elections in 1993, Son Sen was closer to Mok than he was to Sary during the 1980s. This is perhaps less true as an ideological matter and has more to do with the physical deployment and functional role for the movement of the three "lieutenants." Son Sen and Mok largely stayed behind enemy lines and inside Cambodia proper, conducting the kind of military campaigns described in the next chapter.

What eventually became the second united front consisted of the PDK, the Khmer People's National Liberation Front (KPNLF), and the Front Uni National pour un Cambodge Indépendant, Neutre, Pacifique et Coopératif (FUNCINPEC). On paper, the KPNLF, established on October 9, 1979, looked like a "dream team" of former democrats, military members untainted by Republican corruption or CPK bloodthirstiness, with long political careers, in some cases going back to the end of the colonial period. Commonly dismissed as "Republicans," invoking the corruption of the Lon Nol regime that succeeded Sihanouk after his overthrow, the KPNLF's upper echelons in fact demonstrated a diversity of political and military experience that is missed when the party is painted with such a broad political brush. Heder argues that out of the initial thirty-one top leaders, seventeen of them boasted university education or work experience going back to the 1940s, including being leading members of the colonial-era Democrat Party. They had little or no relationship with the Lon Nol regime. The next five leaders (in terms of generational cohort) supported Sihanouk's ouster but opposed the Khmer Republic, as did the next generational cohort. The fourteen non-civilian leaders of the KPNLF had military positions under Sihanouk or under Lon Nol but, apart from Thach Reng and Dien Del, largely stayed out of politics. A number of these leaders had spent time abroad, with four of them operating along the Thai-Cambodian border during the Khmer Rouge era and eight of them even living under (and miraculously surviving) Khmer Rouge rule during that period.⁴⁶

FUNCINPEC was founded on March 21, 1981, by Norodom Sihanouk while commuting between palaces of exile in Beijing and Pyongyang. He sought common cause with the MOULINAKA (Mouvément pour la Liberation Nationale du Kampuchéa, or Movement for the National Liberation of Kampuchea) resistance forces and eventually met Son Sann (KPNLF) and Khieu Samphân, together establishing the Coalition Government of Democratic Kampuchea (CGDK) in 1982 with Sihanouk as president. At around the same time, the merging of smaller resistance armies associated with FUNCINPEC, including MOULINAKA, resulted in the establishment of the Armée Nationale Sihanoukiste (ANS) and its eventual successor, the Armées Nationale pour Khmer Indépendent (ANKI). FUNCINPEC's relations with its CGDK partners was never smooth, and it was often seen as the "softest" of the three partners. But that reflected a focus on the organization of its camp system and its preference for—and comparative advantage in—playing the political game rather than acquitting itself on the battlefield. After Sihanouk stepped down in 1989 (and gave up his party membership in 1991), he was succeeded by Nhiek Tioulong, and then by his own son Ranariddh in 1992, who led FUNCINPEC to victory in the 1993 UNTAC (United Nations Transitional Authority in Cambodia) elections.

The first two meetings between Ieng Sary and KPNLF leader Son Sann (សុីន សាន) established little of substance. In September 1979, acceding to Thai requests that they discuss a military counterattack against the Vietnamese army and the political prospects for reconciliation, Pol Pot met with Son Sann and his military representative, Pi Tureth. (Ieng Sary had gone to the United Nations.) Pol Pot shook Son Sann's hand but embraced Pi Tureth, as the two had been schoolmates. Tureth still had not understood that his classmate, whom he still knew as Saloth Sâr, had metamorphosed into the "brutal Pol Pot." After discussing the military situation, Son Sann rose and spoke in English, ostensibly for the benefit of the Thais. He requested that no news about this meeting be disseminated; he needed time to explain this contorted potential alliance to his supporters.⁴⁷

The following March, while Son Sann and Khieu Samphân both happened to be in China, the PRC authorities arranged for them to meet in Beijing. In May they finally sat down, but Son Sann, this time speaking in both French and Khmer, asserted that he was not there to bargain. He demanded that he "replace" the Democratic Kampuchea leadership and have the power to raise a new government of his choosing. Son Sann was no dummy, and although he believed that the Cambodian people would never accept a restored DK government, he was equally certain that the PDK would seek to colonize any united front of which it was a part. He wanted nothing to do with that process, he said.

> As I have already told you, we cannot be unified. No one [in my party] would agree [to work with DK]. I've asked my people from the west to the east and from the south to the north, and they said "no." If [I] agree to work with you, the people [who support me] would all go and defect to Heng Samrin [of the PRK]. . . . Therefore, what I can tell you now is that we should allow the military from both sides [to] work together quietly and fight against the enemy. I ask that you give me the role to play politics on your behalf. Please think about it. If you agree with my request, we should go to China together so that they know you have agreed to give me the role to play politics on your behalf.

Then Son Sann added, "I say we cannot be unified and work together."[48]

The two met again on January 26, 1981, when Son Sann repeated his demands, to which Khieu Samphân responded that any change from the "Democratic Kampuchea" government could lead to a loss of its UN seat. The DK side offered to take the number two spot in the coalition, but Son Sann demanded that the DK be removed from the government altogether and concentrate on the military aspects of the struggle against Vietnam.[49] Sometime in April of that year, Son Sann sent fellow Khmer Krom, former FANK division commander, and bon vivant Dien Del (one of the few FANK generals who had demonstrated his military acumen in fighting the Khmer Rouge during the Khmer Republic) to negotiate on his behalf. Although he seemed to get along better with his counterparts across the table, he punted when it came to articulating a political solution and protested that he did not have the power to agree to a deal on his own. Again, the talks went nowhere.[50]

On June 12, 1981, Ieng Sary met with Dien Del. There appears to have been some movement as a result of their conversation. Dien Del said, "The purpose of today's discussion is to form a coalition government, and it can follow the name of the government of the Democratic Kampuchea." Sary chimed in that "the political program of the Front is not the political program to build socialism; it is for our nation to survive," but neither side was ready to negotiate the details at that point.⁵¹ Nevertheless, the momentum, sluggish as it may have appeared to the ever patient Thais brokering the deal, continued. At the sixth meeting of a special ad hoc committee on October 4, 1981, the following formulation was hammered out:

1. The Coalition Government of Democratic Kampuchea must have a firm stance of unity. No side has exclusive rights over this Government.
2. The Coalition Government of Democratic Kampuchea must be based on the trilateral principle with trilateral structure and trilateral composition.
3. All the important questions must be decided by the Cabinet based on the consensus principle which is the tradition of the Cabinet.

In addition, the three parties agreed to link these three principles to the structure of power as well as the composition of the Coalition Government of Democratic Kampuchea.⁵²

By the beginning of November, the Chinese had given their blessing. On June 22, 1982, Son Sann's nationalist Khmer People's National Liberation Front and the Royalist FUNCINPEC joined the PDK to form the Coalition Government of Democratic Kampuchea. In John Pilger's tongue-in-cheek formulation, "[The CGDK was] neither a coalition nor a government: nor was it democratic, nor was it in Kampuchea."⁵³

The united front of a decade earlier was thus, in a sense, reborn. Of course, nobody operated under the assumption that the CGDK was anything other than a political marriage of convenience, if that. Even the actual declaration of the founding of the CGDK was bereft of any principles or policies; its content was procedural rather than substantive. Indeed, neither the KPNLF nor FUNCINPEC had any constitutional texts at the time they joined the CGDK.

Initially, the KPNLF and FUNCINPEC were also disadvantaged because they "started from scratch along the Thai-Cambodian border," while the PDK had "left behind a national network of political operatives and military units."⁵⁴ This was also underscored by their disparity in troops: the Khmer Rouge *reportedly* commanded a force of 35,000, while the KPNLF's count stood at 11,000, and the FUNCINPEC/ANS (Armée Nationale Sihanoukiste)/ANKI forces numbered only 5,000.⁵⁵ This was crucial because, insofar as united front tactics were ineffective or needed to be leveraged by force, military activity was integral to

Figure 3.2. Individual united front members' publications.

marginalizing the PRK (later the State of Cambodia/SOC and its military, the Cambodian People's Armed Forces/CPAF), which in turn "demonstrate[d] the political impossibility of [the] exclusion of the PDK."[56] Even wobbly KPNLF victories such as at the Battle of Svay Chek (ស្វាយចេក) from October to November 1989 were in large part due to the CPAF being distracted by their battles against the NADK over Pailin. Without NADK support in the Battle of Kampong Thom, ANS forces collapsed spectacularly.[57] On the ground, military forces attached to two or more of the coalition partners would organize joint operations or engage in information sharing on "objective" topics such as topography and terrain, but individual combatants would rarely mix.[58]

Ultimately, at its core, the second united front (as well as a future, post-1991 attempt at the formation of a third) was just like the first a decade earlier.[59] David Ashley, as ever, puts it best: "The KR viewed FUNCINPEC's offer to join the coalition of anti–Hun Sen parties, the National United Front, in precisely the same way as it had viewed similar alliances with the Royalists in 1970-75 and 1982-91—not as an end to the war against a foreign-backed 'puppet' regime but as a tactic to increase the means to wage it. They saw joining the Front as a way to gather additional 'national' forces, regain legitimacy and enable the world to provide them with aid."[60] In any case, given Beijing's long history of supporting Sihanouk, the PDK was in no position to refuse, even if it wanted to. As in the 1970s, the Cambodian communists made a virtue out of necessity with the goal of eventually dominating the coalition. In the meantime, it would secure its relationship with another key actor, the Thai military.

The Khmer Rouge's Not So Secret Secret Weapon

It cannot be overstated that the Cambodian resistance would not have survived without support from the Royal Thai Army. A key individual in this endeavor was Special Colonel Chavalit, the chief of Tactical Operations Center (TOC) 315 305, which dealt with overall army operations. His principal mandate was to protect Thailand's border from any future incursions by the People's Army of Vietnam (PAVN) or Kampuchean People's Revolutionary Armed Forces (KPRAF). His first order of business was the creation of a new unit subordinate to TOC 315, code-named Task Force 838 (TF 838), under Kasem Thammakul, the commander of TF 506. TF 838 was charged with being the covert

RTA liaison and providing support for Cambodian forces opposed to PAVN. In fact, it had earlier saved the Khmer Rouge movement, with Kasem personally ferrying Ieng Sary and others from Poipet to the Bangkok airport in January 1979, from where Sary would continue on to Beijing.

In the early 1980s, as the refugee camps to be described in the next chapter were first multiplying and then consolidating, TF 838 found itself taking on an outsized role in managing an ever more complex and challenging security situation along the Thai-Cambodian border. Drawing personnel from his 1 Special Forces Regiment, Chavalit assigned three groups to Task Force 838. Of these, one group (divided into three teams split among Sokh Sann, Ampil, and O'Bok) focused on supporting the KPNLF, one company-sized element supported the Royalist ANS, and the third group acted as an observer with the more reclusive Khmer Rouge.

Throughout the 1980s and 1990s, TF 838 proved to be the conduit that allowed the Khmer Rouge to extend its control, its management, and the physical movements of its leaders from Cambodian to Thai soil relatively unmolested and shielded from outside interference. The task force acted as a go-between for any police-related matters within the system of Khmer Rouge–operated camps, which managed the entry into and exit from these camps.[61] The commanders of the various Khmer Rouge "corridors" would make fortnightly visits to the Thai capital to coordinate their operations with the 838 command.[62] TF 838 also guarded Pol Pot's headquarters in Trat.[63] Moreover, in Anlong Veng, *Ta* Mok was himself protected by TF 838 until he was taken into Thai custody.[64] The extent to which TF 838 was willing to accommodate the Khmer Rouge (on the not unreasonable calculus that there was no viable outcome without the PDK)—and, indeed, Pol Pot himself—is illustrated in the task force's backdoor stage-managing of the four-party talks at Pattaya in 1989. As Kenneth Conboy recounts:

> [RTA chief] General Suchinda realized that any SNC [Supreme National Council] decisions that did not include the Khmer Rouge were destined to fail. And while there were two Khmer Rouge delegates in the SNC, the only one who could truly speak for that faction was Pol Pot himself. He was a pariah, however, and could not be seen in public, much less join the SNC in person. Suchinda had a solution. He instructed Task Force 838 to fetch Pol Pot from his safe house on the border near Trat . . . [and bring

him by chopper] to Pattaya, [where he was] then taken in a blacked-out van to the resort where the SNC had gathered. Tucked away inside a hotel room, he was provided with earphones and allowed to secretly listen to the deliberations taking place at an adjacent hall. His comments to the proceedings were surreptitiously fed to the Khmer Rouge delegates on the SNC, and they were thereby able to authoritatively offer their misgivings, and promises, with their leader's full knowledge and consent.[65]

Bangkok's treatment of the Khmer Rouge ended up paying dividends. First and foremost, it secured Beijing's promise to cease funding the insurgent Communist Party of Thailand. But there was also a significant financial upside for the RTA in this arrangement, as Thai military commanders became extremely wealthy through "taxes" (that is, kickbacks) on shipments of everything from lumber to gemstones brought across the border from PDK-held areas inside Cambodia. A United Nations official noted that the lumber trade had grown so "rapacious" that huge swaths of picked-over western Cambodia resembled a "moonscape."[66]

This relationship, in which the Khmer Rouge received logistical support from Thailand and the Thais extracted lumber, gems, and various taxes on other monies from the Khmer Rouge, extended to allowing the Khmer Rouge safe passage to deposit and withdraw funds from Thai banks ("more than enough, it is thought, for the rebels to continue the fight indefinitely," asserted the *New York Times*). These were "obtained from selling concessions to Thai lumber barons and gem traders, and ... Thai bankers act[ing] as a go-between for the rebels' accounts in Switzerland and the Caribbean." A classified 1992 Thai intelligence report put the estimate at more than $1 billion in concessions granted by the Khmer Rouge to Thai logging companies. This was so lucrative that when the Chinese wound down aid to the Khmer Rouge in 1994, the latter were able to continue their operations solely on financial arrangements brokered by the Thai military.[67]

Although an open secret among the political class in Bangkok and Phnom Penh, TF 838–PDK cooperation received some unwelcome scrutiny after the discovery by Thai national police of twelve warehouses along the Thai-Cambodian border that held a cache of an estimated 1,500 tons of Khmer Rouge military equipment. When police commanders initially suggested that it was a Khmer Rouge stockpile, the RTA perhaps gave the game away by asserting that it belonged to *them* (that is, the Thai military commanders themselves), even though the warehouses were guarded by Cambodians.⁶⁸

Although TF 838 was disbanded after the 1993 UNTAC-sponsored elections, it reappeared in 1994 to forcibly repatriate some 25,000 Cambodian refugees fleeing the State of Cambodia military's offensive on Pailin, in a coordinated operation with the Khmer Rouge. One Thai military ranger said that "when senior Khmer Rouge officials travel via our checkpoint, 838 will inform us ahead of time." According to Thai rangers, "at least 14 task forces of Unit 838—each with between 10 and 15 men—were still deployed on the border." By 1993, TF 838 had already garnered unwanted attention via its involvement in a Khmer Rouge seizure of twenty-one United Nations officials in Preah Vihear that year.⁶⁹

Pol Pot's New Headquarters

Perhaps the most important single contribution to Khmer Rouge longevity by TF 838 was its role in maintaining the security and thus the integrity of Pol Pot's base of operations along the Thai-Cambodian border throughout this period. Immediately after the Vietnamese invasion, Pol Pot alternated his time between Cambodia's jungles and banquet halls in Beijing and Pyongyang. He also spent a fair amount of time abroad for medical treatment. Brother Number 1 had long suffered from malaria as well as an extremely painful intestinal ailment. According to a former Khmer Rouge soldier, "he would spend hours on the toilet."⁷⁰ In late 1984, in response to the Vietnamese offensive, Pol Pot and his entourage escaped into Thailand.

Supported by local Thai authorities, Pol Pot was able to establish a comprehensive administrative base of operations. Throughout the organizational life of the PDK, "Office 87" (known by as many aliases as Manson family members: Office 870, 870, 87, 99, 101, 131) was shorthand for Pol Pot and/or the very top leadership. This included Nuon Chea, Son Sen, and Khieu Samphân, who would also stay at Office 87/870. Up until 1979, Pol Pot and his top lieutenants had been collectively referred to by their subordinates as "the Organization" (អង្គការ), "the Revolutionary Organization" (អង្គការបដិវត្តន៍), "the Upper Organization" (អង្គការលើ), or, occasionally, simply as "the Party" (បក្ស) in order to distinguish them from other nodes of functional or regional authority. But in the 1980s and onward, the shorthand for this nexus of politics was one of these numerical aliases, most often "Office 87,"

100   CHAPTER 3

referring to Pol Pot's code number for radio communications during the civil war of the 1970s; "87" could also be used in communications to give it extra gravitas.[71] Office 87/870 was where decisions regarding matters that could not be resolved at lower levels were made.[72]

Office 87/870 was a compound constructed of wooden huts that housed military strategic planning, foreign policy, economics, social affairs/health policy, and communications/propaganda. Altogether the staff numbered more than one hundred, and there were large venues for meetings. Pol Pot would receive "daily summaries of broadcasts from foreign radio stations and translations from Thai and Western newspapers." Pol Pot himself lived farther up the mountain in a compound that was "off-limits to all except the *montagnard* bodyguards, protected by yet another minefield and a ditch full of sharpened bamboo stakes, patrolled day and night by a special security battalion."[73] If Pol Pot sought a meeting, he had direct lines to each of the sections. Policies and news from the various sections were assembled and framed by Pol Pot himself and then broadcast in the form of a "situational analysis."

The location of the compound remained a closely guarded secret; even one of Pol Pot's former security guards at Office K1 during the Democratic Kampuchea era wasn't privy to the location of Office 131.

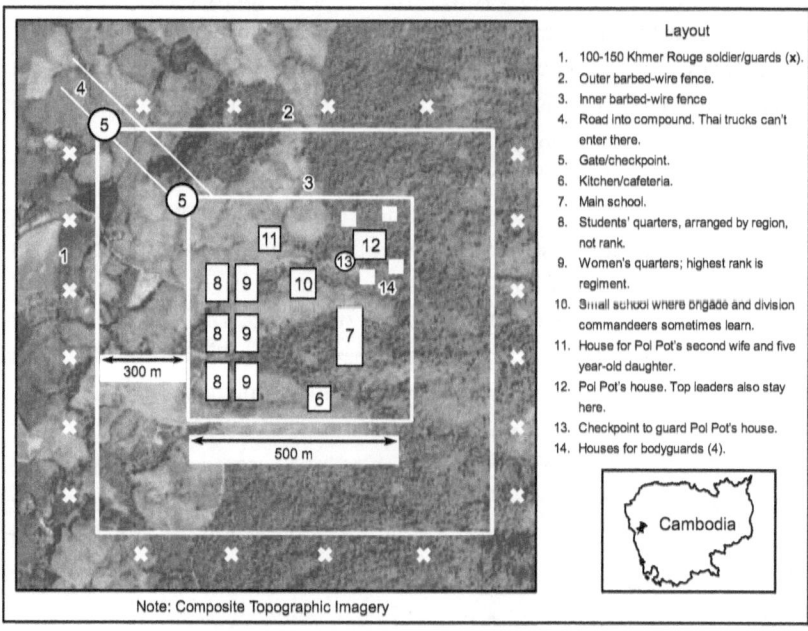

FIGURE 3.3. Layout of Pol Pot's headquarters 87/870, 1990. Gordon Thompson.

"I did not know exactly where [the] leaders were residing; we just knew the code numbers and received [and reported] from [Pailin]," he told an interviewer.⁷⁴ Over time, "Office 131" reverted back to the traditional code marking Pol Pot's base of operations: Office aka. Zone 87/870.

Office 87/870 was perched on a slightly raised piece of land, just higher than the rice fields that surrounded it, cradled by mountains. One could hear a nearby pagoda bell and see Thai villagers maintaining the paddy fields.⁷⁵ Its serene landscape belied its role as the epicenter for political education that would be a key part of PDK strategy to mobilize the population within Cambodia. Liberation was to be achieved through infiltration of and nocturnal rule over the villages by NADK guerrillas. According to this logic, as goes the countryside, so go the urban areas. Toward this end, Pol Pot dispatched "small cells of highly trained cadres [to infiltrate] hundreds of villages throughout Cambodia."⁷⁶ "Big meetings" for the leadership, down to the rank of NADK division commander, were held twice a year.⁷⁷ There were also special seminars that were simply referred to as "going to studies in the department-section-level of older brothers/big shots" (ទៅរៀនថ្នាក់មន្ទីរមុខធំ).

Although "Brother Number 2" Nuon Chea slept most nights at 87/870, his office (as well as a second residence) was thirty minutes away by car at the foot of Phnom Kbal Lan, at Ang Tek (អាងទឹក)⁷⁸ in Special Military Battlefield Command 505—the "prohibited zone"—which he headed. Corridor 505 was a highly restricted zone located at a narrow pass at the foot of Phnom Thom (ធំ), spanning (from east to west, Cambodia into Thailand) the villages of Peam Ta, Veal Rolim, O'Ronung, O'Tataok/Stung Tatok, O'Samril, Chamlong, Romeang, O'Rumcheik, O'Damcheik, O'Choam, Stung Touch, Phum Kropeu Pi, and Kampong Sala.⁷⁹ At 505, Nuon Chea taught politics to PDK cadres all the way down to the group (ក្រុម) level, using teaching materials written by Pol Pot, and in the same manner.⁸⁰ These were pared-down versions of what was taught at 87/870 and largely transmitted orally. (Written materials were provided only down to the level of the regiment commanders.) As one cadre admitted, "I'm illiterate as are most commanders at the battalion level."⁸¹ These classes were held more often, around every two to four months. One noteworthy senior official at 505 was former Tuol Sleng commander Duch, who had by now changed his name to Hang Pin.⁸²

Son Sen would spend time in and around Corridor 505 intermittently throughout the 1980s, even as he commanded Corridor 1001 far to the east. His stature at this stage was not simply—or, to some colleagues, even primarily—based on his military prowess, which may explain his connection to 505 and to Pol Pot's headquarters more generally. Reflecting his tendency—born of not misplaced self-confidence—to distance himself from "the Center," Mok spent a greater amount of time in the theater of war, although moving far more freely than Son Sen to and from Thailand, given Mok's deep and extensive connections with the RTA.

Command and Control from Office 87/870

Meetings held at Office 87/870 also provided opportunities to handle essential cash disbursements to the various NADK divisions. Field commanders attended meetings at 87/870 at least once a year. The content of these seminars (as well as operating funds) would be transmitted downward, as illustrated by the case of *Ta* Beth, who eventually rose to fifth in the NADK hierarchy (commanding Divisions 305 and 405) and was physically located the farthest from 87/870. His wife, who was based in O'Damcheik (អូរដំបេក), made regular trips to Thailand to deposit cash in a bank there. *Ta* Beth would "pocket . . . some of this money" and instruct his wife to deposit the rest, transported by a Thai car and driver. *Ta* Beth would go to Thailand and Pailin every six months or so to receive education and new instructions. Simply getting to the meeting was an arduous task. An NADK defector told an interviewer:

> *Ta* Beth travels through the mountains and the forests and does not take . . . the roads. . . . [H]e often gets rides on woodcutters' tractor[s], crosses [National Route 4], and reaches his base on oxcarts. Whenever he goes, he usually take[s] a 50 men-strong escort along . . . walking or riding on elephants, tractors or oxcarts, depending on what is available, down to Kao Sla [កោះស្លា]. On his way back from Thailand, *Ta* Beth [would] pass new instructions to commanders based in these areas. . . . [Upon his return] he usually organizes a meeting which may last up to 10 days, from 7 to 11 am and from 2 to 4 pm. Teaching documents are brought from the border and are copied, read and commented [on]. At these sessions, buffaloes or cows are killed and participants bring from their respective sector bases soft drinks, coconuts and cards to play and have some good time[s] together. On these occasions, *Ta* Beth also distributes funds to his commanders to finance their

activities. These training sessions concern only upper-level cadres [regiment commanders and above]. ... Middle-ranking officers [battalion and company commanders] are ... taught separately [in] working meetings [ប្រជុំធ្វើការ].[83]

Money was necessary but not sufficient for success. There had to be a political message to build up each of these groups, recruit people to the PDK's cause, and try to outmaneuver its united front partners. Put simply, the PDK's *political* goal was to reestablish its viability and legitimacy as a governing force in post–Democratic Kampuchea Cambodia, to be explored in the next two chapters. The focus of policy at this time was the survival of the movement within an environment of political flux and military insecurity.

Much as the Vietnamese invasion in early 1979 was a throwback to the escape from Phnom Penh to the *maquis* following 1963, so was the post-1979 (re)establishment of Office 87/870 a throwback to Office 100 in the early to mid-1960s in the highlands of Ratanakiri. Once again, the CPK/PDK found itself in the forests, isolated and relying on crafting a political message to mobilize the population on whose backs it would ride back to power. And much as in the 1970s, the united front was a fig leaf, but a necessary one, for the time being. Ieng Sary's role was ascendant (although not for terribly long thereafter). Just as the Khmer Rouge colonized the united front from within during the early to mid-1970s, it would need to dominate the second united front through superior organizing capabilities and military prowess. This was where Son Sen and *Ta* Mok would come to the fore. But all these leaders recognized that in order to grab hold of the reins once again, the PDK had to rely on its ability to structure the refugee camps along the Thai-Cambodia border. These camps would provide the logistics, the command and control, and the bodies necessary to fight a prolonged guerrilla war, prevail politically, and ultimately vanquish its united front allies.

Chapter 4

Command and Control in the Shadows and on the Periphery, 1985–1989

> We must protect our base as we did in Ratanakiri: plant piles, bamboo spikes, and set up booby trap after booby trap. It was important for us to return to our primary principles: people's war and guerrilla war.
>
> —Phi Phuon, quoted in Henri Locard, *Jungle Heart of the Khmer Rouge*

Ghost towns are unnerving places, confusing the metaphysics of space and time in a tangible way, making it impossible to look away or to deny what can no longer be seen. The dustbowl of a border-crossing hamlet—Choam Sangam (ជាំសាងាំ)—is one such place. It is not a textbook "ghost town" per se. It has functioning market stalls, a guesthouse, and even a shiny, decadent casino that shatters the otherwise serene landscape of the Dângrêk Mountains. It boasts signs marking the location of Pol Pot's trial and the place where Son Sen was buried, but the actual physical evidence is long gone. Even Brother Number 1's own cremation site, a somewhat shabby affair, is located steps away from a steady accumulation of garbage behind one of the stalls along the main road, along with a desiccated spirit house that, despite constantly being stocked with food, appears to be itself on the verge of starvation. Taken together, it would be unsettling if it weren't so pathetic.

One of the strangest and most discombobulating effects comes from trying to imagine the kind of complex, dynamic operations that occupied this space a generation ago, as even the most insignificant tangible objects—files,[1] meeting rooms, mess halls, radio trucks—have been reduced to dust by the elements or swallowed up by the forests. Even more unnerving is how time and space have been flattened. What we see today makes 1990s Choam Sangam look no different from Phnom Kulen, the Khmer Rouge base area between 1970 and 1975. Both have been reclaimed by the forest, and the dusty solitude in each gives no indication that the two spectral locations were key nodes for the entire CPK/PDK network—a successful combination of political messaging, logistics, and military activity—in the 1970s and the 1990s, respectively.

Much of the military activity managed by these two sites, two decades apart, was quite similar. But there was one significant difference. In the 1970s civil war, the CPK corralled entire villages into collective farms and thus organized the social organization and food production necessary to nourish its troops and starve the enemy. After 1979, however, denied the same kind of vast swaths of governable land inside Cambodia, the centers for organization and support for the movement were located *outside* Cambodia. In the 1980s, the PDK leveraged the growing archipelago of refugee camps along the Thai-Cambodian border to build up its formidable military organization—and, somewhat less successfully, its political messaging—*inside* Cambodia. These efforts rested on a grassroots political program to penetrate rural villages and recruit soldiers, and they were managed by an extensive command and control system, the subject of this chapter.

It is important to note that, as in the early to mid-1970s, the movement at this point was anything but monolithic—ironic, given the totalitarian instincts of Pol Pot and Nuon Chea. Of course, the Center ruled with an iron fist, but the implementation agents on the ground did not have the luxury of blindly adhering to orthodoxy as interpreted by Office 87/870. Rather, it was the PDK's own requirement that "the leading cadre in each base area ["region"/កំបន់ or "corridor"/ច្រក in PDK parlance] must be highly responsible for the attributes of their base areas."[2] Indeed, the areas controlled by Ieng Sary, Son Sen, and *Ta* Mok were dramatically different, largely conforming to their own biases with regard to united front and, eventually, class struggle.

Confronting and Sidestepping the Past

The immediate political challenge facing the PDK was to win back support from the Cambodian population, first for their guerrilla insurgency and eventually for their return to national power. This was far easier said than done. According to a cadre notebook of the time, the Khmer Rouge had few illusions about the degree of popular support for their movement: "The situation of the population at the beginning of the dry season [of] 1979 is divided, one part still supports us while another is against us and is waiting out to see [what happens]. But by the end of 1979, the proportion of the population that is opposing us and waiting out is diminishing."[3] At this point, the PDK was banking on Khmer hatred of the Vietnamese to work in its favor. Yet such a passive fount of support was insufficient for the task at hand. Some contrition, however disingenuous, was necessary.

Thus Pol Pot saw fit to apologize for the mistakes of the Democratic Kampuchea period. In the spirit of Marxist-Leninist self-criticism, he avowed in a mid-1980s address several "errors," including the policy of outlawing money, food shortages from rural collectivization, executions instead of reeducation, and overworking the population.[4] He acknowledged:

> [Mistakes were made] from various factors of ours. On the one hand, base people, new to power for the first time, came and ran the whole country. They had little experience, and had to learn while they were running the country . . . [and] three years was too short a time to become experienced and straighten out the fault according to our target. However . . . in those three years we fought both to build our nation and to hold against internal and external enemies and we have gained experiences all along. . . . [T]he reconstruction of the country was being shifted onto the right track. In addition, the rice production for 1978–79 was fair and would be able to take care of the people's need and also enable them to be masters of themselves. In the battle against the enemies inside and outside the country, on the one hand we were successful in getting rid of the enemies, but on the other we, from the top to bottom, were somewhat excessive. . . . We have learned our lessons. This lesson is for ourselves and our ranks in the future to avoid as much as possible the mistakes we made during the formation of socialism in those three years. . . . Democratic Kampuchea is truly nationalist. . . . It dares to sacrifice everything.[5]

This seems, at best, ambivalent, but there was enough in the message to mollify critics of the Khmer Rouge and even bring them into the movement.[6] Beneath the surface, though, there were strong echoes of the way things were in the 1970s. In an internal October 12, 1981, "guiding view," for instance, Pol Pot (still at this time referred to as "870") explained that the very name "CPK" would be used only "internally" and even then only in "certain contexts." Instead, "the terms Government of

Democratic Kampuchea, the Patriotic and Democratic Front of Great National Union of Kampuchea, [and] the National Army and Guerrillas of Democratic Kampuchea" were to be used instead. On January 17, 1982, Son Sen articulated the same message: "We have now stopped using the term Communist Party of Kampuchea" and "any terms which belong too obviously to the old communist regime" that would "lead others to suspect that we haven't changed"—this even though the term "comrade" (មិត្ត) was still being used.⁷ *Plus ça change.*

Rebuilding and Reorganizing the Military

Creating a military force out of thin air was nothing new to Son Sen or to *Ta* Mok. They had spent a good part of the 1960s creating what would eventually become the Revolutionary Army of Kampuchea (កងទ័ពរំដោះកម្ពុជា), starting with loyal hill tribesmen and growing it with escapees from the urban areas and other people on the political margins. The difference was that this time around, it was not a civil war

FIGURE 4.1. Khmer Rouge soldier with hill tribesman and his family. Naoki Mabuchi.

revolving around the question of which Cambodian movement would secure power. This time the question was an existential one: How do Cambodians avoid becoming consumed by Vietnam? Son Sen and Mok did not have the luxury of time. They did, however, have the benefit of extensive experience. Unlike the KPNLF and to some extent FUNCIN-PEC, the new National Army of Democratic Kampuchea (NADK) had a sophisticated idea of what they were doing.

The post-1979 NADK relied on foot soldiers and built up its ranks using a series of methods that drew on an equally diverse set of motivations. Some recruits were persuaded to join through regular appeals to nationalism. Others signed up somewhat serendipitously, simply through bumping into the Khmer Rouge in the forest. A number joined because of the unrelenting boredom of farm life and the sense of helplessness from being trapped in perpetual war.[8] Some volunteered because they believed joining the NADK was the most effective way of opposing what they saw as mistreatment by Vietnamese troops and PRK officials and soldiers. Still others did so because they liked the snappy new uniforms or the "great guns" of the NADK troops.[9] Recruits

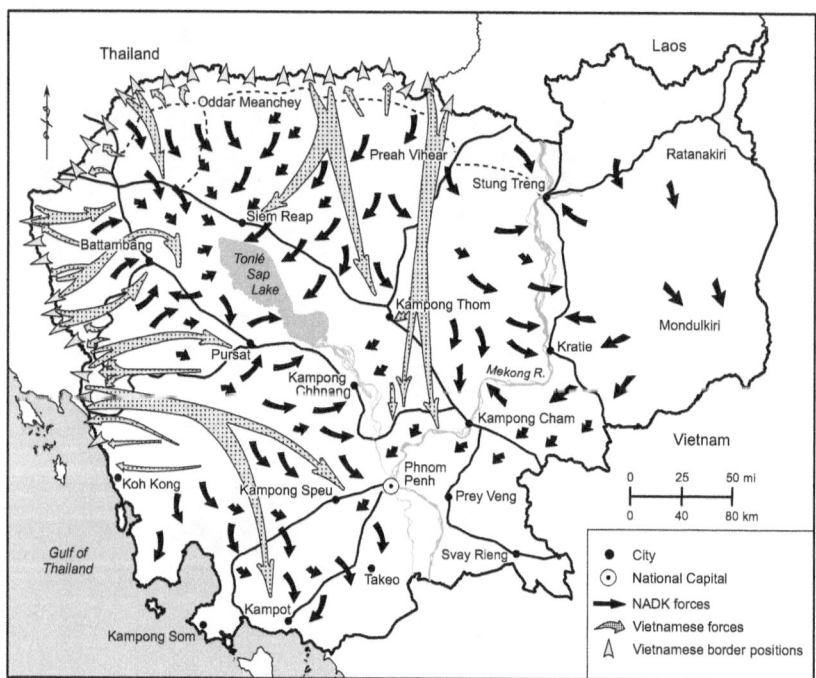

FIGURE 4.2. Troop movements, 1985–1988. Map by Gordon Thompson from *NADK Magazine* 4, no. 25 (October 1989): 23.

often went through a short probationary period before they were issued a weapon, but that lasted only a few months at most. This was very different from the recruitment process for the Vietnamese-backed People's Republic of Kampuchea, which relied on forced conscription, tempered by bribery.

By the mid-1980s, Mok and Son Sen had re-created a widely if thinly spread network of military operations that stretched from the Thai border to locations approaching Phnom Penh and as far away as Cambodian provinces bordering Vietnam.[10] Infiltration corridors linked battlefields back to the Thai border, where troop supplies were less vulnerable to attack and units could regroup, often by retreating into Thailand itself. Although the situation was dynamic over time as leaders' positions shifted, military units were absorbed into one another, and conditions on the ground led to changes within those individual units, it is possible to sketch a general picture of the Khmer Rouge military command. The image that emerges is one of extensive organization and deployment throughout Cambodian territory during the 1980s and 1990s. This buildup was never decisive in pushing out Vietnam, but it did make possible the organizational rebirth of the Khmer Rouge which would have seemed fantastical just a few years before. Indeed, some 30 percent of NADK ranks joined after 1979.[11]

FIGURE 4.3. Khmer Rouge troops inside Cambodia, 1983. Naoki Mabuchi.

NADK military units were subdivided as follows:

One division (កងពលធំ) = three brigades
One brigade (កងពលតូច) = three regiments (one for transport)
One regiment (វរសេនាធំ) = three battalions
One battalion (វរសេនាតូច) = three companies
One company (អនុសេនាធំ) = three sections
One section (អនុសេនាតូច) = three groups
One group (ក្រុម) = three *puok*
One *puok* (ពួក) = three soldiers[12]

Specialized units included:

Transportation unit = one battalion
Special forces (កងពិសេស) unit = one battalion, special military operations
Medical unit (not organized as a discrete unit)
Radio/transmission personnel
Ground troops/"installing unit" (កងទំពាជើង) = intelligence, propaganda, and psyops (ចិត្តសាស្ត្រ)[13]

There were five people at the very top in the chain of command from the division to the battalion level: a political commander (ប្រធាន, or committee chairman) and his deputy (ranked one and three), a military commander (មេបញ្ជាការ) and his deputy (ranked two and four), and a commander of logistics (ranking deputy). If a political commander was killed, he was replaced by his (functional) deputy, not the next person in the chain of command; that is, the number-one-ranked cadre was replaced by the number-three-ranked cadre. If the number-two-ranked cadre was killed, he was replaced by his deputy, the number-four-ranked cadre. This kept politics and strategy focused and undiluted, with politics trumping military concerns.[14] The tertiary cadre was in charge of economics.[15]

In Son Sen's and Mok's configuration, the (mostly male) military units were supported by (mostly female) supply units. In the absence of modern transport and the destruction of much of Cambodia's infrastructure due to war and neglect, these women braved the footpaths through the jungle. Describing one of these supply corps, a supply unit member recalled that her unit was composed of unmarried women in their twenties and thirties who had become separated from their

FIGURE 4.4. Female Khmer Rouge porters inside Cambodia, 1983. Naoki Mabuchi.

families in the confusion surrounding the Vietnamese invasion. They would carry food and supplies (and the ubiquitous hammocks, since they slept in the trees during their forays into the jungle) for up to a week at a time (principally during the dry season, when fighting was at its height), escorted by armed soldiers. Back in their home bases, they slept ten people to a hut, which they had also built when not planting crops. When they married, they would have to leave the unit and be assigned other work.[16]

In sharp contrast to the Democratic Kampuchea period, medical care was reasonably good, considering the circumstances. In 2020 one veteran Khmer Rouge doctor recalled:

> I was in a central hospital which was under control of Pol Pot . . . so they provided enough food and medicine for the patients. We got most medicines from China, Thailand[,] and we treated patients effectively and efficiently. There were lots of patients with severe injuries from the fighting and each of the patients were given pork, chicken, [and other] food to eat, [and received] good medicines. Although none of the doctors had a salary . . . we worked very smoothly and it was very easy to [manage] people then . . . even better than nowadays.[17]

Other field hospitals also received largely uniform praise from those who worked in or who were treated by them.[18]

Food that was collected was stored at a logistics unit of organization (អង្គការកំស្បការ). Soldiers were provided with resources to forage on their own; one recounted that "salt, sugar, fish-sauce, glutamate, tobacco [were] all bought from local villagers and through them. We were also given fishing nets and were allowed to hunt wild animals."[19] An NADK cadre at the time also noted that ordinary people worked and ate family-style at home, while soldiers lived together in each unit. Soldiers did not collect a salary, drawing instead from a free-supply system. If a soldier went to Thailand, his expenses would be paid for by the ranking soldier accompanying him. Monetary transactions were conducted in Thai baht. There was a corresponding easing of restrictions from what had been the case under Democratic Kampuchea. As the cadre described it: "We had more freedom; soldiers could listen to any radio broadcast they wanted; we had more freedom to talk. People ate and worked individually and could grow their own crops."[20] Crops were harvested to feed the communities as well as the NADK forces they supported. A rule of thumb was that eighty to one hundred peasants could support twenty soldiers.[21]

The dry season (October to February) tended to favor the Vietnamese, so the NADK forces used that time to stock up on supplies, especially food. During the day, soldiers could even don civilian clothes and eat, purchase supplies, and otherwise interact with the local population without fear that they would be reported to the (non-PDK) authorities. Sharp-eyed and -eared villagers could identify NADK soldiers because of their comparatively courteous language as well as their hairstyles, in addition to their solid-green Chinese-supplied khakis. The rainy season tended to favor guerrilla warfare, but it was a challenge even for combat-hardened NADK soldiers. One told an interviewer: "The forest is very dense, we have only one [trail] to get to the base; it is impenetrable otherwise, too thick. We cut a tunnel in the vegetation to get access to the camp.... [D]uring the rainy season, the forest is flooded so we move around in boats we captured ... [from] the *Yuon*."[22]

The year 1985 also saw the emergence of ghostly NADK guerrillas who might otherwise have been lost forever to the forest. Groups of five to ten people would rise up out of the shadows with maybe one or two small guns between them that they used for hunting "paddy birds." They would open the birds' stomachs and use the seeds that the birds had consumed to plant their own rice. In some cases, they possessed neither knives nor scissors; thus "their hair had grown, so had their

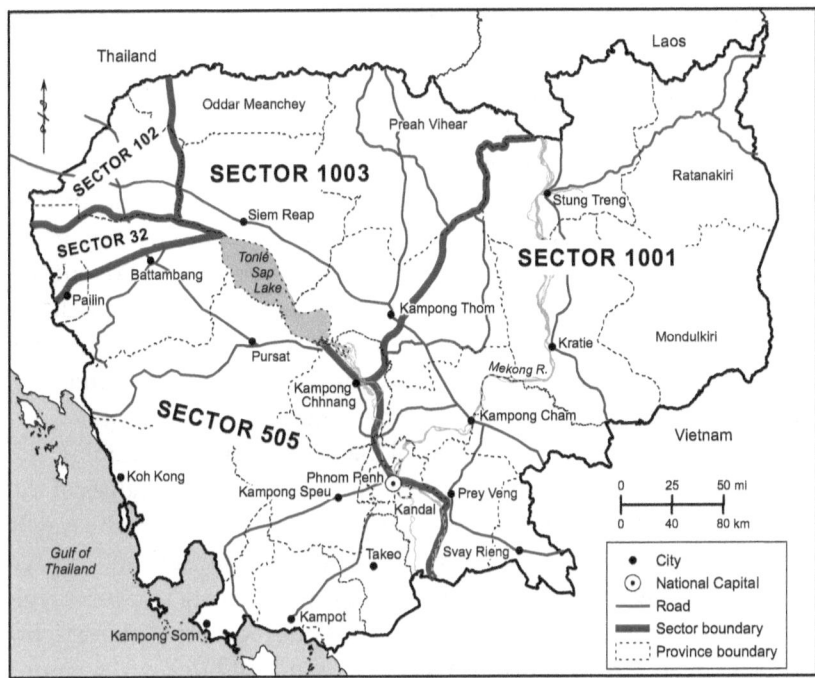

FIGURE 4.5. Principal NADK military corridors, 1985–1993. Gordon Thompson.

beard[s], they almost ran out of clothes and just had pieces of cloth or even nothing, they really looked like jungle people [មនុស្សព្រៃ]."[23]

That winter, PAVN forces launched an offensive. One of their actions (known as "K5") was to seal off the Thai-Cambodian border—aimed at preventing the infiltration of CGDK troops and supplies into Cambodia by denying resistance bases in Thailand access into the country. Son Sen's headquarters for Corridor 1001 was forced to relocate to Thailand,[24] while *Ta* Mok's Corridor 1003 forces were driven across the northern border with Thailand to Choam Sla (ជាំស្លា), moving back only quasi-permanently to Anlong Veng in 1990. But although the respective corridors' HQs moved across the border, extensive military operations continued apace within Cambodia.

The PDK Political Program on the Ground

Hand in hand with these military operations was a focused effort to politically educate Cambodians located in NADK-held areas. For Mok, but even more so for Son Sen, the goal was not simply to secure military victories but also to establish the political foundations on which the PDK could ultimately vanquish the non-communist resistance parties making up the balance of the united front. To survive in such conditions and politically outflank its NCR allies, it was essential for NADK units to establish mutually supportive relations with the local population. "Holding" a village required a relatively constant troop presence, something made particularly challenging after the 1984–85 Vietnamese offensive.[25] The PDK responded by drawing from their pre-1975 CPK playbook. Initially they sought out village and commune leaders who were wounded veterans and could no longer serve at the front or older people who were unable to fight. This changed as recruitment imperatives to fill military ranks expanded to include forming broader networks of in-country political support.

The PDK would identify political classes of people, including the durable Khmer Rouge concept of "base people," indecisive "allies of the base people," the patriotic but silent bourgeoisie, and those who might be anti-Vietnamese but who were also anti-communist,[26] and engage them to actively support the PDK. This meant adhering to a strict regimen of organizational discipline, ostensibly placing politics above fighting. The logic was "practice" (អនុវត្ត) → "war" (សង្គ្រាម) → "weapon" (អាវុធ) → "mouth" (មាត់).[27]

FIGURE 4.6. Khmer Rouge soldiers interacting with villager inside Cambodia, 1983. Naoki Mabuchi.

Once they had identified like-minded villagers, solders would instruct them to practice the "three don'ts": don't give supplies to the enemy, don't enlist in K5, and don't cooperate with the Vietnamese administration or the military. If these were internalized by a village family patriarch or matriarch, then the next step was for them to develop the "four tasks": propagandize the "three don'ts" among the immediate family (ស្មុលគ្រួសារ), the heads of the extended family (ស្មុលក្រុមគ្រួសារ), the core of the village (ស្មុលភូមិ), and the core of the militia (ស្មុលឈ្មប). The goal was to recruit waverers (ប្រជាជនមជ្ឈិម) or those ignorant of (ប្រជាជនខ្សោយ) or otherwise hostile to the PDK program. Given the traditional enmity between the Khmer and the Vietnamese, these were not especially difficult principles to communicate to villagers and secure their buy-in. Still, it took some three years, from 1985 to 1988, for this program to metastasize effectively. Each PDK cadre was provided with a form on which to keep track of the progress his unit had made in implementing the "three don'ts" in his area of operations.[28]

NADK troops would not simply pay for all the goods that they received from the peasants; they would deliberately pay higher prices than those demanded by the government, while also encouraging the peasants to refuse to sell to the government. At the same time, they sought to disarm local authorities militarily and politically under the "two destroys" strategy: destroy the military state authority and destroy the civilian state authority.[29] They could do this because they already knew the individuals who made up the network of pre-1979 rural CPK cadres and could contact them discreetly, often wearing civilian clothes and disguising themselves as "traders to buy rice or cows or chicken [in order to] gather intelligence on the defense forces, government troops, their size, [and] location."[30]

After identifying political targets—group leaders (មេក្រុម), village leaders (មេភូមិ), commune leaders (មេឃុំ), militia commanders, intelligence agents (ប្រជាឈ្មប), or soldiers—the NADK would seek to capture them and take them away for reeducation. An interviewee recalled: "When we catch one of them, we take him to our base and educate him about DK policy and convince him to stop cooperating with the government.... Often when he returns he is arrested or, if not, he is not considered trust[worthy] any longer by the government—so he can stay in his position but the government loses confidence in him and stop[s] using him. The government's power weakens."[31] Such education could last from one month to half a year.

These comparatively benign policies were punctuated by the terror tactics for which both Son Sen and Mok were well known. An interviewee recounts how, for instance, the Khmer Rouge beheaded Sok Chheang, a commander who fought for the Vietnamese-backed regime, "stuck [his head] on a bamboo [pole], and told the Prey Kadouich [ព្រៃកដូច] villagers that Sok was working for [Vietnam] and said, 'don't do like Sok.'"[32] The PDK also punished their own. NADK soldiers and the officers responsible for them could incur serious penalties if they did anything to erode rural support for the movement. The worst thing a Khmer Rouge combatant could do was to kill a villager. (The second was stealing or selling one's weapon.) A first offense was met with scorn within the soldier's unit; a second resulted in group criticism and struggle; while a third would result in interrogation, imprisonment, and often execution. Adultery was also taken very seriously, and if it occurred regularly among a group of soldiers, their commanding officer would be held liable (i.e., executed as a deterrent measure). The same sliding scale of punishments existed for treason or betrayal of information. Significantly, from a united front perspective, such treasonous behavior with Vietnamese or PRK forces was seen as *less* of a crime than conducting oneself in the same manner with the KPNLF (akin to a "worm coming into our flesh").[33]

The civilian administrative apparatus was modeled on the military one. Each area had a five-person leadership group. The ranking division chief was responsible for the entire division, and his or her functional portfolio was politics. The second division chief focused on military/security issues. The third-ranking committee member managed the economy, which essentially revolved around supplying the military and civilian populations with food and other basic supplies. As in the DK period, the fourth-ranking leader looked after social affairs and health-related issues. The fifth-ranking cadre handled cultural and educational matters, such as schooling for the children, insofar as this was possible. (Teachers were exempt from normal peasant work.) Propaganda and ideological indoctrination comprised a broader portfolio and were managed more collectively. These "civilian" organizational units were grafted onto the Khmer Rouge military alongside the chain of command described earlier. Individuals of the military group—say, a brigade economics officer—would report to his civilian counterpart, the fourth-ranking division cadre responsible for the economy. The division chief was responsible for the entire area and reported directly to Pol Pot from 1979 until his 1997 fall from power.[34]

Civilian organization was also a part of governance. Although military terms of art were often used, the district, as we have just seen, was distinct from the military brigade. The top administrators were the civilian "division" (កងពល) leaders, who were appointed by the district chief. (In Anlong Veng, for example, he or she was appointed directly by Mok.) These leaders were recruited and promoted largely on ability and experience rather than on political or ideological criteria. They were placed in charge of some two hundred to three hundred families, mostly women and children, as their husbands and older sons had been recruited into the military. There were many of these civilian "division" leaders, and the organization under their control had military monikers, like "military unit 502."

At the very bottom of these units were the individual households. At this level, one family would "control" or keep an eye on two or three other families. The next level up was the group leaders (បេក្រុម), a grouping of a dozen families. This grouping was managed by a two-person team of a leader and a deputy leader, chosen from the twelve families. There would be nominations, based on experience, ability to read or write, and recommendations from "the Organization," for these two leaders which were made by the leaders at the next level up: brigade (មេកងពលតូច). The families would then attend a meeting and vote, via a show of hands, among the nominees. The winners would become the leader and the deputy leader at the group leader level.

As noted previously, the brigade was the next organizational level. This, too, was handled by two people, a leader and a deputy leader, who were nominated (according to the same criteria just described) by the next-highest administrative level and voted on by the villagers. The brigade leader was responsible for five group leaders—comprising sixty families—and ensured that policy was implemented effectively. These group leaders reported directly to the civilian "division" leaders.

Although this appears somewhat rigid, the people knew these leaders by name (and unit number), and Mok himself would often bypass the chain of command—driving his own vehicle and making himself available to villagers to resolve issues and solve problems. Insofar as policy trickled down to this level, it was of a fairly basic hand-to-mouth variety. For instance, the committee member in charge of social and health policy managed a health care unit (ក្រុមពេទ្យ) that had representatives all the way down to the group leader and individual family levels. Villagers who had some sort of rudimentary medical skills were chosen to be part of this group, which in addition to treating civilians would also go to the front to take care of wounded soldiers.[35]

Since Son Sen and Mok were continuing a *people's* war, mobilization involved the entire population under NADK control. Peasant support allowed guerrillas to disappear into the local populations, thus "providing water in which the fish could swim," in Maoist parlance. Food, logistical assistance, and medical care were provided by organized peasant groups. Areas also had transportation units. (In Anlong Veng, it was known as Office 55.)[36] As a rule, such transport units were overwhelmingly made up of female peasants, whose husbands and sons were often away fighting on the front lines.[37]

Peasants were also mobilized to carve bamboo to produce sharp *punji* stakes used for booby traps against the Vietnamese as well as to provide a secure perimeter around Khmer Rouge villages. Villagers were tasked with producing up to five hundred of these a day. Next to actual weapons, *punji* sticks were the second-most-important fighting tools for the Khmer Rouge soldiers. Whether mixed in among the grass or planted in concealed pits, upon impact they "would often break apart into small pieces that would get lodged in the human body. These pieces were extremely difficult to remove and most soldiers who survived these spikes suffered prolonged recovery as the injuries were slow to heal."[38] Indeed, a key factor in Khmer Rouge warfare at the time was not to kill enemy soldiers but to seriously wound them so that they would become a burden to their unit. In some areas, bamboo *punji* sticks were replaced by iron caltrops that could be reused and simply scattered in tall grass.

However extensive the network of village organization within Cambodia was, the principal resources for food, supplies, logistics, medicine, and training weren't in Cambodia at all. They were in Thailand, embedded in the refugee camps strung along the border.

The Refugee Camp System: KPNLF and FUNCINPEC

For Son Sen, Mok, and their subordinates to succeed inside Cambodia, the Thai-Cambodian border camps were essential as rearguard supply areas. Effective management of these camps was vital for command and control of armed forces and civilian mobilization on the Cambodian battlefields and behind enemy lines. The border had been almost hermetically sealed during the Pol Pot era, which made it practically impossible to flee the bloodshed taking place in Cambodia between 1975 and 1979. When it was opened in the wake of the Vietnamese invasion, "the exodus," in Elizabeth Becker's words, "was a stampede."[39] By the end of the year, there were some 100,000 Cambodian refugees living in the Nong Samet (also known as 007) and Nong Mak Mun/Chumrom Chas encampments, with a smaller ragtag group of Khmer Rouge soldiers seeking sanctuary there as well.[40]

Initially, in the four months between October 1979 and January 1980, Thailand accepted Cambodian refugees without restriction, allowing them to stay until they could be resettled or chose to return to Cambodia. They were held at United Nations High Commission for Refugees (UNHCR) facilities like Khao I Dang (ខាវអ៊ីដាង), located squarely within Thailand. But this policy was unsustainable. By 1980, the scale of the undertaking, the geopolitical conditions, regional power shifts (particularly the lack of any genuine buffer between Vietnamese forces and Thai territory), and domestic Thai politics had complicated the situation considerably. This was reflected in Thai authorities' general neglect of, even contempt for, these refugees. Their draconian policies had their effect, as measured by the decline in the number of refugees who made it into Thailand from across the Cambodian border.[41]

Many Cambodians voted with their feet and turned instead to non-UNHCR camps. This provoked a corresponding complication of the social, economic, and political situation on the ground. Mason and Brown describe camps "split into two distinct spheres—the holding centers within Thailand and the volatile no-man's land called simply 'the border.'"[42] Any ambiguity within this system of UNHCR and Khmer resistance camps created a vital gray zone outside the purview of international law and the institutions formed to adjudicate it. One could argue that from 1979 until late 1984, there were three distinct domains connected to the refugee camp system. First, there were the military command structures and troop bivouacs of the KPNLF, FUNCINPEC/MOULINAKA/ANS, and NADK, which were separate from the civilian population and located either in Cambodia or closest to its border with Thailand. Second, there were civilian populations, either straddling the border or proximate to it. Eventually there also were the UNHCR camps entirely inside Thai territory. In most forward areas, international agencies were barred and had only daytime access to the civilian areas along the border. And although the political officials and cadres of the various movements had access to civilian areas, they rarely visited, instead residing in separate military areas and compounds. This was to maintain their security and freedom of movement and to avoid making the civilian areas legitimate targets for Vietnamese attack.

In the words of Josephine Reynell, "the people from the camps inevitably become associated with resistance groups."[43] Indeed, the civilian refugee population became "a necessary adjunct for the warriors,"[44] a pool for recruitment but at the same time often an unwanted burden in the view of the military forces. W. Courtland Robinson lays out a

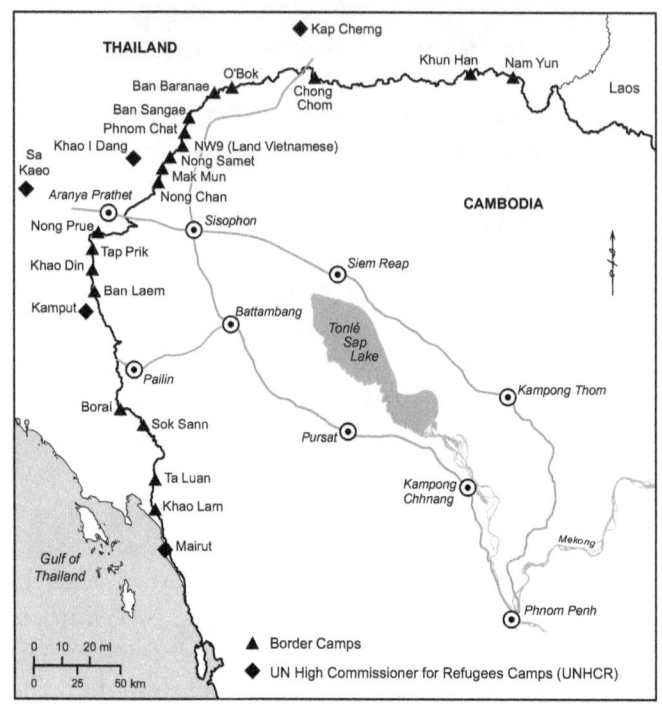
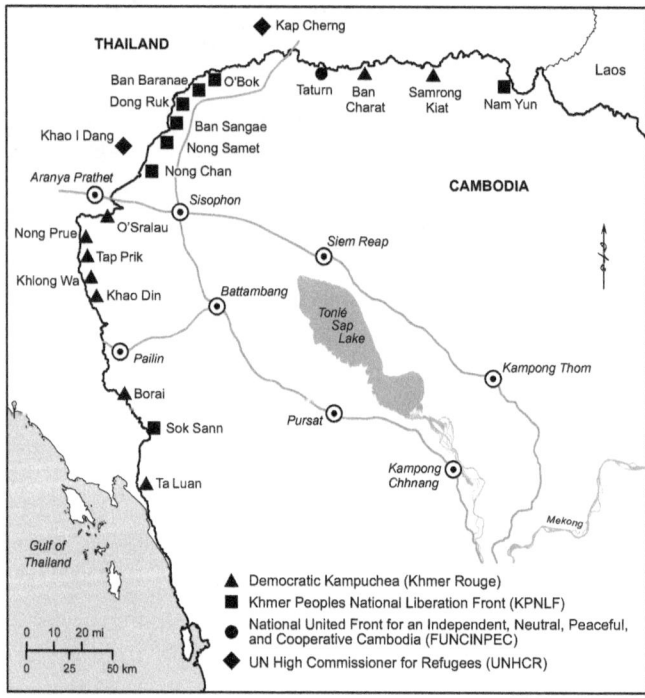

FIGURE 4.7. Consolidation of refugee camps by coalition partner. *Upper map*, 1980; *lower map*, 1984.

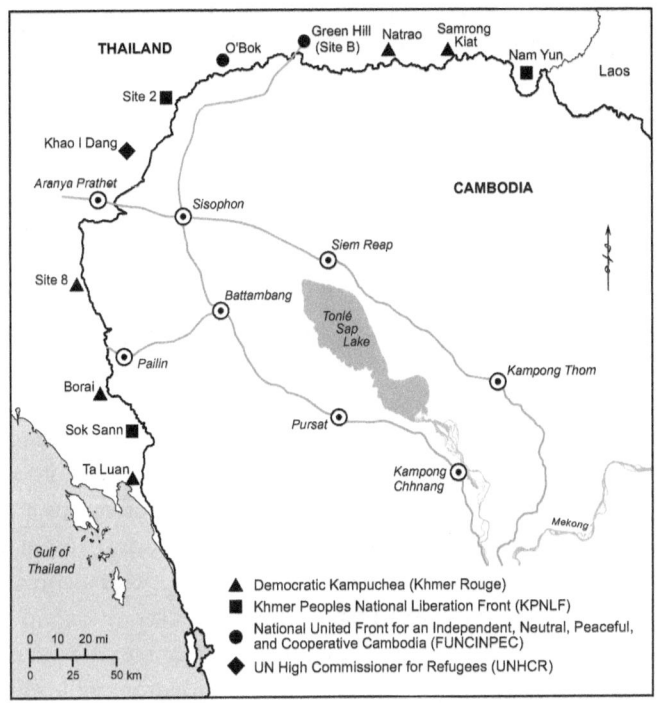

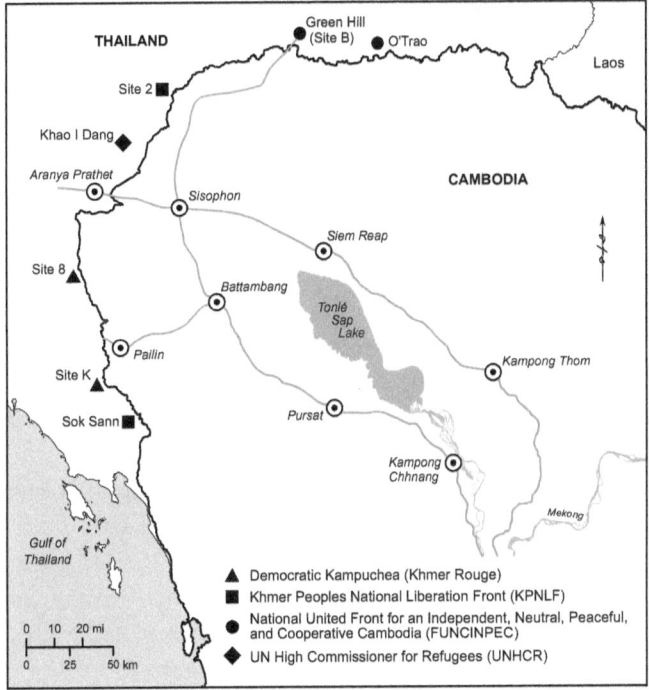

FIGURE 4.7. (Continued) *Upper map*, 1985; *lower map*, 1991. Maps by Gordon Thompson from Cortland W. Robinson, "Double Vision: A History of Cambodian Refugees in Thailand."

useful typology: "refugee camps" (assisted by the aid community), "remote camps" (partially militarized locales with some limited penetration by international actors), and "satellite camps" ("front-line camps, military training camps, and rudimentary hospital camps, to which aid organizations also had no access").[45]

In 1981, just as Son Sen was emerging from his "walkabout" in the Cambodian jungles, the United Nations Border Relief Operation (UNBRO) was put in charge of managing the camps. Beginning in 1983, and continuing through the 1984–85 dry season offensive, a series of Vietnamese military operations led to the evacuation of existing camps and a reconfiguration of their residents. By the late 1980s, governance and managerial differences among the archipelago of camps along the Thai-Cambodian border had become pronounced and impossible to ignore. This variation was not based on topography or demographics but rather on which united front participant managed the camp in question. The PDK outmatched its NCR united front partners on each of these dimensions, giving the Khmer Rouge an incomparable advantage in fighting Vietnamese forces and, presumably, winning back the hearts and minds of the population inside Cambodia.

The KPNLF Camps

Ironically, the NCR camps compared negatively to those run by the Khmer Rouge. Observers were unable to deny that

> the only camps along the Thai/Cambodian border in which people are kept in by force are the camps belonging to the non-communists, particularly Site 2, Sokh Sann, and Site B. In all of the KR camps, with the exception of their show camp at Site 8, there is simply nothing keeping them in their respective camps. They are in fact wandering all over the countryside going from one satellite to another. ICRC [the International Committee of the Red Cross] has even reported members of the KR going to Sokh Sann and then returning to their original KR camp as they found the discipline significantly harsher with the NCR. ICRC incidentally maintains that the camp in which there is the least regard for individual human rights is the KPNLF [camp] at Sokh Sann closely followed by the Sihanoukist camp at Site B.[46]

The main KPNLF camps were Site 2 and Sokh Sann. The largest of the Thai-Cambodian border camps, Site 2, which by 1987 had 160,000 inhabitants, was created by combining the Ban Sangae, Dong Rek, Sam Lor Chnganh, Nong Chan (Camp 511), Nam Yun, Nong Samet, and O'Bok camps.[47] This configuration was a response to the refugee crisis, itself a response to military offenses by the Vietnamese between 1984 and 1986. Nestled about eighty kilometers to the north of Aranyaprathet, Site 2 was not particularly blessed by geography or an abundance of natural resources. Located along a vulnerable stretch on the Thai-Cambodian border, it suffered from a lack of groundwater and insufficient rain to provide adequate supplies for the camp population. This made Site 2 dependent on UNBRO for its water supply. In addition, the soil was devoid of tree cover and not particularly nutrient rich. Small thatch huts were crowded together and separated by pools of stagnant water, breeding malarial mosquitoes. Waste collection and disposal were also a challenge, the mismanagement of which did little to enhance living conditions. Site 2 was, by most accounts, a Dickensian mess.[48]

There was also a considerable degree of violence, and it was not unheard of to find decapitated bodies (or just the heads) of persons accused of thievery or spying dumped nearby. Shield Asia, a private security firm hired to conduct a study of conditions within the camp, found that "a potentially dangerous and tragic situation is in the making at Site 2... [with] domestic crimes, including rape, child rape and molestation of minors, incest, petty theft, actual and grievous bodily harm, gang warfare, juvenile delinquency, suicide, oppression of ethnic religious or political minorities [soon to] assume uncontrollable proportions."[49] One UNBRO security officer at Site 2, Stephane Rousseau, said: "It's not just a cut here or there. They're stabbed multiple times, twenty to thirty times. People are [axing], knifing, throwing grenades, and hitting each other in record numbers."[50] Sokh Sann was no better. According to one on-the-ground assessment, "the human rights violations in the KPNLF camp at Sokh Sann may be the worst in the refugee system." There were reports that "KPNLF members [were] leaving Sokh Sann ... to go to the KR camp at Site-K."[51]

The mismanagement (or, rather, lack of management) of the KPNLF camps translated into sluggishness (at best) on the military front. For most of the 1980s, Thai Task Force 838 had to move mountains to get the NCR to expend the smallest effort in maintaining a modicum of resistance to Vietnamese troops. At one point Thai Special Colonel Boon-rod Somthateven placed the factional leaders within the KPNLF under house arrest to get them to lead their party. At another, they finally incentivized KPNLF troops to "verifiably destroy" enemy ordnance by providing three hundred baht for an enemy rifle, five thousand for artillery pieces, and fifteen thousand for tanks, along with "a social fund ... to pay out 2,500 baht for light injuries, double that for more serious wounds." Unsurprisingly, gains were modest, and the TF 838 leadership was increasingly irate over the heat they were taking for the nonperformance of the NCR.[52]

By late 1987, "the KPNLF [had] practically ceased to exist." One close observer recalls that "the KPNLF commanders practically abandoned their men in the field. ... [T]hey stayed in Thailand and enjoyed their lives." In a sense, they closely resembled the military ethic of Lon Nol's Khmer Republic troops in the early to mid-1970s, who were "busy with women and drinking in Phnom Penh"—and in fact, many of the KPNLF commanders had been Khmer Republic ones. "They ... never learn," the observer lamented.[53]

FUNCINPEC/ANS Camps

FUNCINPEC camps did not suffer from the challenges brought about by the sheer scale of the KPNLF system or by its depths of poor management. Rather, they seem to have suffered from more benign neglect, as if the MOULINAKA and its eventual umbrella organization, the ANS, were an absentee landlord.

Site B, just nine kilometers inside Thailand's Surin province, first congealed into an identifiable camp in 1981. Comprising initially a cluster of smaller camps, Site B went through several evolutions: in 1983 it was the "O'Smach camp" and later the "Tatum camp," and in 1984 it was "Camp David" and the "Ban Baranae" camp, before it settled into what was the Site B location in mid-1985. Site B grew constantly from an initial population of 850 to, by August 1989, some 63,535 residents. It was managed by FUNCINPEC and its military arm, the ANS, and occupied a relatively attractive part of the countryside, "set among heavily jungled hills, with plentiful shade provided by an abundance of trees." Most of the residents were from the Cambodian provinces of Battambang, Siem Reap, and Oddar Meanchey. As in other camps, a large portion of the male workforce was recruited into a military organization, in this case the ANS. By the late 1980s, the camp had been divided into twenty-eight sections, each of which oversaw some five hundred families. Leaders were appointed by the central administration, directing, with UNBRO assistance, "all internal security, primary educational programs, and services ... operat[ing] on well-defined lines of authority."[54]

FUNCINPEC authorities did not mobilize their camp's denizens for the anti-Vietnamese War effort even remotely to the scale of their Khmer Rouge counterparts. As one observer notes: "These guys—the ANS—they weren't fighting very much. They were just waiting around, and they were sort of just injected into politics. And I think the way they saw it was: the Khmer Rouge were carrying water for so long, it was going to go on until it wasn't," that is, until there was a settlement.[55] Unlike Site 2, which was steeped in misery, Site B was well run but lacked military agency. In early 1988, TF 838 concluded that they not only would need to train KPNLF and ANS troops but also would need to fight alongside them. This led to the creation of TF 909, "a new secret unit composed of ninety-eight members of the RTA Special Forces" that was led by Ny Kân, Son Sen's brother, himself. ANS and KPNLF regiments would be assigned six-person teams from TF 909.[56]

The KPNLF and FUNCINPEC/ANS camps simply existed in the present, the former in wretched squalor and the latter in relative comfort, neither of which allowed them to hold up their respective military ends within Cambodia proper. The Khmer Rouge camps, by contrast, were both better organized and equipped to support military operations within Cambodia. This was not only the case with the Ieng Sary-run Site 8, which was unique as a propaganda window into the "reformed" Khmer Rouge, but also with the far more utilitarian Khmer Rouge camps more generally.

Khmer Rouge Camps

Utilitarian did not necessarily mean "friendly," either for outside observers or for refugees inside the Khmer Rouge camps. Most of them seem to have exhibited equal parts misery and fear, at least to foreign observers. "Visits to KR camps," as Dennison Lane describes them, "were distinctly unsettling undertakings. The inhabitants of the KR camps were not funny people.... [H]ere were no smiles, and the dress was either black or Chinese army green.... There were weapons and military equipment everywhere." Nevertheless, during the 1983 Vietnamese spring offensive, when given the choice of relocating to whichever camp they wanted, "a distinct majority of the refugees elected to remain with the Khmer Rouge."[57] It is not a coincidence that the residents of the Khmer Rouge camps tended to be made up of the "base people" (that is, those classes that were lionized during Democratic Kampuchea, identifiable in 1979 photos for being incongruously well fed), while those in the NCR camps tended to be "new people" (who were treated with deliberate neglect and were far more likely to be killed or carried off by disease during the same period).[58]

By 1989, the four Khmer Rouge–affiliated camps along the Thai-Cambodian border were Borai, Ta Luan/Site K, O'Trao (within the region controlled by *Ta* Mok), and Site 8, the "Potemkin village" camp under Ieng Sary. The Borai camp (estimated population 7,600) was located about twenty-five miles from Trat, precariously situated adjacent to a winding eleven-kilometer path surrounded by Thai villages whose inhabitants resented the commotion created by travelers to and from Borai (and sometimes took to shooting at vehicles navigating said path). Borai was more "Spartan" compared to other camps along the border, although it boasted houses made with bamboo walls, as opposed to the thatch used at most of the other camps. Its ten subdivisions were under the unambiguous command of a forty-something Khmer Rouge official straight out of central casting, Brother Tia, who was described as an "inveterate bureaucrat" to such a degree that he neglected military matters because they got in the way of effective camp administration. Borai was also the site of significant economic activity in the gem trade. The Khmer Rouge, according to a person familiar with the trade in gemstones, made about one hundred million Thai baht every five or six months from taxing "the thousands of individuals" engaged in the ruby trade (at a rate of eight hundred to one thousand baht each).[59] Indeed, a complicating factor in conceptualizing the worldview of these leaders has to do with their relationships with capitalism, not simply at Borai but at other Khmer Rouge sites. Altogether the Borai camp system housed twenty thousand civilians and seven thousand soldiers, who operated in Pursat, Maung, and Kampong Chhnang provinces.[60]

The Ta Luan camp was run by a young cadre named Tuan. As at other "open" Khmer Rouge camps, the primary method of punishing criminal and antisocial behavior was through reeducation and self-criticism, but with the evaluation of the accused solely in the hands of a five-person justice committee. This committee—consisting of Tuan, the head of the medical department, and the three section chiefs—meted out justice based on a unanimous verdict. That said, Ta Luan seems to have had looser rules guiding the social relations within its borders, particularly with regard to the very un-KR practice of drinking alcohol.

Ta Luan was closed in 1989 and placed under the strict control of Thai marines. Its inhabitants, and those of Borai, were relocated to a camp system called Site K (also known as the Koh Kong or Southwest battlefield). Site K itself was built after the other camps and located at the end of a remote access road. It housed some ten thousand to twelve thousand residents. About two kilometers long and half a kilometer wide, Site K was vulnerable to shelling and rocket attacks. It was run by thirty-seven-year-old *Loc* Chay, "a thin and very intense man, who found it distinctly difficult to smile." (He was killed when a tree struck by lightning fell on him.) His main gripe was with his loss of control once the camp came under the auspices of UNBRO and the unspecified problems that would bring in the future. Indeed, as things were still in flux with Site K, it became clear that there were several strands of jurisdictional authority that were complicating governance, including the distribution of effective antimalarial medications.[61] Upon hearing of plans to consolidate the southern Khmer Rouge border camps—Ta Luan, Borai, and their associated sub-camps—into the UNBRO-administered Site K at the beginning of 1989, Chay took more than two thirds of Ta Luan's six thousand residents back across the border into Cambodia on the reasoning that "the Khmer Rouge don't want to lose control of their civilians.... [T]hey are a vital military asset."[62]

O'Trao, also referred to as the North Sisophon battlefield, was a constellation of some seven satellite camps that radiated out from the UNBRO-associated main O'Trao camp. It was a fairly simple affair, with thatch huts scattered among the unkempt grasses. Altogether, the O'Trao system was estimated to house more than nine thousand troops and another forty thousand civilians.[63] Militarily, O'Trao was connected

FIGURE 4.8. Khmer Rouge cadre lining up recruits, Phnom Malai, 1979. Steve Heder.

to the Khmer Rouge military base at O'Panko. East of O'Trao was the Khmer Rouge military camp of Chong Kor, with a population of six thousand, under the authority of Son Sen, with which O'Trao engaged in considerable trade. Another camp under Son Sen—outside of the auspices of the UN—called Surniki, was not far from where Ta Mok had a residence at Ban Charat. The site was to some degree under his influence as well. Specific NADK divisions associated with O'Trao were Divisions 616, 785, and 906 (consisting mostly of porters).[64] Mok was acknowledged by observers as overseeing the operations of the O'Trao system. Military forces out of O'Trao operated in Oddar Meanchey, Siem Reap, and Preah Vihear provinces.

In addition, there was an unknown number of people under PDK control in camps on Thai soil to which UNBRO and the ICRC had no access. This number was estimated to be as high as 150,000, giving "a total Khmer Rouge strength along the border of 220,500, that is, almost a quarter of a million people on the border alone."[65] Each of the "open" camps (but not including the operations around Phnom Malai and Pailin) was actually part of a combination of UNBRO-assisted camps, military camps within Cambodia, and closed support camps that included logistical personnel and the families of the military camp residents.

Khmer Rouge camps (apart from Site 8, as we shall see, and to a lesser extent O'Trao) were truly dark, surreal places, in which the only color was "provided by the red and white checkered sarong worn by the KR." Children's eyes had a "dead" quality, and their faces were those of "ghosts."[66] An observer recalled, in a December 1980 trip to Borai, that "the children were unsmiling; there was no crying, either. It was eerily silent. . . . It wasn't just the children who didn't smile, of course. *Nobody* smiled."[67] Naturally the misery of living in the camps was part of the appeal of the Khmer Rouge. One observer cited as a way of understanding the PDK calculus Eric Hoffer's contention that "a movement retains its vigor only so long as it can offer nothing in the present" in favor of the future.[68]

And yet, by the early 1980s, observers could not avoid the conclusion that "the KR is the only organization capable of providing the four necessities of life—food, shelter, clothing, and security—and accordingly, there being no alternative, people join the KR."[69] This was the conventional wisdom along the Thai-Cambodian border, if not in Washington, DC. Journalists on-site at the time, however, had no illusions. Mary Kay Magstad, a veteran reporter who covered the Cambodian refugee crisis (as well as Myanmar's military crackdown and the Rwandan genocide, and who would subsequently open the Beijing bureau for National

Public Radio in 1996) and was no fan of the Khmer Rouge, recounts the words of a senior Western border aid official: "The Khmer Rouge are very clever. They have an aim, and a tactic to reach that aim. [Site 8] today is the best-managed camp along the border. The administration seems to really care for the people and seems to have their support."[70] In fact, Site 8 was as complex an organization as it was unique.

Ieng Sary, Site 8, and Sector 102

Located two kilometers inside Thailand, in Prachinburi province, PDK-controlled Site 8 housed evacuees from the Nong Pru, O'Sralau, Tap Prik, Klong Wah/Bung Beng, and Khao Din refugee camps.[71] It was a key backstop for Khmer Rouge military activity within Cambodia, particularly around Pailin and Phnom Malai. Originally, Site 8 was envisioned as a means to control the population and to draw on manpower for the battlefield. The camp committee was led by Sok Saeng.[72] He was empowered by Office 87/870 to prohibit the creation of markets, the operation of religious centers, and the ability of residents to marry at will, and to ensure that education follow a strict DK curriculum. None of that came to pass, much to the chagrin of the PDK leadership, as "Site 8 was in contradiction with the DK policy line because people there enjoyed more freedom."[73] This was somewhat distinct from 102, in which Site 8 was embedded, which, although a civilian camp, was "organized military style" and contained an "inside office" (បន្ទប់ក្នុង) that was off-limits to all but the top leadership.[74]

Site 8's "contradiction" had everything to do with Ieng Sary. Sary, along with Thai forces that ultimately controlled the camp, transformed Site 8 into something radically different: a model showcase for the Khmer Rouge. Much of what was special about Site 8 (estimated population 32,000) had to do with Ieng Sary's recognizing the importance of standing out among other united front allies by putting a positive public face on the movement. As a civilian who wittingly left military matters to others, he gambled on politics, and the skills that he had honed throughout his notably non-military professional career, particularly after 1970, served him well here.

To that end, Site 8 served as the face that Sary's wing of the PDK wanted to show the outside world—to prove that they were "les nouvelles Khmères Rouges," in Christophe Peschoux's tongue-in-cheek words.[75] "Here, against a backdrop of dramatic limestone cliffs," as Nic Dunlop describes the scene, "huts [were] neatly laid out on a bed of red laterite." Unlike at other Khmer Rouge camps, "visitors to Site 8 would be mobbed by throngs of smiling children selling trinkets and souvenirs," and "journalists were permitted to walk through the gates manned by the Thai military to wander at will." Residents also "replaced their black uniformity with garish colors of varying hue"; they "smiled and could approach foreigners and talk apparently freely." There was even "a bustling black market [selling] anything from talcum powder to Coca-Cola."[76]

And it was also here that the formal conduct of foreign affairs was handled by Ieng Sary and his staff. Sary had situated the PDK's foreign affairs office in Malai, nestled squarely within the no-man's land between the refugee camps and the military bases. This ambiguous geographic, legal, and political space provided the PDK leaders opportunities to build up their bases of operations; Sary used it to establish a de facto foreign ministry infrastructure and a conduit for commerce and trade in the same area where the Chinese had established their first embassy in exile back in early 1979. Vietnamese offensives, however, would occasionally push its operations into Thai territory, so when delegations visited Pailin, the foreign affairs infrastructure would move there.[77]

The atmospherics were probably best captured by Henry Kamm, whose observations are worth quoting at length:

> A table, decorated with flowers and greenery[, was] placed under a handsome thatched vaulted roof, hot coffee [was served].... A courteous young man speaking flawless French collected our passports to issue us visas. Mine was returned bearing the only visa in longhand I have ever received.... The Khmer Rouge guest-house was the very latest in jungle luxury. It was clearly modeled on the sumptuous hunting lodges to which the French planters of the past invited guests for weekend shoots.... [There were] four guest bungalows and paths linking them to the bath-houses, toilets, dining pavilion, meeting lodge and communications shack.... Soldiers swept the entire camp daily.... In front of each bungalow, our attentive hosts had placed trays of glasses, a thermos of hot water, a packet of Chinese tea and packs of American cigarettes.... Vases of bamboo ... were filled with fresh flowers.... The plates of fruit brought from Bangkok were renewed each day.... The best Thai beer, Johnnie Walker Black Label Scotch, American soft drinks and Thai bottled water were served.[78]

More substantively, Site 8 was the setting for the PDK to showcase its commitment to good governance, providing the PDK an opportunity to govern on a scale unattainable inside Cambodia since 1979 and not possible again until 1989. And it provided Sary with a potentially effective political power base to demonstrate to the united front (and possible future coalition partners) as well as the international organizations that the Khmer Rouge were in fact capable of benign rule. But it was ultimately a gamble on Sary's part: insofar as Site 8 reflected Ieng Sary's "liberal" approach to PDK governance, it would raise the suspicions of his more orthodox colleagues in the PDK.

Site 8 provided education (starting at six years of age); a first-grade class of 5,801 students initially enrolled, but enrollments dramatically decreased in later grades such that by seventh (the last) grade, there were only 140 students.[79] Health care, under *Loc Y*, could be measured by the presence of a three-hundred-bed-capacity military hospital at Site 85.[80] Site 8 also contained a prosthetic limb factory and workshop that supplied a substantial number of the prosthetics used by civilians and soldiers along the Thai-Cambodian border as a result of hidden land mines and war-related injuries, respectively.[81] Markets were generally open from 7:00 to 10:00 a.m., but when foreign delegations visited the camp, they stayed open all day. Indeed, all the things that distinguished Site 8—colorful clothing, religious events, and so on—were ramped up for foreign consumption.[82]

Behind the scenes, of course, things were far more complicated—and tense. Sary recruited servants and staff from the ranks of the NADK, often people who had worked in B1 between 1975 and 1979 with the foreign language or other skills necessary to make a good impression on their guests. They did not receive adequate (re)training, however, and were petrified of Sary ("he didn't speak very much but he was 'strong' [ឡាំង]") and Thirith ("when I made a mistake she looked as if she was going to stab me"), not even daring to make eye contact with them.[83]

And it was difficult for Sary to carve out an independent power base along the Pailin-Malai corridor as Son Sen and Mok had in their respective military corridors—simply because so many senior Khmer Rouge leaders spent time or transited through there. Indeed, in 1996, the area was the site for the final sequence of events that led to the implosion of the movement. Whatever power Sary enjoyed there was thus political, not military, in nature. As Sary himself recounted: "I had political power in Malai. I have been kept away from military power since the beginnings of the movement. Pol Pot has always maintained me outside military matters. Pol Pot was very 'Titoste' [*sic*] at the time. I favored instead other alternatives integrating the role of the intellectuals. Pol Pot deprived me of military power in Malai ... As [early as when] he returned from France in 1955, Son Sen badmouthed me [to] Pol Pot, criticized my rich peasant origins and contrasting them with his middle-peasant background."[84]

This criticism continued into the 1980s, with Son Sen pointing out Sary's "excessive tendencies toward 'liberalism.'"[85] NADK commander Ny Kân was particularly hostile to this "liberalizing" trend, underscoring some of the ideological dissent in the leadership's ranks.[86]

Sary was in a very difficult position. Given the martial nature of the movement, he was being marginalized by his more hard-line colleagues. He rightly recognized that his value lay in his diplomatic and economic connections rather than in any battlefield prowess. Thus, Sary sought to enhance his position within the Khmer Rouge ranks by doing what only he could: changing the image of the movement in the eyes of the world by showcasing a well-run camp that defied any association with the dark years of Democratic Kampuchea.

Front 32

Front 32 was the quasi-military area associated with Division 320 (as well as Divisions 948, 705, and 531) within the Central Northwest and Special Battlefield Command area.[87] Although it was geographically close to Site 8 (and Sector 102), it could not have been more different, thus underscoring Site 8's uniqueness as well as Ieng Sary's precarious position within the Khmer Rouge leadership. It was even more severe than 102, according to a cadre based at 32: "The word is that 102 is an easier place to be than 32. It's easier in that the people at 102 are able to preserve their customs. They have [*wats*] [វត្ត, temples] and marriages and contact between villages. It's different from 32 in that 32 is much more strict."[88] Front 32 was led by Ny Kân (and Chea Rin, his civilian counterpart), the former chief of protocol in Ieng Sary's Foreign Ministry during the Democratic Kampuchea period. Yet despite this connection, Ny Kân's primary attachment seems to have been to his brother Son Sen.[89] In fact, Sary and Ny Kân had a falling-out when Sary accused the latter of not coming to his aid during a Vietnamese attack. This negative sentiment extended to Son Sen, whose already poor relations with Sary were further strained from that point onward.[90]

Mistrust, suspicion, and innuendo were rife within Front 32 and contributed to an uncertain political situation that engendered instability. A cadre who had been put in charge of Sector 408 (within Front 32) warily observed:

> The Sector 32 cadres, in fact all the cadres, remember everything about people's backgrounds, and they don't forget bad biographies. In my case, because I was an East Zone cadre [the Eastern

Zone's leaders were accused of being Vietnamese agents toward the end of the Democratic Kampuchea period], they say behind my back that the *Yuon* were able to take Kampuchea because the East Zone cadres were good, but were instead *Yuon* agents. They never openly said I was an enemy because I was from the East Zone, but they kept taking away my power a bit at a time until I was completely separated from the masses.[91]

Front 32 had a sophisticated incarceration infrastructure, which had little direct oversight; in the words of one cadre: "I was never able to resolve the case of anyone who was being held at *Ta* Chan's place. I didn't even dare to try."[92] There was good reason not to. *Ta* Chan (កាច័ន្ទ) was none other than Mam Nay (ម៉មណៃ), the chief interrogator of Tuol Sleng during the Democratic Kampuchea period. A tall, pockmarked, "almost albino man"[93] who "always wore a long-sleeved shirt buttoned up tight so his associates could not see his ringworm-infected skin,"[94] Chan was described by Nate Thayer—no delicate flower himself—as "'the most frightening-looking character' he had ever seen."[95] When Thayer—who knew exactly who Chan was but didn't let on—asked him his occupation, Chan replied, "I slaughter pigs!"[96] Chan's swagger was so pronounced that he brushed off accusations by Son Sen of being counterrevolutionary and petty bourgeois because Chan insisted on growing his crops in the middle of footpaths. After Son Sen unceremoniously retreated from Front 32 in 1996, Chan boasted that he made 100,000 baht from his cornfield, was indeed planting corn in the footpaths, and was even increasing his acreage so that he could plant whatever he wanted, wherever he wanted.[97]

There were two dimensions that contributed to the military-civilian/diplomatic tensions between the management of Sector 32 and the efforts by Site 8 leaders to cement the public image of the Khmer Rouge as a benign governing force. The first was the political disagreements between Ieng Sary and Ny Kân as to the degree to which it was desirable to have Site 8's "public image" deviate from Khmer Rouge orthodoxy. The second had to do with tensions between the military function of Sector 32 and its relationship with the Displaced Persons Protection Unit (DPPU), a paramilitary unit created in 1988 and charged with providing security on the Thai-Cambodian border, specifically maintaining the integrity of camp boundaries and repelling bandits. Individual infractions by soldiers were minor, as there was an effective mechanism to check weapons at the camp. More frequent, but still quite rare, were efforts by soldiers to avoid returning to the front. Police-related matters that involved Khmer Rouge soldiers were referred to, and handled by, Task Force 838.[98] The prominence of TF 838 points to the degree to which Site 8 was embedded within the larger cluster of military-based Khmer Rouge operations, which was both a function of the ongoing military hostilities within that stretch of borderland and a potential contributing factor to it.

Preparing for the Next Stage

By decade's end, a reinvigorated Khmer Rouge had established an extensive and increasingly sophisticated organizational infrastructure in many places along the Thai border and inside Cambodia. The bar was not high when it came to management of the refugee camps, but in demonstrating their organizational abilities in the management of theirs, the Khmer Rouge were able to play up the notion that, as a movement, they were uniquely qualified to lead the population under their control into a future that was an emphatic negation of their present misery. As late as July 1992, an UNTAC report described NADK combatants as being "obviously well-fed and in apparently good physical condition, in contrast to the KPNLF troops cantoned in Thmar Puok [ថ្មារពួក], many of whom were scrawny and sickly."[99] The Khmer Rouge thus provided a clear signal that they were the best-organized and militarily most formidable component of their post-Vietnamese invasion united front conglomerate. Held up against their united front counterparts, they demonstrated a superior capacity to be socially responsive and non-elitist; this, they hoped, would suggest their political potential vis-à-vis compromised and corrupt electoral competitors, be they designated enemies or coalition partners. The reemergence of the PDK as a viable movement in the early 1980s was thus nothing short of remarkable—if deeply troubling.

But organizing, managing, and ultimately exploiting an anarchic and seemingly impossible situation along the border with Thailand was only a preliminary step. The camps had provided an essential logistical network as well as a potentially mobilizable (and, following the defeat of Vietnam, redistributable) force to populate the interior of Cambodia and enhance the power of the PDK/NADK militarily. But they did not, as we shall see in the next chapter, offer the same boons at the ballot box.

Chapter 5

An Unattainable Political Space, 1990–1993

> Pol Pot and the others were very good at making theory in terms of 10-point elements, the 8-this, the 6-that and all the rest of it, but when it came to the basic question of how to end the war they didn't have an answer.
>
> —Former cadre from NADK Division 450, from an interview with Steve Heder

The Khmer Rouge always operated in the shadows. It was a movement replete with hidden hierarchies and sophisticatedly constructed figureheads. Aliases abounded. Local executions were carried out under cover of darkness or away from populated areas and were never announced. Its most sophisticated torture complex, Tuol Sleng, was so secret that once somebody entered—that is, saw the site with their own eyes—they *had* to be killed. When one wrongly accused cadre was sent to be tortured and subsequently executed, he was reprieved not simply or even primarily because he was innocent but because he had not yet been taken to S-21.[1] Even conversations among top cadres after 1975 were conducted in hushed tones, leading some to argue that this was a sort of unsettling idiosyncratic tic that the PDK elite had been socialized into. It was just as likely a simple survival mechanism. Secrecy was an extraordinarily potent form of control for the CPK, and the movement used it effectively.

This behind-the-scenes maneuvering extended to local elections in CPK-held areas in the early 1970s. For the most part, the CPK had avoided placing its existing officials at the grassroots level. Rather, the CPK wielded its power by discreetly installing members in key positions at the district level and above. Some masqueraded as FUNK representatives responsible for overseeing local elections, thus enabling the CPK's influence to trickle down through levels of governance via covert means. For instance, in Kampong Thom, Pol Pot's home province, district committees in charge of establishing the local FUNK commune-level administration—which in turn selected village chiefs—were headed covertly by CPK district secretaries who were outwardly FUNK representatives. In other places, like in Mok's Takeo, village chiefs were appointed by CPK "liberated units" (កងរំដោះ). The village chief, in turn, selected the deputy and the third member of the leadership troika, responsible for economics. These three organized people "into units and groups, selecting unit chiefs and group chief to control those members."[2]

Such maneuvers occurred at a remove from the people being governed. Where elections determined the commune and village leadership, the results appear to have been seen as being transparent and fair. As a result, there was little opposition to the tightening of security measures by these local cadres. Indeed, in the rare instances when the clandestine CPK cadres found themselves working at the village or commune level, they were under strict orders to behave in ways that would not alienate the local population but instead gain their trust and support.[3]

None of this earlier groundwork, whether in the early 1970s or the late 1980s, would prepare the PDK for competitive UNTAC (United Nations Transitional Authority in Cambodia) elections slated to take place in 1993 under the terms of the 1991 Paris Peace Agreements. Electoral campaigning, political showboating, and the flexing of military muscle came to supplant the united front strategy which had paved the way to power for the PDK, effectively cutting the ground from beneath its feet. Unless the PDK was fully ensconced in power, it did not perform well in the cold light of day. The decision to enter the electoral political fray in the early 1990s, and the disastrous outcome for the movement, made this all too obvious. Infighting within the PDK during this volatile period only made matters worse. For our three lieutenants, distrust and clashes over the party's direction eventually led to Ieng Sary being sidelined altogether, Son Sen scrambling to find favor within the leadership, and *Ta* Mok devolving into dangerous extremism. In this new and unfamiliar political space, the stage was set for the Khmer Rouge to self-destruct.

The Khmer Rouge Plays at Peace

After the turmoil of the 1970s, Cambodia in the 1980s experienced a period of relative albeit austere calm. Under the regime of the Kampuchean People's Revolutionary Party (KPRP), reinstalled in power by

Hanoi following Vietnam's invasion of Cambodia, the country—now renamed the People's Republic of Kampuchea (PRK)—began a process of reconstruction that involved revitalizing the economy and reinstating cultural and religious freedoms. For the time being, the Khmer Rouge, themselves regrouping under the cover of the Coalition Government of Democratic Kampuchea (CGDK), were held at bay.

The 1987 meeting on the outskirts of Paris between PRK prime minister Hun Sen and CGDK head Norodom Sihanouk opened the door to reconciliation between the ruling regime and the government-in-exile.[4] But the talks wore on for years. The Vietnamese delegation finally called what had essentially been Washington's and Beijing's bluff, laying bare that they were, in fact, supporting the Khmer Rouge and warning that if NADK troops entered Phnom Penh again, that would be on the United States and China. As noted in chapter 3, international support was vital in the formation of the united front; insofar as the Khmer Rouge would prevail on the battlefield against its united front allies in the vacuum left behind by the Vietnamese, such an anticipated outcome forced the international community to shift gears and reach a peace accord.

This occurred on October 23, 1991. After years of negotiations, nineteen countries—including the five permanent members of the UN Security Council—produced the framework for peace better known as the Paris Agreements or, more officially, the Agreement on a Comprehensive Political Settlement of the Cambodia Conflict. Signed by the four warring Cambodian factions—FUNCINPEC, KPNLF, the CPP (Cambodia People's Party, the new name adopted by the KPRP in 1991), and the PDK—as well as seventeen other concerned nations, the agreements marked the official end of the Cambodian-Vietnamese War. Among its protocols, it mandated the demobilization of the factions' respective militaries and authorized the creation of the UNTAC, the provisional body intended to administer peace in Cambodia in the lead-up to multiparty elections.[5]

The Khmer Rouge entered this transitional period in a manner that is perhaps best described as that of a leopard trying—but unable—to change its spots. They had seized the opportunity created by the departure of the Vietnamese to launch military operations, if only for the sake of gaining political leverage. For instance, the Battle of Pailin, which began on September 9, 1989, was deemed a significant victory by the Khmer Rouge despite the heavy casualties they suffered because it "earned them inclusion in the negotiating process."[6] And they had initially appeared willing to participate in the elections, with Ieng Sary purportedly expected to stand as a candidate.[7]

138   CHAPTER 5

This apparent vacillation between the Khmer Rouge's desire to attain power through legitimate political means, on the one hand, and violent ones, on the other, is best explained by a document obtained from a defector from Mok's forces in 1987. Dated December 2, 1986, and titled "What Is the Virtue, the Quality, the Reality, and the Responsibility of Democratic Kampuchea in the Past, Present, and Future?," the report offers a remarkable insider's glimpse into the worldview of the Khmer Rouge then that allows us to trace the motivation behind their actions over the coming years. Notably, the document uses "they/them" (គេ) throughout to refer to, as the translator's note clarifies, "the non-Communist Cambodian resistance factions allied with Democratic Kampuchea in the CGDK."[8]

It begins by drawing a line in the sand between the PDK forces and "them"—that is, those seeking the "venomous and evil political objective of annihilating Democratic Kampuchea, poison[ing] our cadres, our ranks, our people, and the world." Pointedly, the document does not

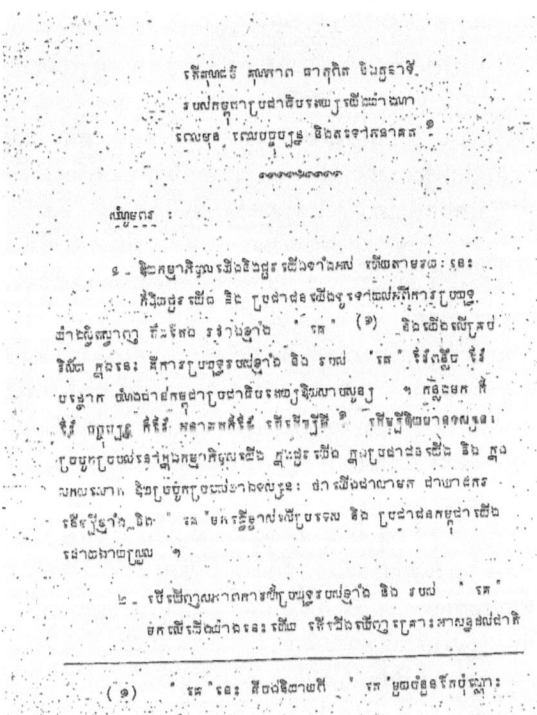

FIGURE 5.1. "What Is the Virtue, the Quality, the Reality, and the Responsibility of Democratic Kampuchea in the Past, Present, and Future?" 1986. Steve Heder.

distinguish between the Vietnamese, who sought to "swallow Cambodia," and those within the united front. "The so-called 'they,'" it proclaims, "is a group in the international front opposing the Soviets and the Vietnamese. . . . This group is also active, like the Vietnamese, in attacking Democratic Kampuchea on the political front. And it has many means, many kinds of the [sic] means, in this matter, to confuse our ranks, our people and the world. It operates by firmly organized plans and coordination . . . to become masters of Cambodia." Indeed, "they," as the document continues, would simply hand over Cambodia like "putting roasted meat on a tray and handing it over to the Vietnamese."[9]

The report goes on to describe the various classes within the Cambodian populace and the history of Democratic Kampuchea since its struggles in the *maquis* in the 1960s, noting its achievements (and a few shortcomings) and concluding that, compared to a number of other and larger countries, "the true character of Democratic Kampuchea is far higher. . . . Democratic Kampuchea has never violated or abused anybody." It also outlines the contours of the PDK outlook and the measures necessary to uphold it. These included, first, understanding that the battle against "they/them" was ideological ("of mind, of brain"); the goal was to win the hearts and minds of the people as opposed to winning on the battlefield. The PDK was also to aggressively utilize all forms of propaganda—"indoctrination, radio, magazines, leaflets, [in-person] meetings, public denouncements"—in order to underscore that it was the principal line of defense against not simply the Vietnamese but also those who would return to the old ways of exploitation. Additionally, the sanctity of the PDK's leadership ranks was to be maintained; suggestions that "the Democratic Kampuchea [receive] a facelift" or that "there must be the removal of this or that person" were to be rejected. Finally, the PDK was to pursue a no-holds-barred approach in its actions, which were to be guided by particular understandings of certain terms: "In the struggles which follow one another, we use secret form[s], open act[ions], half open act[ions], unlawful act[ions], lawful act[ions], and half-lawful act[ions]; we fight and build forces in remote areas and cities according to the political slogan 'National Democracy and Economy.' We use 'Economy' as a means to incite and mobilize the people in the remote areas, 'Democracy' to mobilize people in the middle level such as students and intellectuals, and 'Nation' in order to mobilize front forces in the upper level."[10]

In spelling out how the Khmer Rouge saw themselves and the direction of the movement during that period, the document illustrates just how far from reality their vision continued to be along multiple historical, political, economic, and social dimensions—and this even after the movement had suffered one decisive rout. The Khmer Rouge evidently remained unrepentant about their track record, particularly between 1975 and 1979; to them, that time was but a blip in the movement's thirty-year existence. They also appeared to have learned little about the unpopularity of, and fear engendered by, the class struggles of the past; class struggle was, after all, a feature, and not a bug, of the movement. The document thus stands as a "smoking gun" showing that, to the Khmer Rouge, the united front strategy was a strategy against which vigilance was essential. A notion like "democracy" was therefore not much more than a mobilization tactic to ensure the triumph and longevity of the movement, and a shift back to violent class struggle was never wholly out of the picture.

Given this outlook, it is thus not surprising that the PDK took the Paris Agreements as a chance to expand their political power by using their domestic coalition partners and international supporters to weaken the position of the State of Cambodia (SoC, the name that the PRK adopted after 1989). A summary of PDK communications from the period describes the PDK as having signed the agreements "on the basis of the presumption that the best way to ensure its survival and future prospects was to use them as a device by which to achieve a maximum say in Cambodia's pre-election administration." And as far as the UNTAC-sponsored elections were concerned, the PDK, staying true to form, saw them as but one means among many to achieve the "full blown and legalized reentry by the PDK into Cambodian political life"[11]—the denial of which, in the early 1960s, had led to the radicalization of the CPK in the *maquis* in the first place.

Pol Pot appears to have been confident of electoral victory, insisting that the PDK sign the Paris Agreements even as the NADK was to be largely demobilized under its terms.[12] *Ta* Mok, conversely, remained vehemently opposed, stewing in silence for the time being.[13] Tensions between the two became evident at an enlarged meeting at Office 87/870 around early November 1991, where Pol Pot articulated what PDK policy should be moving forward:

> The meeting in late 1991 brought together all the division committees. Pol Pot, Nuon Chea and Son Sen all attended, but only Pol Pot expressed opinions. . . . *Ta* Mok also attended this as all previous such meetings but did not speak. At this meeting Pol Pot

said that the problem of Cambodia had now been solved and so all the 4 factions had to disarm and we were to get our people to come down from Thai soil and to find them land on which they could farm and thus sustain themselves. The people were free to go wherever they wanted, but we would just point out areas in our respective sectors . . . where there was land available, land did not have an owner. . . . Our entire army was to be disarmed, none would be maintained, but some of the army would be converted into a police force to work with the other factions under UNTAC.

The Paris Agreements stipulated the demobilization of 70 percent of the NADK and the disarmament of the remaining 30 percent. Divisions such as 450 and 519 drew down as ordered, but in a foreshadowing of the PDK's eventual refusal to abide by the Paris Agreements, those in Corridor 1001 and, particularly, Corridor 1003 pointedly refused to do so.[14] The reason was obvious: both corridors were, by 1991, under the command of *Ta* Mok.

Ta Mok's Rise, Son Sen's Fall

Although *Ta* Mok's ascent within the Khmer Rouge had been slower than those of its other leaders, his position by the early 1990s was unsurpassed except by Pol Pot and possibly Nuon Chea. This period saw a consolidation of the military under Mok, leading to a corresponding increase in his power. Figure 5.2 illustrates the sheer number of NADK divisions under his control, which surpassed those of any other similarly ranked PDK leader.

By 1991, Mok was in charge of not only Corridor 1003 but also Corridor 1001, which had initially been under Son Sen's command. The two were later combined and renamed Corridor 1008 (also, erroneously, sometimes referred to as "1005").[15] Mok's protégé, Rân, replaced Son Sen's own, San, in the leadership reshuffle.[16]

This merger of the two corridors under Mok was purportedly possible thanks to "Son Sen relinquish[ing] total command of this area . . . because he was too preoccupied with political duties."[17] Yet as noted previously, Son Sen's brief was likely doomed to failure from the beginning, and his inability to secure Corridor 1001 sufficiently almost certainly contributed to his removal from its command. Insofar as one could speak of a "front" in a guerrilla war, Corridor 1001 was the Khmer Rouge's most vulnerable. Spanning northeastern and eastern Cambodia,

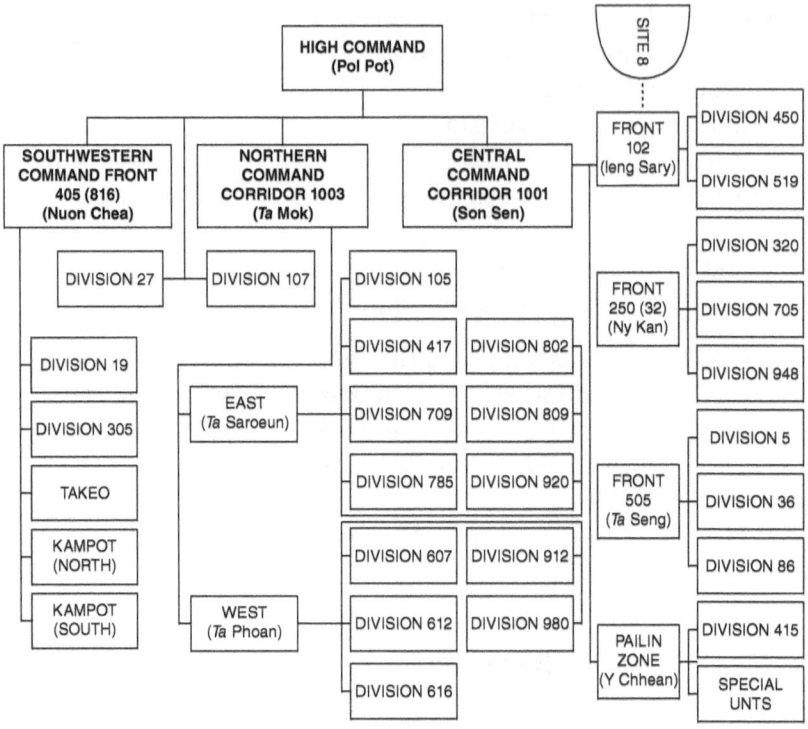

FIGURE 5.2. NADK order of battle, early 1990s.

it was the most directly exposed to both Vietnam and Laos, and thus bore the greatest likelihood of engagement with the enemy. Back in 1983, forces operating in Corridor 1001 were getting clobbered by the Vietnamese, and in December 1984, during the dry season offensive, much of the area making up Corridor 1001 was overrun by People's Army of Vietnam forces. This is not to say that other Khmer Rouge commanders then—*Ta* Mok in Corridor 1003, Nuon Chea in Sector 505, and Ny Kân in Front 32—were faring considerably better, but the difference was striking enough to get the attention of Pol Pot and Nuon Chea. Corridor 1001 was finally abolished in August 1992, with Pol Pot criticizing Son Sen for not demonstrating sufficient commitment to the PDK's military mission and political goals. Relieved of his position as NADK commander in chief and sent to undergo "reeducation" that same year, Son Sen was "reduced," as Heder puts it, "to a voiceless cipher."[18]

While Son Sen's apparent military failings were one reason for his fall from favor in the 1980s, there was also the simple fact that he was not terribly well liked. As mentioned in the introduction, his acerbic tongue was a constant source of friction between him and his colleagues; nobody could feel warmly toward someone who didn't hesitate to deride others as a "tamarind grown out of a piece of shit."[19] And certainly there was no love lost between Son Sen and *Ta* Mok, either. One well-placed NADK officer recounts that "when the KR evacuated Phnom Penh in the face of the Vietnamese invasion in January 1979, Son Sen dispatched a truckload of KR gold to the Thai border. *Ta* Mok commandeered the vehicle, killing the driver." One can only imagine what Mok did with that truckload of gold, but Son Sen, it seems, did not let go of the incident. Once Mok took over Corridor 1001, according to the same NADK officer, "Son Sen refuse[d] to supply *Ta* Mok from ... stocks [located in Thailand] or to tell him where they [were] located. The two despise[d] each other; moreover, Son Sen fe[lt] that *Ta* Mok's undisciplined troops waste[d] ammunition."[20]

Facing increasing unpopularity and the risk of marginalization from the PDK's center, Son Sen began to explore the completely alien territory of working within a political system that exceeded the Khmer Rouge's political worldview—one built on fair and free elections. In what could be interpreted as an attempt to curry favor with Pol Pot, who at the time appeared (delusionally) enthusiastic about upcoming UNTAC elections, Son Sen even went so far as to "signal ... that PDK was not worried about plans for the formation of a CPP-FUNCINPEC coalition government,"[21] and to assume responsibility for handling relations with the other Cambodian factions in anticipation of the elections. But such efforts in fact resulted only in even more criticism against him and deepened perceptions of his political unreliability, as his handling of Khieu Samphân's arrival in Phnom Penh in November 1991 was to show.

Khieu Samphân's return to Phnom Penh appeared, in part at least, to be a genuine attempt by the PDK to enter the political process. But it was also a reaction to Sihanouk's arrival in the capital just a few weeks earlier, not long after the Paris Agreements were signed. Flying in from Beijing, accompanied by Chinese diplomats, Sihanouk basked in the adulation of the crowds that lined the streets from the airport all the way to his villa. Almost immediately after, the mercurial prince began praising Hun Sen and condemning the Khmer Rouge. The latter, feeling that they had been hoodwinked and sold down the river, acted swiftly to mitigate the crisis. In a manner reminiscent of the CPK's successful takeover of GRUNK in 1973, Khieu Samphân was sent to Phnom Penh under Pol Pot's orders to, as Serge Thion puts it, "play the game, do everything to maintain an opening into the Phnom Penh system, whereas we, in the forest, shall maintain our forces, to filter in and destroy the enemy grip from within."[22]

After meeting with Pol Pot at Office 87/870 in Thailand, Samphân boarded a flight to Phnom Penh. He had reason to believe he would receive a statesman-like welcome, even if not as grandiose as the one that greeted Sihanouk. Prior to escaping into the *maquis* and joining the Khmer Rouge in 1967 following a final Sangkum-led leftist purge, Samphân had been an elected member of the Cambodian legislature, and he may have hoped that at least some pockets of the population recalled his then genuine-seeming idealism, moderation, and incorruptibility during the early 1960s. Samphân may also have had reason to think that his old reputation would serve the PDK well at this particular juncture, perhaps even allowing him to feel a mild sense of triumph.

But he could not have been more wrong. Upon his arrival, Samphân greeted well-wishers with a smile that conveyed equal parts arrogance and tone-deafness, at least in retrospect. He and his entourage, which included Son Sen (who had earlier been sent to the capital to prepare the visit), snaked through the city, arrived at their villa, and began making themselves at home. An excitable group of people was milling around the perimeter, initially a modest assemblage of protesters, journalists there to document the historic event, and police responsible for maintaining order. Although there does not seem to have been a key inciting moment, at one point the crowd became agitated and things rapidly escalated into violence—with the police demonstrably doing little to stop it. The crowd eventually breached the room in which Samphân was hiding. Overwhelming his North Korean security detail, the crowd pounced, and one protester hit Samphân with a metal bar, drawing blood. He was provided with a pair of men's underwear in lieu of gauze to put over his bleeding head and left the compound aboard an armored car amidst a hail of sticks and stones.[23] Both Samphân and Son Sen were then whisked back to the airport and put on a return flight to Bangkok.

Hun Sen, who was almost certainly behind them, cast the protests as an expression of the will of the people. "You see, nobody wants them here," he declared. But if the event was a political fiasco for the Khmer Rouge, making them look weak and incompetent, it was a personal one for Son Sen. Even if, as some speculate, Samphân's high-profile trip was Pol Pot's brainchild, he was quick to pass the blame onto Son Sen. After all, it had been Son Sen's responsibility to manage pre-election relations with the CPP, FUNCINPEC, and KPNLF, and it was he who had secured guarantees of safety for Samphân in anticipation of the Phnom Penh trip from the SoC's vice minister of the interior.[24] In fact, Son Sen, having arrived in Phnom Penh a week prior to Samphân, had apparently gotten wind of a possible demonstration but did not take any action. For the ever mistrustful Pol Pot, "that raised [further] suspicions about Sen's loyalty."[25]

Son Sen's mismanagement of this trip was a high-profile, embarrassing failure that garnered him the type of attention from PDK leadership one generally sought to avoid. The Khmer Rouge was not a movement in which failure was easily forgiven, as Son Sen knew better than just about anybody. Out of fear of falling even further in the eyes of Brother Number 1, he sought to mitigate his situation by swinging back to the more familiar hard-line militancy that had defined most of his career. But as the next chapter will show, his efforts amounted to little.

Ieng Sary, Unmoored and Alone

If Son Sen during this period can best be described as hanging onto power by the skin of his teeth, Ieng Sary had neither skin nor teeth to even speak of. The 1980s had been increasingly unkind to him. Although he managed to hold on to a supervisory role in foreign relations until 1984, he was being outflanked by Khieu Samphân on the foreign policy front and found himself downgraded to chair of the economics and finance committee in 1982, with a focus on Chinese foreign aid. The eventual termination of Chinese assistance in the early 1990s severely undercut Sary's position even further, and Khieu Samphân's proximity to Pol Pot as political secretary (akin to the Chinese *mishu*, 秘书) gave him greater authority than Sary could hope for.

In addition to his uncanny discipline in never slow-walking an order no matter how morally repugnant or distasteful ("he would always produce the required brief on time and could always be relied upon to do what his superior told him"),[26] Khieu Samphân was also adept at situating himself close to the locus of power without becoming a victim of that proximity. Ieng Sary lamented that his "significant diplomatic tasks" had been transferred to Khieu Samphân, whom Pol Pot could completely control.[27] Samphân thus remained the outward, public face of the Khmer Rouge, even as he was little more than an appendage of

Pol Pot. Samphân's gradual eclipse of Sary in the 1980s signaled that Pol Pot himself was largely done with his brother-in-law. Khieu Samphân even took control of Sary's traditional role in managing the united front, going so far as to combine these two portfolios.[28]

As his services as Khmer Rouge foreign minister were being curtailed, Sary became involved in the illicit cross-border trade in timber and gemstones. In a December 1981 document on national income generation, the Democratic Kampuchea government laid out several anticipated income streams that would make up the national budget: fishing, timber, minerals and precious stones, tourism, and business taxes.[29] Out of all of these, only timber and gemstones were viable income-generating commodities and were therefore critical to funding the movement while it remained in the opposition. They became even more crucial after Beijing ceased its foreign aid to the PDK/NADK.

A myth emerged in the foreign press during the 1990s that Sary eventually amassed a gemstone-funded local fiefdom that made him the de facto warlord of Pailin, over which Sary simply had no authority, even though a former Foreign Ministry cadre, Y Chhean, commanded a division based there. Journalistic innuendo connected Sary to the sale of concessions in ruby-rich Pailin, for a time the only Cambodian municipality under Khmer Rouge administration, to rapacious foreign mining interests. This steady revenue stream, coupled with generous Chinese aid, allegedly gave Sary personal control over several million dollars from his base at Malai—even as he slipped further down the PDK's chain of command.[30]

The reality was somewhat more complicated. The gemstone and logging trade began around 1984 in Samlaut under *Ta* Tith and in Malai under *Ta* Dorn (later extending to Pailin under Y Chhean). Border areas like Borai charged individual gem miners $560 for right of access, and in these small zones the Khmer Rouge were pocketing some $5 million.[31] Areas deeper inside Cambodia were even more profitable. A former aide to Sary estimated that profits were in the neighborhood of 60 million Thai baht ($2.4 million) from Malai, between 300 and 600 million baht ($12 to $24 million) from Samlaut, and 1 billion baht ($40 million) from Pailin.[32] "Economic cadres" policed these areas and punished those who violated the terms of agreement, helping to pre-empt "mid-level corruption and ensure all the money appears to end up in central funds."[33] This money was pooled and redistributed among the various Khmer Rouge leaders. The revenue from Malai was the lowest of the three, and after 1994, it was Y Chhean and not Ieng Sary who handled the gemstone trade.³⁴ This point became moot by 1995, as Pailin's soil had been fully mined for gemstones. This ended the gem trade and left logging the chief generator of income for the Khmer Rouge.³⁵

Both the foreign affairs and commercial portfolios were valuable ones within the context of international recognition, but they were also precisely those that were most suspect within the orthodox Khmer Rouge worldview, amounting to something of a poisoned chalice. Moreover, Sary was not personally above suspicion. By 1984, both Pol Pot and *Ta* Mok had accused him of demonstrating "enemy tendencies" by failing to quash commercial activities seen as contrary to the PDK's general line, as was the case in Site 8.³⁶ Political differences between Sary and Pol Pot continued through 1987.³⁷ Things eventually became personal, as Pol Pot had abandoned his first wife, Khieu Ponnary, who had been suffering from mental incapacity since 1968. When Pol Pot then married a second, much younger wife, Sary complained: "He also didn't invite me to his wedding, to the wife that Son Sen found for him, this new wife who was originally in Ny Kân's area. I said to Pol Pot, what the hell do you need a new wife for, at your age? What's more, I had always argued that if we were going to continue to fight a war, we had to be strict about not allowing too much family life."³⁸

Even his plan to forge an unlikely bond with *Ta* Mok in the 1980s through an arranged marriage petered out when Sary's son determined that Mok's daughter was "not exactly to his taste."³⁹ By mid-decade, "Where is Ieng Sary?" became a standard question among Cambodia watchers.⁴⁰ By the next, Sary had become almost completely sidelined and without resources. As he described it:

> I was effectively removed . . . starting in 1990. This was the year when the Chinese ceased completely to provide assistance. Following this, I was deprived of resources. *Ta* Mok controlled the forest in the north, timber resources he estimated at 600 million . . . baht. I have often requested Mok to provide me resources but he has never accepted. During a meeting he has even criticized me for having begged resources from him. And this despite the fact that I have never neglected him in the sharing of resources I was receiving from China.⁴¹

If Sary had not been alienated from PDK leadership the way he came to be, would his diplomatic talent and skill at managing the united front have better ensured the party's participation in the UNTAC elections for a chance to come to power through legal and peaceful means? One can only speculate. What the Khmer Rouge's history does show, however, is that, with Sary more or less out of the picture, the movement cast aside the façade of political cooperation it had put on and returned eventually to the means of obtaining power it seemed to know best: violence.

Electoral Failure for the Khmer Rouge

By April 1992 the PDK's view of UNTAC had started to become a bit more jaundiced. Even as Son Sen and Khieu Samphân remained confident that they could still "wrest some immediate benefit from [UNTAC]," leadership sentiment—led not unexpectedly by Mok—on the futility of the agreements and participating in the elections began to grow. This took a decisive turn by that fall. As Heder recounts:

> At the end of August there was another meeting of the older PDK leaders, which took place at the same time as a gathering of leading PDK and NADK cadre from throughout Cambodia. A "debate" is said to have occurred among the veterans, in which Mok reportedly announced that he had been right to think that the Agreements were "useless," and that it was now demonstrated that UNTAC would not and could not be turned around. Pol Pot is said to have indicated concurrence with this "hardline" assessment, and so-called "liberals," including Khieu Samphân, are said also to have shifted their position in Mok's direction. Moreover, Mok is said to have enjoyed the strong support of several "young [T]urks" among the second echelon.[42]

Pol Pot sided with Mok in "Decision 30-4," which held that the NADK would "resum[e] . . . full-fledged conventional warfare in north-central Cambodia with militarization of people's war everywhere."[43] Following the meeting, Mok, with the power vested in him through his control of the new Corridor 1008, proceeded to intensify military operations. UNTAC lacked a mechanism to ensure parties' compliance with the Paris Agreements, and when the Khmer Rouge leadership turned against the peace process, NADK forces unleashed a flurry of attacks against UNTAC targets, disrupting UNTAC's attempts at national stabilization. On May 3, 1993, the NADK undertook the largest military action during the UNTAC period when it attacked the town of Siem Reap in the early morning hours. The body count was small, but according to the UN-appointed Siem Reap governor, Benny Widyono, "if the main objective had been to create panic and fear, the attackers had been extremely successful."⁴⁴

NADK troops were also transformed into civilian administrators in PDK-controlled "division villages." With the Vietnamese withdrawal and breakdown of the Paris Accords and UNTAC mission, the PDK raced to repopulate "liberated areas" under their control. NADK organization was replicated as the structure of governance down to the district, commune, and village levels. Residents were tasked with building villages and starting agricultural production under the administration of NADK authorities, who disbursed food rations, tools, and land. The idea was to once again carve out as much of the countryside as a base for PDK operations as possible and renew support for the movement there.⁴⁵

But Pol Pot's calculus was off. A combination of savage misrule fifteen years earlier with widespread war fatigue among the population (and also, significantly, within NADK ranks) left the Khmer Rouge with no real electoral base. As Heder puts it, "The PDK leadership consistently misinterpreted popular dislike of SoC and tactical popular accommodation with its own armed forces as evidence of positive, dedicated support just waiting to be tapped and manifested in various ways, including through a 'free and fair' election." And despite exhortations from the top to be more "political," NADK's guerrilla insurgents–*cum*–would-be electoral activists "could only advance to the extent that they relied on military means, and only under circumstances where Cambodian villagers had no political alternatives other than living with SoC or supporting the PDK against SoC."⁴⁶

What was becoming increasingly evident to the Khmer Rouge was KPRP-turned-CPP prime minister Hun Sen's own political machinations among the Cambodian populace. Himself a former Eastern Zone Khmer Rouge cadre who defected from the movement in 1977 to join Vietnamese-sponsored forces, Hun Sen was no stranger to the way the Khmer Rouge worked and what they were capable (or not capable) of. Enjoying the incumbent advantage of what had been the ruling regime prior to this period of transition, Hun Sen savvily deployed the "widespread and persistent use of SoC state apparatus to conduct [the] political campaigns of the CPP in which state employees—police, armed forces, and civil servants—were mobilized for CPP electioneering."⁴⁷ It was a masterstroke by Hun Sen that further embittered the Khmer Rouge against UNTAC. To them, Hun Sen's maneuverings, and indeed their very possibility, was all "pre-arranged" by those who sought to despoil them of their electoral chances.[48]

The PDK's inability to gain an electoral foothold was no less due to the fact that by the early 1990s, FUNCINPEC had decisively outflanked the PDK on the political front. FUNCINPEC may have been less militarized than either of its CGDK partners or the CPP, but the battlefield preoccupations of the latter two parties worked in FUNCINPEC's favor, giving it increased opportunities to establish its primacy on the political front. The party was also more adept than both the KPNLF and PDK at doing underground political work in the countryside to cultivate its popularity. FUNCINPEC had made early contact with and incorporated a variety of spontaneously arising anticommunist, anti-Vietnamese movements that had sprung up in various parts of the country after January 1979 and thereafter quietly built a network that spread into many parts of the country. Relying on Sihanouk's name, they promoted the argument that whereas the PRK were merely pawns of the Vietnamese, the PDK perpetrators of genocide, and the KPNLF haunted by the ghost of the bellicist Lon Nol, Sihanouk had under his watch held the Vietnamese at bay, opposed genocidal communism, and kept the country out of war.

This "ideology" (of moderation) was promulgated by the former members of ANKI (Armées Nationale pour Khmer Indépendent, the successor of the ANS), which FUNCINPEC had earlier disbanded. Having laid down arms, these erstwhile soldiers were thus freed up to concentrate on political work, particularly in the more heavily populated areas of Cambodia. Of course, this resulted in ANKI's abandonment of areas in Siem Reap/Oddar Meanchey and Kampong Thom to the NADK, which consequently led to the NADK expanding the territory under its control. If many saw this as a sign of FUNCINPEC's decline, it was only because they conflated military activity with political work. Much of the groundwork was in fact being done to secure FUNCINPEC's eventual victory at the ballot box in the 1993 UNTAC elections even while vast areas of the countryside remained under Khmer Rouge control.[49]

Thus, for all the effort and rhetoric in the service of politics taking precedence over military strategy, the PDK was never able to establish a dominant political presence within the postwar, post–Paris Agreements, pre–UNTAC elections period. It had all been for naught. When the polls finally opened between May 23 and 28, 1993, more than 90 percent of eligible Cambodians voted. FUNCINPEC achieved an unambiguous victory among the twenty parties that had registered to compete for political office. The results, released on June 10, saw FUNCINPEC winning 45 percent of the popular vote and 58 of the 120 contested seats for a new constituent assembly; the CPP attained 38 percent of the popular vote and 52 seats.[50] The Khmer Rouge, having chosen a return to arms over participation in the electoral process, were not represented in the final tally.

Regressing Forward

The elections were a profound inflection point for all the political actors involved, for Cambodia's position in the international order, and for the Cambodian people. Despite the many security challenges faced throughout the electoral process, more than nine tenths of the electorate voted in what was by far the most democratic election in Cambodian history, before or since. For the Khmer Rouge, however, it was an unmitigated failure. Once FUNCINPEC brokered a power-sharing agreement with the CPP not long after the UNTAC elections wrapped up, the PDK's electoral prospects were reduced to nil. An attack against Pol Pot's headquarters launched by the new FUNCINPEC-CPP coalition in August 1993 resulted in the capture of a major NADK arms depot and Pol Pot's retreat to Anlong Veng, burning the PDK's bridges with FUNCINPEC and the CPP beyond repair and further weakening the Khmer Rouge's position to the point that Brother Number 1 could no longer deny it. And in the face of Cambodia's reemergence on the world stage, no longer an isolated country wracked by genocidal turmoil and UN sanctions but one with a single coalition government that held a clear mandate, international aid to the Khmer Rouge had completely dried up.

Failing at this test of its strength as a political party and forced to search for other sources of revenue, the Khmer Rouge returned to a form of self-reliance not unlike in its early days in the *maquis*. To the movement's leadership, there was only one direction left to take. If the Khmer Rouge could not dominate and consume the united front through electoral means, the movement would shift, inexorably, to a way in which they could, in their own minds, eventually dominate the political process: class struggle. And in the midst of this renewed turmoil, as they were "turning and turning in the widening gyre," our three lieutenants would each meet different fates, with Ieng Sary defecting from the PDK, Son Sen hunted down, and *Ta* Mok—despite all his zeal for the movement—confronting an unbreachable schism with Brother Number 1 himself.

Chapter 6

Back to Basics
Scorched-Earth Class Struggle, 1994–1997

> It's true that Ta Mok and Son Sen don't get along—they have very different levels of education—but they do agree when it comes to killing.
>
> —Suong Sikoeun, from an interview with Steve Heder

In January 2014 I was conducting interviews along the northern Thai-Cambodian border, gleaning information on the Khmer Rouge's last days from those who had lived it. The approachability I had enjoyed in past years eluded me on that occasion, as potential interlocutors politely but firmly refused my attempts to engage them. At Anlong Veng, something akin to a muzzled, faintly judgmental Greek chorus of weathered, unsmiling locals fixated on my team with vaguely menacing thousand-yard stares. Finally, a shopkeeper broke the silence, explaining that the residents of Anlong Veng had deepened their distrust of outsiders after being betrayed by journalists who, despite assurances of anonymity, had quoted them by name and broadcast their non-pixilated images on television. Throwing out a final non sequitur as a desperate "Hail Mary," I asked him if he knew any of *Ta* Mok's former troops. He responded that many of them—whom he referred to as "Division 8"—had been transferred to frontline positions along the contested Thai-Cambodian border area around the Preah Vihear temple.[1] Hoping a change of venue might help with my research, and since I had already paid for the car and driver, I decided to travel there the following day.

Accessing *prasat* Preah Vihear from its base requires riding in the back of a flatbed truck along a winding road to the top of a plateau some 1,700 feet above the surrounding Cambodian plain. Along the way, Khmer fellow passengers threw cigarettes and candy to a gaggle of scrawny soldiers, some of them barefoot, chasing the truck. While at the summit, my research assistant and I saw these same young men playing a game of volleyball while we had lunch at a small restaurant. I asked the proprietress, "Are these soldiers in Division 8?" She chuckled, explaining that they were harmless boys deployed as rearguard troops along the foxholes nearby. Division 8, she continued, was an elite corps located midway down the mountain and positioned as frontline troops, deep in the bush, to deter the Thai.

We hired two motorcycles and rode to the Division 8 camp. Stepping past the all but invisible (and unguarded) entrance, we saw two soldiers walking toward us, one covered in traditional Buddhist tattoos and the other a bare-chested jarhead type straight out of central casting. They shook their heads, laughed at the absurdity of our having suddenly appeared in their world, and finally asked, between snorts, "What are you two even *doing* here? Don't you know that this is completely off-limits?" We responded that we were eager to learn about Division 8, to which they replied, still laughing, that we had to leave immediately. I knew they were serious but couldn't resist asking, "Does that mean we can't interview you?" They laughed even harder, waving us off. "*Of course* that means you can't interview us!"

Although we left the camp without incident, there was an almost tangible eeriness to the encounter. In a different time (say, a few years before) or place (as little as a few hundred steps away) from where we were, these very same soldiers might easily have executed us and buried our bullet-riddled bodies, as had happened to other foreign "interlopers" described later in this chapter. Rather than feel disappointment that we did not get the interview, I felt an overwhelming sense of relief that we got out of what could have been a dicey situation. But I also came away with something important and unique: I had stumbled upon an impossible juxtaposition of knee-slapping jocularity and deadly serious menace. This was as close as I would come to *experiencing* the otherworldly atmospherics of the dark, self-contained world spun by *Ta* Mok and his troops after 1993. For by then, Mok had gone down a path of increasing violence and destruction that turned him into a juggernaut of force from which even Pol Pot was not safe.

To be sure, Mok had merely—albeit enthusiastically—been toeing the line of class struggle that the Khmer Rouge had taken up again following their spectacular failure to secure any legitimate political gains during the UNTAC-led transition years. If the period between 1979 and

1982 saw the PDK returning to a strategy they were familiar with—the united front—the period between 1994 and 1997 likewise saw them returning to the also familiar strategy of class struggle once they realized that the united front approach was no longer tenable. Over the course of these three years, the Khmer Rouge carried out scorched-earth policies, extrajudicial killings, and political purges that were as bloody as, if not more so than, those that took place in the 1970s.

Yet there were contextual differences, of course, between the Khmer Rouge's two periods of class struggle. For one, the Khmer Rouge were not at the helm of the state in the 1990s the way they were in the late 1970s. Instead, the country was now led by Sihanouk's son Norodom Ranariddh and CPP head Hun Sen in an uneasy co-prime ministership. Although Ranariddh was de facto prime minister-elect, secessionist threats from Cambodia's eastern provinces led by CPP leaders and Hun Sen's claims of electoral fraud compelled Sihanouk and his son, with the acquiescence of the UNTAC chief Yasushi Akashi and the enthusiastic support of former colonial power France, to agree to this arrangement for the sake of upholding the country's political stability and allowing the UN a fig leaf to exit Cambodia. Over the next three years, the relationship between the two co-prime ministers devolved into a zero-sum competition for power which the PDK exploited—and was in turn exploited by.

Different as well were the positions of our three lieutenants within the Khmer Rouge's leadership. As detailed in the previous chapter, *Ta Mok* was enjoying top dog status, Son Sen struggling to retain a modicum of influence, and Ieng Sary scarcely a presence. The combined upshot of their respective trajectories—destruction, death, defection—all but ensured that the path the Khmer Rouge set itself on in the early 1990s was one of no return.

Class Struggle Redux

By late 1994, it became clear to even the most stubborn Khmer Rouge leaders that they were truly outside the political process and that the united front had failed. That year a document was circulated as a "draft plan" for the PDK's future.[2] It called for a set of new policies that would not simply signal the collapse of the united front; it would also change the PDK program on the ground in the direction of class struggle to a degree not seen since the Democratic Kampuchea period. The document itself was a dissemination of a study session from August and

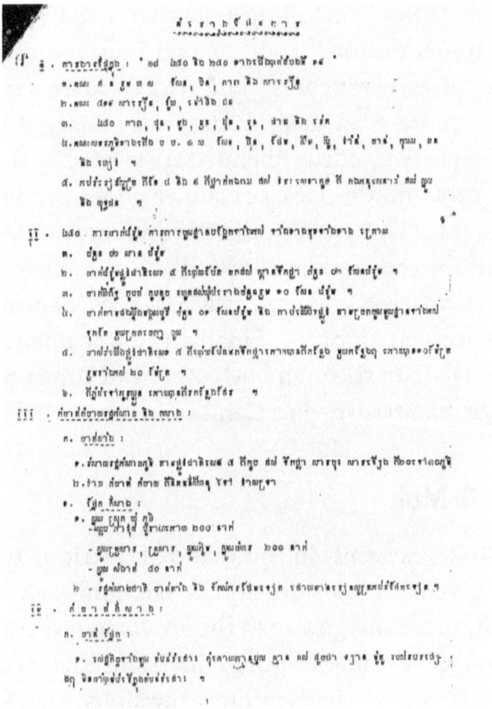

FIGURE 6.1. "Draft Plan," 1994. Steve Heder.

September of that year involving cadres "from the level of division to battalion, from company to cores and combatants."

This document first called for Division 450 to plant some 2 million *punji* stakes "to defend all bases both at the front and at the rear." Specifically, it instructed that 200,000 of them were to be planted along National Route 5 from Poipet to the bridge at Teuk Thla (ទឹកថ្លា). Another 100,000 were to be placed around small and large ponds up to the Samraong (សំរោង) commune. Still another 100,000 were to be placed along the Mongkolborei (មង្គលបុរី) River, and soldiers were ordered to "cut trees to close all routes going into the base areas[,] leaving only one access route." Crews were also to dig ditches up to ten meters long in two areas on Route 5 between Poipet and Teuk Thla as well as between Phnom Thom and Au Snguon (អូរស្ងួន).

Second, it ordered the dissolution and elimination of all state authorities along Route 5 from Kroup to Teuk Thla and to "eliminate and scatter" (កម្ទាត់កម្ចាយ) SoC officials from Nikom Sihanouk to Veal Trea (វាលត្រា). At the same time, it called for the strengthening of village-level PDK "cores," including a quota of two hundred people "as traditional weapons militia," another two hundred as "family cores, families, village cores, overt cores," and fifty to act in a covert capacity.

Perhaps even more ominously, cadres were charged with ensuring that "the whole economy of the liberated areas has deep and solid roots, for example[,] cars, motorcycles, consumer goods are unnecessary for the liberated areas." There were calls to eliminate "rationism," or private accumulation, and to increase production so that all individuals could support themselves and gradually ease the financial burden associated with continued fighting. Finally, the document called for an elimination of pacifism through both overt and covert reeducation.

Class struggle had returned to Cambodia.

Terror under *Ta* Mok

By this time, Mok was firmly in command of Corridor 1008, headquartered in Anlong Veng.[3] Mok's deputy So Saroeun was chairman of the Zone 1008 committee and governed the area along with Vice Chairman San and committee members Ngun, Nhân, and Khaev. Logging operations effectively financed Mok's military divisions, with Mok maintaining tight control over them; he decided which Thai timber companies to sell to, and even which trees to cut. Revenue would then be distributed to the divisions and from there down to the regiments. In order to maintain these operations, Mok nurtured contacts with the Thai military individuals and businessmen, primarily through Arun Sawat, a nephew of Thai military strongman Chaovalit Yongjaiyut. True to his extensive use of his network Arun Sawat was the father-in-law of one of Mok's daughters.[4]

Vibrant cross-border commercial contacts notwithstanding, Corridor 1008 was the site of radical socioeconomic policies similar to those previously carried out, as noted in chapter 2, in the 1970s. Indeed, Mok, as described earlier, had told senior Corridor 1008 combatants in 1994 that "the situation had changed back to 1975 and so we have to use the tactics of 1975."[5] A January 1992 PDK document illustrates the Khmer Rouge's renewed focus during this period on targeting economic activity and associated groups of the Cambodian population that fell beyond the purview of party ideology. Titled "Heighten the Spirit of Vigilance and Eliminate the Enemy's Pacification Moles in Our Zones and Ranks"[6] and signed by Pol Pot (using the code name "101"), this document called for a ratcheting-up of the identification and neutralization of "enemies," which included "people making their living cutting down trees and collecting vines; those contacting us on trade and business matters on both large and small scales; those in the gem trade; those selling draught animals, heartwood and the like." The document outlined that "there [were] to be no concessions, no negotiations, no contacts, and no mutual money-making [nor] establishment of any sort of peaceful interrelationship" with such individuals. Instead, the PDK was to undertake a "conscientious re-education about this internally [through a] solid and firm organization from top to bottom."[7]

Such organization went down to the immediate family level. Trade was reordered into units based on particular industries. For instance, there was a unit that would trade with Thai merchants for rice and material, mostly cloth, and a woodcutting unit that would cut down trees and sell the timber to Thai commercial interests. All these operations were based on barter, as money (mostly Thai baht) was generally not used until 1993, and even then sparingly.[8] Some new Khmer Rouge banknotes were being printed, but they appear to have been limited in circulation.

Given that the PDK was no longer receiving foreign aid from Beijing, these policies enabled the PDK to ensure its self-sufficiency. But they also guaranteed PDK control over goods and services, as befitted a war zone. Mok himself sealed off Anlong Veng and made sure that nobody could enter or leave without his permission, and characteristically put relatives in charge of key "state" functions.[9] He also deployed NADK troops to carry out scorched-earth policies all along Routes 6 and 68, forcibly relocating residents and setting the surrounding landscape on fire. And under Pol Pot's orders, burnings were also carried out in Varin (វ៉ារិន), Sre Snam (ស្រែស្នំ), Puok (ពួក), and elsewhere to "wipe out the puppet state power."[10]

Yet Mok was not completely overbearing in his orthodoxy, at least as far as the local economy was concerned. An ex–Khmer Rouge commander recalled that even as "the one-legged northern zone commander is unpredictable, temperamental, and brutal ... he [had] alternatively encouraged and halted free market trading in his zone." Mok also closed down his commercial sawmills to set an example for the people and to show that he was one of them.[11] Moreover, the good relations he sought to cultivate with the Anlong Veng community over the years may have mitigated some of the potential for discontent. As an interviewee describes, back in the 1980s, Mok was "funny and well-liked. He's liked because he supports and protects everyone around

Figure 6.2. Khmer Rouge banknotes, ca. 1993. Photographs by the author.

him, [providing] supplies, food, soap, everything." Mok even opposed what he saw as random acts of violence against the poor peasant class, the vanguard of the movement.[12]

Others deemed threats to the movement, however, did not escape Mok's renowned brutality. As noted previously, Mok had deployed Division 912 forces to kill any Royal Government of Cambodia authorities they encountered along Route 68 for the purposes of cutting off intelligence channels with Phnom Penh. This same reason purportedly accounted for attacks earlier in the 1990s on trains and other modes of public transport, though the Khmer Rouge also stood to gain materially from what were basically acts of literal highway robbery. In mid-June 1990, for instance, a train was stopped by around one thousand Khmer Rouge troops south of Phnom Penh. Three days prior, the Khmer Rouge had circulated leaflets advising private individuals not to take the trains, warning that "nationalist soldiers will cut off the communications lines of the enemy, including the railway line." The leaflets proclaimed, "If people do not observe this warning, the nationalist soldiers cannot be held responsible for the damage to property and life." Even with this warning, and despite a government escort of about a hundred soldiers, the incident resulted in significant casualties: at least seven government employees and some dozen passengers were killed, with another fifty-two wounded. Those who were spared were forced to carry the plunder—weapons, rice, motorcycles, TV sets, radios, and the like—to Khmer Rouge camps around Phnom Voal (ភ្នំវាល់) and Phnom Boko (ភ្នំបូកោ), the principal PDK base in the area.[13]

Apart from attacks on government forces, the Khmer Rouge also targeted non-Khmer groups from neighboring countries still residing in Cambodia. In 1993 they attacked ethnic Vietnamese fishermen whose families had been living around Tonlé Sap for generations. Altogether some thirty-three men, women, and children were massacred, with another two dozen wounded.[14] Ethnic Lao were also targeted. Since 1979 there had been close to three thousand Cambodians of Lao ethnicity living in Anlong Veng. These Lao Cambodians had been absorbed into *Ta* Mok's and Son Sen's forces. Although they had requested to be demobilized in 1993, lack of progress on this front led them to attempt joining up with FUNCINPEC commander General Nhek Bun Chhay sometime between 1995 and 1996. When news of this potential merger leaked to Mok, he doubled down on surveillance of the ethnic Lao, targeting representatives located in Ratanakiri, Mondulkiri, and Steung Trâng provinces and issuing an order to all Khmer

Rouge division commanders to arrest and eliminate anyone "identified as betrayer/traitor of the KR organization."[15] Ten people—including five Lao Americans—were rounded up and killed. Some of the Lao officers managed to escape, but a dozen of their family members were executed and buried in a mass grave.

Such extrajudicial killings were carried out ostensibly in the name of class struggle, of purging the country of elements antithetical to the Khmer Rouge's warped vision of what it should look like. But they were as much efforts to grasp at the power that had eluded the Khmer Rouge at the ballot box. As if hell-bent on proving to the FUNCINPEC-CPP government and to the rest of the world that they were still in the game, the Khmer Rouge carried out attacks on civilians when and where they could. At the beginning of 1994, a reward was offered for capturing and killing foreigners. One Khmer Rouge official recalled that the reward was 600,000 baht. The orders were to "negotiate if negotiations are possible, but afterwards, kill. Particularly westerners, Europeans."[16]

This targeting of foreigners quickly became a signature act of the Khmer Rouge, who appeared intent on demonstrating that they did not fear killing anyone—consequences be damned—who "violated Cambodian sovereignty." The year 1994 alone saw the kidnapping and murder of the Englishman Robert Bundred and a Thai companion in January; American aid worker Melissa Himes in March; Hong Kong residents Dominic Chappelle and his girlfriend, Kellie Wilkinson—co-owners of a café in Kampong Som—along with their friend Tina Dominy in April; Belgian tourists Michel Baran and his wife, Nathalie Roobaert, in May; Frenchman Jean-Michel Braquet, Englishman Mark Slator, and Australian David Wilson in July; and German tourist Tobias Wolf in December.[17]

The immediate circumstances surrounding these abductions and murders were generally innocuous—which made their occurrence all the more chilling. Chappelle and Wilkinson, for instance, were abducted when their hired taxi was stopped by the Khmer Rouge on National Route 4 on their way back from Phnom Penh. Their remains were found in a nearby village months later. Wolf, a teacher, was vacationing from Taiwan when he was intercepted on a motorcycle near the border on December 8.

Baran and Roobaert were sightseeing on the Thai-Cambodian border adjacent to the Preah Vihear temple. They were last seen in the parking area around noon. Subsequent investigations determined that the couple, accompanied by a Thai ranger, had approached the border checkpoint and requested permission from the two Khmer Rouge soldiers there to sneak in and visit Preah Vihear. The area was controlled by Chhon (aka Khon) and the temple complex by Koy, both under Saroeun's Division 800, firmly under Mok's command. Permission was granted, but at approximately 2:00 p.m., the couple were arrested and interrogated under the suspicion that they were spies. Their captors communicated with Pol Pot and *Ta* Mok and received orders to execute the pair. Baran was then stabbed. There was also the sound of guns being fired, and it later emerged that a comrade (*mit*) Ton had shot him as well. According to one well-connected Khmer Rouge official, once they killed Baran, they threw his body over "a high crevasse," whereupon Roobaert reportedly took her own life rather than face certain execution.

The kidnapping and killing of Braquet, Slator, and Wilson occurred during a train journey from Phnom Penh to Kampot. Khmer Rouge soldiers stopped their train in what the engineers called "an average attack," plundered the train, and marched some twenty hostages to their base in Phnom Voal. The Khmer Rouge released photos of the three Westerners on August 8 and started announcing a range of ransoms, anywhere between $50,000 and $150,000 in gold for each prisoner. The provincial military chief of Kampot, General Eng Hong, offered to secure the release of the three prisoners for a cool million dollars after having earlier proposed selling photos of the hostages to journalists for $800. Perhaps inevitably, negotiations spiraled out of control. On August 19 a link was set up to provide a grim radio interview with the hostages, who were suffering from malaria, dysentery, and the growing certainty that they would be killed. Their remains were found on October 30. In a typically horrific detail, the Khmer Rouge captors had cut their hostages' Achilles tendons to prevent them from escaping.

One of the last Western hostage cases came some two years later with the March 26, 1996, abduction of Christopher Howes and his Cambodian interpreter Huon Hourth just north of Siem Reap at Preah Ko. Howes had been working as a mine-clearing expert for the Mines Advisory Group. At 9:00 a.m., Howes and his Cambodian team were taken into custody. Initially, Howes was told he would be released to negotiate the terms for freeing his team. He refused to leave them. In response, the Khmer Rouge released all but one of the Cambodians and Howes at 2:00 that afternoon. Internally, a comrade Tem received word of Howes's capture from a radio transmission. He subsequently met with Mok, who in turn met with Pol Pot, who gave the verbal order that "arrangements be made"; these apparently included shooting Howes in the back of the head after he had been invited to share a meal with his captors. Making this even more excruciating for the families of the victims was that there had been no confirmation of the execution, and for some two years they held on to the faint hope that he might still be alive.

Although the body count of foreigners is minute compared to the number of Cambodians murdered by the Khmer Rouge, the focus of the foreign media on these cases contributed not insignificantly to the image of the Khmer Rouge as a force still to be reckoned with.

One individual who was intimately involved in the negotiations to return foreigners captured by the Khmer Rouge argues that, at the time, "the lives of those people could have been saved by a peaceful approach." In his opinion, "the Khmer Rouge organization was interested in building up funds for their cause. . . . [T]hey were [strapped] for cash" once the last vestiges of Chinese aid dried up and would have done anything to refill their coffers.[18] Such desperate measures apparently extended to the trafficking of foreigners' bones. Sometime in 1998, a woman running a palm wine shop in Anlong Veng, prompted by a flyer offering "everlasting wealth" to anyone who handed over the remains of Howes, offered up for purchase her collection of human bones (which she claimed to be Howes's), respectfully wrapped in expensive cloth. This woman was believed to be a broker for several senior (by then former) Khmer Rouge officials who had heard that foreigners' bones could bring a fortune. It was not surprising, therefore, that such remains were scavenged by these entrepreneurs, thereby ending up in macabre venues like the Anlong Veng wine shop rather than where the victims had been killed or in the possession of their loved ones.

Son Sen Flounders

One thing that *is* perhaps surprising about this period of burnings and bloody killings is that it all happened against the backdrop of the NADK hemorrhaging personnel and continued infighting among the PDK leadership. NADK troop strength had been cut in half since 1989 as a result of defections following the Vietnamese withdrawal, the 1993 elections, and a general weariness with continuing the civil war into a second decade. Corridor 1008's forces were in fact down to between two thousand and three thousand troops overseeing a civilian population of about thirty thousand, extending through Preah Vihear, Siem Reap, Kampong Thom, Kampong Cham, Kratie, Steung Trâng, Ratanakiri, and Mondulkiri provinces. Corridor 1008 units in Division 616 and Division 785 had largely ceased to exist, while divisions 802 and 612 were down to one regiment each. Divisions 801 and 980 were also reported to be considerably undermanned, and division 415, located in Pailin and by then the largest and best, was undersupplied ammunition-wise, thanks to being denied ammunition by Thai authorities and Son Sen's continuing refusal to let Mok use the old 1001 cache in Trapeang Kol.[19]

With Sary sidelined, the PDK leadership was separated into two groups: a northeastern front under Pol Pot and *Ta* Mok and a southernwestern front under Nuon Chea and Son Sen.[20] This geographical division only worsened relations between *Ta* Mok and Son Sen, and NADK troops began taking sides. One such cadre was Men Kaev, who had long been associated with Son Sen. Growing disenchanted with Mok, Kaev disobeyed his orders to attack Preah Vihear and Steung Trâng. On January 15, 1994, Mok responded by arresting Kaev. Kaev, however, managed not only to escape but also to persuade some twenty-one of his men in Siem Reap to defect with him, his wife, and his children. This outcome must have been embarrassing for Son Sen, as his former aide gave up all sorts of valuable information to foreign authorities on the Khmer Rouge's depleted troop strength and low ammunition stocks.[21]

Unlike Mok, the "warlord of Anlong Veng," who was, although feared, also respected, Son Sen—preening, arrogant, and aloof—did not engender much goodwill among the people he was assigned to govern. In 1994 he inherited the new, fully militarized Front 450, which encompassed territory around Pailin and Malai and combined Sectors 102 and 32, formerly under Ieng Sary. Stinging from his failure to succeed in the world of politics not too long before and anxious to prove himself to Pol Pot, he imposed ultra-hard-line policies that harked back to the Democratic Kampuchea era:

> All local institutions were no longer elected but instead appointed which meant that Son Sen filled them with his relatives and his bunch [បក្សពួក]. The market was closed, as were all the shops and noodle stores, and the goods were confiscated even from the smallest trader who in some cases lost tens of thousands of baht. Cars were also confiscated for common use, and ultimately so were the ox-carts[,] which became a major issue. Son Sen said 80%

of everything had to be for the battlefield and 20% for solving one's livelihood. The temple was dissolved and the monks were made to serve as porters for the army.... [E]ven watching soap operas on the television could be interpreted as diverting attention from fighting. Trade was considered in the same light because those involved in petty trading weren't working as ammunition porters or making *punji* stakes. And so because of these measures the people saw the situation as reverting back to the 3-year period. From what we know, there was even a plan to confiscate televisions, bicycles, motorcycles, jewelry, etc. but it had not yet been implemented.[22]

These policies were a volte-face from the comparatively liberal ones Ieng Sary had implemented, and residents felt no reason to cultivate the kind of personal loyalty to Son Sen that they felt toward Sary. In fact, they preferred Ny Kân, Son Sen's younger brother, who had led Front 32, over Son Sen himself. A cadre from Division 450 recalled that "before Son Sen came to this area, Ny Kân wasn't like this: he wasn't so strict and was well liked by the people. But after Son Sen came in 1994, Ny Kân had to follow him as both his commander and his older brother." And Son Sen's renewed brutality did him no favors either. He dubbed those who disagreed with his policies "pacification agents" (សន្តិសម្បុទ្ធ) or, more ominously, "rotten cadres" (កម្មាភិបាលស្រួយ/ រលួយ—invoking images of rotten or swollen flesh).[23] Invectives aside, "the main trouble under Son Sen," according to another former member of Division 450, "was the killing, there was lots of killings, both within the ranks and of the people in the forest.... Son Sen did have his own ideas but never succeeded in carrying them out, primarily because he was too vicious. If anyone opposed him, they would be accused of treachery and killed, but killed in a quiet, subtle, sweet manner. In this, Son Sen is like Pol Pot whereas *Ta* Mok is open and loud-mouthed about things."[24]

Division commanders within Front 450 likewise bristled at Son Sen's hard-line approach. Y Chhean, who was commander of Division 415 in Pailin at the time, recalled that he "was convinced that fighting by this method would not be possible and suggested that [the PDK] change its policy." While he believed that "communism if done properly is good," he nonetheless thought that "their way was not the appropriate response to our problem which is to find peace."[25] Things came to a head when, in early June 1996, Son Sen issued a circular to confiscate oxcarts from the population after catching two peasants using them to illegally export timber to Thailand. The local commanders, including Y Chhean and Sok Pheap (commander of Division 450 in Malai), simply refused to carry out the order.²⁶

Pol Pot learned of this incident in mid-July and received an appeal by Y Chhean and Sok Pheap to resolve the issue. Brother Number 1 refused the request and invited "415 and 450" to a meeting with Son Sen in Malai instead. Y Chhean and Sok Pheap refused, and *Ta* Mok, enraged at their intransigence, was dispatched by Pol Pot to "handle" the situation. On July 23, a meeting was held at Son Sen's headquarters, with Sok Pheap and other local participants attending while Y Chhean remained in Pailin. Although it took the form of a criticism/self-criticism session, Son Sen and Mok "mentioned only their [good] qualities and not their faults," to the chagrin of the local participants.²⁷ Son Sen also used the opportunity to boast that "he was the only one to strictly apply the political line of the party and that the cadres and people do not respect it properly." He did, however, make sure to point out that it was a policy made by "99" (that is, Son Sen, Nuon Chea, and *Ta* Mok combined). Mok added that if the policies continued "until the end of the world" (ដល់ភ្លើងនេះកល្ប/កប្ប), so be it. When a woman who had known Mok since the 1970s asked, "If we apply the [DK] Government's line to burn down the buildings of the enemy administration in the villages, and that in the process villagers' houses get destroyed, if for instance the house of my father is burnt too, what do I do?," Mok dryly responded, "Too bad for your father" (ខឹ ឪប៉ាទៅ ខ្ញុំរស់).²⁸ The woman shook her head; in the twenty years she had known Mok he had not changed one bit.²⁹

Discussions continued for two more days, but they eventually reached a stalemate, with Mok and Son Sen "insist[ing] on the absolute sacrifice to the struggle and a rejection of private property." To break the impasse, *Ta* Mok used his position as commander of Corridor 1008 to summon Sok Pheap to a military meeting in Pailin that, as chief of Division 450, he was duty bound to obey. He had hoped that with Pheap in Pailin, Son Sen's efforts might wear down the local authorities in Malai, who could not look to Pheap as an advocate on their behalf. They also tried to sandbag Y Chhean. Though Pheap and Chhean were able to maneuver themselves into an additional set of meetings, discussions broke down once again.³⁰

In the early morning of August 7, Y Chhean came across a telegram "from 99" ordering that six people—himself, Sok Pheap, as well as his brothers Nhiep, Ny, Rin, and Kaen—be "smashed" (កម្ទេច, that is, executed). Between August 8 and 10, Mok, Nuon, and Son Sen ordered simultaneous attacks on Malai and Pailin. But Front 250, which had been ordered to do so, refused to carry out the orders. The next evening, Mok and crew ordered tanks based in Banteay Ti-pir (បន្ទាយទី២) to shell Au Sampoar (អូរសំពារ) and troops from Khla Ngoap (ខ្លាងាប់) to attack Malai. They also stood down. But on the evening of August 13, three rockets (possibly launched by Division 948) hit the house where Son Sen had been staying.

Almost in a panic, *Ta* Mok and Nuon Chea solicited Mok's contacts in the gem trade (along with a personal appeal from Nuon Chea to Y Chhean's wife) to get them safely across the Thai border to Phnom Koi, even while Son Sen remained in Malai. Once safely there, Mok unleashed a torrent of invective, promising that he would "destroy Pailin, everybody there, including babies in their hammocks," and sent a telegram to Pol Pot advising him of the situation. As for Son Sen, he had four of his own bodyguards murdered the morning after his house was shelled because "they knew many secrets about his life as well as their evacuation plan." He then escaped to Thailand with his family before reentering Cambodian territory, reaching Samlaut by August 15. Ny Kân also reached Samlaut on August 15 and, a week later, commanded his Division 270 to attack Division 250. But Y Chhean and Sok Pheap surrounded and disarmed Division 270, allowing its troops to scatter but keeping its officers, including Ny Kân, under armed guard.[31] Ny Kân would escape Pailin in December after "working on the guards and getting them on his side."[32]

Ieng Sary Defects

The revolt by NADK troops against their commanders was unprecedented. But the situation was more dire than simple rebellion. Y Chhean and Sok Pheap had begun the ultimate act of mutiny: negotiations with the Royal Government of Cambodia, with the aim of coming to some sort of settlement that would ensure their safety while allowing them to counter Son Sen, *Ta* Mok, and Nuon Chea. Back on June 10, 1996, Lay Vireak, the Division 12 commander of the Royal Cambodian Armed Forces (RCAF), had met with NADK Division 450 deputy commander Bou Sareth to formalize a ceasefire. On August 1 and 2, Chhean and Pheap were given a promise from Hun Sen, recorded on tape, that if they defected, they would be able to keep their property, their positions (transferred to the CPP), and, perhaps more importantly, their lives.

Up till this point, Hun Sen and Norodom Ranariddh had been closely watching NADK movement not only for the sake of monitoring the Khmer Rouge insurgency overall, but also in the hopes of recapturing defecting Khmer Rouge to shore up their positions vis-à-vis one another. As Benny Widyono observed: "Ironically the imminent demise of the KR movement, which means peace for the entire country is finally within sight, instead sparked a new rivalry between the two protagonists over defecting KRs. The incomplete integration in the army, which before only existed for knowledgeable people, was out into the open with both sides parading as many ex-KR commanders being wined and dined as possible."[33]

Hun Sen's and Ranariddh's responsibilities toward the Khmer Rouge were split north and south of the dividing line of National Route 5. While Ranariddh was responsible for those hard-line Khmer Rouge in Anlong Veng and Preah Vihear, Hun Sen focused on the more moderate, albeit wilier, Khmer Rouge faction in Pailin and Malai and the former Nuon Chea forces in the south.[34] This division of labor meant that Hun Sen, with the willing defection of Y Chhean and Sok Pheap along with the troops under their command, met with greater success in NADK recapture efforts. Perhaps his greatest triumph on this count, however, was securing the defection of Ieng Sary.

As described in chapter 5, the hardening of positions within the Khmer Rouge leading up to and following the Paris Agreements resulted in Ieng Sary's increasing irrelevance and vulnerability. A combination of exposure to ideologies and economic incentives that deviated from Khmer Rouge orthodoxy made Sary the foremost exemplar of the "united front" strategy among senior leaders, and by that juncture in the Khmer Rouge's history, that put him squarely outside the leadership orbit and, indeed, in opposition to it. By the middle of 1991, Ieng Sary had been stripped of all power within the movement, and sometime between 1993 and 1994 he had fled Malai for Pailin.[35] When the Khmer Rouge high command was reorganized in 1994, Ieng Sary was absent from it. This completed his failure to become an effective king of a mountaintop and thus a genuine powerbroker.

Still, Ieng Sary appeared to the Khmer Rouge leadership to wield some influence yet, as Pol Pot suspected him to be the ringleader behind Y Chhean and Sok Pheap's insubordination. A former Khmer Rouge interviewee recalls that "KR radio accuse[d] Ieng Sary of being a traitor for refusing to implement an order to collectivize property in Malai District."[36] But although Ieng Sary's son Savut supposedly took part in the negotiations between Hun Sen, Y Chhean, and Sok Pheap, Sary was in fact not present.³⁷ He had been hospitalized in Bangkok with a heart condition for most of the prior two years, and was effectively out of the loop on commanding his own area, let alone the upper Khmer Rouge ranks which he had been frozen out of.

The defectors nonetheless found Ieng Sary indispensable. As ex-deputy commander of Division 705 Phon Phaen explains: "We wanted to join with the government as people reconciling the nation.... We turned to Ieng Sary because we understood that even though he was in the [leadership], he took a middle road [ផ្លូវកណ្ដាល] and it was for this reason that his power had been reduced. But Ieng Sary lacked [forces and energy, កម្លាំង] and so depended on Sok Pheap and Y Chhean, which led to [Divisions] 415 and 450 controlling 250 rather than 250 being an equal partner."³⁸ Thus on August 6, 1996, Y Chhean met with Ieng Sary, who was still convalescing in a hospital in Bangkok, for the first time in four years. Sary told him that he had to fight against the remaining Khmer Rouge leadership: "I told him if you do not fight, you will die, but if you fight, you have a chance to win—you are not sure to win, but you have a chance."³⁹ The next day, Chhean learned that Pol Pot had ordered his arrest; the day after, Divisions 415 and 450 expressed support for their "leader," Ieng Sary.

Chhean and Pheap eventually persuaded Ieng Sary to leave his hospital bed in Thailand and return to Cambodia. This he did on August 13, following intensive negotiations with Hun Sen on his behalf, and established the reconciliation-oriented Democratic National Union Movement (DNUM) political party two days later. The drama would, however, continue to play out for some weeks afterward, as Sary insisted on amnesty as a condition for his surrender.⁴⁰ The story of Ieng Sary as an active Khmer Rouge leader—no matter how diminished he had become by that point—ended with Ieng Sary committing his forces to a reconciliation on September 16 and control of them being handed over to the Royal Government of Cambodia on November 7.⁴¹ Armed with a pardon from Sihanouk himself (which took weeks if not months of intensive negotiations to obtain), Sary hung up his PDK spurs and joined the establishment he had spent a lifetime opposing.⁴²

Heart of Darkness

The defections of 1996 affected the Khmer Rouge on several counts. As Timothy Dylan Wood puts it, given the importance of the area for gems and timber, "the loss in the northwest was felt financially; in addition, [losing] an elite DK leader as well as 15,000 soldiers and civilians was a military and political blow."[43] In response to these defections and subsequent others,[44] and as his suspicions of his colleagues started to escalate, Pol Pot doubled down. Policies became even more strict in the areas under their control, sharply curtailing freedom of movement and trade with Thailand. Command posts were fortified, and suspected spies were executed.[45]

As had been the case exactly two decades earlier, the Khmer Rouge were beginning to turn on their own in earnest. Following a high-level meeting in November 1996, Division Commander Von, along with the other ranking cadres summoned to the meeting, were killed when they drove over land mines deliberately laid by Khmer Rouge hard-liners to prevent their defection.[46] Others, including the chairman of Division 990, Comrade Phorn, the deputy chairman of Division 980, Comrade Ri, as well as a regimental-level cadre, Comrade Sai, were killed on the An Seh battlefield by mines as well. Kheum Ngun, a Khmer Rouge cadre, recounted that these mines had been deployed by *Ta* Saroeun's men and that Phorn in particular had been targeted because he "didn't carry out the burning" of houses in Varin district which Saroeun, under Pol Pot's instructions, had ordered.[47]

FIGURE 6.3. Pol Pot's bunker, Kbal Tonsaong. Photograph by the author.

It is perhaps worth stepping back for a moment to contemplate the mindset of Pol Pot at this point. Sequestered away in Kbal Tonsaong, the highlands site to which he had retreated in 1994 following an attack on Anlong Veng by RGC (Royal Government of Cambodia) forces, Pol Pot was isolated from on-the-ground realities and associates he was close with, including veteran Jaraï and other upland Khmer combatants whose families had served as his bodyguards for over three generations. Those around him nonetheless kept Pol Pot physically safe and allowed him to focus on the supposed "big picture," which very much involved a dusted-off DK-era playbook for how to survive in the face of political challenges.

Pol Pot was never one for genuine self-reflection, and his splendid isolation in Kbal Tonsaong only reinforced his own sense of what was right and proper. Being secluded in this way must have taken him back to the formative years in the *maquis*, where the Khmer Rouge had gestated from an unpromising band of urban exiles to the rulers of the nation in only a dozen years. Certainly his bunker itself was nothing terribly fancy, although it was far better than anything he had lived in during the 1960s. It was built in the early 1990s from reinforced concrete, with gold reserves (painted black to evade detection, or so the rumor went) in the cellar, punctuated by an incongruous pastel blue squat toilet. The location of the bunker was secure from a military point of view—with escape routes to the east and to the west, and the Thai border just to the north—and intoxicating from a contemplative one. Quite apart from the strategic advantage of being able to look over the Cambodian countryside all the way to the horizon, it offered a perch where—devoid of unwanted distractions or other stimuli—it was possible to erase the rough edges of past history and surrender to the power of ideas and convictions, a real-life Kurtz-like stronghold.

Such convictions included the necessity of unleashing class struggle against his most dangerous enemies: his decades-long political associates Son Sen, *Ta* Mok, and Nuon Chea. The machinations of Hun Sen and Ranariddh were successful in exploiting Pol Pot's natural tendency toward suspicion, even (or especially) against those who were closest to him. Hun Sen was particularly adept at this, offering coveted positions to associates of Son Sen and Mok and almost certainly attempting to contact them (and if not, creating incentives for FUNCINPEC to do so)—all of which further aggravated Pol Pot's paranoia.[48]

After all, it had been the actions—or inactions—of his top lieutenants that led to the precipitous decline of a movement that should have been guaranteed success by historical materialism. Pol Pot had interpreted Marx correctly and done his due diligence, had he not? The Khmer Rouge had pursued for more than two generations, undiluted and unbound and by the book, their own turbocharged version of Marxism (លទ្ធិម៉ាក្សនិយម). But then, there were these lieutenants of his. Son Sen and Nuon Chea had been in charge of territory they had let fall into the hands of the enemy—those defecting divisions, that RGC—against which he had been so vigilant. Surely there was some kind of perfidy going on with those two. And *Ta* Mok—*Ta* Mok's *entire* Corridor 1008 apparatus could not prevail against two errant divisions? He must also be disloyal.

Exit Son Sen

The furious competition between Hun Sen and Norodom Ranariddh for total power had a profound effect on PDK politics, little of it good. Since assuming office, Hun Sen had consistently outmaneuvered Ranariddh, and FUNCINPEC leaders began siding with Hun Sen. Consequently, Ranariddh increasingly relied on advisers who had previously served as military commanders on the Thai border and had worked with the Khmer Rouge. Being "bitter enemies of the CPP," these former commanders urged Ranariddh to split with the CPP, to form an alliance with the Khmer Rouge, and to rally all anti-CPP forces to its banner.[49]

The Khmer Rouge were paying close attention as the two co-prime ministers went after each other in a display of strength vis-à-vis the Khmer Rouge themselves, first by having dueling meetings with former Khmer Rouge soldiers (Hun Sen on September 24, 1996, Ranariddh the very next day).[50] The rivalry between Hun Sen and Ranariddh eventually broke down into actual armed conflict, while the Khmer Rouge looked on from the sidelines of Anlong Veng.[51] The former KPNLF Division 12 had scored some victories in bringing over ex-Khmer Rouge in Phnom Malai and Thmar Puok, while Hun Sen prevailed over the former Khmer Rouge south of Phnom Malai and in the Samlaut area, which included Ny Kân, Meas Muth, and Kaev Pung. Y Chhean in Pailin somehow managed to remain neutral.[52] Eventually, that July, Hun Sen would mobilize "his" ex-Khmer Rouge defectors alongside CPP veterans willing to join hands to attack FUNCINPEC forces in a coup against Ranariddh.

There was a tacit understanding among some in the government that a distinction existed "between the leadership group (Pol Pot, Nuon Chea, *Ta* Mok, Ieng Sary, *and perhaps Son Sen* and Khieu Samphân)" on the one hand and lower tiers of leaders on the other who could be reconciled in some fashion to the new political system.[53] This phrasing suggests that even within the first group there were divisions that could be exploited—potentially linked to Son Sen and Khieu Samphân, and possibly even Nuon Chea. Moreover, as early as June 1996, the Cambodian government received intelligence that Son Sen (as well as Nuon Chea and Khieu Samphân) had less confidence in the efficacy of a military strategy than did *Ta* Mok and Pol Pot.[54]

It is impossible to imagine that Pol Pot, already a boiling-over vessel of suspicion, did not assume that something serious was afoot among his remaining top lieutenants, and that from this point he began to view them with increasing skepticism. His existing paranoia was almost certainly reinforced by the very public post-defection reconciliation between Ieng Sary and Hun Sen in Pailin in August, and in Malai the following February.[55] This further exacerbated Pol Pot's already escalating distrust of Son Sen. Hun Sen exploited these tensions masterfully, announcing on November 16, "I . . . thank . . . Ranariddh for providing support to the way I handled this matter including measures to end talks with Son Sen, whose troops are in the process of breaking away."[56] Whether or not this was true is irrelevant, for it accomplished two things. First, it signaled to Pol Pot—accurately or not—that Son Sen was seeking a separate peace. Second, it painted Ranariddh as someone so morally bankrupt that he would negotiate with the worst of the worst Khmer Rouge leaders.

Ten days later, reports emerged that Son Sen had fled once more to Samlaut after his son was imprisoned by Y Chhean, who was seeking to draw out as many of his former combatants in Anlong Veng as he could as a way to increase his own leverage. Perhaps fearing that Son Sen would explore some sort of arrangement to secure his son's release, Pol Pot began to doubt Son Sen's loyalty even more. The following month, Son Sen's brother Ny Kân defected—at that point the highest-ranking NADK commander to do so.[57]

More worrisome defections were occurring in real time. Son Sen's other brother, Son Chhum, had also defected, as had Mok's son-in-law and former head of the DK navy Meas Muth. All of these men joined the RGC on December 18, 1996. By this time Pol Pot had already formulated plans to kill Son Sen and *Ta* Mok (and Nuon Chea) for their failure to quell the rebellion of NADK forces in Pailin and Malai.[58] This was not a spur-of-the-moment decision, but it does appear that even Brother Number 1 was vacillating on the timing of the deed if not the deed itself. As early as October 1996, Pol Pot had appointed a cadre,

Mao, to go west and shoot Mok, Nuon Chea, and Son Sen and burn their bodies to destroy any evidence. This did not pan out. Next, Pol Pot arranged for gasoline stocks to be prepared so that the three could be ambushed and burned alive. When this, too, did not move forward, he ordered the house arrest of Mok, Nuon, and Son Sen, during which "they were not allowed to go anywhere . . . to do anything."[59] To further underscore their fall from grace in Pol Pot's eyes, he convened a congress in February 1997 to rearrange the top leadership. Unilaterally, without any discussion, he assigned *Ta* Saroeun as the chairman in waiting, with *Ta* San as his military commander.

Incredibly, while all of this was happening, Pol Pot *and* Son Sen were setting up negotiations with the FUNCINPEC arm of the RGC to secure the release of Son Sen's son and others, although the two disagreed over the depth and scope of the concessions they were prepared to make. A dozen or so RGC negotiators were on their way to talks with Long Tern and Kheum Ngon on Valentine's Day when they were ambushed by troops loyal to Pol Pot. According to Kheum: "Pol Pot had arranged for Saroeun, San, and a force of 200 men to surround the area without letting me know. While I was talking to and bringing them, arranging to meet [the RGC delegates], Saroeun went to . . . capture [them and] shot the helicopter team." Several RGC negotiators were shot and killed, and Pol Pot, as Kheum recounts, attempted to shift the blame of the botched negotiations onto Kheum himself.[60]

Brutal as it was, the ambush represented Pol Pot's attempts to bring his commanders to heel in the midst of defections left, right, and center. The last straw for him may have been when Ranariddh told the UN that the RGC had entered into talks with Khmer Rouge hard-liners, including *Ta* Mok, independently of Brother Number 1. In June 1997, Pol Pot reportedly summoned Son Sen and Nuon Chea from their homes near Darm Russey (ដើមប្ញស្សី) to Kbal Tonsaong, prevailing on them "to do some work for the struggle." When, upon returning, they reported this to Mok, he balked at the order. Pol Pot concluded that Mok was therefore in cahoots with the RGC.[61] If this was the case with someone as hitherto unassailable as Mok, how trustworthy could Son Sen or even Nuon Chea possibly be? So again he ordered their execution on June 9.

In the wee hours of the morning on June 10, Pol Pot sent his forces to kill *Ta* Mok, Nuon Chea, and Son Sen. According to an eyewitness:

[The executioners] were commanded by *Ta* Roeun [General So Saroeun] and *Ta* San [General Nhem San] . . . who received orders directly from Pol Pot. The soldiers reached my house first, woke me, and warned me, "When you hear something, stay calm and do not do anything. When you see the incident, do not fight back." The whole area was already surrounded as two cars, packed full of soldiers, drove toward the residences of Son Sen and Nuon Chea, one to each house. . . .(After one car went to shoot at Son Sen's house), another car went to capture Nuon Chea, his wife, their daughter, two grandchildren (one boy and one girl), an older granddaughter, and their adopted daughter. . . .*Ta* Mok had left five days before the attack on Son Sen in order to stay at his lakeside house in Anlong Veng. *Ta* Mok, Son Sen, and Nuon Chea had plans to move down from the mountain, and *Ta* Mok had already moved.[62]

Nuon managed to escape the firefight and fled to the Thai border, having anticipated that Pol Pot's actions could not be resolved once Mok realized that he had been one of the targets. Son Sen, however, was not so lucky.

Coup de Grâce

Mok's reaction to Pol Pot's attack was swift, characteristically ruthless, and politically savvy. Early the next day, according to one source, Mok sent out bogus feelers about negotiating a reunification of the Khmer Rouge leadership ranks, surrendering power and control of the military to Pol Pot. He invited Pol Pot, Nuon Chea, and Khieu Samphân to negotiate, but "99" instead sent the same three commanders—Saroeun, San, and Khorn—initially charged with killing Mok and Son Sen, not daring to come himself.[63] Mok also ordered that the bodies of Son Sen and Yun Yat be exhumed and brought to Srah Chhouk (ស្រះឈូក), where he had built a sawmill years before in the service of the cross-border timber trade. This public venue allowed Mok to make the case that Pol Pot had betrayed the people and the movement, and that he therefore must be arrested and brought to justice. Then he cremated the bodies.

Mok then began to rally forces for a counterscharge against Pol Pot. Kheum Ngun, smarting from Pol Pot's attempt to blame him for the deaths of RGC negotiators in February, sought out the forces still loyal to Pol Pot that were preparing to attack and kill Mok as well as officers aligned with him in the hopes of resolving the situation. Kheum's efforts, however, were to no avail. As he recounted: "I called San to meet me and told San that 'you should arrange to withdraw your forces' because San and Saroeun had arranged forces since 10 o'clock the previous day to climb the hills with the aim of shooting at me, shooting at *Ta* [Mok]. So, San returned to Division 920, because it was Division 920 which had prepared to shoot, which had climbed the hills. But when he got there... San instead prepared additional forces. Because San and Saroeun were in-laws."⁶⁴

Things escalated quickly. An ex-soldier from the former Corridor 1001 recounts: "I first saw the movement of soldiers across this village here and I wondered why? Then I asked a friend who lives here too... and he said that there was a dispute between *Ta* Mok and Pol Pot. Then I asked him again, what should we do? Where should we go? He replied that when parents fight each other, they do so just for a short time and that they may eventually get along well again, so we should simply wait and see what happens."⁶⁵ But as it turned out, the soldiers did not have long to wait.

On June 19, 1997, Pol Pot and Mok's armies, distinguished by their uniforms (the former wore darker green khakis, the latter lighter, "tree leaf"-colored fatigues), clashed at Kbal Tonsaong on a mountain known locally as "Phnom (Mountain) 200," a place where explosives had once been manufactured.⁶⁶ Although both sides brought Kalashnikovs, rocket launchers, anti-tank guns, and other artillery, only around a dozen or so were killed (or, in the interviewee's vernacular, "dumped" or "[with] eyes closed") or injured, as Mok's intention was to capture, not kill, Pol Pot.⁶⁷ By this time, Pol Pot—"yoked in a hammock and saddled with an oxygen tank"—had retreated through the forest to the Thai border while broadcasting from a radio truck that it was in fact Son Sen who had betrayed the Cambodian people.⁶⁸ He was accompanied by Chan Youran, Mak Ben, Kao Bunheng, In Sopheap, and, among others, Khieu Samphân, Meas Son, "Muon" (his wife), Mul (his daughter), five bodyguards, and other Khmer Rouge cadres. Samphân was captured and, not long afterward, so was Pol Pot, at Peuy, near Choam Pranong, Thailand.⁶⁹ Mok had fixed his guns on a stream he knew Pol Pot was going to follow to the border; he had also asked the Thai military to refuse Pol Pot and his troops passage, and they had complied.⁷⁰ Pol Pot's leadership of the movement ended then and there. As a Khmer journalist put it the following year, "'Year Zero' has... ended."⁷¹

Finale

Ta Mok's moment in the sun was dramatic but short. He presided over the trial of Pol Pot in Anlong Veng on July 25, 1997, which was reported on around the world thanks to the presence of the journalist Nate

Thayer at the proceedings. Mok used that opportunity to brag to Thayer that catching Pol Pot was something of a "turkey shoot":

> Immediately after Pol Pot smashed Son Sen, I took Son Sen's body and held a big meeting. I declared Pol Pot's crimes. And that's why the army and people united to capture and smash Pol Pot with everything over in 2 days. Pol Pot had forces of 2 Divisions—920 and 801—who planned to smash me. With Saroeun [from] 801, San [from] 920, Nuon [from] 920, Khon [from] 801, and Se Ban. That's all I want to inform you about the events of 9 June to 15 June, in fact only 2 days, 9 and 10 June, and [by] 11 June it was all over. And for the other few days, it came from all these gentlemen [laughs and gestures to people in the room, including the interpreter] who got scattered, fled, were afraid, and some were captured by Pol Pot . . . the intellectuals. It took 3 more days to gather them up.[72]

Mok assumed overall control of the movement, forming a standing committee of his own people—Nhorn, Kheum Ngon, Khem, Tem, and Nuon Nov—and pursuing policies that continued the radical turn of the preceding several years. This was particularly true when it came to implementing policies against free enterprise and in the direction of increased militarization, a sort of "war communism." Joining him was, inevitably, Khieu Samphân, reprising his role as "Moloch's poodle" to the person he had denounced just days before during his retreat into the forest with Pol Pot.

Pol Pot died on April 15, 1998, of apparent heart failure while serving a lifetime prison sentence. (Rumors swirled that he had been poisoned by, alternatively, the CIA, Hun Sen, the Thai military, and anybody else who would have wanted him dead.) Mok eulogized him thus: "He is nothing more than cow shit. Actually, cow shit is more useful because it can be used as fertilizer."[73] Following his July 7 coup the year before against his co-prime minister, Ranariddh, Hun Sen, no longer handicapped by a two-front political battle, could concentrate on "mopping up" Khmer Rouge forces, and he set his sights on Mok.

On May 4, 1998, *Ta* Mok retreated to Kbal Tonsaong while fifteen thousand refugees crossed over into Thailand's Sisaket province and formed two "refugee camps" under Mok's control. Several of Mok's standing committee designees defected on December 4, while Nuon Chea and Khieu Samphân did so on Christmas Day. In the meantime, Mok—holed up at the Nga-Saam (ង្គាស្ងំ) Pass—was protected by Thai

FIGURE 6.4. Final resting places of *Ta* Mok (top) and Pol Pot (bottom). Photographs by the author.

CHAPTER 6

Special Unit 838 and one infantry battalion. They were invited to a meeting at Chhorng Sangum Pass, but were detained there, taken back to Anlong Veng, and helicoptered to Phnom Penh. Since just about everyone else had already defected, Mok no longer served any purpose to the RGC besides, perhaps, as a game trophy representing the vanquished.[74] He died in custody in 2006 and was cremated in Anlong Veng, where he remains a "favorite son," a folk hero to this day.

Conclusion

"Pure Socialism"

> Forget the myths the media's created about the White House. The truth is, these are not very bright guys, and things got out of hand.
>
> —Hal Holbrook (as Deep Throat) in
> *All the President's Men*

A decade after Son Sen's execution and Mok's victory over Pol Pot, and a year after Mok died in custody, it was time for Nuon Chea to face his own reckoning. By the mid-2000s, Nuon was living modestly and largely anonymously in Phsar Prum (ផ្សារព្រំ) village, outside the city of Pailin on the Thai-Cambodian border. In 2007 the ECCC authorized his detention and began to plan his arrest with utmost secrecy.[1] Because it was illegal to arrest people past sundown (to avoid association with the dreaded "knock in the middle of the night"), authorities scheduled his apprehension for daybreak on September 19, 2007. This meant slipping out unnoticed from Battambang, the second-largest city in Cambodia, at midnight.

Unfortunately for the ECCC team, their plans had somehow been leaked.[2] The special operation quickly devolved into a media circus, with an extended convoy of press vehicles in tow. They descended upon the village and prepared for the breach, establishing three concentric security perimeters—on the off chance they met armed resistance—with only the immediate arresting party authorized to penetrate all three. Entering the traditional Khmer raised wooden house, they were met by Nuon, in his pajamas and accompanied by his wife. He bid the arrest team "good morning" in English and offered them breakfast.

180 CONCLUSION

Compelled to accept the circumstances of his arrest, Brother Number 2 was instructed to change out of his nightclothes. With his valet, Thet Sambath,³ who ended up accompanying him to Phnom Penh, Nuon discussed which patterned boxer shorts he should put on. A member of the arresting party recalled that he appropriately chose the striped ones.

As this was happening, Nuon's young grandson had somehow slipped through all three security perimeters, taken his place in the middle of the action, and asked what was going on.

"Grandpa's going away for a while, to Phnom Penh," Nuon said.

"Are you going with *that*?" asked the grandson, pointing to the Royal Cambodian Air Force Mil Mi-8 now docked outside.⁴

"Yes, I've decided to travel by helicopter."

"Can I go with you?"

"No, you should stay here with Grandma," Nuon answered, referring to his wife, Ly Kimseng.

The child replied, loud enough for everyone to hear, "I don't *want* to stay with Grandma. *GRANDMA IS A BITCH* (យាយ កាច ឆ្កាស ណាស់)!"⁵

Thus unfolded the beginning of the end to one of the darkest chapters in the history of Cambodia and the world—the "pure socialist" revolution poised to exceed all that had come before.

Surpassing the Russian and Chinese Revolutions

Revolutionaries rarely succeed. Those who do find that subsequent governance is brutally challenging. The strategies, experience, and skills necessary to foment a revolution—to overturn state, society, and economy—run into the inelegance of actual governance. Storming the palace does not guarantee effective day-to-day bureaucratic management of it. Destroying the ancien régime's train tracks is not at all the same as ensuring, post-revolution, that the trains run on time. Attacking market fundamentals is not even remotely as complex as managing a perceived equitable distribution of resources and ensuring economics-based regime legitimacy. Working alongside comrades in arms in the same foxhole is fundamentally at odds with mobilizing elements of non-revolutionary society to rebuild the state after the enthusiasm of revolutionary victory fades from view.

The Russian Bolsheviks inherited a movement without effective institutions or even an effective blueprint for governance. One of the most remarkable aspects of the Soviet Union is that it survived its first five years when everything was so deeply and profoundly in flux. Fundamental questions—from government-party relations, the role of nationalism and governance over multiethnic republics, peasant support, external relations with Europe and Asia, even fundamentals like global communism versus "revolution in one country"—were all being hotly debated and imperfectly formulated against the backdrop of a precipitous withdrawal from the Eastern Front, subsequent Allied invasion of the USSR, the Russian Civil War, and intense infighting among Vladimir Lenin's successors as the old man become increasingly incapacitated. Atrocities like the New Economic Policy and establishing diplomatic relations with Great Britain were necessary evils, as was the rise of Stalin, his tying all these loose ends together through his deep understanding of Marxism, his extraordinary talents as a bureaucrat par excellence, and, of course, his singular ruthlessness.[6]

The Chinese Communist Party was in far, far better shape than its Russian counterpart when Mao Zedong's armies rode into Beijing in early 1949 and declared the establishment of the People's Republic that October. The extraordinary legitimacy of a revolution that reunified China after a generation of debilitating, anarchic warlord rule and fought the United Nations coalition led by the United States to a stalemate on the Korean Peninsula after a century of imperialist humiliation allowed the Chinese Communist Party to rebuild the country by mobilizing (and then disenfranchising) the bourgeoisie, installing a technocratic elite, and establishing durable, gargantuan centralized ministries. Moreover, this was a regime that understood the importance and variability of local conditions, and it delegated a significant amount of decision-making to local cadres throughout its continent-sized landmass. Although initially reliant on scattered remnants of the ancien régime, the new authorities could superimpose their vision, and the two remained compatible as they evolved in the direction of what would be a natural progress toward Marxist (and Maoist) statehood. In fact, the Chinese communists were so successful in taking over the country that they beat their own timetable by several years.

But by the same token, they also faced a premature reckoning with history. By the mid- to late 1950s, Mao was becoming increasingly preoccupied with what he saw as a betrayal of the revolution. Technocratic expertise was edging out revolutionary élan ("redness"), and the government was beginning to eclipse the party as China increasingly resembled its Soviet counterpart and moved away from China's own indigenous Marxist apparatus forged during its rise to power from

CONCLUSION

1921 through 1949. Counterrevolutionary classes continued to be present, even within the socialist society that he and his colleagues had fashioned at great cost. Even more than had been the case in the Soviet Union, Mao saw the compromises to his vision as sowing the seeds of the destruction of the Marxist experiment to which he had devoted his entire career. As ideologically charged actions against these tendencies begot economic chaos and political unease, Mao doubled down against what he deemed "revisionism," a dilution, a betrayal of the revolution, and moved increasingly leftward, unleashing the Anti-Rightist Campaign, the Great Leap Forward, the Socialist Education Movement, and ultimately the Cultural Revolution.

And yet, by the early 1970s, widespread cynicism had replaced seemingly boundless revolutionary enthusiasm; foreign policy revolved around rapprochement with China's existential opponent, the United States; and amidst centrifugal elite politics, a pragmatic political line threatened (and eventually supplanted) the more radical vision that was closer to Mao's own heart and political proclivities. It was thus at this historical moment, as noted in the introduction, that Mao met with the new victors of the Cambodian revolution, advising them to resist compromising their beliefs and essentially telling them that they

FIGURE 7.1. Khmer Rouge leaders meet with Mao Zedong, June 1975. CPA Media Pte Ltd / Alamy Stock Photo.

held the key to an unadulterated revolutionary society that China had been unable to deliver.

Mao needn't have worried. This obsession with the unforgiving laws of inexorable progress among Khmer Rouge leaders goes all the way back to the 1950s. A former student of Ieng Thirith recalls that during an oral examination in 1955, she asked him whether a two-headed snake was better than a one-headed snake. He responded that the two-headed snake was better because it had two brains. Thirith corrected him by explaining that a two-headed snake would be bogged down by two different sets of opinions, rendering it indecisive, and thus would be unable to move forward as rapidly as a one-headed snake.[7]

Pol Pot and Ieng Sary embodied the requisite arrogance to bulldoze through any impediments that would prevent the imposition of this pure vision onto the Cambodian state they had just liberated. And by the time they visited Mao in Beijing, they had already started doing so. In this sense, the sheer ambitiousness of emptying cities and eliminating class distinctions (and the physical liquidation of exploiting classes) that made up Year Zero came as close to an experiment for the viability of Marxist governance in its purest form as history was ever likely to see. Only in the laboratory of Democratic Kampuchea were conditions so perfectly aligned for testing out a Marxism that was ultra-orthodox and über-radical, unalloyed and unadulterated.

The modest intellectual talents of the Khmer Rouge's top leadership arguably *enhanced* this natural experiment. Their mediocrity manifested itself in an unquestioning arrogance, a lack of self-reflection, and an utter rejection of the need for, or desirability of, adaptability. And akin to the force of physics, it is precisely this mediocrity that nurtured the possibility, even the inevitability, of a radical class-based politics so completely bereft of nuance and without the slightest concern for mitigating circumstances. Top PDK leaders were too unimaginative to pull any punches, to stray from the blueprint. Mediocrity was not responsible for the shortcomings of the Khmer Rouge's policies; it was responsible for their very *makeup*.

The Sweep of History

Given this extraordinary opportunity to establish such unadulterated conditions for Marxist governance within a real-world context, how did the CPK regime fare from 1975 to 1979 on the policy front? Terribly, as it turns out. If, as Marxist doctrine goes, property created classes and classes were responsible for exploitation as well as uneven and unfair distribution of societal production, then with the abolition of property and of classes, the result should be efficient production and distortion-free distribution of goods and services. That is not what happened in Democratic Kampuchea.

Despite the conventional wisdom, it would be historically inaccurate to assert that Cambodia was a land of plenty before the 1970s.[8] If that had been true, there would likely not have been the series of circumstances—beginning with the Samlaut Rebellion of 1967—that put into motion the events that led to the CPK victory of 1975. The reality for many of Cambodia's peasants was that they were perhaps a harvest or two away from starvation. Moreover, the quality of life in the countryside was generally miserable. One can make the somewhat controversial argument that life for the "base people," that is, the poor peasantry, particularly in the underdeveloped regions of the country, was at least comparable before and after 1975.

The "Four-Year Plan in All Fields" sought to change this and transform the country overnight. During this time, Sary sought to draw international support and legitimacy for the regime, Mok oversaw and enforced the slave labor of the Cambodian people, and Son Sen and his apparatus "smashed" those who fell short. But the plan flopped nonetheless. Owing to a combination of impossible targets that were determined by doctrine—and not by scientific agricultural laws, let alone local conditions—and enforced by the state's well-developed coercive capacity, particularly from 1976 onward, the state failed in its most fundamental objective: feeding its own population. Democratic Kampuchea did export substantial amounts of its rice harvest abroad,[9] but it is not clear whether it would have significantly changed starvation conditions at home. To be sure, flawed export policies are hardly necessary as an explanation for the widespread starvation during the Democratic Kampuchea period; its agriculture policy—the bedrock of the regime's future success—was sufficiently flawed on its own.[10]

At the same time, a dramatic increase in manufacturing was very much seen as an aspirational, even necessary, goal, given the doctrine of self-sufficiency. The official crest of Democratic Kampuchea placed manufacturing, which was generally limited to textiles, crafts, rubber, and other traditional areas of Cambodia's pre-1975 economy, above agriculture. Indeed, the goal of increasing agricultural output was to provide the material conditions for development of a manufacturing capacity and eventually industrial transformation. With the failure of requisite agricultural stocks, none of these other initiatives could move forward.[11]

CPK cadres also mobilized the population and employed human wave tactics to build infrastructure with decidedly mixed results. At one extreme were projects like the retrofitting of the petroleum facilities at Kampong Som, which became a dark comedy of errors as Chinese expatriate managers and workers marveled at the incompetence and inconsistencies exhibited by their Cambodian colleagues. Much of that was due to a combination of a lack of training (to avoid creating an intellectual class) as well as the fact that today's manager could be, and often was, tomorrow's victim of the continually ongoing purge of CPK ranks. At the other extreme was the Krang Leav airfield, built by the slave labor of demobilized soldiers and eventually—under even more harsh conditions—victims of the Eastern Zone purge, overseen by Son Sen and Mok. And yet the quality of the basic infrastructure was so good that barely a blade of grass exists on the immaculate tarmac. Somewhere in between lay projects like the Trapeang Thma (ត្រពាំងថ្ម) and the January 1st/January 6th dams, which were tens of miles long (all built by hand), and which, perhaps inevitably, became inoperable because of the hubris of privileging revolutionary zeal over technical competence.[12]

Many, although by no means all, of these projects included direct involvement of the Khmer Rouge military, whether for mobilization, enforcement, or, in some cases such as Krang Leav, participation. Son Sen and Mok thus were responsible for operationalizing these keystone Khmer Rouge policies during the Democratic Kampuchea period. Ieng Sary was largely divorced from overseeing all this, although he exploited these projects by leading numerous delegation visits abroad, where he used these "successes" to legitimize the regime among potentially sympathetic governments (Sweden, Singapore), much as he had, earlier on, enticed Cambodian expatriates to return to the motherland.

Given all the foregoing—given that the conditions for the doctrinally specified success of an ultra-orthodox Marxist revolution were so favorable—the failure of the Khmer Rouge could, to its leaders, be chalked up to one and only one reason: enemies on the outside and on the inside seeking to undermine it. In chapter 2 we saw how class struggle played out in the Democratic Kampuchea era, with Son Sen and *Ta* Mok in leading roles. In chapter 6 we saw it play out in the mid-1990s, again with Son Sen and Mok taking charge. In the latter case, most of the conditions facing the PDK were considerably less conducive to

CONCLUSION

movement success. By 1994, the international situation was not at all auspicious for the PDK, and yet it continued to undertake draconian policies that closely resembled those it had undertaken from 1975 to 1979. This second coming of class struggle did not last long enough to provide a robust comparison, but what is at least equally important here is that the PDK's response to external conditions was demonstrably inelastic: whether the international context was favorable or not, CPK/PDK policies were the same.

Images of the refugee camps along the Thai-Cambodian border from 1979 onward do not provide much of a visual illustration of class differences. Indeed, what we do see can be quite distorted. There are images of relatively healthy Khmer Rouge refugees who were the "base people." Standing in contrast to the often more malnourished "new people"/former city dwellers/bourgeoisie, this traditionally exploited class clearly had fared better than the emaciated walking corpses that CPK class enemies had become. By then, distinctions between peasants and proletarians were largely irrelevant, as the CPK engaged in a form of "war communism" that continued to flatten class distinctions. But that did not mean that such distinctions were completely absent. In fact, the KPNLF and FUNCINPEC, and particularly the Vietnamese-led SoC, provided all the class enemies the PDK needed. For much of the 1980s, however, the first two were opportunistically accepted by the Khmer Rouge as its united front partners. But as CPK/PDK policies became more draconian around 1994, anybody who resisted—as had been the case in the 1970s—was by very definition a class enemy.

As we have seen, for the first half of the post-1979 period, Ieng Sary was instrumental in forging and maintaining the legitimacy and viability of the PDK in securing the second united front, while Mok provided the military victories the PDK needed to translate into political power within that united front framework. Son Sen likewise leaned into his role as battlefield commander but started tacking toward a more political role by the late 1980s and early 1990s. His attempt to transform the PDK into a credible political force to compete with if not colonize an electoral system (as it had in the early 1970s vis-à-vis the united front) met with dramatic failure. Pol Pot himself seems to have wavered but eventually soured on the entire electoral experiment, more closely aligning himself with Mok, who had been contemptuous of the entire united front and electoral strategies from the get-go.

And so, even though the situations facing the CPK/PDK in 1975 and 1994 could not have been more different, the response was identical:

shifting to violent class struggle. After all, objective conditions could not possibly have any impact on the only possible course of action. Although one's conclusions must remain speculative, it is reasonable to assume that to his last breath, Pol Pot believed that his movement was the only one to have maintained the purity necessary to inevitably succeed. All who had come before had compromised and ultimately failed the logic of historical materialism, betraying the promise of Marxism. Or as Pol Pot himself maintained throughout his life, *nobody*—including Ieng Sary and Son Sen—got it right because they ended up watering it down.

But of course, he didn't get it right either. That is because he failed to see the conundrum inherent in successful revolutionary movements: the vast chasm between the revolutionary rise to power on the one hand and the mundane realities of governance on the other. The Khmer Rouge leaders sought to resolve this profound challenge—how to preserve ideological purity and revolutionary transformation within a functioning state that requires political trade-offs and compromises, predictability, institutional integrity, and sound economic policies—by denying its very existence. In doing so, by refusing to acknowledge the moderate political space crucial for effective, viable governance, the Khmer Rouge condemned itself to two—and *only* two—distinct courses of action: to united front and, when that was no longer viable, to class struggle.

The friability of this universe of action made the extinction of the Khmer Rouge as inevitable as—to Marx, Lenin, Mao, and Pol Pot—that of capitalism. In the end, the movement was not simply a heartless victimizer on a historic scale; it was itself ultimately a victim of the equally pitiless, unsentimental sweep of history. Its ideologues—Pol Pot and Nuon Chea—as well as its enforcers—Ieng Sary, Son Sen, and *Ta* Mok—have become little more than historical cautionary tales.

In History's Wake

And yet their efforts have not entirely disappeared. In January 2013, I spent an entire morning interviewing Yung Moeun (យង់ មឿន), Pol Pot's former cook.[13] Her story is instructive, if not exactly typical. In the mid-1960s she was enrolled as a student in a school in Kampong Cham, where her brother was a teacher. But by the time of the 1967 Samlaut Rebellion, her "anticolonial feelings" had spurred her to join the movement in Ratanakiri. After Lon Nol came to power in 1970, she joined an army unit of female CPK soldiers in Sector 42 in the old Northern Zone. These young female (ស្រី) troops were tasked with motivating families to allow their children to join the revolution. They also worked on producing agricultural products and food for the (male) soldiers while simultaneously managing the rear/base areas while the male soldiers fought at the front.

By 1973 Moeun was appointed chief of the female combatant units for Area 304 as well as in Area 31. She was responsible for Sector 43's five districts (Steung Trâng, Chamkar Leu, Kampong Siem, Tang Kok, and Baray), and became secretary of Tang Kok (កងឃុំកក). Moeun attributed her success to her personality, which was—indeed—quite effervescent.[14] She volunteered that she would always try (though she did not always succeed) to prevent people from being "sent away" by moving them around to other areas she administered. She referred to herself as an "intuitive" revolutionary, not a dogmatic one.

Moeun remained in this area until 1975. Following April 17, she moved to Tang Kok district and went to work with Ieng Sary at the Foreign Ministry's "curved house" (ផ្ទះវៀកខ) at B1. She received training and was subsequently dispatched to Beijing, where her husband, Pich Chean, was ambassador. She was first consul, in charge of political, economic, and internal affairs; she was also, more pointedly, the CPK secretary of the embassy, responsible for the thousand or so Cambodians—civilian and military—studying in China. Moeun said that during that time she never communicated directly with 87/870 but she did with Ieng Sary, as did her husband. Whereas the ambassador did so for issues of government and administration as it related to the Foreign Ministry, she corresponded with Sary on internal CPK matters. When I asked her to describe a typical day or a typical week, Moeun's response made it sound oppressively bureaucratic (memos, logistics, attending to the minutiae of Chinese protocol, down to who sits next to whom at what tables, and so on).[15]

But what became astonishingly clear over the course of the interview was how much affection Moeun still had for Pol Pot. His staff loved him, she gushed, because he was never boring or uninspiring, as other officials could often be. He was "always interesting." Brother Number 1 also apparently had a very dry sense of humor and would use it to great effect. For instance, as Moeun recounted, Pol Pot would never criticize somebody for doing something; rather, he would say the opposite in an expression of irony, and people would immediately understand. When we chatted about Pol Pot's legacy, her response was deeply resonant with the sentiments of days of yore: "The spirit of Pol Pot is to be against Vietnam.... [T]his spirit still exists, but not with everybody." After our formal interview concluded, we had lunch at her restaurant in Anlong Veng, where she waxed nostalgic about the absence of corruption during the Pol Pot era and the clarifying simplicity of life back then, at least for her.

While Moeun was clearly a swooning revolutionary romantic, if not quite an ideologue, other former Khmer Rouge officials were more opportunistic. At the time of Ieng Sary's defection in 1996, entire armies were coming over to the CPP or FUNCINPEC sides, promised amnesty and, in some cases, a position within the government. Of course, this was a practice that had come from the very top. Some two decades earlier, Hun Sen—who had lost an eye during the final 1975 offensive on Phnom Penh—was part of a group of Eastern Zone Khmer Rouge commanders under So Phim who saw the grim writing on the wall and, in order to avoid what increasingly seemed like certain death during the great purge of the Eastern Zone, defected over the border to Vietnam.

From the mid-1990s onward, many key Khmer Rouge officials exploited the opportunities provided by Hun Sen's self-touted "win-win" strategy of enticing Khmer Rouge to likewise defect and become part of the Cambodian government or, at the very least, be granted amnesty. Y Chhean and Sok Pheap barely escaped with their lives after talks with *Ta* Mok broke down, as recounted in chapter 6.[16] They were instrumental in getting Ieng Sary himself to defect. Y Chhean eventually rose to become the secretary of state within the Ministry of National Defense, while Sok Pheap became undersecretary of state.[17] Former Khmer Rouge air force commander Sou Met resided in Battambang and served as an adviser to Hun Sen's Ministry of Defense. General Pol Saroeun, once vice chair of the Khmer Rouge Eastern Zone General Staff, which included supervision over the zone-level S79 Security Office, became supreme commander of the Royal Cambodian Armed Forces and thereafter senior minister for special missions. General Kun Kim, who spent the Democratic Kampuchea era as chair of the Tbaung Khmum district Security Office in the zone's Sector 21, took up the position of deputy supreme commander of RCAF and chief of the RCAF Mixed General Staff, and subsequently senior minister for special missions, first vice chairperson of the National Committee for Disaster Management, and secretary-general of the Cambodian Veterans Association.[18] And, of course, Kè Pauk defected in 1998 and served as a general in the Cambodian military until his death in 2002. There are many more.

This political proximity of current and recent leadership to the Khmer Rouge legacy is a source of awkwardness, with a decidedly sinister edge. The ECCC had been created to take on cases of crimes against humanity leveled at Kaing Guek-Eav (Case 001) and those of Ieng Sary, Nuon Chea, Khieu Samphân, and Ieng Thirith (Case 002), with no small amount of resistance and foot-dragging on the part of Hun Sen.[19] Subsequent attempts to bring others to trial—the previously mentioned Sou Met and Meas Muth (Case 003) as well as Ao An, Yim Tith, and Im Chæm (Case 004)—were deemed by Hun Sen a bridge too far.[20] As a 2020 Open Society report notes: "The 003 and 004 series of cases have been divisive since the day the international co-prosecutor announced his decision to pursue them. The government of Cambodia has been vocal that it does not wish the cases to proceed and the Cambodian officials on the court have taken every decision available to them to deliver that result." Indeed, as the report continues, the standoff between the Cambodian and international sides "reached a new height of legal absurdity when the two co-investigating judges issued separate and contradictory closing orders." Instead of either an indictment that would send the case to trial or an order that would dismiss the case, "the Cambodian judge issued a dismissal order and the international judge issued an indictment for genocide and crimes against humanity."[21] But with the deaths of the defendants, it is a practical certainty that these and other cases will never be heard.

Embedding History in the Everyday

The imprint left by the Khmer Rouge movement is not limited to the individual lives and deaths of these and other high- and mid-level cadres. It extends across and all the way down to the bottom of Cambodia's social system. In 2006 the anthropologist Krisna Uk described life in O'Neang (អូរណាង) village in Pailin province, Ieng Sary's former power base, which was at its core a continuation of Khmer Rouge life and livelihood. O'Neang sits perched along, and reined in by, the K5 land mine belt, and its physical character and politics are intimately associated with the unexploded ordnance laid down by the Khmer Rouge over the prior two decades. The village, established in 1998 by ten Khmer Rouge cadre families who feared retaliation if they returned to their home villages, had grown to twenty-five times that size within a few years. This influx had not diluted the founding families' political power; indeed, it had provided them more outlets through which to exercise and reinforce their dominance. In addition to having procured the best land for themselves, the founding villagers had been in the Khmer Rouge military units that scattered the surrounding land mines (at a rate of two hundred per day, sometimes for months on end), so they knew exactly where they were buried—an extraordinarily potent example of informational asymmetry that greatly disadvantaged the newer settlers.[22]

While real power eventually became concentrated among four or five former Khmer Rouge families, the two individuals with the largest landholdings, whom Uk calls "Big Sister" (formerly the cadre tasked with forcibly moving the population from the southeastern part of the country to the Northwest Zone) and "Big Brother," sit at the pinnacle of village power and politics. As Uk observes, these individuals "have built their political authority on their background, reputation and present connections beyond the village boundaries. They hold decision-making power over all social and economic matters in the village and the role of the [official] village chief is thus essentially a clerical one. The brotherhood among the village elite is forged in the history of the Khmer Rouge—its members have all been involved in the DK regime and resistance against the Vietnamese."[23]

Even the new socioeconomic relationships have incorporated old Khmer Rouge repertoires, in this case class struggle, where "class" has been flipped to benefit the economic "haves" and the struggle is now simply over raw political power. For example, in July 2003, following a dustup with Big Sister, Mom, a poor farmer, was weeding her land when she stepped on a land mine. What made this more disturbing than simply another tragic land mine accident is that the land "had *already been cleared* by a national clearance agency."[24] In other words, it was placed there after official hostilities ended but at a time when parochial conflict became the coin of the local realm.

In another case, a peasant named May took a shortcut, trespassing on Big Sister's land, to which the latter responded by stabbing May in the eye, warning her, "Be careful, don't be too strong" (ប្រយ័ត្នកុំ ខ្លាំងពេក). It had been downhill for May ever since then, noted Uk, as she became "both socially marginalised and subject to frequent intimidation.... The walls of the house they now occupy have been scrawled with curses telling her to leave and Big Sister's son sometimes sleeps beneath the building in order to spy on her."[25]

CONCLUSION

O'Neang is not a one-off. Even in the border camps described in chapter 4, Mary Kay Magstad observed in the 1980s that "one Khmer Rouge family in Site Two camp (run by the KPNLF), still praises Khmer Rouge policies. The father was a Khmer Rouge sub-district officer. When he argues with neighbors, he has been heard to say, 'If it were still [the] Pol Pot [era], I'd kill you.'"[26] According to Uk, Ieng Sary's—and subsequently Nuon Chea's—former stronghold of Pailin also "remains a KR fiefdom where former leaders hold significant influence over the political and social life of the area in which some former KR practices [are allowed] to survive."[27] Although one must be careful about generalizing too much from a part of the country with a larger than usual concentration of former Khmer Rouge cadres—that requires a book of its own—it does tell us that the half-life of the Khmer Rouge was not extinguished by the arrest of Nuon Chea, described at the beginning of this chapter. The Communist Party of Kampuchea's legacy—the lifetime of efforts forged by the likes of Ieng Sary, Son Sen, and *Ta* Mok—continues to endure, living on like Hydra's teeth strewn about the rust-red Cambodian soil.

Selected Glossary

Angkar (អង្គការ): the Organization
Angkar Leu (អង្គការលើ): the upper echelon of the CPK
Angkar Padevat (អង្គការបដិវត្តន៍): the Revolutionary Organization
Anlong Veng (អន្លង់វែង): town in Oddar Meanchey province, stronghold of Mok
B1: Ministry of Foreign Affairs
B30: tempering facility under the Ministry of Foreign Affairs
B32: tempering facility under the Ministry of Foreign Affairs
baht: Thai unit of currency
"base people" (អ្នកមូលដ្ឋាន): politically privileged demographic of peasants living in liberated areas during the Cambodian civil war, 1970-1975
Boeng Trabek (បឹងត្របែក): tempering facility under the Ministry of Foreign Affairs
Borai Khmer Rouge refugee camp
"brother" (បង): traditional form of informal address for (male) peers
chhlôp (ឈ្លប): youth militia
Chhrang Chamreh (M1, B60/ច្រាំងចម្រេះ): tempering facility under the Ministry of Foreign Affairs
Corridor 1001 (ច្រក១០០១): area under Son Sen's control from the early 1980s until 1991; subsequently combined with 1003 to form Corridor 1008
Corridor 1003 (ច្រក១០០៣): area under Mok's control from the 1980s until 1991; subsequently combined with 1001 to form Corridor 1008
Corridor 1005 (ច្រក១០០៥): refers (incorrectly) to 1008
Corridor 1008 (ច្រក១០០៨): consolidated area (combining 1001 and 1003) under Mok after 1991
Dângrêk Mountains (ភ្នំដងរែក): mountain range marking the northern Cambodian border with Thailand
Eastern (បូព៌ា) Zone: Democratic Kampuchea subnational unit of government bordering Vietnam that took the brunt of pre-1979 border skirmishes; led by Sao Phim until his purge in 1978
Front 32 military counterpart of Site 8/Sector 102
Jaraï (ចារាយ): highland minority group closely associated with the CPK beginning in the 1960s

SELECTED GLOSSARY

K5 Project (ផែនការកណ្ដ): Vietnamese/PRK plan to seal off guerrilla infiltration routes between 1985 and 1989

Kbal Tonsaong (ក្បាលទន្សោង): site of Pol Pot's bunker and final hideaway in the Dângrêk Mountains

Khao I Dang (ខាវអ៊ីដាង): United Nations High Commission for Refugees (UNHCR) facility, unaffiliated with Cambodian factions

Khmer Issarak (ខ្មែរឥស្សរៈ): "liberated" or "free" Khmer; anticolonial Khmer forces based in Cambodian countryside

Khmer Krom (ខ្មែរក្រោម): "Lowland Khmer": ethnic Khmer from southern Vietnam

Khmer Leu (ខ្មែរលើ): "Highland Khmer"

Khmer Rouge (ខ្មែរក្រហម): term coined by Norodom Sihanouk to refer to the Cambodian communists

Khmer Rumdas/Khmer Rumdoh (ខ្មែររំដោះ): "Royalist" Khmer, 1970–1975; CPK coalition partner

Khmer Sâr (ខ្មែរស): "White Khmer" (same as Royalist Khmer), 1970–1975; CPK coalition partner

khsae (ខ្សែ): personal network (literally "string/cable")

Malai (ម៉ាឡៃ): western Cambodian town that, along with Pailin, was Ieng Sary's base of operations

Mondulkiri (មណ្ឌលគិរី): northeastern province, early site of CPK headquarters

"new people" (អ្នកថ្មី): urban evacuees sent to the countryside in 1975 and placed at the very bottom of the CPK political hierarchy

nôkôrôbal (នគរបាល): the secret police system

Northwest (ពាយ័ព្យ) **Zone:** Democratic Kampuchea subnational unit of government led by Nhim Ros (purged 1976) and subsequently by Kè Pauk

O'Trao Khmer Rouge refugee camp

Office 100 Pol Pot's pre-revolutionary base of operations

Office 87/870 (99, 101, 131): Pol Pot's post-1979 office(s)

Om (អុំ): term of high respect toward people older than one's parents

Pailin (ប៉ៃលិន): traditional gemstone-mining province in northwest Cambodia and site of Ieng Sary's power base

Phnom Kulen (ភ្នំគូលេន): CPK base area during the Cambodian civil war (1970–1975)

phum (ភូមិ): village

Preah Vihear (ព្រាសាទព្រះវិហារ): temple on the Thai-Cambodian border

puok (ពួក): group

Ratanakiri (រតនគិរី): northeastern province, early site of CPK headquarters

Samlaut (សំឡូត): site of 1967 peasant rebellion that animated the CPK

SELECTED GLOSSARY

sàntĭbal (សន្តិបាល): secret police under the Khmer Rouge (literally "keeper of peace")

sàntĭsok (សន្តិសុខ): state security bureaucracy

Site 2: KPNLF refugee camp

Site 8/Sector 102: Khmer Rouge refugee camp (under Ieng Sary)

Site B: FUNCINPEC refugee camp

Site K/Koh Kong: Khmer Rouge refugee camp

Sokh Sann/Sok San: KPNLF refugee camp

Southwest (និរតី) Zone: Democratic Kampuchea subnational unit of government led by Mok

Ta (តា): "grandfather"/term of high respect

Ta Khmau/B64 (តាខ្មៅ): capital of Kandal province and site of B1 work camps

Ta Luan: Khmer Rouge refugee camp

Tuol Sleng (ទួលស្លែង)/S21: torture and confession (and, briefly, execution) center in southwestern Phnom Penh, 1976–1979

"uncle" (ពូ): traditional Cambodian form of respectful address to a superior

Yuon (យួន): derogatory term for Vietnamese

Zone (ភូមិភាគ): Highest subnational administrative level in Democratic Kampuchea

NOTES

Introduction

1. Chandler, *Tragedy of Cambodian History*, 311.
2. E3_106_EN.PDF, interview transcript, Steve Heder with Ieng Sary, December 17, 1996, 41.
3. Ashley, "The End of the Revolution," 1.
4. Chandler, *Brother Number One*; Short, *Pol Pot*; and Becker, *When the War Was Over*.
5. Ashley, "The End of the Revolution," 2.
6. Comintern, *Protokoll des Vierten Kongresses der Kommunistischen Internationale*, cited in Riddell, "The Origins of the United Front Policy."
7. Trotsky, *The First Five Years of the Communist International*.
8. Karl Marx and Friedrich Engels, "Appeal to the Central Committee of the Communist League," quoted in Kolakowski, *Main Currents of Marxism*, 1:302.
9. Kolakowski, *Main Currents of Marxism*, 1:304.
10. The slogan "if someone is very hungry, the Angkar [organization] will take him where he will be stuffed with food" (បើមនណាហ្យានខ្លាំងអង្គការនឹង នាំទៅកន្លែងសម្បូរហូបចុក) is a warning to people that if they complain about hunger, they will swiftly be killed and, by implication, fertilize the ground in which they are buried. Locard, *Pol Pot's Little Red Book*, 204.
11. Kolakowski, *Main Currents of Marxism*, 3:38.
12. Burgler, *The Eyes of the Pineapple*, 67.
13. The Cambodian delegation included Pol Pot; Ieng Sary; Ney Saran, aka Ya (sinicized as Ming Shan); Siet Chhe, alias Tum (sinicized as Du Mu); and Chhěum Sàm-aok, alias Pâng (sinicized as Peng). As Ya had been handling CPK supply lines coming through the Northeast and Tum was or was about to become an RAK General Staff vice chairperson, this delegation seems to have had arranging PRC military aid as a major agenda item. Pâng was there as Pol's chief aide at 87/870 Office S71. See also https://www.eccc.gov.kh/sites/default/files/documents/courtdoc/00183246-00183280_E3_1596_EN-35.TXT.pdf. English translation: https://digitalarchive.wilsoncenter.org/document/122052.
14. Yang, *Biography of Ai Siqi* [艾思奇传].
15. Mao Zedong, "Speech at the Hangzhou Conference," December 21, 1965. Mao was in fact referring to the Chinese Communist Party's relationship with *its* united front partner, the Nationalist Party.

16. Interview Number 4 (Sauv Kim Hong), Kao I Dang, February 29, 1980, in "Interviews with Kampuchean Refugees at Thai-Cambodia Border," Steve Heder's private collection.

17. Chandler, Kiernan, and Boua, *Pol Pot Plans the Future*, 125.

18. See, inter alia, Steinmo and Thelen, *Structuring Politics*; Pierson, "Increasing Returns, Path Dependence, and the Study of Politics"; Kalyvas, *The Logic of Violence in Civil War*; and Staniland, *Networks of Rebellion*.

19. See, for example, Chandler, Kiernan, and Boua, *Pol Pot Plans the Future*.

20. Peschoux, interview with V, April 1990.

21. UNCOHCHR, "Talk with Om Van," Phum Dong, Malai, January 26, 1997, Steve Heder's private collection.

22. Heder, "Khieu Samphân and Pol Pot," Steve Heder's private collection.

23. Interview of Long Norin (Secretary General of DNUM), Phum Dong, Malai, January 24, 1997, Steve Heder's private collection.

24. "Information from Mr. Phi Phuon aka Cheam," Interviews conducted at Phum Dong Village, Phnom Malai, Banteay Meanchey Province, September 27, 1996, 12, Steve Heder's private collection.

25. Chandler, *Brother Number One*; Short, *Pol Pot*. See also Becker, *When the War Was Over*.

26. Ashley, "The End of the Revolution," 2.

27. For the sake of full disclosure, I worked as a consultant for the Ieng Thirith defense team at the ECCC from 2010 to 2011.

28. Conversation with Steve Heder. By this point Thirith was suffering from acute dementia, which ultimately exempted her from prosecution.

29. Lest this be interpreted as an exoneration of Sary, let me be clear that the moral case for Sary's guilt by association is unassailable. He did enforce—or allow to be enforced—purges that took place within the Foreign Ministry, as well as other actions that directly or indirectly led to the deaths of hundreds, even thousands, of Cambodians. As we shall see, however, his place in this hierarchy of persecution and death was on a different scale from those of the other individuals discussed in subsequent chapters, particularly Son Sen and *Ta* Mok.

30. Transcription of Ieng Thirith's 1980 audio interview by Elizabeth Becker, 6, Steve Heder's private collection.

31. When people are referred to as "cats" in Cambodia, it means that they are seen as sneaky, untruthful, and not to be trusted. The image of a broken teapot—with its bent spout—indicates that a person is a liar. Interview 21DC01A, Washington, DC, October 10, 2021.

32. Corfield and Summers, *Historical Dictionary of Cambodia*, 166-67.

33. Transcription of Ieng Thirith's 1980 audio interview by Elizabeth Becker, 4.

34. Becker, *When the War Was Over*, 72, 78.

35. Huang, *Factionalism in Chinese Communist Politics*, 8.

36. This, of course, raises one of the biggest questions of all: Since Pol Pot also did not have a mountaintop of his own, what explains *his* dominance? Although a complete answer to this question is beyond the scope of this book,

part of the answer lies in the key role played by Nuon Chea and the complementary roles he and Pol Pot brought to the apex of power in the movement.

37. Conversation with Steve Heder, June 1, 2020.
38. Conversation with Peter Bartu, May 3, 2023.
39. This is captured in an uninterrupted, unedited handheld video I made of the road between the Thai black market stalls all the way to Pol Pot's bunker at Kbal Tonsaong in June 2009. See https://youtu.be/HlqgwiVec24.
40. Interview 20AV05, Anlong Veng, July 5, 2020.
41. Seth Mydans, "Khmer Rouge Said to Execute a Top Aide on Pol Pot's Order," *New York Times*, June 14, 1997.
42. Wood, "Tracing the Last Breath," 207–8.
43. Mertha, *Brothers in Arms*, 40–41.
44. Interview Number 32, Mai Rut, March 15, 1980, in "Interviews with Kampuchean Refugees at Thai-Cambodia Border," 65, Steve Heder's private collection.
45. Locard, *Jungle Heart of the Khmer Rouge*, 81.
46. Conversation with Peter Bartu, May 3, 2023.
47. "The Life and Crimes of Ta Mok," *Phnom Penh Post*, January 16, 1998.
48. Interview 20SR01, Siem Reap, July 6, 2020.
49. Kè Pauk, "Ke Pauk's Autobiography from 1949–1985."
50. Interview 20PL01, Pailin, July 7, 2020.
51. Peschoux, interview with S, August 1990, 5.
52. Heder, *Cambodian Communism and the Vietnamese Model*, 29.
53. Ea, *The Chain of Terror*, 30; Heder and Tittemore, *Seven Candidates for Prosecution*, 100; Becker, *When the War Was Over*, 190–91.
54. Becker, *When the War Was Over*, 190–91; Ea, *The Chain of Terror*, 30.
55. Heder, *Cambodian Communism and the Vietnamese Model*, 139.
56. Interview Number 18, Sakeo, March 8, 1980, in "Interviews with Kampuchean Refugees at Thai-Cambodia Border," 32–33, Steve Heder's private collection.
57. Becker, *When the War Was Over*, 1998 edition, 177.
58. Interview 20SR01, Siem Reap, July 6, 2020; Interview 20PL01, Pailin, July 7, 2020.
59. Interview 20PS01, Pursat, August 14, 2020.
60. Interview of *Ta* Mok by Nate Thayer, undated, Steve Heder's private collection.
61. Martine, *Cambodia*, 96–99.

1. The First United Front

1. https://www.eccc.gov.kh/en/indicted-person/ieng-sary.
2. Corfield and Summers, *Historical Dictionary of Cambodia*, 167.
3. Chandler, *Voices from S-21*, 19.
4. Kiernan, *How Pol Pot Came to Power*, 197.
5. D86/4, Extraordinary Chambers in the Courts of Cambodia, Office of the Co-Investigating Judges (hereafter ECCC), Written Record of Charged Person, Kaing Guek-Eav, alias Duch, August 23, 2007, 4.

6. Interview of Son Sen, April 8, 1980, Steve Heder's private collection.

7. Interview Number 28, Navy Camp 62, Chanthaburi, March 11, 1989, in "Interviews with Kampuchean Refugees at Thai-Cambodia Border," 51, Steve Heder's private collection.

8. The Sangkum Reastr Niyum (សង្គមរាស្ត្រនិយម) was the political party founded by Sihanouk.

9. Short, *Pol Pot*, 161-62.

10. Short, *Pol Pot*, 173.

11. Colm and Sim, *Khmer Rouge Purges in the Mondul Kiri Highlands Region 105*, 11.

12. D91/14, ECCC, Written Record of Interview of Witness, Saloth Ban, December 11, 2007, 3.

13. Uk, *Salvage*, 45.

14. Locard interview with Phi Phuon, quoted in Uk, *Salvage*, 42-43. Although the Jaraï continued as bodyguards for Pol Pot into the 1990s, they were not immune from the destruction wrought by the CPK. Uk, *Salvage*, 45-49.

15. Interview 09AV01, Anlong Veng, June 21, 2009.

16. Interview 15MDK03, Mondulkiri, January 27, 2015.

17. Short, *Pol Pot*, 166-67. Craig Etcheson notes, however, that scholarly opinion on Samlaut is divided. He writes, "I myself believe that the original event was spontaneous, organic peasant unrest, then Ruos [Nhim Ros] recognized the opportunity and piggy-backed on it, only to be over-ruled by Nuon Chea." Personal communication. In either case, the result was less than it otherwise might have been for the CPK at that point in its rise to power.

18. Conboy, *The Cambodian Wars*, 48.

19. Kiernan, "The Samlaut Rebellion and Its Aftermath," 10.

20. Mao, *A Single Spark Can Start a Prairie Fire*.

21. Gray, "Swimming to Cambodia: Part One," in *Swimming to Cambodia*, 28.

22. Rust, *Eisenhower and Cambodia*, 229, 277.

23. Heder, *Cambodian Communism and the Vietnamese Model*, 144.

24. Kiernan, "Pol Pot and the Kampuchean Communist Movement."

25. A historical term for Vietnam/Vietnamese that remained the general term for them after official and popular nationalism settled on it as the name for both in twentieth-century Vietnam, during which time it became increasingly racialized in Khmer discourse and considered derogatory among Vietnamese.

26. Kuong, "Report on the Communist Party of Kampuchea," 31.

27. Richardson, *China, Cambodia, and the Five Principles of Peaceful Coexistence*, 70-71, 72.

28. Colm and Sim, *Khmer Rouge Purges in the Mondul Kiri Highlands Region 105*, 22.

29. D91/10, ECCC, Written Record of Interview of Witness, Phy Phuon, December 5, 2007, 3; Short, *Pol Pot*, 172.

30. Locard, *Jungle Heart of the Khmer Rouge*, 94.

31. D91/10 ECCC, Written Record of Interview of Witness, Phy Phuon, December 5, 2007, 3; Short, *Pol Pot*, 172.

32. Colm and Sim, *Khmer Rouge Purges in the Mondul Kiri Highlands Region 105*, 25.
33. Short, *Pol Pot*, 176-77. Phi Phuon places Sary at K5 along with Pol Pot and Son Sen. Locard, *Jungle Heart of the Khmer Rouge*, 91.
34. D91/10, ECCC, Written Record of Interview of Witness, Phy Phuon, December 5, 2007, 3; Colm and Sim, *Khmer Rouge Purges in the Mondul Kiri Highlands Region 105*, 24.
35. D95, ECCC, Written Record of Charged Person, Kaing Guek-Eav alias Duch, July 15, 2008, 2; D233/7, ECCC, Written Record of Interview of Witness, In Sopheap, September 28, 2009, 3; and Le Minh Khai, "Ieng Sary and Radio Stung Treng," *Le Minh Khai's SEAsian History Blog*, https://leminhkhai.blog/ieng-sary-and-radio-stung-treng/.
36. Richardson, *China, Cambodia, and the Five Principles of Peaceful Coexistence*, 69.
37. Doreen Chen, "Documents Reveal Khmer Rouge-Era Roles of Ieng Sary and Khieu Samphân," *Cambodia Tribunal Monitor*, January 30, 2013, https://cambodiatribunal.org/2013/01/30/documents-reveal-khmer-rouge-era-roles-of-ieng-sary-and-khieu-samphan/.
38. D199/21, ECCC, Rogatory Letter Record of Civil Party Boramy Svay, June 9, 2009, 3-4.
39. Richardson, *China, Cambodia, and the Five Principles of Peaceful Coexistence*, 70-71, 76.
40. D199/14, ECCC, Rogatory Letter Record of Civil Party Martine Lefeuvre, June 2, 2009, 2-3.
41. Richardson, *China, Cambodia, and the Five Principles of Peaceful Coexistence*, 72.
42. D167, ECCC, Written Record of Interview of Witness, Suong Sikoeun, May 6, 2009, 3.
43. D115/4, ECCC, Tribunal de Grande Instance de Dijon Written Record of Witness Deposition, Laurence Picq, October 31, 2008, 2.
44. Corfield and Summers, *Historical Dictionary of Cambodia*, 156-57, 194.
45. Richardson, *China, Cambodia, and the Five Principles of Peaceful Coexistence*, 76-77; Heder and Tittemore, *Seven Candidates for the Prosecution*, 76; D91/3, ECCC, Written Record of Interview of Witness, Long Norin, December 4, 2007, 3, 8; D91/10, ECCC, Written Record of Interview of Witness, Phy Phuon, December 5, 2007, 4.
46. D115/4, ECCC, Tribunal de Grande Instance de Dijon, Written Record of Witness Deposition, Laurence Picq, October 31, 2008, 3.
47. "Material on Ieng Sary," 1, Steve Heder's private collection.
48. D91/24, ECCC, Written Record of Interview of Witness, Saloth Ban, December 11, 2007, 3.
49. Short, *Pol Pot*, 176; Colm and Sim, *Khmer Rouge Purges in the Mondul Kiri Highlands Region*, 25.
50. Locard, *Jungle Heart of the Khmer Rouge*, 81, 95, and fn. 27.
51. Short, *Pol Pot*, 212.
52. D166/117, ECCC, Written Record of Interview of Witness, Khoem Sâmhuon, March 6, 2009, 3-4.
53. Burgler, *The Eyes of the Pineapple*, 40.

54. D86/5, ECCC, Written Record of Charged Person, Kaing Guek-Eav alias Duch, October 7, 2007, 11. This could be mistaken for Sdok Saat (ស្តុកស្អាត) village.

55. Short, *Pol Pot*, 252.

56. D87, ECCC, Written Record of Charged Person, Kaing Guek-Eav alias Duch, June 2, 2008, 5–6; D86/7, ECCC, Written Record of Charged Person, Kaing Guek-Eav alias Duch, October 7, 2007, 11; D86/23, ECCC, Written Record of Charged Person, Kaing Guek-Eav alias Duch, June 2, 2008, 6; and D86/10, ECCC, Written Record of Charged Person, Kaing Guek-Eav alias Duch, September 5, 2007, 3.

57. D86/5, ECCC, Written Record of Charged Person, Kaing Guek-Eav alias Duch, October 7, 2007, 11.

58. D95, ECCC, Written Record of Charged Person, Kaing Guek-Eav alias Duch, July 15, 2008, 2; D233/7, ECCC, Written Record of Interview of Witness, In Sopheap, September 28, 2009, 3.

59. Interview 14PL05, Pailin, December 30, 2014.

60. Short, *Pol Pot*, 175.

61. Short, *Pol Pot*, 178–79.

62. David Ashley translation of Nate Thayer's interview with *Ta* Mok and Nuon Chea, 13, Steve Heder's private collection.

63. Short, *Pol Pot*, 175.

64. D46, ECCC, Written Record of Charged Person, Kaing Guek-Eav alias Duch, April 1, 2008, 3.

65. Sarin, "Nine Months in the Maquis," 54.

66. D86/7, ECCC, Written Record of Charged Person, Kaing Guek-Eav alias Duch, October 7, 2007, 10.

67. D86/23, ECCC, Written Record of Charged Person, Kaing Guek-Eav alias Duch, June 2, 2008, 3; D86/7, ECCC, Written Record of Charged Person, Kaing Guek-Eav alias Duch, October 7, 2007, 11.

68. Kiernan, *How Pol Pot Came to Power*, 315.

69. D86/27, ECCC, Written Record of Charged Person, Kaing Guek-Eav alias Duch, May 5, 2008, 14.

70. Kiernan, *How Pol Pot Came to Power*, 326–27.

71. D86/7, ECCC, Written Record of Charged Person, Kaing Guek-Eav alias Duch, October 7, 2007, 10.

72. Interview Number 29, Lonh (aka Lorn), member of the Kampong Som city Standing Committee, Navy Camp 62, Chanthaburi, March 12, 1980, in "Interviews with Kampuchean Refugees at Thai-Cambodia Border," 55, Steve Heder's private collection.

73. Short, *Pol Pot*, 173.

74. Burgler, *The Eyes of the Pineapple*, 41.

75. D119, ECCC, Written Record of Charged Person, Kaing Guek-Eav alias Duch, November 25, 2008, 8. Kè Pauk, reportedly terrified, hid under a bed once confronted with the news.

76. Bizot, *The Gate*, 250.

77. D123/2 ECCC, Written Record of Interview of Witness, Chhouk Rin, May 21, 2008, 2–3.

78. Interview Number 31, Mai Rut Holding Center, March 15, 1980, in "Interviews with Kampuchean Refugees at Thai-Cambodia Border," 64, Steve Heder's private collection.

79. D123/2 ECCC, Written Record of Interview of Witness, Chhouk Rin, May 21, 2008, 2-3.

80. William N. Harben, Association for Diplomatic Studies and Training Foreign Affairs Oral History Project, 1998, 58-59, emphasis added, https://www.adst.org/OH%20TOCs/Harben,%20William%20N.toc.pdf?_ga=2.55948331.1296246245.1561081605-268390464.1561081605.

2. Before and After Year Zero

1. David Ashley, "Brief Conversation with It Sâm, Deputy Commander of Small Division 92, Big Division 980," February 26, 1995, Steve Heder's private collection.

2. Telephone interview with Ambassador Kenneth Quinn, March 5, 2015. The regions (កំបន់) where the burning was taking place were Military Region (MR) 203 (Regions 23 and 24), MR 405 (Regions 13 and 35), and MR 697 (Region 25). Michael Vickery disagrees with Quinn's suggestion of uniformity but may be overstating his own case. Vickery, *Cambodia, 1975-1982*, 87.

3. Colm and Sim, *Khmer Rouge Purges in the Mondul Kiri Highlands Region 105*, 35.

4. Quinn, "The Origins and Development of Radical Cambodian Communism," 86.

5. Craig Etcheson, personal communication.

6. Interview 15, Sakeo, in "Interviews with Kampuchean Refugees at Thai-Cambodia Border," 28, Steve Heder's private collection.

7. Interview Number 18, Sakeo, March 8, 1980, in "Interviews with Kampuchean Refugees at Thai-Cambodia Border," 33, Steve Heder's private collection.

8. Interview Number 14 (Khem), Sakeo, March 7, 1980, in "Interviews with Kampuchean Refugees at Thai-Cambodia Border," 23-25, Steve Heder's private collection.

9. Interview Number 14 (Khem), Sakeo, March 7, 1980, in "Interviews with Kampuchean Refugees at Thai-Cambodia Border," 23-25, Steve Heder's private collection.

10. Interview Number 29 (Lonh aka Lorn), Navy Camp 62, Chanthaburi, March 12, 1980, in "Interviews with Kampuchean Refugees at Thai-Cambodia Border," 54, Steve Heder's private collection.

11. Interview Number 18, Sakeo, March 8, 1980, in "Interviews with Kampuchean Refugees at Thai-Cambodia Border," 36, Steve Heder's private collection.

12. Quinn, "The Origins and Development of Radical Cambodian Communism," 86.

13. Quinn, "The Origins and Development of Radical Cambodian Communism," 32, 33.

14. Interview Number 14 (Khem), Sakeo, March 7, 1980, in "Interviews with Kampuchean Refugees at Thai-Cambodia Border," 23–25, Steve Heder's private collection.
15. Interview 15MDK02, Mondulkiri, January 27, 2015.
16. Interview 15MDK02, Mondulkiri, January 27, 2015.
17. Interview Number 18, Sakeo, March 8, 1980, in "Interviews with Kampuchean Refugees at Thai-Cambodia Border," 36, Steve Heder's private collection.
18. Quinn, "The Origins and Development of Radical Cambodian Communism," 82, 85–86.
19. Interview 21DC01D, Washington, DC, November 7, 2021.
20. Quinn, "The Origins and Development of Radical Cambodian Communism," 76.
21. Quinn, "The Origins and Development of Radical Cambodian Communism," 76.
22. Quinn, "The Origins and Development of Radical Cambodian Communism," 84.
23. Colm and Sim, *Khmer Rouge Purges in the Mondul Kiri Highlands Region*, 33.
24. Quinn, "The Khmer Krahom Program to Create a Communist Society in Southern Cambodia," 2, 6.
25. Quinn, preface to "The Khmer Krahom Program," 7.
26. Colm and Sim, *Khmer Rouge Purges in the Mondul Kiri Highlands Region*, 34.
27. Heder, "From Pol Pot to Pen Sovan to the Villages," 4.
28. Heder, "From Pol Pot to Pen Sovan to the Villages," 5.
29. Heder, "From Pol Pot to Pen Sovan to the Villages," 5–6.
30. ECCC, "List of S-21 Prisoners," https://www.eccc.gov.kh/en/s-21-prisoner-list.
31. Ea, *The Chain of Terror*.
32. Interview 21DC01D, Washington, DC, November 7, 2021.
33. Nate Thayer, https://natethayer.typepad.com/blog/kr-personalities-ieng-sary/, emphasis added.
34. D143, ECCC, Written Record of Interview of Witness, Suong Sikoeun, March 12, 2009, 3.
35. Heder, Interview of Ieng Sary, December 17, 1995, 6, Steve Heder's private collection. The CPK also surreptitiously accepted aid from North Korea.
36. There were also at least two visitor reception houses directly managed by the Foreign Ministry: House Number 1, which was near Wat Phnom, and House Number 2, which became the Hôtel Le Royal (where the waitstaff alone numbered between fifty and sixty). There were also guesthouses in Svay Rieng, Kampong Thom, Kampong Chhnang, Siem Reap, Battambang, Pursat, and Kampong Som. Mertha, *Brothers in Arms*, 38.
37. Mertha, *Brothers in Arms*, 38.
38. Charles McDermid, "Looking Back at the 1979 People's Revolutionary Tribunal," *Phnom Penh Post*, January 26, 2007, https://www.phnompenhpost.com/national/looking-back-1979-peoples-revolutionary-tribunal.
39. In its obituary for Ieng Sary in 2013, even *The Economist* identified him as "Brother Number 3"—again greatly inflating his power and influence vis-à-vis those of Son Sen and other past Khmer Rouge leaders. "Ieng Sary," *The Economist*, April 6, 2013.

40. D91/26, ECCC, Written Record of Interview of Witness, Suong Sikoeun, December 19, 2007, 4.

41. D91/14, ECCC, Written Record of Interview of Witness, Saloth Ban, December 11, 2007, 3.

42. D168, ECCC, Written Record of Interview of Witness, Suong Sikoeun, May 7, 2009, 8.

43. D89, ECCC, Written Record of Charged Person, Kaing Guek-Eav alias Duch, June 24, 2008, 3.

44. Princess Sisowath Ayravady, "Declaration (Fait à Paris, le 22 Octobre 1989)"; and "Camp de reeducation de Beng Trebek sous la direction des Khmer Rouge (KR) dd Février 1977 au Janvier 1979," undated, in "Material on Ieng Sary," 9–10, Steve Heder's private collection.

45. "Material on Ieng Sary," 10, 13, Steve Heder's private collection. Sean An's actual relationship with Sary remains murky.

46. D89, ECCC, Written Record of Charged Person, Kaing Guek-Eav alias Duch, June 24, 2008, 3.

47. D107/3, ECCC, Written Record of Interview of Witness, Phy Phuon, September 21, 2008, 4.

48. D233/14, ECCC, Written Record of Interview of Witness, Toch Vannarith, December 22, 2009, 5–6.

49. Interview Number 4 (Ong Thing Hoeung and Sauv Kim Hong), Kao I Dang, February 29, 1980, in "Interviews with Kampuchean Refugees at Thai-Cambodia Border," 9, Steve Heder's private collection.

50. Interview Number 4 (Sauv Kim Hong), (and presumably also) Kao I Dang, February 29, 1980, in "Interviews with Kampuchean Refugees at Thai-Cambodia Border," 12, Steve Heder's private collection. This was after the purge of Pang and Savorn in mid-1978, and some of the Boeng Trabek units did come under the authority of B1.

51. "Material on Ieng Sary," 15, Steve Heder's private collection.

52. D91/3, ECCC, Written Record of Interview of Witness, Long Norin, December 4, 2007, 4.

53. Heder and Tittemore, *Seven Candidates for Prosecution*, 86.

54. D91/3, ECCC, Written Record of Interview of Witness, Long Norin, December 4, 2007, 8.

55. D199/20, ECCC, Rogatory Letter Record of Civil Party Thiounn Prasith, June 8, 2009, 4/8.

56. D91/26, ECCC, Written Record of Interview of Witness, Suong Sikoeun, December 19, 2007, 4.

57. "Material on Ieng Sary," 17, Steve Heder's private collection. The removal of these cadres to B1 was akin to Sary's assignment to Beijing: denied a mountaintop, the cadres were deprived of their power bases by being sent there. This also had the effect of further contaminating B1 as a nest of "no-good elements."

58. D87, ECCC, Written Record of Charged Person, Kaing Guek-Eav alias Duch, June 2, 2008, 4.

59. D86/10, ECCC, Written Record of Charged Person, Kaing Guek-Eav alias Duch, September 5, 2007, 4.

60. "Open Letter from Suong Sikoeun to Laurence Picq," October 5, 1996, published in the *Phnom Penh Post*, November 15–28, 1996.

61. Short, *Pol Pot*, 275.

62. So did Sary's loyalty to Brother Number 1, as well as the sheer heft of the Foreign Ministry as an A-list institution in a regime filled with C- and D-grade ministerial and other organizational units.

63. ECCC Closing Order Case 002/01n, Judgment.

64. Khieu Samphân was awarded his doctorate in economics, with a thesis titled "Cambodia's Economy and Industrial Development," from the University of Paris in 1959. See Khieu Samphân, "Cambodia's Economy and Industrial Development," trans. Laura Summers, Data Paper Number 111, Southeast Asia Program, Department of Asian Studies, Cornell University, March 1979. It has often been erroneously linked to the eventual economic program of Democratic Kampuchea, to which it bears little, if any, resemblance. It should also be noted, if in passing, that Khieu Samphân did not interact with Pol Pot in France, having arrived some two years after the latter had already returned to Cambodia.

65. Material on Ieng Sary, 13, Steve Heder's private collection.

66. Hou Youn defended his doctoral thesis in economics, titled "La Paysannerie du Cambodge et Ses Projects de Modernisation," at the University of Paris on December 14, 1955. See Galway, "Specters of Dependency."

67. Short, *Pol Pot*, 63.

68. Hou Youn was one of the first top leaders sanctioned by the regime not long after it was established, ostensibly because he opposed the abolition of currency and the lack of non-ideological incentives in economic planning. It is unclear whether he was "liquidated" at S21; there are credible alternative versions that he died trying to escape from rural detention/reeducation or even of disease.

69. Chanda, "When the Killing Had to Stop," 22.

70. Short, *Pol Pot*, 63.

71. D117, ECCC, Written Record of Charged Person, Kaing Guek-Eav alias Duch, November 19, 2008, 10; D200/9, ECCC, Written Record of Witness Interview, Norng Sophàng, March 28, 2009, 7.

72. From 1973 to 1975, before creation of the General Staff, the regional party committees controlled the brigades.

73. Chandler, *Voices from S-21*, 20.

74. In describing the village, Heder recalls that "even in the second decade of the twenty-first century, it was the back of beyond. Dogpatch. Nothing. Nowheresville. Like that place where I and my father grew up on the Iowa-Missouri border, where I look out the window and think if I still had to live here, I'd wake up every morning and cry. The Cambodian version of Livonia, Missouri." Personal conversation.

75. Corfield and Summers, *Historical Dictionary of Cambodia*, 194.

76. Heder, "From Pol Pot to Pen Sovan to the Villages," 11.

77. D88, ECCC, Written Record of Charged Person, Kaing Guek-Eav alias Duch, June 3, 2008, 4.

78. Chandler, *Voices from S-21*; Kiernan, *The Pol Pot Regime*; Hinton, *Why Did They Kill?*; Hinton, *Man or Monster?*; Tyner, *The Politics of Lists*.

79. ECCC, Trial Chamber—Trial Day 33, Case No. 001/18-07-2007-ECCC/TC, Kaing Guek-Eav, June 24, 2009; see also Ea, *The Chain of Terror*; and ECCC Co-Prosecutors' Closing Brief E457/6/1, Case 002/02, May 18, 2017.

80. Ea, *The Chain of Terror*, 31.
81. Chandler, *Voices from S-21*.
82. D88, ECCC, Written Record of Charged Person, Kaing Guek-Eav alias Duch, June 3, 2008, 7. Overall communications between Standing Committee members remained truncated: although Son Sen could contact Kè Pauk and other zone leaders directly, he could not do so with Mok, Pheum, or Foreign Minister Ieng Sary. All these communications had to go through Nuon Chea.
83. D86/8, ECCC, Written Record of Charged Person, Kaing Guek-Eav alias Duch, November 22, 2007, 6; and D87, ECCC, Written Record of Charged Person, Kaing Guek-Eav alias Duch, June 2, 2008, 3.
84. D86/24, ECCC, Written Record of Charged Person, Kaing Guek-Eav alias Duch, April 2, 2008, 2; D95, ECCC, Written Record of Charged Person, Kaing Guek-Eav alias Duch, July 15, 2008, 7.
85. D225, ECCC, Written Record of Charged Person, Kaing Guek-Eav alias Duch, October 20, 2009, 4.
86. D86/9, ECCC, Written Record of Charged Person, Kaing Guek-Eav alias Duch, November 29, 2007, 3.
87. D86/10, ECCC, Written Record of Charged Person, Kaing Guek-Eav alias Duch, September 5, 2007, 2.
88. D86/9, ECCC, Written Record of Charged Person, Kaing Guek-Eav alias Duch, November 29, 2007, 15.
89. D86/24, ECCC, Written Record of Charged Person, Kaing Guek-Eav alias Duch, February 19, 2008, 4.
90. D86/24, ECCC, Written Record of Charged Person, Kaing Guek-Eav alias Duch, February 19, 2008, 3.
91. D86/7, ECCC, Written Record of Charged Person, Kaing Guek-Eav alias Duch, October 7, 2007, 6.
92. D87, ECCC, Written Record of Charged Person, Kaing Guek-Eav alias Duch, June 2, 2008, 4.
93. D91/26, ECCC, Written Record of Interview of Witness, Suong Sikoeun, December 19, 2007, 4. Sary also had the reputation of deferring to his wife, Ieng Thirith. D167, ECCC, Written Record of Interview of Witness, Suong Sikoeun, May 6, 2009, 5.
94. Locard, *Jungle Heart of the Khmer Rouge*, 82–83. It is clear that Phi Phuon was no fan of the couple but reserved most of his contempt for Yun Yat: "She was angry about a trifle and was very hard on those around her for everything related to discipline, relationships with people and the smallest details of everyday life, such as clothing, food, or hygiene" (82).
95. Panh with Bataille, *The Elimination*, 256–57.
96. D86/27, ECCC, Written Record of Charged Person, Kaing Guek-Eav alias Duch, May 5, 2008, 12.
97. Chandler, *Voices from S-21*, 20.
98. D123/3, ECCC, Written Record of Interview of Witness, Chhouk Rin, July 29, 2008, 4.
99. Becker, *When the War Was Over*, 191. Democratic Kampuchea had six zones (ក្រុមភាគ): Northern, Northeast, Northwest, Eastern, Southwest, and Western, the last having been hived off from the larger original Southwest Zone

and was headquartered in Kampong Chhnang. There were also several special administrative units, including Phnom Penh, the Kratie autonomous sector (Sector 505), the Siem Reap/Oddar Meanchey autonomous sector (Sector 106), and the Preah Vihear autonomous sector (Sector 103). The port city of Kampong Som (formerly Sihanoukville) was directly controlled by the Center (through Mok's son-in-law Muth). Zones were divided into regions/sectors (តំបន់), which were further divided into districts (ស្រុក), then into sub-districts/communes (ឃុំ) or cooperatives (សហករណ៍), and finally individual villages (ភូមិ). Zone secretaries were automatically on the Central Committee, but only three—Southwest Zone commander *Ta* Mok, Eastern Zone commander So Phim, and special zone commander Vorn Vet—were on the Standing Committee.

100. Ea, *The Chain of Terror*, 26.
101. Becker, *When the War Was Over*, 190.
102. Heder, "From Pol Pot to Pen Sovan to the Villages," 8.
103. Becker, *When the War Was Over*, 190, 308; Heder, "From Pol Pot to Pen Sovan to the Villages," 8.
104. Skinner, *Marketing and Social Structure in Rural China*.
105. Becker, *When the War Was Over*, 190.
106. Kiernan, *The Pol Pot Regime*, 87–88.
107. D210/12, ECCC, Interview of Heng Teav, 4
108. Interview of *Ta* Mok by Nate Thayer, undated, Steve Heder's private collection.
109. Mertha, *Brothers in Arms*, 33.
110. Heder, "From Pol Pot to Pen Sovan to the Villages," 9.
111. Its military divisions were 310 and 450. Chandler, *Voices from S-21*, 62.
112. Its military divisions included 920. Colm and Sim, *Khmer Rouge Purges in the Mondul Kiri Highlands Region 105*, 45.
113. Colm and Sim, *Khmer Rouge Purges in the Mondul Kiri Highlands Region 105*, 50–51, 65–66.
114. D86/27, Interview of Duch, ECCC Transcripts, 17; D86/7, ECCC Transcripts, 10–11; but according to D427, para. 891, Nuon Chea took control of the Northeast and Eastern Zones after purges of their secretaries.
115. Heder, "From Pol Pot to Pen Sovan to the Villages," 11.
116. Heder, "From Pol Pot to Pen Sovan to the Villages," 11.
117. Kè Pauk, "Ke Pauk's Autobiography from 1949–1985."
118. Kè Pauk, "Ke Pauk's Autobiography from 1949–1985."
119. Becker, *When the War Was Over*, 250.
120. D86/7, ECCC, Written Record of Charged Person, Kaing Guek-Eav alias Duch, October 7, 2007, 11.
121. Interview Number 23, Sa Keo, Um Samang, from Region 21, Eastern region, March 10, 1980, in "Interviews with Kampuchean Refugees at Thai-Cambodia Border," 45, Steve Heder's private collection.
122. Short, *Pol Pot*, 178.
123. D123/3, ECCC, Written Record of Interview of Witness, Chhouk Rin, July 29, 2008, 4–5; D234/21, ECCC, Written Record of Witness Interview, Chhouk Rin, November 26, 2009, 3.
124. Short, *Pol Pot*, 385.

125. D166/166, ECCC, Written Record of Interview of Witness, Kè Pich Vannak, June 4, 2009, 9.
126. D123/2, ECCC, Written Record of Interview of Witness, Chhouk Rin, May 21, 2008, 7.
127. D166/166, ECCC, Written Record of Interview of Witness, Kè Pich Vannak, June 4, 2009, 9.
128. Short, *Pol Pot*, 386.
129. D166/166, ECCC, Written Record of Interview of Witness, Kè Pich Vannak, June 4, 2009, 10.
130. D166/166, ECCC, Written Record of Interview of Witness, Kè Pich Vannak, June 4, 2009, 10–11.
131. D234/21, ECCC, Written Record of Witness Interview, Chhouk Rin, November 26, 2009, 4.
132. "Request for Opening a New Investigation of So Met and Meas Mut," The Investigative Fund website, www.theinvestigativefund.org/files/managed/Cambodia2nd_Intro_Submission.pdf, quoted in Mertha, *Brothers in Arms*, 90, fn. 44.
133. D166/117, ECCC, Written Record of Interview of Witness, Khoem Sâmhuon, March 6, 2009, 7.
134. "Norn Suon called Chey Suon called Chey called Sèn called Sèng: Final Part: Part 6: XII. He Talks about a Number of Older Brothers in the Leading Organization," November 21, 1976, 6–10 (trans. Steve Heder), Steve Heder's private collection.

3. Dusting Off United Front Doctrine, 1979–1984

1. Becker, *When the War Was Over*, 114; Chandler, *Brother Number One*, 63.
2. Osbourne, *Before Kampuchea*, 80.
3. Becker, *When the War Was Over*, 119.
4. "Norn Suon called Chey Suon called Chey called Sèn called Sèng: Final Part: Part 6: XII. He Talks about a Number of Older Brothers in the Leading Organization," November 21, 1976, 6–10 (trans. Steve Heder), emphasis added, Steve Heder's private collection.
5. Interview 20SR01, Siem Reap, July 6, 2020.
6. The term *mika* is somewhat akin to the male equivalent *tapek*, or the gender-neutral prefix "*a-*," or "contemptible" (as in the popular moniker *a-Pot*, "the contemptible [Pol] Pot").
7. Personal communication with colleagues at the ECCC, January 2011.
8. D118, ECCC, Written Record of Charged Person, Kaing Guek-Eav alias Duch, November 20, 2008, 3.
9. Interview with Phon Phaen (Ex-Deputy Commander of Division 705, Now District Vice Governor of Sampeou Luang, Sampeou Luang, Front 250, January 25, 1997, Steve Heder's private collection.
10. D89, ECCC, Written Record of Charged Person, Kaing Guek-Eav alias Duch, June 24, 2008, 3. Ironically, Nên means "thick," "dense," or "dull."
11. Short, *Pol Pot*, 402.
12. Yun, "An Account of Chinese Diplomats," 503–5.

13. Yun, "An Account of Chinese Diplomats," 505.
14. See https://www.youtube.com/watch?v=42BzYMXw8b0 to get a sense of the immediate area.
15. Yun, "An Account of Chinese Diplomats," 512, 518.
16. Locard, *Jungle Heart of the Khmer Rouge*, 168.
17. Chandler, *Voices from S-21*, 19.
18. "Norng Suon called Chey Suon called Chey called Sèn called Sèng: Final Part: Part 6."
19. Kè Pauk, "Ke Pauk's Autobiography from 1949–1985."
20. Chandler, *Voices from S-21*, 20.
21. "NADK PAPERS," 23, Steve Heder's private collection.
22. Becker, *When the War Was Over* 433–436.
23. Thion, *Watching Cambodia*, 131.
24. Chandler, *Voices from S-21*, 20.
25. Steve Heder, Interview of Son Sen, April 8, 1980, Steve Heder's private collection.
26. Dy and Dearing, *A History of the Anlong Veng Community*, 47.
27. Ea, *The Chain of Terror*, 23.
28. Vickery, *Cambodia, 1979–1982*, 86.
29. Vickery compares this with the Eastern Zone, where peasant opposition—which also existed in the Southwest—was met with a modification, an easing of radical policy. Vickery, *Cambodia, 1979–1982*, 87.
30. Interview Number 18, Sakeo, March 8, 1980, in "Interviews with Kampuchean Refugees at Thai-Cambodia Border," 37, emphasis added, Steve Heder's private collection.
31. Interview of *Ta* Mok by Nate Thayer, undated, Steve Heder's private collection.
32. Interview Number 23, Sa Keo, Um Samang, from Region 21, Eastern region, March 10, 1980, in "Interviews with Kampuchean Refugees at Thai-Cambodia Border," 45, Steve Heder's private collection.
33. Locard, *Jungle Heart of the Khmer Rouge*, 162.
34. Interview 20PS02, Pursat, August 15, 2020.
35. Locard, *Jungle Heart of the Khmer Rouge*, 164.
36. Dy and Dearing, *A History of the Anlong Veng Community*, 47.
37. "DK Order of Battle Materials," 2, Steve Heder's private collection.
38. "Brief Conversation with It Sâm, Deputy Commander of Small Division 92, Big Division 980," February 26, 1995, 2, Steve Heder's private collection.
39. Dy and Dearing, *A History of the Anlong Veng Community*, 53.
40. "DK Order of Battle Materials," 10, 2. Sometimes Division 925 was erroneously referred to as 525.
41. The analysis in this section examines the united front from the perspective of the PDK. For a fuller picture of the non-communist resistance, see Conboy, *The Cambodian Wars*.
42. Elizabeth Becker, personal communication.
43. Becker, *When the War Was Over*, 440.
44. Walter Goodman, "Jennings Says U.S. Helps Khmer Rouge," *New York Times*, April 26, 1990. The Jennings report mentioned in the article is available at https://www.youtube.com/watch?v=QxPHarm3Q_E.

45. Whitlock, *The Afghanistan Papers*.
46. Heder, "The National Army for the Liberation of the Khmer Populace and the National Front for the Liberation of the Khmer Populace," pt. 1, 1–13, Steve Heder's private collection.
47. "Minutes of Comrade First Minister P P's Meeting with Son San (Late September 1979)," documents found in Khieu Samphân's Phnom Dângrêk residence.
48. "Comrade First Minister Khieu Samphân's Meeting with Son Sann (Late May 1980)," documents found in Khieu Samphân's Phnom Dângrêk residence.
49. "Comrade First Minister Khieu Samphân's Second Meeting with Son Sann, January 26, 1981," documents found in Khieu Samphân's Phnom Dângrêk residence.
50. "Minutes of Comrade Khieu Samphân's Meeting with Dien Del, May 8, 1981," documents found in Khieu Samphân's Phnom Dângrêk residence.
51. "Meeting with Dien Del, June 12, 1981, from 3:30 to 5:00 PM at His Excellency Nong's House," documents found in Khieu Samphân's Phnom Dângrêk residence.
52. "Supplementary Notes to the Minutes of October 4, 1981," documents found in Khieu Samphân's Phnom Dângrêk residence.
53. Pilger, *Heroes*, 449.
54. Thion, *Watching Cambodia*, 139.
55. Strangio, *Hun Sen's Cambodia*, 29. These numbers were almost certainly higher than the reality on the ground. The Armée Nationale Sihanoukiste (ANS) was FUNCINPEC's military wing, the successor to MOULINAKA.
56. Executive summary of the "Digest and Analysis of Partie of Democratic Kampuchea Public Media from October 1991–October 1992," 2, Steve Heder's private collection.
57. Captain P. Bartu, "Background History on Major Battles in Cambodia after the Withdrawal of the Vietnamese in September 1989," PB/seg, November 19, 1992, 2, 6, Steve Heder's private collection.
58. Peschoux, Interview with CY, March 1990, 4, Steve Heder's private collection.
59. There was one important distinction, as Nhem Boraden points out: "Unlike the period between 1970 and 1975, the Khmer Rouge had to work with other resistance forces that did not plan to leave Cambodia as the Vietnamese troops did in 1972." Nhem, *The Khmer Rouge*, 116.
60. Ashley, "The 'KR' Papers," 4, Steve Heder's private collection.
61. "Summary: the following is the first of two (2) IIRs addressing Khmer Rouge camps. This IIR addresses Site 8," in Lane, The Cambodian Border File, 5.
62. "Debrief of Ex-Senior Khmer Rouge Commander," 5, Steve Heder's private collection.
63. Conboy, *The Cambodian Wars*, 385.
64. Wood, "Tracing the Last Breath," 220–22.
65. Conboy, *The Cambodian Wars*, 312.
66. Philip Shenon, "Pol Pot & Co.: The Thai Connection," *New York Times*, December 19, 1993.
67. Shenon, "Pol Pot & Co."

68. Shenon, "Pol Pot & Co."

69. Sutin Wannabovorn, "Covert Thai Unit 838 Resurfaces," *Phnom Penh Post,* April 8, 1994, https://www.phnompenhpost.com/national/covert-thai-unit-838-resurfaces; Buszynski, "Thailand's Foreign Policy," 724, 731.

70. Peschoux, Interview with V, August 1990.

71. Peschoux, Interview with V, August 1990.

72. Interview with Mao Sam Ouen, Phnom Penh, October 9–10, 1996, Steve Heder's private collection.

73. Short, *Pol Pot,* 413.

74. Interview 14PL01, Pailin, December 28, 2014.

75. Peschoux, Interview with V, November 1990.

76. Roger Normand, "The Teachings of Chairman Pot: At the Khmer Rouge School," *The Nation* (August 27–September 3, 1990), 198, 199.

77. Peschoux, Interview with CY, March 1990.

78. https://www.youtube.com/watch?v=rB5A4xV_RI0.

79. Peschoux, Interview with Khat Sali, Sihanoukville, January 9–10, 1992 (actually 1993); UNTAC Memorandum, "Notes on Interview with NADK 'Self-Demobilizer,' Interview with an NADK defector in Kampot Province," from Christophe Peschoux to Tim Carney via Penny Edwards, January 27, 1993, Steve Heder's private collection.

80. Peschoux, Interview with V, August 1990, Steve Heder's private collection; Interview with Khat Sali, February 1, 1993, UNTAC Memorandum, "Interview with an NADK defector in Kampot Province," from Christophe Peschoux to Tim Carney via Steve Heder, February 5, 1993, Steve Heder's private collection.

81. "February 28, 1995, Interview with Major Heuan Vut, Battalion Commander, Regiment 55, Division 912 in Siem Reap PT," Steve Heder's private collection.

82. Dunlop, *The Lost Executioner,* 207.

83. Peschoux, Interview with KS, Sihanoukville, January 1993; UNTAC Memorandum, "Notes on Interview with NADK 'Self-Demobilizer,' Interview with an NADK Defector in Kampot Province," from Christophe Peschoux to Tim Carney via Penny Edwards, January 27, 1993, Steve Heder's private collection.

4. Command and Control in the Shadows and on the Periphery, 1985–1989

1. See Tyner, *The Politics of Lists,* on how even whispered conspiracy theories became tangible "reality" through the practice of compiling lists, particularly of "strings" (ខ្សែ), or networks, of traitors.

2. NADK Document, "Decisions of the Meeting of 1001 Leading Cadre," January 10, 1992, 3, Steve Heder's private collection.

3. Thayer, "Cambodia: Misperceptions and Peace," 188.

4. Interview 15MDK03, Mondulkiri, January 27, 2015.

5. "What Is the Virtue, the Quality, the Reality and the Responsibility of Democratic Kampuchea in the Past, Present, and Future?" (captured CPK/PDK document), English translation, 17, Steve Heder's private collection.

6. Interview 15MDK03, Mondulkiri, January 27, 2015.
7. Heder, Dossier of Documents: 80–81, 131, 148–50, Steve Heder's private collection.
8. Peschoux, Interview with V, August 1990.
9. UNTAC Memorandum from Deputy Chief, Military Information Branch, to Chief, Military Information Branch, "Interview with Self-Demobilized Soldier—Set Siet," November 11, 1992, Steve Heder's private collection.
10. "VODK Catalogs Years of Failure since SRV Attack," Voice of Democratic Kampuchea (clandestine radio broadcast), January 6, 1985, Steve Heder's private collection.
11. Peschoux, Interviews with V, August 1990. (This is a different document from Interview with V, August 1990.)
12. Peschoux, Interview with CY, March 8, 1990, 3; and Peschoux, Interview with V, August 1990.
13. Peschoux, Interview with V, August 1990.
14. Peschoux, Interview with V, August 1990.
15. Interview 14PL03, Pailin, December 29, 2014.
16. "DK Commanders, Troops Viewed in Visit to Phnom Malai," *China Daily*, November 10, 1984.
17. Interview 20PL07, Pailin, July 20, 2020.
18. Interview 16AV05, Anlong Veng, October 7, 2016.
19. Peschoux, Interview with Khat Sali," UNTAC Memorandum, "Notes on Interview with NADK 'Self-Demobilizer,' Interview with an NADK Defector in Kampot Province," from Christophe Peschoux to Tim Carney via Penny Edwards, January 27, 1993, Steve Heder's private collection.
20. Interview 14PL04, Pailin, December 30, 2014.
21. Interview Number 9, Nong Pru, March 1, 1980, in "Interviews with Kampuchean Refugees at Thai-Cambodia Border," 16, Steve Heder's private collection.
22. Peschoux, Interview with C, August 1990.
23. Peschoux, Interview with V, August 1990.
24. Journal No. 2508-C24, August 17, 1992, Steve Heder's private collection.
25. Heder, "From Pol Pot to Pen Sovan to the Villages," 25; on Vietnamese organization of Cambodian villages, see 21–39; on KPNLF rural organization, see Heder, "The National Army for the Liberation of the Khmer Populace and the National Front for the Liberation of the Khmer Populace," pt. 2, 36–40, Steve Heder's private collection.
26. "What Is the Virtue, the Quality, the Reality, and the Responsibility of Democratic Kampuchea?" 6–9.
27. Peschoux, Interview with V, August 1990.
28. Peschoux, Interview with V, August 1990.
29. Peschoux, Interview with V, August 1990.
30. Peschoux, Interview with R, August 1990.
31. Peschoux, Interview with V, August 1990.
32. Peschoux, Interview with R, August 1990.
33. Peschoux, Interview with V, August 1990.

34. Interview 15MDK 01, Mondulkiri, January 27, 2015; Interview 16AV01, Anlong Veng, October 6, 2016; Interview 15MDK01, Mondulkiri, January 27, 2015.
35. Interview 16AV01, Anlong Veng, October 6, 2016.
36. Interview 14PL06, Pailin, December 31, 2014.
37. Dy and Dearing, *A History of the Anlong Veng Community*, 62.
38. Dy and Dearing, *A History of the Anlong Veng Community*, 63-64.
39. Elizabeth Becker, personal communication.
40. Robinson, "Double Vision," 63.
41. Robinson, "Double Vision," 7, 53-57, 72.
42. Mason and Brown, *Rice, Rivalry and Politics*, 101.
43. Reynell, "Political Pawns," 42.
44. Zolberg, Suhrke, and Aguayo, *Escape from Violence*, 275.
45. Robinson, "Double Vision."
46. "KR-18/Subject: Dealing with Khmer Rouge Numbers," in Lane, Cambodian Border File, 9-10.
47. "Site 2," Thai/Cambodia Border Refugee Camps 1975-1999 Information and Documentation Website, http://www.websitesrcg.com/border/camps/Site-2.html.
48. For an extraordinary account of Site 2, see Lindsay Cole French, "Enduring Holocaust, Surviving History: Displaced Cambodians on the Thai-Cambodian Border" (PhD diss., Harvard University, 1994), https://www.websitesrcg.com/border/documents/French%201994%20Site%20II%20dissertation.pdf.
49. Robinson, "Double Vision," 126.
50. Dunlop, *The Lost Executioner*, 206.
51. "KR-31/Summary: (U) source has occasion to twice drive the road between O'Trao and O'Panko most recently on 3 September. Ta Mok has ordered that all civilians evacuate O'Panko prior to 6 September. Ta Mok is presently residing in a safe house in Amphoe Khukhan," in Lane, Cambodian Border File, 2.
52. Conboy, *The Cambodian Wars*, 236, 245-46, 261.
53. Interview 21DC01A, Washington, DC, October 10, 2021.
54. "A Demographic Study of the Residents of Site 2/Site II, Site B, and Site 8," Thai/Cambodia Border Refugee Camps 1975-1999 Information and Documentation Website, https://www.websitesrcg.com/border/camps/survey-1989.html.
55. Interview 19DC03, Washington, DC, August 2, 2019.
56. Conboy, *The Cambodian Wars*, 261.
57. Lane, "Subject: Dealing with Khmer Rouge Numbers (U)," in Cambodian Border File, 5.
58. Interview, 21DC01A, October 10, 2021.
59. Lane, "KR-24," in Cambodian Border File, 1, 85, 17, 86.
60. Asia Watch, "Violations of the Laws of War by the Khmer Rouge," 6, https://www.hrw.org/reports/pdfs/c/cambodia/cambodia904.pdf.
61. Lane, "KR-25 Appendix J: Administrator Chay," in Cambodian Border File, 43, 350.
62. *Bangkok Post*, May 11, 1989, quoted in Robinson, "Double Vision," 138.
63. Asia Watch, "Violations of the Laws of War by the Khmer Rouge," 5.

64. Lane, "KR-28," in Cambodian Border File, 2.

65. Lane, "Subject: Dealing with Khmer Rouge Numbers (U)," 2.

66. Lane, "KR-24," in Cambodian Border File, 86. O'Trao was in many ways quite different from the Khmer Rouge camps to the south. Residents' clothing was colorful, there were ubiquitous television sets (run on car batteries, as O'Trao did not have electricity), and a leadership management style that was on the "benign" side, at least toward those who were not in its political crosshairs. Lane, "KR-24," 2.

67. Interview 21DC02, Washington, DC, November 21, 2021.

68. Lane, "Subject: Dealing with Khmer Rouge Numbers (U)," 3, 4, 8, and 11, referencing Hoffer, *The True Believer*.

69. Lane, "Subject: Dealing with Khmer Rouge Numbers (U)," 1.

70. Magstad, "Notes on the Khmer Rouge, February–October 1989," 3, Steve Heder's private collection. See, inter alia, Magstad and Hawk, "Khmer Rouge Abuses Along the Thai-Cambodian Border."

71. "A Demographic Study of the Residents of Site 2/Site II, Site B, and Site 8."

72. Lane, "Summary: The following is the first of two (2) IIRs addressing Khmer Rouge camps. This IIR addresses Site 8," in Cambodian Border File, 1–4.

73. Peschoux, Interview with CH, July 1990.

74. Interview of Aek Chun, by Steve Heder, on November 11, 1984, at Samla Changanh, Steve Heder's private collection.

75. Peschoux, *Les "nouveaux" Khmères rouges*.

76. Dunlop, *The Lost Executioner*, 202–3.

77. Widyono, *Dancing in Shadows*.

78. Kamm, *Cambodia*, 179–81.

79. Lane, "Summary," 2.

80. Dennison Lane, "The Following Is a Listing of Items Written during the Period March 1989–November 1989," in Cambodian Border File, 3.

81. Werbrouk, "The Site 8 Artificial Limb Workshop," Steve Heder's private collection.

82. Peschoux, Interview with CH, July 1990.

83. Interview 20SR01, Siem Reap, July 6, 2020.

84. UNCOHCHR, "Talk with Om Van," Phum Dong, Malai January 26, 1997, Steve Heder's private collection.

85. UNTAC, Interoffice Memorandum from Steve Heder to Yasushi Akashi (through Tim Carney), "PDK Leadership and Policy," November 3, 1992, 1, Steve Heder's private collection.

86. Kampuchea, K-A3, DK-B3fl, DK-B5e, DK-Blc, PRK-B3fl, PRK-B3i, talk with Joe de Rienzo, 24.5.85, Steve Heder's private collection.

87. Memorandum from Christophe Peschoux (revised by David Ashley) to David Hawk et al., "First Needs Assessment Mission in the Zones Controlled by the Khmer Rouge Dissident Factions (24–27 January 1997)," 10–11, Steve Heder's private collection; Interview with Mao Sam Ouen, Phnom Penh, October 9–10, 1996, Steve Heder's private collection.

88. Interview of Aek Chun, by Steve Heder, on November 11, 1984, at Samla Changanh.

89. Ny Kân tended not to visit 102 very often and would instead receive his orders from the Supreme Command Site of the National Army of Democratic Kampuchea at Koh Kong, where he presumed Pol Pot (*om di mui*) must be. Interview 20AV01, Anlong Veng, July 5, 2020.

90. UNCOHCHR, "Phon Phaen (Ex-Deputy Commander of Division 705. Now District Governor of Sampoeu Luang), Sampoeu Lang, Front 250," January 25, 1997. Ieng Sary had antagonized a large number of intellectuals who had worked with him at B1 and were happy to be free of him. See "KR Defections," 25, Steve Heder's private collection.

91. Interview of Aek Chun, by Steve Heder, on November 11, 1984, at Samla Changanh.

92. Interview of Aek Chun, by Steve Heder, on November 11, 1984, at Samla Changanh.

93. Dunlop, *The Lost Executioner*, 52.

94. Huy, *The Khmer Rouge Division 703*, 95.

95. Chandler, *Voices from S-21*, 24.

96. Craig Etcheson, personal communication.

97. Memorandum from Christophe Peschoux (revised by David Ashley) to David Hawk et al., "First Needs Assessment Mission in the Zones Controlled by the Khmer Rouge Dissident Factions."

98. Lane, "Summary," 5-6.

99. "Information/Education Division Report on a Visit to Banteay Chhmar, July 16, 1992," 2, Steve Heder's private collection.

5. An Unattainable Political Space, 1990–1993

1. D86/5, ECCC, Written Record of Charged Person, Kaing Guek-Eav alias Duch, September 5, 2007, 4.

2. Quinn, "The Origins and Development of Radical Cambodian Communism," 76.

3. Quinn, "The Origins and Development of Radical Cambodian Communism," 78, 77; Kuong Lumphon, "Report on the Communist Party of Cambodia" (Pak Kommunist Kampuchea) "PCK," submitted to the Republican Government, May 8, 1973, 11.

4. Widyono, *Dancing in Shadows*, 33.

5. Widyono, *Dancing in Shadows*, 34-35.

6. Captain Peter Bartu, "Background History on Major Battles in Cambodia after the Withdrawal of the Vietnamese in September 1989," PB/seg, November 19, 1992, 2, Steve Heder's private collection.

7. Barbara Smith, "Ieng Sary Is a Cambodian, but Others from Kampuchea Krom Are Not—DK," *Cambodia Times*, October 19-25, 1992.

8. "What Is the Virtue, the Quality, the Reality, and the Responsibility of Democratic Kampuchea in the Past, Present, and Future," December 2, 1986 (English translator unknown), Steve Heder's private collection.

9. "What Is the Virtue, the Quality, the Reality, and the Responsibility of Democratic Kampuchea in the Past, Present, and Future?" 4, 5.

10. "What Is the Virtue, the Quality, the Reality, and the Responsibility of Democratic Kampuchea in the Past, Present, and Future?" 14.

11. "Digest and Analysis of Partie of Democratic Kampuchea Public Media from October 1991–October 1992," full digest and analysis, 1, Steve Heder's private collection.

12. Heder, "The Resumption of Armed Struggle," 73–74.

13. UNTAC, Interoffice memorandum from Steve Heder to Yasushi Akashi (through Tim Carney), "PDK Leadership and Policy," November 3, 1992, 2, Steve Heder's private collection.

14. Interview with Mao Sam Ouen, Phnom Penh, October 9–10, 1996, Steve Heder's private collection.

15. Corridor 1008/1005 comprised the following divisions from the former Corridor 1001:

> Division 417 (Kampong Cham province: Steung Trâng, Chamkar Leu, Prey Chhor, Kang Meas, and Kampong Siem districts; Kampong Thom province: Baray district)
> Division 920 (Kandal province: Prek Prasap, Kratie, Snuol, Chhlong, and Sambaur districts)
> Division 709 (Ratanakiri province; Steung Trâng province; Preah Vihear province: Chhep district)
> Division 607 (Preah Vihear province: Rovieng district)
> Division 105 (Mondulkiri province)
> Division 802 ("in the forested uplands," along with divisions 709, 607, and 105, which were carved out of Division 801; Division 709 comprised the former Divisions 108 and 800)

Corridor 1008/1005 also included the following divisions from the former Corridor 1003:

> Division 612 (Preah Vihear province: Koulen, Tbeng, and Choam Khsan districts)
> Division 616 (Kampong Thom province: Staung and Kampong Svay districts)
> Division 785 (Kandal province: Mouk Kampoul district; Kampong Cham province: Choeung Prey district)
> Division 809 (Kampong Cham province: Koh Sotin and Srei Santhor districts; Kandal province: Lovea Em and Kien Svay districts)
> Division 912, Division 980, and Division 946 ([Siem Reap], which contained some of Division 612's forces as a sort of "strategic reserve for Mok" as 612 became part of the UNTAC process)

UNTAC, Interoffice memorandum from Deputy Chief, Military Information Branch, to Chief, Military Information Branch, "Interview with Self-Demobilized NADK Soldier—Cheun Cheam, November 13, 1992, 1; undated, untitled summary report on NADK Order of Battle, 3; and National 3 and "National Army of Democratic Kampuchea High Command: Deployment of Forces of the NADK Divisions and Independent Regiments," August 1991. This source also lists a Division 18 (Thporng, O'Ral, Oudong, and Samrong

Torng districts in Kampong Speu province), which was likely carved out of Division 19, Front 450. Other divisions like 787 and 919 are difficult to pin down with the available data.

16. UNTAC, Interoffice memorandum from Steve Heder to Yasushi Akashi (through Tim Carney), "PDK Leadership and Policy."

17. Debrief of Ex-Senior Khmer Rouge Commander, undated but probably late 1994, Steve Heder's private collection.

18. Heder, "Pol Pot at Bay," 265–66.

19. Undated interview with Nuon Chea, 15, Steve Heder's private collection.

20. Debrief of Ex-Senior Khmer Rouge Commander, undated (but likely late 1994).

21. Heder, "Pol Pot at Bay," 146.

22. Thion, *Watching Cambodia*, 190.

23. Thion, *Watching Cambodia*, 193.

24. Thion, *Watching Cambodia*, 190, 193.

25. Short, *Pol Pot*, 428.

26. Heder, "Khieu Samphân and Pol Pot: Moloch's Poodle," Steve Heder's private collection.

27. Heder, Interview of Ieng Sary, December 17, 1996, 8, Steve Heder's private collection.

28. "Meeting Minutes: Brother Hæm Meets with Chinese Embassy [Officials], December 21, 1987, Nighttime," Khieu Samphân document cache (in author's possession).

29. "National Income Generation, Democratic Kampuchea, December 1981," Khieu Samphân document cache (in author's possession).

30. James Pringle, "Pol Pot Cleans Up Image with Soap Opera," *The Times*, June 6, 1990.

31. Nate Thayer, "Rubies Are Rouge," *Far Eastern Economic Review* (February 7, 1991): 29–30.

32. Interview 20SR01, Siem Reap, July 6, 2020.

33. Thayer, "Rubies Are Rouge."

34. Interview 20SR01, Siem Reap, July 6, 2020.

35. "Meeting with Mr. Sar Kim Lamuth," May 5, 1995, at the Ministry of the Interior (JW/05.05.95), Steve Heder's private collection.

36. UNCOHCHR, "Interview with Mao Sam Oeun, Phnom Penh," October 9–10, 1996, Steve Heder's private collection.

37. UNCOHCHR, "Talk with Om Van," Phum Dong, Malai, January 26, 1997, Steve Heder's private collection.

38. Heder, Interview of Ieng Sary, December 17, 1995, 9, Steve Heder's private collection.

39. "KR Defections," 25, KR Defections File, Steve Heder's private collection.

40. Bekaert, *Cambodian Diary*, 93.

41. UNCOHCHR, "Talk with Om Van," Phum Dong, Malai, January 26, 1997, Steve Heder's private collection.

42. UNTAC, Interoffice memorandum from Steve Heder to Yasushi Akashi (through Tim Carney), "PDK Leadership and Policy," November 3, 1992, 3.

43. Heder, "Pol Pot at Bay," 236–38.
44. Widyono, *Dancing in Shadows,* 83, 98.
45. Waller, LTC, DCMIO, "Memorandum thru the Chief, Military Information for the Force Commander, Notes from a Talk with Christophe Peschoux," September 20, 1992, 2, Steve Heder's private collection; "Digest and Analysis of Partie of Democratic Kampuchea Public Media from October 1991–October 1992."
46. Heder, "Pol Pot at Bay," 35.
47. UN Secretary General, "Fourth Progress Report of the Secretary on UNTAC," 1993, Steve Heder's private collection.
48. "Digest and Analysis of Partie of Democratic Kampuchea Public Media from October 1991–October 1992, 4.
49. Bekaert, *Cambodian Diary,* 56.
50. Bekaert, *Cambodian Diary,* 127.

6. Back to Basics

1. Mok's troops were so well trained that they formed the vanguard of these defensive positions along the hotly contested Preah Vihear corridor.
2. All quotations in this discussion are from the 1994 "Draft Plan," Steve Heder's private collection.
3. US Embassy, "Debrief of Ex-Senior Khmer Rouge Commander," undated (but dated by context to late 1994), Steve Heder's private collection.
4. David Ashley, interview of Siem Chouch, Deputy Commander of Regiment 51, Division 912, and Uy Kim Seng, Deputy Commander of Battalion 990, Regiment 51, May 25, 1995, Puok District, Siem Reap Province (Siem Chouch), Steve Heder's private collection; US Embassy, "Debrief of Ex-Senior Khmer Rouge Commander."
5. David Ashley, "Brief Conversation with It Sâm, Deputy Commander of Small Division 92, Big Division 980," February 26, 1995, Steve Heder's private collection.
6. UNTAC, Interoffice memorandum from Steve Heder to Yasushi Akashi (through Tim Carney), "A January PDK Document, January 20, 1993." As of late 1992, "class struggle" as a coherent theme had yet to make it into the PDK's propaganda. VGNUFC, "Propaganda Themes since April 1992," Steve Heder's private collection.
7. "From Sector 2 MON TEAM, To: HQ UNTAC MON CELL MILINFO, Subject: Questioning of Two NADK Defectors, Chor Von," 2, Steve Heder's private collection.
8. The third-ranking local cadre during the DK period was also responsible for economics. This included everything from growing crops and raising animals to supervising the communal kitchens and canteens to warehousing crops and draft animals. Responsibilities also included receiving goods from the Center and distributing them among the commune as well as extracting surpluses to be sent off to the central warehouses. The commune economic chief supervised his counterparts in the villages, whose tasks were mainly to oversee the village cooks and, most importantly, decide what those surpluses would be. Interview 15MDK01, Mondulkiri, January 27, 2019.

9. "From Sector 2 MON TEAM, To: HQ UNTAC MON CELL MILINFO, Subject: Questioning of Two NADK Defectors."

10. Interview with Kheum Ngun, translation by David Ashley of four tape cassettes recorded by Nate Thayer in Anlong Veng, July 25, 1997, 11, Steve Heder's private collection.

11. "Debrief of Ex-Senior Khmer Rouge Commander," undated (probably late 1994).

12. David Ashley, Interview of Yung Reuan, Commander of Battalion 215, Division 912, Angkor Chum District, Siem Reap, May 24, 1995, Steve Heder's private collection.

13. Peschoux, interview with SS, August 1990; "Khmer Rouge Leave Trail of Blood," *Independent* (London), July 14, 1990.

14. Dunlop, *The Lost Executioner*, 235–36.

15. "Alleged Atrocities against Ta Mok," confidential memo based on interview with a Laotian national, July 23, 1999, 2–3, Steve Heder's private collection.

16. Partial document: confidential interview with Peas Sambath, December 10, 1997, Steve Heder's private collection.

17. The discussion that follows is drawn from Interview 21DC01F, Washington, DC, November 17, 2021; "Highway of Fear," *South China Morning Post*, April 14, 1994; Partial Document: Confidential Interview with Peas Sambath; and William Branigin, "Cambodian Kidnap Scam Profits Officials, Rebels," *Washington Post*, August 17, 1994.

18. Interview 21DC01F, Washington, DC, November 17, 2021.

19. US Embassy, "Debrief of Ex-Senior Khmer Rouge Commander."

20. Suong Sikoeun, "From Pol Pot's Winter to the Malai-Pailin Spring," *Phnom Penh Post*, November 15–28, 1996.

21. US Embassy, "Debrief of Ex-Senior Khmer Rouge Commander."

22. Interview of Suong Sikoeun (assistant to Ieng Sary and ex-Foreign Ministry official) with additional information from Mrs. Toth Kim Seng (ex–Foreign Ministry official and ex-Secretary General of the Red Cross of DK) and Yen (from Division 450).

23. Interview with Long Norin (Secretary General of DNUM); "Yen, Cadre in NADK Division 450," interviews conducted at Phum Dong Village, Phnom Malai, Banteay Meanchey Province, September 27, 1996, Steve Heder's private collection.

24. "Information from Mr. Phi Phuon a.k.a. Cheam," interviews conducted at Phum Dong Village, Phnom Malai, Banteay Meanchey Province, September 27, 1996, 12–13, Steve Heder's private collection.

25. "Talk with Ee Chhien [Y Chhean], January 27, 1997," Steve Heder's private collection.

26. UNCOHCHR, "Talk with Om Van," Phum Dong, Malai, January 26, 1997, Steve Heder's private collection.

27. UNCOHCHR, "Talk with Om Van."

28. Literally, "Father, you die but I live."

29. Interview of Phon Phaen, Ex-Deputy Commander of Division 705, Now District Vice-Governor of Sampeou Luang, Sampeou Luang, Front 250, January 25, 1997, Steve Heder's private collection.

30. UNCOHCHR, "Talk with Om Van."
31. UNCOHCHR, "Talk with Om Van."
32. Interview of Phon Phaen, Ex-Deputy Commander of Division 705, Now District Vice-Governor of Sampeou Luang.
33. Widyono, Confidential Interim Report No. 572, "An Analysis of Recent Developments," 2, Steve Heder's private collection.
34. *Reaksmei Kampuchea*, November 2, 1996, Steve Heder's private collection.
35. "Station Calls on Khmer Rouge Fighters to Return," Phnom Penh National Radio, September 21, 1995, FBIS-EAS-95-186, September 1995, 66–67; "Khmer Rouge Brands Ieng Sary a Traitor," Radio of the Provisional Government of National Union and National Salvation of Cambodia, August 7, 1996, FBIS-EAS-96-154, August 1996, 66.
36. UNCOHCHR, "Talk with Om Van"; UNCOHCHR, "Interviews Conducted at Phum Dong Village, Phnom Malai, Banteay Meanchey Province, September 27, 1996," Steve Heder's private collection.
37. UNOSGRC, "Weekly Report #103 Covering the Period from 2 to 8 September 1996," September 9, 1996, Steve Heder's private collection.
38. Interview of Phon Phaen, Ex-Deputy Commander of Division 705, Now District Vice-Governor of Sampeou Luang, Sampeou Luang.
39. UNCOHCHR, "Talk with Om Van."
40. UNCOHCHR, "Talk with Om Van."
41. Phnom Penh Radio, November 8, 1996, Steve Heder's private collection.
42. Widyono, *Dancing in Shadows*, chap. 13.
43. Wood, "Tracing the Last Breath," 217.
44. For example, in the first two weeks of October 1996, eight Khmer Rouge divisions from Battambang, Banteay Meanchey, and Pursat (Divisions 695, 35, 19, 277, 26, 36, 91, and 305) defected (Claudia Rizzi, "Keo Pong: CPP's Point Man for KR Negotiations," *Phnom Penh Post*, September 20–October 3, 1996), as did the divisions (505, 404, 695, 108, and 469) making up Front 909 (*Cambodia Today*, November 4, 1996) and Front 250 (Divisions 320, 948, 705, and 531) on November 1 (Phnom Penh Radio, November 3, 1996). Hard-line Divisions 611 and 618 also defected in November (*Cambodia Today*, November 11, 1996). The total number is estimated at thirty-six divisions and sub-divisional units having defected, with a total of 17,985 troops integrated into the RCAF (*Cambodia Today*, November 27, 1996).
45. David Ashley, Interview of Siem Chouch, Deputy Commander of Regiment 51, Division 912, and Uy Kim Seng, Deputy Commander of Battalion 990, Regiment 51, May 25, 1995, Puok District, Siem Reap province (Siem Chouch), Steve Heder's private collection.
46. *Reaksmei Kampuchea*, November 10, 1996, Steve Heder's private collection.
47. Interview with Kheum Ngun, translation by David Ashley of four tape cassettes recorded by Nate Thayer in Anlong Veng, July 25, 1997, 8, 10.
48. David Ashley, "The End of the Revolution," 9, Steve Heder's private collection.
49. Rowley, "Second Life, Second Death," 205–6.
50. UNOSGRG, "Monthly Report for November 1996," Steve Heder's private collection.
51. UNOSGRG, "Interim Report No. 572," Steve Heder's private collection.

52. UNOSGRC, "Monthly Report for December 1996," Steve Heder's private collection.

53. Office of the Centre for Human Rights in Cambodia to Thomas Hammarberg, "Your Second Mission—Amnesty to Ieng Sary and Other DK Leaders" and "Suggested Draft Statement on the Issue of Amnesty to Ieng Sary and Other Figures or Senior Cadres of Democratic Kampuchea (Khmer Rouge)," November 14, 1996, Steve Heder's private collection.

54. UNOSGRC, "Weekly Report #103 Covering the Period from 2 to 8 September 1996."

55. Widyono, *Dancing in Shadows*, chap 11.

56. Radio Phnom Penh, November 16, 1996, Steve Heder's private collection.

57. Christine Chaumeau, Reuters, "CPP Gains Some Ground in Competition for Defectors," *Phnom Penh Post*, December 27, 1996-January 9, 1997.

58. David Ashley, "The 'KR' Papers: An Analysis," 3, Steve Heder's private collection.

59. Interview with Kheum Ngun, translation by David Ashley of four tape cassettes recorded by Nate Thayer in Anlong Veng, July 25, 1997, 10.

60. Interview with Kheum Ngun, translation by David Ashley of four tape cassettes recorded by Nate Thayer in Anlong Veng, July 25, 1997, 10-11.

61. Wood, "Tracing the Last Breath," 207.

62. Wood, "Tracing the Last Breath," 208-9.

63. Ta Mok eventually had the three (along with Saroeun's wife) arrested and put in small cages, where they were starved, deprived of sleep, and exposed to the elements. They died in agony a month later. "Alleged Atrocities against Ta Mok," confidential memo based on interview with a Laotian national, July 23, 1999, 3.

64. Interview with Kheum Ngun, translation by David Ashley of four tape cassettes recorded by Nate Thayer in Anlong Veng, July 25, 1997, 11.

65. Interview 20AV05, Anlong Veng, July 5, 2020.

66. Interviews 20AV03 and 20AV04, Anlong Veng, July 5, 2020.

67. Interviews 20AV04, Anlong Veng, July 5, 2020, and 20PL01, Pailin, July 7, 2020.

68. Wood, "Tracing the Last Breath," 210, 209.

69. Interview 20AV04, Anlong Veng, July 5, 2020.

70. Interview 20AV04, Anlong Veng, July 5, 2020; Interview 20PL01, Pailin, July 7, 2020.

71. Dunlop, *The Lost Executioner*, 259.

72. Interview of Ta Mok by Nate Thayer, undated, Steve Heder's private collection.

73. "Ta Mok, Khmer Rouge Head Facing Genocide Trial, Dies," *New York Times*, July 21, 2006. I deliberately use the word "shit" because that is almost certainly the term Mok used. It is an uncanny parallel to Mao's description of intellectuals during the 1940s Yan'an era. See Gao Hua, *How the Red Sun Rose: The Origins and Development of the Yan'an Rectification Movement, 1930–1945*, trans. Stacey Mosher and Guo Jian (Hong Kong: Chinese University Press, 2018), 746.

74. Wood, "Tracing the Last Breath," 220-22.

Conclusion

1. ECCC, Criminal Case File 002/14-08-2006, Investigation 002/19-09-2007, Provisional Detention Order, https://www.eccc.gov.kh/sites/default/files/documents/courtdoc/Provisional_Detention_Order_Nuon_Chea_19092007_ENG.pdf.

2. Craig Etcheson recalls: "That was such a bizarre comedy of errors, from start to finish. About a week before the operation, senior Ministry of Interior officials started calling international journalists, offering to sell a hot tip on a big upcoming story; none of those [journalists] took them up on the offer, but it meant the jig was already up, and at the court we started to get deluged with requests for comment. Meanwhile, local journalists operated on a somewhat different set of ethics, and proceeded to purchase prime seats to cover the event, at the end of the road leading to Nuon's house, at the helicopter landing site not far away, at the military air base at Pochentong [airport] where the chopper returned with Nuon, at the gate of the military base, at the gate of ECCC compound through which Nuon was brought, and at the door of the court building where Nuon was to be arraigned, among others. In the wee hours on the morning of the arrest, while I was monitoring the operation from Phnom Penh, I realized that Thet Sambath was broadcasting live from Nuon's house, narrating the anticipated arrival of the arresting officers. That motivated me to send an urgent message to Steve Heder, who was on the arrest team, even then creeping through the jungle approaching Nuon's house, telling him that they should expect to be greeted by journalists, perhaps live on camera. Moreover, the local Pailin authorities had of course been informed of the operation, and being loyal former cadres of the beloved Upper Brothers, they in turn had informed Nuon and Samphân. It was crazy." Personal communication.

3. Thet Sambath's parents had been executed on Nuon Chea's orders. Decades later, in the process of gathering the material that eventually became the movie *Enemies of the People* (dir. Rithy Panh), Sambath ended up being "adopted" by Nuon, even as the latter was unrepentant about having signed off on the execution of Sambath's parents. Nuon told the arresting officers that Sambath was his nephew, thus enabling Sambath to accompany Nuon on the helicopter and even into the preliminary hearing with the co-investigating judges, where a staff member of the national co-investigating judge recognized him and exclaimed, "What are YOU doing here?!" To further complicate matters, "Sambath's book, *Behind the Killing Fields* (with Gina Chon), was his revision of an autobiography that Sambath had stolen from Nuon, who complained bitterly about it. 'Where are my royalties?!' he repeatedly demanded of his attorneys." Craig Etcheson, personal communication.

4. A video of these events is available at https://www.youtube.com/watch?v=xxFXq60WEK4.

5. Steve Heder, personal communication.

6. Kotkin, *Stalin*, vol. 1, chap. 8.

7. Personal communication, June 16, 2024.

8. Osbourne, *Before Kampuchea*, chap. 13.

9. E457/6/1, ECCC, Case File No. 002/19-09-2007/ECCC-TC, Co-Prosecutors' Closing Brief, 123–25, https://www.eccc.gov.kh/sites/default/files/documents/courtdoc/%5Bdate-in-tz%5D/E457_6_1_Redacted_EN.pdf.

10. Chandler, Kiernan, and Boua, *Pol Pot Plans the Future*, 33.

11. Chandler, Kiernan, and Boua, *Pol Pot Plans the Future*, 33.

12. Mertha, *Brothers in Arms*, chap. 4; and E457/6/1, ECCC, Case File No. 002/19-09-2007/ECCC-TC, Co-Prosecutors' Closing Brief, 708. Trapeang Thma alone was twenty-two kilometers (over thirteen and a half miles) long. Surprisingly, the CPK had started to institute what might have been a modest but successful commercial trading regime. Largely existing apart from the policy areas emphasized by the regime, the CPK started trading with a small but growing number of partners in addition to its two largest destinations, China and North Korea. As noted elsewhere, Democratic Kampuchea even founded a trading company based in Hong Kong and planned to do the same in Singapore. Modest though it was, international commerce showed the potential for some modicum of success, unlike the dramatic failure of agriculture, and, as it turned out, defense. See Mertha, *Brothers in Arms*, chap. 5.

13. Real name Yung Yem, but she went by Yung Moeun.

14. This was not true for every interlocutor who came calling. See Norén-Nilsson, "Children of Former Khmer Rouge Cadres."

15. Interview 13AV01, Anlong Veng, January 3, 2013; Norén-Nilsson, "Children," 463.

16. See also Ouch Sony, "20 Years On, Historic Khmer Rouge Defection Remembered," *Cambodia Daily*, August 9, 2016, https://english.cambodiadaily.com/editors-choice/20-years-historic-defection-remembered-116447/.

17. "PM Hun Sen: Win-Win Policy Is Possible Thanks to Y Chhean and Sok Pheap," *Fresh News Asia*, October 24, 2020, https://m.en.freshnewsasia.com/index.php/en/localnews/19830-2020-10-24-06-39-20.html.

18. "Cambodia's Dirty Dozen: A Long History of Rights Abuses by Hun Sen's Generals," Human Rights Watch report, June 28, 2018, https://www.hrw.org/report/2018/06/28/cambodias-dirty-dozen-long-history-rights-abuses-hun-sens-generals.

19. Steve Heder, personal communication. Thirith was eventually determined to be unable to stand trial because of mental incapacity.

20. Ciorciari and Heindel, *Hybrid Justice*, chap. 6. Meas Muth, one of Ta Mok's sons-in-law who defected in 1996, was commander of Division 164 and of the navy during the Democratic Kampuchea period. Ao An (អាវ អាន) was deputy secretary of Democratic Kampuchea's Central Zone and secretary of said zone's Sector 41. Prior to having been involved in the gemstone trade in Malai, Yim Tith (យឹម ទិត្យ) worked as secretary in Sector 13 of the Southwest Zone and, as Mok's forces expanded to manage politically suspect zones, extended his reach into the Northwest Zone. He was accused of overseeing the imprisonment, torture, and execution of thousands of individuals in both places. Im Chæm (អុឹម ចែម) also supervised purges of the Northwest Zone and, together with *Ta* Tith, is responsible for as many as 560,000 deaths, according to court documents. See Julia Wallace, "The Bucolic Life of a

Cambodian Grandmother Accused of Mass Killings," *New York Times,* February 24, 2017.

21. Open Society Justice Initiative, "Recent Developments at the Extraordinary Chambers in the Courts of Cambodia: Deadlock Continues in Ao An Case," January 2020, 2, https://www.justiceinitiative.org/uploads/54dc3814-d6c0-49ea-976c-1d4be896418f/briefing-eccc-recent-developments-20200109.pdf.

22. Uk, "Local Perceptions and Responses to Risk," 7, 16, 20, and fn. 35. In a personal communication Craig Etcheson adds: "Much if not most of the K5 land mine belt was laid by the PRK and Vietnamese. And the KR would often watch the dragooned people laying the mines by day, then come in at night and move them, much to the misfortune of the K5 workforce." In either case, the Khmer Rouge knew where the land mines were.

23. Uk, "Local Perceptions and Responses to Risk," 15.

24. Uk, "Local Perceptions and Responses to Risk," 17, emphasis added.

25. Uk, "Local Perceptions and Responses to Risk," 18.

26. Magstad, "Notes on the Khmer Rouge, February–October 1989," 3, Steve Heder's private collection.

27. Uk, "Local Perceptions and Responses to Risk," 16.

Bibliography

Primary Sources

From Steve Heder's Private Collection

"Alleged Atrocities against Ta Mok." Confidential memo based on interview with a Laotian national, July 23, 1999.
Ashley, David. "Brief Conversation with It Sâm, Deputy Commander of Small Division 92, Big Division 980," February 26, 1995.
Ashley, David. "The End of the Revolution," April 1998.
Ashley, David. Interview of Siem Chouch, Deputy Commander of Regiment 51, Division 912, and Uy Kim Seng, Deputy Commander of Battalion 990, Regiment 51, May 25, 1995, Puok District, Siem Reap Province (Siem Chouch).
Ashley, David. Interview of Yung Reuan, Commander of Battalion 215, Division 912, Angkor Chum District, Siem Reap, May 24, 1995.
Ashley, David. "The 'KR' Papers: An Analysis."
Ashley, David. Translation of Nate Thayer's interview with *Ta* Mok and Nuon Chea.
Bartu, Captain Peter. "Background History on Major Battles in Cambodia after the Withdrawal of the Vietnamese in September 1989," November 19, 1992.
"Camp de Reeducation de Beng Trebek sous la Direction des Khmer Rouge (KR) dd Février 1977 au Janvier 1979," undated. In "Material on Ieng Sary."
"Debrief of ex-senior Khmer Rouge Commander," undated [probably late 1994].
"Digest and Analysis of Partie of Democratic Kampuchea Public Media from October 1991–October 1992." Full digest and analysis.
"DK Order of Battle Materials."
"Draft Plan," 1994.
Executive summary of the "Digest and Analysis of Partie of Democratic Kampuchea Public Media," October 1991–October 1992.
"February 28, 1995, Interview with Major Heuan Vut, Battalion Commander, Regiment 55, Division 912 in Siem Reap PT."
"From Sector 2 MON TEAM, To: HQ UNTAC MON CELL MILINFO, Subject: Questioning of Two NADK Defectors, Chor Von."
Heder, Steve. Dossier of Documents: 80–81.
Heder, Steve. Interview of Ieng Sary, December 17, 1995.
Heder, Steve. Interview of Son Sen, April 8, 1980.
Heder, Steve. "The National Army for the Liberation of the Khmer Populace and the National Front for the Liberation of the Khmer Populace," part 1, July 1983.

BIBLIOGRAPHY

"Information/Education Division Report on a Visit to Banteay Chhmar, July 16, 1992."
"Information from Mr. Phi Phuon aka Cheam."
Interview Number 4 (Ong Thing Hoeung and Sauv Kim Hong), Kao I Dang, February 29, 1980.
Interview Number 4 (Sauv Kim Hong), Kao I Dang, (presumably) February 29, 1980.
Interview Number 9, Nong Pru, March 1, 1980.
Interview Number 14 (Khem), Sakeo, March 7, 1980.
Interview Number 18, Sakeo, March 8, 1980.
Interview Number 23, Sa Keo, Um Samang, from Region 21, Eastern Region, March 10, 1980.
Interview Number 28, Navy Camp 62, Chanthaburi, March 11, 1989.
Interview Number 29 (Lonh aka Lorn), Navy Camp 62, Chanthaburi, March 12, 1980.
Interview Number 31, Mai Rut Holding Center, March 15, 1980.
Interview Number 32, Mai Rut, March 15, 1980.
Interview of Aek Chun, by Steve Heder, on November 11, 1984, at Samla Changanh.
Interview of Long Norin (Secretary General of DNUM), Phum Dong, Malai, January 24, 1997.
Interview of Phon Phaen (ex-Deputy Commander of Division 705, now District Vice-Governor of Sampeou Luang, Sampeou Luang), Front 250, January 25, 1997.
Interview of Suong Sikoeun (assistant to Ieng Sary and ex-Foreign Ministry official) with additional information from Mrs. Toth Kim Seng (ex-Foreign Ministry official and ex-Secretary General of the Red Cross of DK) and Yen (from Division 450).
Interview of *Ta* Mok by Nate Thayer, undated.
Interview transcript, Steve Heder with Ieng Sary, E3_106_EN.PDF, December 17, 1996.
Interview with Ambassador Kenneth Quinn, March 5, 2015.
Interview with Khat Sali, February 1, 1993, UNTAC Memorandum, "Interview with an NADK defector in Kampot Province," from Christophe Peschoux to Tim Carney via Steve Heder, February 5, 1993.
Interview with Kheum Ngun. Translation by David Ashley of four tape cassettes recorded by Nate Thayer in Anlong Veng, July 25, 1997.
Interview with Long Norin (Secretary General of DNUM), Phum Dong Malai, January 1, 1997.
Interview with Mao Sam Ouen, Phnom Penh, October 9–10, 1996.
Interview with Nuon Chea, undated.
Interview with Phon Phaen (ex-Deputy Commander of Division 705, now District Vice Governor of Sampeou Luang), Sampeou Luang, Front 250, January 25, 1997.
Interviews Conducted at Phum Dong Village, Phnom Malai, Banteay Meanchey Province, September 27, 1996.

"Interviews with Kampuchean Refugees at Thai-Cambodia Border: Prepared for Ishiyama Committee Annual Report 1980, February–March 1980." Journal No. 2508-C24, August 17, 1992.
Kampuchea, K-A3, DK-B3fl, DK-B5e, DK-Blc, PRK-B3fl, PRK-B3i, talk with Joe de Rienzo, 24.5.85.
KR Defections File.
Magstad, Mary Kay. "Notes on the Khmer Rouge, February–October 1989."
Material on Ieng Sary File.
"Meeting with Mr. Sar Kim Lamuth, May 5, 1995, at the Ministry of the Interior (JW/05.05.95)."
Memorandum from Christophe Peschoux (revised by David Ashley) to David Hawk et al., "First Needs Assessment Mission in the Zones Controlled by the Khmer Rouge Dissident Factions (24–27 January 1997)."
NADK Document, "Decisions of the Meeting of 1001 Leading Cadre," January 10, 1992.
NADK PAPERS File.
"National Army of Democratic Kampuchea High Command: Deployment of Forces of the NADK Divisions and Independent Regiments," August 1991.
"Norn Suon called Chey Suon called Chey called Sèn called Sèng: Final Part: Part 6: XII. He Talks about a Number of Older Brothers in the Leading Organization," November 21, 1976, 6–10. Translation by Steve Heder.
Office of the Centre for Human Rights in Cambodia to Thomas Hammarberg. "Your Second Mission—Amnesty to Ieng Sary and Other DK Leaders" and "Suggested Draft Statement on the Issue of Amnesty to Ieng Sary and Other Figures or Senior Cadres of Democratic Kampuchea (Khmer Rouge)," November 14, 1996.
Partial Document: Confidential Interview with Peas Sambath, December 10, 1997.
Peschoux, Christophe. Interview with C, August 1990.
Peschoux, Christophe. Interview with CH, July 1990.
Peschoux, Christophe. Interview with CY, March 1990.
Peschoux, Christophe. Interview with Khat Sali, Sihanoukville, January 9–10, 1992 [*sic;* actually 1993].
Peschoux, Christophe. Interview with KS, Sihanoukville, January 1993 (SHA).
Peschoux, Christophe. Interview with R, August 1990.
Peschoux, Christophe. Interview with S, August 1990.
Peschoux, Christophe. Interview with SS, August 1990.
Peschoux, Christophe. Interview with V, April 1990.
Peschoux, Christophe. Interview with V, August 1990.
Peschoux, Christophe. Interview with V, November 1990.
Peschoux, Christophe. *Les "nouveaux" Khmères rouges: Enquête (1979–1990)—Reconstruction du mouvement et reconquête des villages.* Paris: L'Harmattan, 1992.
Princess Sisowath Ayravady. "Declaration (Fait à Paris, le 22 Octobre 1989)" in "Material on Ieng Sary."
Reaksmei Kampuchea, November 2, 1996.
Reaksmei Kampuchea, November 10, 1996.

"Subject: Dealing with Khmer Rouge Numbers (U)."
"Talk with Ee Chhien, January 27, 1997."
Transcription of Ieng Thirith's 1980 audio interview by Elizabeth Becker.
UN Secretary General. "Fourth Progress Report of the Secretary on UNTAC," 1993.
UNCOHCHR [United Nations Cambodia Office of the High Commissioner for Human Rights]. Interviews Conducted at Phum Dong Village, Phnom Malai, Banteay Meanchey Province, September 27, 1996.
UNCOHCHR. Interview with Mao Sam Oeun, Phnom Penh, October 9–10, 1996.
UNCOHCHR. "Phon Phaen (Ex-Deputy Commander of Division 705. Now District Governor of Sampoeu Luang), Sampoeu Lang, Front 250," January 25, 1997.
UNCOHCHR. "Talk with Om Van," Phum Dong, Malai, January 26, 1997.
UNOSGRC. "Weekly Report #103 Covering the Period from 2 to 8 September 1996," September 9, 1996.
UNOSGRC. "Monthly Report for December 1996."
UNOSGRG. "Monthly Report for November 1996."
UNTAC (United Nations Transitional Authority in Cambodia). Interoffice memorandum from Deputy Chief, Military Information Branch, to Chief, Military Information Branch, "Interview with Self-Demobilized NADK Soldier—Cheun Cheam," November 13, 1992.
UNTAC. Interoffice memorandum from Steve Heder to Yasushi Akashi (through Tim Carney), "A January PDK Document," January 20, 1993.
UNTAC. Interoffice memorandum from Steve Heder to Yasushi Akashi (through Tim Carney), "PDK Leadership and Policy," November 3, 1992.
UNTAC. Memorandum from Deputy Chief, Military Information Branch, to Chief, Military Information Branch, "Interview with Self-Demobilized Soldier—Set Siet," November 11, 1992.
UNTAC. Memorandum, "Notes on Interview with NADK 'Self-Demobilizer,' Interview with an NADK Defector in Kampot Province," from Christophe Peschoux to Tim Carney via Penny Edwards, January 27, 1993.
"US Embassy Debrief of Ex-Senior Khmer Rouge Commander," undated [late 1994].
VGNUFC (Voice of Democratic Kampuchea). "Propaganda Themes since April 1992."
"VODK Catalogs Years of Failure since SRV Attack," Voice of Democratic Kampuchea (clandestine radio broadcast), January 6, 1985.
Waller, Robert E., LTC, DCMIO. "Memorandum thru the Chief, Military Information, for the Force Commander, Notes from a Talk with Christophe Peschoux," September 20, 1992.
Werbrouk, Filip. "The Site 8 Artificial Limb Workshop: A Humanitarian or Military Aid Programme? A Study of Aid to a Khmer Rouge Camp on the Thai-Cambodian Border," April 1987.
"What Is the Virtue, the Quality, the Reality, and the Responsibility of Democratic Kampuchea in the Past, Present, and Future?" December 2, 1986 (English translator unknown).

Widyono, Benny. Confidential Interim Report No. 572, "An Analysis of Recent Developments."

"Yen, Cadre in NADK Division 450."

From the Extraordinary Chambers of the Courts of Cambodia Archives

D46, Office of the Co-Investigating Judges, Criminal Case File 002/14-08-2006, Investigation 002/19-09-2007-ECCC-OCIJ, Written Record of Charged Person, Kaing Guek-Eav alias Duch, April 1, 2008.

D86/4, Office of the Co-Investigating Judges, Criminal Case File 002/14-08-2006, Investigation 001/18-07-2007-ECCC-OCIJ, Written Record of Charged Person, Kaing Guek-Eav alias Duch, August 23, 2007.

D86/5, Office of the Co-Investigating Judges, Criminal Case File 002/14/2006, Investigation 001/18-07-2007-ECCC-OCIJ, Written Record of Charged Person, Kaing Guek-Eav alias Duch, September 5, 2007.

D86/7, Office of the Co-Investigating Judges, Criminal Case File 002/14-08-2006, Investigation 001/18-07-2007-ECCC-OCIJ, Written Record of Charged Person, Kaing Guek-Eav alias Duch, October 7, 2007.

D86/8, Office of the Co-Investigating Judges, Criminal Case File 002/14-08-2006, Investigation 001/18-07-2007-ECCC-OCIJ, Written Record of Charged Person, Kaing Guek-Eav alias Duch, November 22, 2007.

D86/9, Office of the Co-Investigating Judges, Criminal Case File 002/14-08-2006, Investigation 001/18-07-2007-ECCC-OCIJ, Written Record of Charged Person, Kaing Guek-Eav alias Duch, November 29, 2007.

D86/10, Office of the Co-Investigating Judges, Criminal Case File 002/14-08-2006, Investigation 001/18-07-2007-ECCC-OCIJ, Written Record of Charged Person, Kaing Guek-Eav alias Duch, September 5, 2007.

D86/23, Office of the Co-Investigating Judges, Criminal Investigation 002/19-09-2007-ECCC-OCIJ, Written Record of Charged Person, Kaing Guek-Eav alias Duch, June 2, 2008.

D86/27, Office of the Co-Investigating Judges, Investigation 001/18-07-2007-ECCC-OCIJ, Written Record of Charged Person, Kaing Guek-Eav alias Duch, May 5, 2008.

D87, Office of the Co-Investigating Judges, Criminal Investigation 002/19-09-2007-ECCC-OCIJ, Written Record of Charged Person, Kaing Guek-Eav alias Duch, June 2, 2008.

D88, Office of the Co-Investigating Judges, Criminal Investigation 002/19-09-2007-ECCC-OCIJ, Written Record of Charged Person, Kaing Guek-Eav alias Duch, June 3, 2008.

D89, Office of the Co-Investigating Judges, Criminal Case File 002/19-09-2007-ECCC-OCIJ, Written Record of Charged Person, Kaing Guek-Eav alias Duch, June 24, 2008.

D91/3, Office of the Co-Investigating Judges, Criminal Case File 002/14-08-2006, Investigation 002/19-09-2007-ECCC-OCIJ, Written Record of Interview of Witness, Long Norin, December 4, 2007.

BIBLIOGRAPHY

D91/10, Office of the Co-Investigating Judges, Criminal Case File 002/14-08-2006, Investigation 002/19-09-2007-ECCC-OCIJ, Written Record of Interview of Witness, Phy Phuon, December 5, 2007.

D91/14, Office of the Co-Investigating Judges, Criminal Case File 002/14-08-2006, Investigation 002/19-09-2007-ECCC-OCIJ, Written Record of Interview of Witness, Saloth Ban, December 11, 2007.

D91/24, Office of the Co-Investigating Judges, Criminal Case File 002/14-08-2006, Investigation 002/19-09-2007-ECCC-OCIJ, Written Record of Interview of Witness, Saloth Ban, December 11, 2007, 3.

D91/26, Office of the Co-Investigating Judges, Criminal Case File 002/14-08-2006, Investigation 002/19-09-2007-ECCC-OCIJ, Written Record of Interview of Witness, Suong Sikoeun, December 19, 2007.

D95, Office of the Co-Investigating Judges 002/19-09-2007-ECCC-OCIJ, Written Record of Charged Person, Kaing Guek-Eav alias Duch, July 15, 2008.

D107/3, Office of the Co-Investigating Judges, Criminal Case File 002/14-08-2006, Investigation 002/19-09-2007-ECCC-OCIJ, Written Record of Interview of Witness, Phy Phuon, September 21, 2008.

D115/4, Tribunal de Grande Instance de Dijon, Written Record of Witness Deposition, Laurence Picq, October 31, 2008.

D117, Office of the Co-Investigating Judges, Criminal Case File 002/14-08-2006, Investigation 001/19-09-2007-ECCC-OCIJ, Written Record of Charged Person, Kaing Guek-Eav alias Duch, November 19, 2008.

D118, Office of the Co-Investigating Judges, Criminal Case File 002/14-08-2006, Investigation 002/19-09-2007-ECCC-OCIJ, Written Record of Charged Person, Kaing Guek-Eav alias Duch, November 20, 2008.

D119, Office of the Co-Investigating Judges, Criminal Case File 002/14-08-2006, Investigation 001/19-09-2007-ECCC-OCIJ, Written Record of Charged Person, Kaing Guek-Eav alias Duch, November 25, 2008.

D123/2, Office of the Co-Investigating Judges, Criminal Case File 002/14-08-2006, Investigation 002/19-09-2007-ECCC-OCIJ, Written Record of Interview of Witness, Chhouk Rin, May 21, 2008.

D123/3, Office of the Co-Investigating Judges, Criminal Case File 002/14-08-2006, Investigation 002/19-09-2007-ECCC-OCIJ, Written Record of Interview of Witness, Chhouk Rin, July 29, 2008.

D143, Office of the Co-Investigating Judges, Criminal Case File 002/14-08-2006, Investigation 002/19-09-2007-ECCC-OCIJ, Written Record of Interview of Witness, Suong Sikoeun, March 12, 2009.

D166/117, Office of the Co-Investigating Judges, Criminal Case File 002/14-08-2006, Investigation 002/19-09-2007-ECCC-OCIJ, Written Record of Interview of Witness, Khoem Sâmhuon, March 6, 2009.

D166/166, Office of the Co-Investigating Judges, Criminal Case File 002/14-08-2006, Investigation 002/19-09-2007-ECCC-OCIJ, Written Record of Interview of Witness, Kè Pich Vannak, June 4, 2009.

D167, Office of the Co-Investigating Judges, Criminal Case File 002/14-08-2006, Investigation 002/19-09-2007-ECCC-OCIJ, Written Record of Interview of Witness, Suong Sikoeun, May 6, 2009.

BIBLIOGRAPHY 233

D168, Office of the Co-Investigating Judges, Criminal Case File 002/14-08-2006, Investigation 002/19-09-2007-ECCC-OCIJ, Written Record of Interview of Witness, Suong Sikoeun, May 7, 2009.

D199/14, Rogatory Letter Record of Civil Party Martine Lefeuvre, June 2, 2009.

D199/20, Rogatory Letter Record of Civil Party Thiounn Prasith, June 8, 2009.

D199/21, Rogatory Letter Record of Civil Party Boramy Svay, June 9, 2009.

D200/9, Office of the Co-Investigating Judges, Criminal Case File 002/14-08-2006, Investigation 002/19-09-2007-ECCC-OCIJ, Written Record of Witness Interview, Norng Sophàng, March 28, 2009.

D210/12, ECCC Interview of Heng Teav.

D225, Office of the Co-Investigating Judges, Criminal Case File 002/14-08-2006, Investigation 001/19-09-2007-ECCC-OCIJ, Written Record of Charged Person, Kaing Guek-Eav alias Duch, October 20, 2009.

D233/7, Office of the Co-Investigating Judges, Criminal Case File 002/14-08-2006, Investigation 002/19-09-2007-ECCC-OCIJ, Written Record of Interview of Witness, In Sopheap, September 28, 2009.

D233/14, Office of the Co-Investigating Judges, Criminal Case File 002/14-08-2006, Investigation 002/19-09-2007-ECCC-OCIJ, Written Record of Interview of Witness, Toch Vannarith, December 22, 2009.

D234/21, Office of the Co-Investigating Judges, Criminal Case File 002/14-08-2006, Investigation 002/19-09-2007-ECCC-OCIJ, Written Record of Witness Interview, Chhouk Rin, November 26, 2009.

D369/6, Office of the Co-Investigating Judges, Criminal Case File 002/14-08-2006, Investigation 002/19-09-2007-ECCC-OCIJ, Written Record of Witness, Chuon Thi, March 2, 2010.

D427, Office of the Co-Investigating Judges, Closing Order, Case File No. 002/19-09-2007-ECCC-OCIJ. https://www.eccc.gov.kh/sites/default/files/documents/courtdoc/D427Eng.pdf.

Extraordinary Chambers in the Courts of Cambodia, Closing Order Case 002/01n Judgment. https://www.legal-tools.org/doc/4888de/pdf/.

Extraordinary Chambers in the Courts of Cambodia, Co-Prosecutors' Closing Brief E457/6/1, Case 002/02, May 18, 2017. https://www.eccc.gov.kh/sites/default/files/documents/courtdoc/%5Bdate-in-tz%5D/E457_6_1_Redacted_EN.pdf.

Extraordinary Chambers in the Courts of Cambodia Office of the Co-Investigating Judges, Criminal Case File 002/14-08-2006, Investigation 002/19-09-2007-ECCC-OCIJ, Written Record of Interview of Witness, Long Norin, December 4, 2007.

Extraordinary Chambers in the Courts of Cambodia, Trial Chamber—Trial Day 33, Case No. 001/18-07-2007-ECCC/TC Kaing Guek-Eav, June 24, 2009.

From Khieu Samphân's Phnom Dângrêk Residence

"Comrade First Minister Khieu Samphân's Meeting with Son Sann (Late May 1980)."

"Comrade First Minister Khieu Samphân's Second Meeting with Son Sann, January 26, 1981."

"Meeting Minutes: Brother Hæm Meets with Chinese Embassy [Officials], December 21, 1987, Nighttime."
"Meeting with Dien Del, June 12, 1981, from 3:30 to 5:00 PM at His Excellency Nong's House."
"Minutes of Comrade First Minister P P's Meeting with Son San (Late September 1979)."
"Minutes of Comrade Khieu Samphân's Meeting with Dien Del, May 8, 1981."
"National Income Generation, Democratic Kampuchea, December 1981."
"Supplementary Notes to the Minutes of October 4, 1981."

From Other Sites

Kè Pauk. "Ke Pauk's Autobiography from 1949–1985." Document on file with DC-CAM. https://d.dccam.org/Archives/Documents/Biography/Biographies_Autography_Ke_Pauk.htm.
"Khmer Rouge Brands Ieng Sary a Traitor." Radio of the Provisional Government of National Union and National Salvation of Cambodia, August 7, 1996, FBIS-EAS-96-154.
Kuong Lumphon. "Report on the Communist Party of Cambodia" (Pak Kommunist Kampuchea), "PCK," submitted to the Republican Government, May 8, 1973. Personal papers of David Chandler.
Lane, Dennison. The Cambodian Border File.
"Summary: the following is the first of two (2) IIRs addressing Khmer Rouge camps. This IIR addresses Site 8."
"Station Calls on Khmer Rouge Fighters to Return." Phnom Penh National Radio, September 21, 1995, FBIS-EAS-95-186, September 1995.

In-Country/Author Interviews

Interview 09AV01, Anlong Veng, June 21, 2009.
Interview 13AV01, Anlong Veng, January 3, 2013.
Interview 14PL01, Pailin, December 28, 2014.
Interview 14PL03, Pailin, December 29, 2014.
Interview 14PL04, Pailin, December 30, 2014.
Interview 14PL05, Pailin, December 30, 2014.
Interview 14PL06, Pailin, December 31, 2014.
Interview 15MDK01, Mondulkiri, January 27, 2015.
Interview 15MDK02, Mondulkiri, January 27, 2015.
Interview 15MDK03, Mondulkiri, January 27, 2015.
Interview 16AV01, Anlong Veng, October 6, 2016.
Interview 16AV05, Anlong Veng, October 7, 2016.
Interview 19DC03, Washington, DC, August 2, 2019.
Interview 20AV03 Anlong Veng, July 5, 2020.
Interview 20AV04, Anlong Veng, July 5, 2020.
Interview 20AV05, Anlong Veng, July 5, 2020.
Interview 20SR01, Siem Reap, July 6, 2020.
Interview 20PL01, Pailin, July 7, 2020.

Interview 20PL07, Pailin, July 20, 2020.
Interview 20PS02, Pursat, August 15, 2020.
Interview 21DC01A, Washington, DC, October 10, 2021.
Interview 21DC01D, Washington, DC, November 7, 2021.
Interview 21DC01F, Washington, DC, November 17, 2021.
Interview 21DC02, Washington, DC, November 21, 2021.

Secondary Sources

Becker, Elizabeth. *When the War Was Over: Cambodia and the Khmer Rouge Revolution*. New York: PublicAffairs, 1998.
Becker, Elizabeth. *When the War Was Over: The Voices of Cambodia and Its People*. New York: Simon & Schuster, 1986.
Bekaert, Jacques. *Cambodian Diary: A Long Road to Peace, 1987–1993*. Bangkok: White Lotus, 1998.
Bizot, François. *The Gate*. New York: Vintage, 2004.
Brown, MacAlistern, and Joseph J. Zasloff. *Cambodia Confounds the Peacemakers, 1979–1998*. Ithaca: Cornell University Press, 1998.
Bultmann, Daniel. *Inside Cambodian Insurgency: A Sociological Perspective on Civil Wars and Conflict*. Farnham, Surrey: Ashgate, 2015.
Burgler, R.A. *The Eyes of the Pineapple: Revolutionary Intellectuals and Terror in Democratic Kampuchea*. Nijmegen Studies in Development and Cultural Change. Nijmegen: Nijmeegs Instituut voor Comparatieve Cultuuren Ontwikkelingsstudies (NICCOS), 1990.
Buszynski, Leszek. "Thailand's Foreign Policy: Management of a Regional Vision." *Asian Survey* 34, no. 8 (August 1994): 721-37.
"Cambodia's Dirty Dozen: A Long History of Rights Abuses by Hun Sen's Generals." Human Rights Watch, June 28, 2018.
Chanda, Nayan. *Brother Enemy: The War after the War*. New York: Collier, 1986.
Chanda, Nayan. "When the Killing Had to Stop." *Far Eastern Economic Review*, (October 29, 1976): 20-23.
Chandler, David P. *Brother Number One: A Political Biography of Pol Pot*. Boulder: Westview Press, 1999.
Chandler, David P. *The Tragedy of Cambodian History: Politics, War, and Revolution since 1945*. New Haven: Yale University Press, 1991.
Chandler, David P. *Voices from S-21: Terror and History from Pol Pot's Secret Prison*. Berkeley: University of California Press, 1999.
Chandler, David P., Ben Kiernan, and Chanthou Boua, eds. *Pol Pot Plans the Future: Confidential Leadership Documents from Democratic Kampuchea, 1976–1977*. Monograph 33. New Haven: Yale University Southeast Asia Studies.
Ciorciari, John D., and Anne Heindel. *Hybrid Justice: The Extraordinary Chambers in the Courts of Cambodia*. Ann Arbor: University of Michigan Press, 2014.
Colm, Sara, and Sorya Sim. *Khmer Rouge Purges in the Mondul Kiri Highlands Region 105*. Documentation Series no. 14. Documentation Center of Cambodia, Phnom Penh, 2009.

Conboy, Kenneth. *The Cambodian Wars: Clashing Armies and CIA Covert Operations*. Lawrence: University Press of Kansas, 2013.

Corfield, Justin, and Laura Summers. *Historical Dictionary of Cambodia*. Asian/Oceanian Historical Dictionaries no. 43. Lanham, MD: Scarecrow Press, 2003.

Dunlop, Nic. *The Lost Executioner: A Journey to the Heart of the Killing Fields*. New York: Walker & Company, 2006.

Dy Khamboly and Christopher Dearing. *A History of the Anlong Veng Community: The Final Stronghold of the Khmer Rouge Movement*. Documentation Series no. 20. Phnom Penh: Documentation Center of Cambodia in Collaboration with the Ministry of Tourism, Kingdom of Cambodia, 2014.

Ea, Meng Try. *The Chain of Terror: The Khmer Rouge Southwest Zone Security System*. Documentation Series no. 7. Phnom Penh: Documentation Center of Cambodia, 2005.

French, Lindsay Cole. "Enduring Holocaust, Surviving History: Displaced Cambodians on the Thai-Cambodian Border." PhD dissertation, Harvard University, 1994.

Galway, Matthew. "Specters of Dependency: Hou Yuon and the Origins of Cambodia's Marxist Vision (1955–1975)." *Cross-Currents: East Asian History and Culture Review* 1, no. 31 (2019). https://escholarship.org/uc/item/1bk8d0h4.

Gottesman, Evan. *Cambodia after the Khmer Rouge: Inside the Politics of Nation Building*. New Haven: Yale University Press, 2003.

Gray, Spalding. *Swimming to Cambodia: The Collected Works of Spalding Gray*. London: Picador, 1987.

Harben, William N. "The Association for Diplomatic Studies and Training Foreign Affairs Oral History Project," 1998, 58–59. https://www.adst.org/OH%20TOCs/Harben,%20William%20N.toc.pdf?_ga=2.55948331.1296246245.1561081605-268390464.1561081605.

Heder, Stephen R. "Khieu Samphan and Pol Pot: Moloch's Poodle," undated.

Heder, Stephen R. "Pol Pot at Bay: People's War and the Breakdown of the 1991 Paris Agreements." PhD dissertation, School of Oriental and African Studies, London, 1999.

Heder, Stephen, and Brian D. Tittemore. *Seven Candidates for Prosecution: Accountability for the Crimes of the Khmer Rouge*. Documentation Series no. 4. Phnom Penh: Documentation Center of Cambodia, 2004.

Heder, Steve. *Cambodian Communism and the Vietnamese Model: Imitation and Independence, 1930–1975*. Bangkok: White Lotus, 2004.

Heder, Steve. "From Pol Pot to Pen Sovan to the Villages." Paper presented to the International Conference on Indochina and Problems of Security and Stability in Southeast Asia, Chulalongkorn University, Bangkok, June 19–21, 1980.

Heder, Steve. "The Resumption of Armed Struggle by the Party of Democratic Kampuchea: Evidence from the National Army of Democratic Kampuchea 'Self-Demobilizers.'" In *Propaganda, Politics, and Violence in Cambodia: Democratic Transitions under United Nations Peace-Keeping*, ed. Steve Heder and Judy Ledgerwood, 73–113. Armonk, NY: M. E. Sharpe, 1996.

Hinton, Alexander Laban. *Man or Monster? The Trial of a Khmer Rouge Torturer.* Durham: Duke University Press, 2016.

Hinton, Alexander Laban. *Why Did They Kill? Cambodia in the Shadow of Genocide.* Berkeley: University of California Press, 2004.

Hoffer, Eric. *The True Believer: Thoughts on the Nature of Mass Movements.* New York: Harper Perennial Modern Classics, 2010.

Huang, Jing. *Factionalism in Chinese Communist Politics.* New York: Cambridge University Press, 2000.

Huy Vannak. *The Khmer Rouge Division 703: From Victory to Self-Destruction.* Documentation Series no. 3. Phnom Penh: Documentation Center of Cambodia, 2003.

Ith Sarin. "Nine Months in the Maquis." In Tim Carney, "Communist Party Power in Kampuchea," Data Paper 106, 34–41. Ithaca: Southeast Asian Studies Program, Department of Asian Studies, Cornell University, January 1977.

Kalyvas, Stathis N. *The Logic of Violence in Civil War.* New York: Cambridge University Press, 2002.

Kamm, Henry. *Cambodia: Report from a Stricken Land.* New York: Arcade, 1999.

Kiernan, Ben. *How Pol Pot Came to Power: Colonialism, Nationalism, and Communism in Cambodia, 1930–1975.* New Haven: Yale University Press, 2004.

Kiernan, Ben. "Pol Pot and the Kampuchean Communist Movement." In *Peasants and Politics in Kampuchea, 1942–1981,* ed. Ben Kiernan and Chanthou Boua, 227–317. London: Zed Press, 1982.

Kiernan, Ben. *The Pol Pot Regime: Race, Power, and Genocide in Cambodia under the Khmer Rouge, 1975–79.* New Haven: Yale University Press, 1996.

Kiernan, Ben. "The Samlaut Rebellion and Its Aftermath, 1967–1970: The Origins of Cambodia's Liberation Movement, Part 1." Imprint no. 4, Monash University, Melbourne, 1975.

Kolakowski, Leszek. *Main Currents of Marxism.* Vol. 1. *The Founders.* New York: Oxford University Press, 1978.

Kolakowski, Leszek. *Main Currents of Marxism.* Vol. 3. *The Breakdown.* New York: Oxford University Press, 1978.

Kotkin, Stephen. *Stalin.* Vol. 1. *Paradoxes of Power, 1878–1928.* New York: Penguin, 2015.

"The Life and Crimes of Ta Mok." *Phnom Penh Post,* January 16, 1998.

Locard, Henri. *Jungle Heart of the Khmer Rouge: The Memoirs of Phi Phuon, Pol Pot's Jarai Aide-de-Camp, and the Role of Ratanakiri and Its Tribal Minorities in the Cambodian Revolution.* NIAS Monographs no. 157. Copenhagen: Nordic Institute of Asian Studies, 2023.

Locard, Henri. *Pol Pot's Little Red Book: The Sayings of Angkar.* Chiang Mai: Silkworm Books, 2005.

Magstad, Mary Kay, and David Hawk. "Khmer Rouge Abuses Along the Thai-Cambodian Border." [Washington, DC]: Asia Watch Committee; available from Human Rights Watch, 1989.

Mao Tse-tung [Mao Zedong]. *A Single Spark Can Start a Prairie Fire.* Peking: Foreign Language Press, 1953.

Mao Zedong, "Speech at the Hangzhou Conference, December 21, 1965." https://www.marxists.org/chinese/maozedong/1968/5-172.htm.
Martine, Marie Alexandrine. *Cambodia: A Shattered Society*. Translated by Mark W. McLeod. Berkeley: University of California Press, 1994.
Marx, Karl. *The Eighteenth Brumaire of Louis Bonaparte*. New York: Die Revolution, 1852.
Mason, Linda Hunter, and Roger Brown. *Rice, Rivalry, and Politics: Managing Cambodian Relief*. Notre Dame: University of Notre Dame Press, 1983.
McDermid, Charles. "Looking Back at the 1979 People's Revolutionary Tribunal." *Phnom Penh Post*, January 26, 2007. https://www.phnompenhpost.com/national/looking-back-1979-peoples-revolutionary-tribunal.
Mertha, Andrew. *Brothers in Arms: Chinese Aid to the Khmer Rouge, 1975–1979*. Ithaca: Cornell University Press, 2014.
Nhem, Boraden. *The Khmer Rouge: Ideology, Militarism, and a Revolution That Consumed a Generation*. Santa Barbara: Praeger, 2013.
Norén-Nilsson, Astrid. "Children of Former Khmer Rouge Cadres." *Peace Review: A Journal of Social Justice* 23 (2011): 462–68.
Osbourne, Milton. *Before Kampuchea: Preludes to Tragedy*. Bangkok: Orchid Press, 2006.
Panh, Rithy, with Christophe Bataille. *The Elimination: A Survivor of the Khmer Rouge Confronts His Past and the Commandant of the Killing Fields*. London: Clerkenwell Press, 2013.
Pierson, Paul. "Increasing Returns, Path Dependence, and the Study of Politics." *American Political Science Review* 94, no. 2 (June 2000): 251–67. https://doi.org/10.2307/2586011.
Pilger, John. *Heroes*. Cambridge, MA: South End Press, 2002.
Pringle, James. "Pol Pot Cleans Up Image with Soap Opera." *The Times*, June 6, 1990.
Quinn, Kenneth. "The Khmer Krahom Program to Create a Communist Society in Southern Cambodia," US Department of State, US Consulate Can Tho (Vietnam) (19 February 1974). https://www.ambassadorkennethquinnarchive.org/media/cms/The_Khmer_Krahom_Program_to_Create__772B3E1D6BE91.pdf.
Quinn, Kenneth. "The Origins and Development of Radical Cambodian Communism." PhD dissertation, University of Maryland, College Park, 1982.
"Request for Opening a New Investigation of So Met and Meas Mut." The Investigative Fund. www.theinvestigativefund.org/files/managed/Cambodia2nd_Intro_Submission.pdf.
Reynell, Josephine. "Political Pawns: Refugees on the Thai-Kampuchean Border." Refugee Studies Programme, University of Oxford, 1989.
Richardson, Sophie. *China, Cambodia, and the Five Principles of Peaceful Coexistence*. New York: Columbia University Press, 2009.
Riddell, John. "The Origins of the United Front Policy," *International Socialism* 130 (2011). http://isj.org.uk/the-origins-of-the-united-front-policy/.
Robinson, W. Courtland. "Double Vision: A History of Cambodian Refugees in Thailand." Asian Research Center for Migration, Institute of Asian Studies, Chulalongkorn University, July 1996.

Rowley, Kelvin. "Second Life, Second Death: The Khmer Rouge after 1978." In *Genocide in Cambodia and Rwanda: New Perspectives*, ed. Susan E. Cook. New Brunswick, NJ: Transaction Publishers, 2006.
Rust, William J. *Eisenhower and Cambodia, Covert Action, and the Origins of the Second Indochina War*. Lexington: University Press of Kentucky, 2016.
Shawcross, William. *The Quality of Mercy: Cambodia, Holocaust and Modern Conscience*. New York: Simon and Schuster, 1984.
Shenon, Philip. "Pol Pot & Co.: The Thai Connection—A Special Report; In Big Threat to Cambodia, Thais Still Aid Khmer Rouge." *New York Times*, December 19, 1993.
Short, Philip. *Pol Pot: Anatomy of a Nightmare*. New York: Henry Holt, 2005.
Skinner, G. William. *Marketing and Social Structure in Rural China*. Ann Arbor: Journal of Asian Studies Monographs, 2010.
Slocomb, Margaret. *The People's Republic of Kampuchea, 1979–1989: The Revolution after Pol Pot*. Chiang Mai: Silkworm Books, 2003.
Staniland, Paul. *Networks of Rebellion: Explaining Insurgent Cohesion and Collapse*. Ithaca: Cornell University Press, 2014.
Steinmo, Sven, and Kathleen Thelen, eds. *Structuring Politics: Historical Institutionalism in Comparative Analysis*. New York: Cambridge University Press, 1992.
Strangio, Sebastian. *Hun Sen's Cambodia*. New Haven: Yale University Press, 2014.
Thayer, Nate. "Cambodia: Misperceptions and Peace." *Washington Quarterly* 14, no. 2 (Spring 1991): 179–91.
Thayer, Nate. "Khmer Rouge, Cambodian Government Suffer Memory Failure in Court: This Might Help." *Nate Thayer* (blog), December 8, 2011. https://natethayer.typepad.com/blog/kr-personalities-ieng-sary/.
Thayer, Nate. "Rubies Are Rouge." *Far Eastern Economic Review*, February 7, 1991: 29–30.
Thayer, Nate. "12 Entries Categorized 'KR Personalities-Ieng Sary.'" *Nate Thayer* (blog). https://natethayer.typepad.com/blog/kr-personalities-ieng-sary/.
Thion, Serge. *Watching Cambodia: Ten Paths to Enter the Cambodian Tangle*. Bangkok: White Lotus, 1993.
Trotsky, Leon. *The First Five Years of the Communist International*. Vol. 2. Moscow: State Publishing House, 1924.
Tyner, James A. *The Politics of Lists: Bureaucracy and Genocide under the Khmer Rouge*. Morgantown: West Virginia University Press, 2018.
Uk, Krisna. "Local Perceptions and Responses to Risk: A Study of a Cambodian Village." Master's thesis, University of Cambridge, 2006.
Uk, Krisna. *Salvage: Cultural Resilience among the Jorai of Northeast Cambodia*. Ithaca: Cornell University Press, 2016.
Vickery, Michael. *Cambodia, 1979–1982*. Chiang Mai: Silkworm Books, 1984.
Whitlock, Craig. *The Afghanistan Papers: A Secret History of the War*. New York: Simon & Schuster, 2021.
Widyono, Benny. *Dancing in Shadows: Sihanouk, the Khmer Rouge, and the United Nations in Cambodia*. New York: Rowman & Littlefield, 2008.

Wood, Timothy Dylan. "'Tracing the Last Breath': Movements in Anlong Veng." Doctoral thesis, Rice University, 2009.

Yang Su. *Biography of Ai Siqi* [艾思奇传]. 2nd ed. Kunming: Yunnan Education Publishers, 2002.

Yun Shui. "An Account of Chinese Diplomats Accompanying the Government of Democratic Kampuchea's Move to the Cardamom Mountains." Translated by Paul Marks. *Critical Asian Studies* 34, no. 4 (2002): 502-6.

Zolberg, Aristide R., Astri Suhrke, and Sergio Aguayo. *Escape from Violence: Conflict and the Refugee Crisis in the Developing World*. New York: Oxford University Press, 1989.

Index

abduction, 160, 161
abuse, 139, 215, 224
accusation, xxiii, 20, 60, 73, 123, 126, 132–133, 135, 147, 164, 167, 224, 225
adultery, 72, 116
AEK (Khmer Students' Association), xv, 24
Afghanistan, xviii, 90, 211
agriculture, xviii, xxii, 15, 17, 47, 49–50, 60, 105, 111–112, 133, 141, 149, 184–185, 188, 219, 224
aid, xix, 57, 83, 90–91, 98, 122, 129, 146, 151, 157, 160, 162, 197, 204
Akashi Yasushi, 154, 215, 217–219
alias (*nom de guerre*), ix, xxi–xxiv, 14, 18, 20–22, 35, 40–41, 43, 59, 63, 66–67, 69, 73, 82–83, 89, 99, 101, 135, 161, 197–199, 201–203, 205–209, 216
alliances, 3–6, 35, 43–44, 48, 52–53, 66, 80, 90, 92, 96, 103, 114, 171. *See also* united front
amnesty, 12, 168, 189, 222
Angkar, 35, 51, 193, 197
ANKI (Armées Nationale pour Khmer Indépendant), xv, 92, 94, 150
Anlong Veng, xi, xix, 16, 21, 87, 89, 97, 113, 117–118, 151–152, 156–157, 159, 162–163, 167, 170–172, 174–175, 178, 189, 193, 199–200, 210, 213–214, 216, 220–222, 224
ANS (Armée Nationale Sihanoukiste), xv, 96–97, 119, 124–125, 150, 211
anticolonial, 21, 187, 194
anticommunist, 48, 55, 114, 150
anti-Vietnamese, 34, 150
Aranyaprathet, 123
armies, xvi, 2, 19, 33, 42, 45, 49, 63–64, 76, 83–84, 87–90, 92, 96, 107–108, 123, 142, 164, 175–176, 181, 188–189
arms, xxv, 25, 32, 36, 42, 44, 68, 150–151, 180, 199, 204, 208–209, 224

arrests, xix, xx, xxii, 12–13, 14, 23, 38, 44–45, 60–61, 67, 74–76, 86, 115, 123, 160–161, 163, 168, 173, 179–180, 192
artillery, 124, 175
ASEAN, 90
Asia, xii, 30, 61, 90, 123, 181, 206, 214, 224
assistance, 37, 118, 124, 145, 147
atrocities, 181, 220, 222
Aural Mountains, 42

Ban Baranae, 120, 124
Bangkok, 83, 97–98, 130, 144, 168, 214
banknotes, ix, 36, 157–158
banks, 36, 47, 64, 84, 98, 102, 106
Banteay Meanchey, 198, 216, 220–221
Baran, Michel, 160–161
bases, xxii, 3, 7, 14, 22–23, 29, 33, 36, 39, 41–42, 62, 64, 82, 88–89, 99, 101–102, 104–106, 111–115, 125, 127, 128–130, 131, 146, 149, 152, 155, 159, 161, 184, 186, 188, 190, 193–194, 205, 223
Battambang, xvii, 2, 32, 41, 43, 59, 68, 83–84, 108, 113, 121, 124, 179, 189, 204, 221
Becker, Elizabeth, xii, 70, 86, 90, 119, 197–199, 207–210, 214
Beijing, xviii, 6, 14, 35–39, 53, 61, 63, 83, 85, 92, 96–99, 128, 137, 143, 146, 157, 181, 183, 188, 205
betrayal, 24, 39, 65, 75, 116, 152, 160, 174–175, 181–182, 187
Boeng Trabek, 60, 75, 193, 205
Borai, 120–121, 126–128, 146, 193
borders, xi–xii, xviii, xxii, xxv, 3, 25, 29, 36, 47, 65, 68, 70–71, 73–74, 80, 83–84, 87–89, 91, 94, 96–99, 102–105, 108–109, 113, 118–119, 120, 122, 123, 126–129, 131, 133–134, 143, 146, 152, 156, 160, 166, 170–171, 174–175, 179, 186, 189, 192–194, 198–200, 202–206, 208, 210–211, 213–215

INDEX

bourgeois, 8, 25, 29, 31, 56-57, 59, 63-64, 73, 77, 85, 114, 133, 181, 186
Braquet, Jean-Michel, 160-161
brutality, 2, 8, 10-11, 20, 41, 55-56, 66, 69, 72, 74, 79, 92, 157, 159, 164, 173, 180
Brzezinski, Zbigniew, 90
Bundred, Robert, 160

cadre, ix, xi, 8, 10-11, 35, 37, 43-44, 51, 53-54, 56, 60-61, 66-68, 71-74, 76, 82, 84-85, 88, 101, 103, 105, 110, 112, 115-116, 119, 126-127, 132-133, 135-136, 138, 146, 148-149, 155-156, 163-165, 169, 172, 175, 181, 185, 190-191, 205, 212, 219-220, 222-224
Caldwell, Malcolm, 86
camps, ix, xviii-xix, xxv-xxvi, 5, 25, 59, 66, 80, 92, 97, 103, 105, 112, 118-134, 153, 159, 176, 186, 192-195, 200, 202-203, 205, 211, 214-215
Cần Thơ, 46-47
Canton (Guangzhou), 37
capitalism, 1, 3, 5, 7, 48, 126, 187
capture, 9, 18, 21, 38, 51, 70, 76, 112, 115, 129, 151, 160-162, 173-176, 199, 212
Cardamom Mountains, 84
Cercle Marxiste, xvii, 14, 63
CGDK (Coalition Government of Democratic Kampuchea), 92, 94, 113, 137-138, 150
Chamkar Leu, 73, 188, 217
Chan (Mam Nay), xxi, 66, 75, 132
Chandler, David, 3, 68, 197-199, 206-210, 216, 224
Chavalit Yongjaiyut (Yongchaiyudh), 89, 96-97, 156
checkpoints, 99-100, 161
"chewing," 68
Chhit Choeun, xxiii, 21. *See also* Mok
chhlôp, 41, 193
Chhrang Chamreh, 59-60, 193
children, 11, 18, 21, 23, 31, 37, 41, 55, 67, 76, 116-117, 123, 128, 130, 159, 163, 180, 188, 224
China/Chinese, xvi-xviii, xxii, 1, 6-9, 14-15, 18, 24, 30, 33, 35-36, 38-40, 42, 49, 57, 71, 76, 83-84, 87, 90, 92-94, 111-112, 125, 130, 137, 143, 145-147, 162, 180-183, 185, 188, 197-198, 200-201, 208, 213, 218, 220, 222, 224

Chinese Communist Party, xv, 33, 37, 181, 197
Choam Sangam, 104-105
Choeung Ek, 56, 67
Chou Chet, 43
CIA, 34, 61, 176
civilian, xxi, 25, 41, 91, 112, 115-119, 126-127, 129, 131-133, 149, 160, 162, 169, 188, 214
civil war, xxi, xxvi, 1, 9, 23, 39-40, 42, 62, 71, 100, 105, 107, 162, 181, 191, 193-194, 198
clandestine, xxi, 29, 37, 49, 136, 213
class struggle, vi-vii, xviii-xix, 1, 3-8, 11-12, 17-20, 23-26, 39-46, 49, 52, 59, 61, 63-65, 70, 72-73, 77-78, 82, 87-88, 105, 140, 151-154, 156, 160, 170, 186-187, 191, 219
coalition, xv, ix, 3, 35, 38-39, 52, 54, 63, 88, 92-94, 96, 120, 131, 134, 137, 140, 143, 151, 181, 194. *See also* united front
collectivization, xviii, xxi, 18, 47-51, 55, 58, 73, 99, 105-106, 116, 167
colonialism, vii, 14, 21, 24, 27, 35, 54, 91, 93, 103, 154, 184, 187, 194
communes, xxi, 35, 39, 51, 71, 88, 114-115, 136, 149, 155, 208, 219
communism, xv-xviii, 1, 5-7, 10, 14, 20, 22, 24, 27, 29-31, 33-36, 40, 44, 52, 62, 80, 85, 96, 98, 107, 114, 122, 138, 150, 164, 176, 181, 186, 192, 194, 197-200, 203-204, 210, 216
confessions, ix, xxii, 19-20, 23, 60-62, 66-67, 67, 69, 77, 82, 85-86, 195
cooperatives, xxi, 39, 49, 51, 59, 71, 120-121, 208
corridors, ix, xix, xxiii, 46, 65, 87, 89-90, 97, 101, 105, 109, 113, 131, 141-143, 148, 156, 162-
corruption, 91, 146, 134, 189
CPAF (Cambodian People's Armed Forces), xv, 96
CPK (Communist Party of Kampuchea), xv, xvii-xviii, xxi-xxiii, 1-4, 6-9, 11-12, 15-16, 18-26, 30-45, 47-57, 59, 62, 64-66, 71-73, 77-80, 82-84, 88, 91, 103, 105-106, 114-115, 135-136, 140, 143, 183-186, 188, 193-194, 197, 200, 204, 212, 224

INDEX 243

CPP (Cambodian People's Party), xv, 137, 143, 145, 149–151, 154, 160, 166, 171, 189, 221–222
crime, 2, 12, 14, 58, 116, 123, 126, 176, 190, 199

Dângrêk Mountains, 16, 104, 193–194, 211
death, xx, 11–12, 18, 29, 51–53, 55, 61, 63, 69, 79–80, 85, 88, 154, 174, 176, 178–179, 189–190, 198, 221, 224
defeat, 23, 54, 74, 134
defection, xix, xxii–xxiv, 18, 21, 26, 38, 93, 102, 138, 149, 151, 154, 162–163, 166–169, 171–173, 176, 178, 189, 212–213, 216–222, 224
demobilization, 137, 140–141, 159, 185, 212–213
Democratic Kampuchea, ix, xv–xvi, xviii–xix, xxi–xxiv, xxvi, 1–2, 4, 7–8, 10, 12, 14–15, 18–19, 23, 39, 49, 55–78, 80, 83–88, 92–94, 100, 103, 106–108, 111–112, 120–121, 125, 132–133, 137–139, 146, 154, 163, 183–185, 189, 193–195, 206–207, 211–213, 216–219, 222, 224
demonstrations, 54, 79, 144–145
Deng Xiaoping, 83
denunciations, 53, 56, 139, 176
detentions, 40–41, 59, 75, 178–179, 206, 223
Dien Del, 93
disbursements, 102, 149
displacement, 54, 30, 52, 133, 214
divisions (military), xix, xxiii–xxiv, 19, 23, 40, 64, 67, 71–72, 75, 86, 89, 93, 100–102, 110, 116–117, 128, 132, 135, 140–142, 146, 149, 153, 155–156, 159–161, 163–169, 171, 175, 203, 209–210, 212, 216–221, 224
DNUM (Democratic National Union Movement), 168, 198, 220
Duch (Kaing Guek-Eav), xxi, 19, 40–41, 65–68, 101, 190, 199, 201–202, 205–209, 216

ECCC (Extraordinary Chambers in the Courts of Cambodia), xi, xv, xx, xxvi, 12, 82, 179, 190, 197–209, 214, 216, 223–225
economy, 8, 31–32, 48–51, 53, 55–56, 58, 69–71, 73, 110, 116, 119, 126, 132, 136–137, 139–140, 145–146, 156–157, 167, 180–182, 184, 187–188, 191, 206, 218–219
education, 19, 21, 28, 31, 56, 59, 63, 91, 101–102, 113, 115–116, 124, 129, 131, 157, 216
elections, xvi, xix, xxiii, 24, 26, 91–92, 99, 124, 134, 135–137, 140, 143–145, 147–151, 154, 162–163, 186
Engels, Friedrich, 7, 197
escalation, 19, 39, 53, 144, 169, 172, 175
escape, xvii, 2–3, 28–30, 41–42, 54, 74, 76, 99, 103, 107, 144, 159–161, 163, 166, 170, 174, 189, 206, 214
evacuation, 57–58, 69, 73, 83, 122, 129, 143, 166, 194, 214
executions, xix–xxiv, 2, 15, 18–19, 40, 41, 43–44, 52–53, 55–56, 59, 61, 66, 69, 72–73, 76, 106, 116, 135, 153, 160–62, 166, 169, 173, 179, 195, 199, 212, 214–216, 220, 222–224
exile, 8, 33, 36, 48, 80, 83, 92, 130, 137, 170
expulsions, 4, 6, 43–44, 48, 52, 54–55, 83
extrajudicial killing, 48, 154, 160

factions, xix, 15, 38–39, 97, 123, 137–138, 141, 143, 167, 194, 198, 215–216
factories, 72, 86, 131
FANK (Forces Armées Nationales Khmères), xv, 48, 54–55, 93
FCP (French Communist Party), 14
food, xii, 15, 29, 36, 49–51, 60, 75, 84–85, 91, 98, 104–106, 111–112, 116, 118, 125, 128, 134, 149, 153, 159, 164, 168, 184, 188, 197, 207
France, xvii, 1, 14, 21–22, 28–29, 35–36, 38, 42, 44, 56, 60, 62–64, 92, 130–131, 154, 160, 206, 214
FUNCINPEC (Front Uni National pour un Cambodge Indépendant, Neutre, Pacifique et Coopératif), xv, xviii–xix, xxiii, 91–92, 94, 96, 108, 118–121, 124–125, 137, 143, 145, 150–151, 159–160, 170–171, 173, 186, 189, 195, 211
FUNK (Front Uni National du Kampuchéa), xv, xvii, xxiii, 27, 35–38, 48, 52–54, 59, 135–136

gemstones, 98, 126, 146–147, 157, 166, 168, 194, 224
Geneva Conference/Accords, xvii, 22, 24, 42

INDEX

genocide, 58, 128, 150–151, 190, 222
governance, xxi, 3–4, 9–11, 20–21, 30, 48, 55, 66, 78, 87, 90, 103, 105, 117, 122, 127, 130–131, 133, 136, 149, 156, 163, 180–181, 183, 187
governments, xv–xvi, 6, 15, 29, 32, 35, 37, 45–46, 53, 58, 85, 92–94, 106, 115, 137, 143, 146, 151, 159–160, 165–166, 168, 170–172, 181, 185, 188–190, 193–195, 216, 221
Gromyko, Andrei, 9
GRUNK (Gouvernement Royal d'Union Nationale du Kampuchéa), xv, xvii–xviii, xxi, 35–39, 42, 52–53, 59, 61, 63, 143
Guangzhou (Canton), 37
guerrillas, 2, 29, 31, 80, 84, 101, 103–105, 107, 112, 118, 141, 149, 194

Hanoi, xix, xxii, 27, 33, 37, 44, 90, 137
Harben, William, 45, 203
harvest, 47, 53, 70, 74, 112, 184
headquarters, ix, 16, 24, 30, 49, 75, 84, 88–89, 97, 99–100, 102, 113, 151, 156, 165, 194, 208
health, 20, 100, 116–118, 131, 186
Heder, Steve, v, xi, xiii, xxv–xxvi, 10, 15, 34, 54, 61, 63–65, 69–73, 87, 91, 127, 135, 138, 142, 148–149, 152, 155, 197–206, 208–213, 215–225
Heng Samrin, 93
Ho Chi Minh, 33, 39
hospitals, 21, 71, 111–112, 122, 131, 168
hostages, 160–162
Howes, Christopher, 161–162
Hu Nim, xxi, 39, 42, 53, 62, 79, 83
Hun Sen, xix, xxii, 12, 96, 137, 143–144, 149, 154, 166–168, 170–172, 176, 189–190, 211, 224

ICP (Indochinese Communist Party), xv, 30
ICRC (International Committee of the Red Cross), 122, 128
ideology, 4, 9, 18, 21, 24, 38–39, 41, 48, 54, 64, 91, 116–117, 132, 139, 150, 156, 167, 182, 187, 189, 206
Ieng Sary, ix, xv, xvii–xx, xxii–xxiv, 2, 8–9, 11–16, 18–22, 24–29, 31, 36–42, 44, 56–64, 75–77, 79–80, 82–87, 91–93, 97, 103, 105, 125–126, 129–133, 136–137, 142, 145–148, 151, 154, 163–164, 166–168, 171–172, 183–190, 192, 194–195, 197–199, 201, 204–207, 215–216, 218, 220–222
Ieng Thirith, xx, xxii, 12–14, 37, 41, 62, 82–83, 131, 183, 190, 198, 207, 224
imperialism, 35, 181
imprisonment, xx, 52, 116, 133, 172, 224
income, 146–147, 218
incursion, ix, 33–34, 89, 96
Indochina, xvii, 24, 30, 33, 40, 44
indoctrination, 51, 116, 139
industry, 21, 50, 74, 157, 184, 206
infighting, 136, 162, 181
injuries, 111, 118, 124, 131, 175
insurgency, 3–4, 6, 8–9, 21, 25, 28, 35–36, 52, 80, 98, 105, 149, 167
integration, 131, 167, 221
intellectuals, xxii, 8–10, 15, 28, 36, 42–43, 55–56, 59–61, 63, 65, 70, 73, 77, 82–83, 85, 131, 139, 176, 183, 185, 216, 222
intelligence, 38, 55, 98, 110, 115, 159, 172
interrogate, 40–41, 66–68, 116, 133, 161
invasion, xviii, xxii, 2, 25, 27, 28, 66, 77, 80, 83, 86–88, 90, 99, 103, 111, 119, 134, 137, 143, 181
Issarak, xxiii, 22, 25, 194

Jaraï, 30–31, 40, 170, 193, 200
journalists, xii, xxv, 24, 38, 86, 128, 130, 144, 152, 161, 175, 223
jungle, 19, 25, 28, 32, 55, 83–84, 99, 104, 110–111, 113, 122, 124, 130, 199–201, 207, 210, 223

Kampong Cham, 36, 38, 43, 68, 75, 108, 113, 163, 187, 217
Kampong Chhnang, 22, 41–43, 68, 76, 108, 113, 120–121, 126, 204, 208
Kampong Som (Preah Sihanouk/Sihanoukville), xxii, 33, 43, 68, 72, 89, 108, 113, 160, 185, 202, 204, 208
Kampong Speu, 70, 88, 108, 113, 218
Kampong Thom, 96, 108, 113, 120–121, 136, 150, 163, 204, 217
Kampot, 42–43, 53, 68, 70, 72, 74, 108, 113, 142, 161, 212–213
Kandal, 17, 43, 68, 70, 74, 113, 195, 217
Kang Maozhao, 36

INDEX

Kbal Tonsaong, ix, 16, 18, 169–170, 173, 175–176, 194, 199
Kè Pauk, xxii, 14, 23, 29, 64–65, 73–76, 86–87, 189, 194, 199, 202, 207–208, 210
KGB, 61
Khao I Dang, 120–121, 194
Khieu Ponnary, 14, 62, 147
Khieu Samphân, xii, xix, xxii, 10–11, 16, 39, 42, 62, 79, 84, 91–93, 99, 143–146, 148, 171–172, 174–176, 190, 198, 201, 206, 211, 218
Khmer Hanoi, xviii, 35, 54
Khmer Republic, xv, xvii, 35–36, 38, 45, 48, 52, 54–55, 80, 91, 93, 109, 124
Khmer Rouge, iii, ix, xi, xv, xx, xxii, xxv–xxvi, 1–7, 9–19, 21, 23–25, 27–33, 35, 37–40, 45–49, 52, 54–59, 62–64, 66, 69, 73, 78, 81, 83–85, 87–94, 96–100, 103–109, 111, 114, 116, 118–154, 156–163, 167–176, 182–183, 185–187, 189–195, 199–201, 203–205, 207–208, 210–212, 214–216, 218–222, 224–225
Khmer Rumdas/Rumdoh, 35, 52–53, 194
Khmer Students' Association (AEK), xv, 24
kidnapping, 44, 46, 160–161, 220
Kiernan, Ben, 32, 198–200, 202, 206, 208, 224
killing, xix, 2, 18–19, 32, 46, 48, 53, 55–56, 61–62, 66–67, 73–76, 79, 102, 110, 116, 118, 124, 126, 135, 143, 152, 154, 159–162, 164, 169, 172–175, 192, 197, 206, 223, 225
Koh Kong, 43, 68, 70, 108, 113, 126, 195, 216
Korea, 15, 38, 144, 181, 204, 224
Koy Thuon, xxii, 14, 29, 43, 73–74
KPNLF (Khmer People's National Liberation Front), xviii–xix, xxiii, 91–92, 94, 96–97, 108, 116, 118–125, 134, 137, 145, 150, 171, 186, 192, 195, 213
KPRAF (Kampuchean People's Revolutionary Armed Forces), 96
KPRP (Kampuchean People's Revolutionary Party), 136–137, 149
Krang Leav airfield, 76, 185
Kratie, 37, 43, 51, 68, 108, 113, 163, 208, 217
Kuong Lumphon, 27, 35, 200, 216

labor, 50, 62, 167, 184–185
land, 17, 20, 45, 50, 70, 74, 101, 105, 119, 122, 130–131, 141, 149, 169, 184, 190–191, 225
landlord, 85, 124
land mines, 17, 20, 100, 131, 161, 169, 190–191, 100, 225
Lane, Dennison, xii, xxv, 34, 125, 211, 214–216
Lao/Laos, 30, 60, 68, 80, 87, 89, 108, 113, 120–121, 142, 159–160, 220, 222
legitimacy, 3, 6, 8, 18, 30, 39, 80, 83, 85, 96, 103, 119, 138, 153, 180–181, 184–186
Lenin, Vladimir, 7, 57, 59, 106, 181, 187
liberation, xvi, xviii, 1, 4, 29, 35, 38–39, 47, 50, 83–84, 91–92, 94, 101, 120–121, 136, 149, 156, 183, 193–194, 211, 213
Lin Biao, 9
logistics, 98, 103, 105, 110, 112, 118, 188, 128, 134
Lon Nol, xvii, 33–36, 45, 47–48, 52, 79, 91, 124, 150, 187
Lycée Sisowath, 14, 28

Malai, ix, 84, 127–131, 146, 163, 165–167, 171–172, 194, 198, 213, 215, 218, 220–221, 224
malaria, 27, 42, 52, 79–80, 99, 123, 127, 161
Mao Zedong, ix, xviii, 8–9, 14, 32, 118, 173, 181–183, 187, 197, 200, 212, 215, 217–218, 222
maquis, ix, xvii, 19, 22, 25–26, 28, 30, 40, 42, 55, 65, 79–80, 103, 139–140, 144, 151, 170, 202
markets, 45, 49, 65, 69, 71, 104, 128–130, 157, 163, 180, 199, 208
marriage, 2, 9, 14, 23, 59, 62, 72, 94, 111, 147, 129, 132, 147
Marx, Karl, 7, 171, 187, 197
Marxism, 1, 64, 171, 181, 183, 187, 197
Marxist, 1, 4–5, 7, 9, 28–29, 31, 35, 56, 106, 181–183, 185,
Meas (Khe) Muth (Meas Mut), xxii, 23, 71–72, 87, 89, 171–172, 190, 208, 224
medical, 37, 50–51, 99, 110–111, 117–118, 126–127
Mekong, 47, 68, 72, 113, 120–121

INDEX

military, ix, xv, xviii, xxiii, 14–15, 19–21, 23, 25, 29, 32–35, 37, 40–41, 46, 48–49, 54, 58, 63–64, 68, 70, 74–75, 77, 83, 87, 89–94, 96, 98–103, 105, 107, 109–110, 113–117, 119–134, 136–137, 141–142, 148–150, 156, 161, 163, 165, 169–176, 185–186, 188, 190–191, 193, 197, 203, 208, 211, 213, 217, 219, 223
militias, 22, 42, 115, 156, 193
mining (excavating), 146–147, 194
ministers, xviii–xix, xxi–xxii, xxiv, 2, 12, 14, 19, 25, 37, 39, 53, 57, 59, 61, 73, 79, 83, 86, 137, 145–146, 149, 154, 171, 176, 189, 207, 211
ministries, xviii, xxii, 9, 15, 37, 39, 57–61, 63–64, 76, 80, 82–84, 86, 130, 132, 146, 181, 188–189, 193, 198, 204, 206, 218, 223
minorities, 21, 31, 40, 43, 52, 76, 123, 193
Mok (Ta Mok), ix, xvii–xx, xxii–xxiii, 3, 9, 11–12, 14, 16–26, 28–29, 39–44, 46, 48, 53, 57, 61–67, 69–77, 80, 87–91, 97, 102–103, 105, 107–110, 113, 116–118, 126, 128, 131, 136, 138, 140–143, 147–148, 151–154, 156–157, 159, 161, 163–166, 170–179, 184–187, 189, 192–193, 195, 198–199, 202, 207–208, 210, 214, 217, 219–220, 222, 224
Mondulkiri, 30, 37, 40, 43, 53, 68, 108, 113, 159, 163, 194, 200–201, 203–204, 208, 212–214, 217, 219
money, 1, 24, 51, 64, 90, 98, 102–103, 106, 112, 146, 157
Moscow, xviii, 35, 90
MOULINAKA (Movement for the National Liberation of Kampuchea [Mouvement pour la Libération Nationale du Kampuchéa]), xvi, 92, 119, 124, 211
murder, 2, 46, 86, 160, 162, 166

NADK (National Army of Democratic Kampuchea), ix, xvi, xxiii–xxiv, xxvi, 87, 96, 101–102, 108–110, 112–116, 118–119, 128, 131–132, 134–135, 137, 140–143, 146, 148–151, 157, 162–163, 166–167, 172, 210, 212–213, 217, 219–220
navy, xxii, 72, 75, 88–89, 172, 200, 202–203, 224
NCR (non-communist resistance), xvi, 80, 114, 122–125

negotiations, xxiii–xxiv, 24, 44, 54, 73, 93, 137, 157, 160–162, 166–168, 172–174
Ney Saran, xxii, 40, 67, 73, 197
nôkôrôbal, 40, 194
Norn (Nuon) Suon, xxii, 77–78, 82, 85, 209–210
Norodom Ranariddh. See Ranariddh
Norodom Sihanouk. See Sihanouk
Nuon Chea, xix–xx, xxii–xxiii, 11, 15–16, 19–21, 23, 27, 42–43, 49, 58–59, 61–64, 66–68, 74–77, 82–84, 87, 89, 99, 101, 105, 140–142, 163, 165–167, 170–174, 176, 179–180, 187, 190, 192, 199–200, 202, 207–208, 218, 223
Ny Kân (Kan), xxiii, 58, 84, 86–87, 125, 132–133, 142, 147, 164, 166, 171–172, 216

O'Bok, 97, 120–121
O'Trao, 121, 126–128, 194, 214–215
Oddar Meanchey, 43, 68, 87, 108, 113, 124, 128, 150, 193, 198, 208, 220–221
offensives, xix, 63, 99, 113–114, 122, 125, 129, 142, 189
ordnance, 17, 44, 123, 190
orthodoxy, 5, 15, 18, 59, 72, 82, 105, 131, 133, 147, 157, 167, 183, 185
overthrow, 3, 33, 35, 55, 59, 91

Pailin, 82, 84, 96, 99, 101–102, 113, 121, 128–131, 137, 142, 146–147, 163–167, 171–172, 179, 190, 192, 194, 199, 202, 212–214, 220, 222–223
Paris, xvii, xix, 14, 18–19, 24, 62–64, 77, 136–137, 140–141, 143, 148–150, 167, 205–206
PAVN (People's Army of Vietnam), xvi, 96–97, 113
PDK (Party of Democratic Kampuchea), xvi, xviii–xix, xxi–xxiv, 7, 10, 12, 18, 26, 44, 80, 85, 89–91, 93–94, 96–99, 101, 103, 105–106, 112–116, 122, 128–131, 134–151, 154, 156–157, 159, 162–164, 168, 171, 183, 185–186, 210, 212, 215, 217–219
peasants, 7–8, 16, 21, 31–32, 34, 47, 49–52, 54, 70–71, 73, 85, 88, 112, 115–116, 118, 131, 159, 165, 181, 184, 186, 191, 193–194, 200, 210

INDEX

Phi (Phy) Phuon, 20, 31, 36, 57, 67, 84, 88, 104, 198, 200–201, 205, 207, 220
Phnom Kulen, 39, 105, 194
Phnom Malai, ix, 84, 127–129, 171, 198, 213,
Phnom Penh, xi, xviii–xix, 1, 3–4, 6–7, 12, 14, 19, 23, 25, 28–30, 32, 36, 41, 43, 45, 55, 57–59, 63, 68, 70, 72–76, 79–80, 83, 88–89, 98, 103, 108–109, 113, 120–121, 124, 137, 143–145, 159–161, 178, 180, 189, 195, 199, 204–205, 208, 212, 215, 217–218, 220–223
Pochentong Airport, 62, 72, 223
Poipet, 83–84, 97, 155
police, 32, 41–42, 97–98, 100, 133, 141, 144, 146, 149, 169, 194–195
Pol Pot, ix, xvii–xxiii, 2–4, 6–12, 14–21, 24–25, 27, 29–31, 36–40, 42–43, 49, 57–59, 61–64, 72–73, 75–77, 79, 82, 84, 86–90, 92, 97, 99–102, 104–106, 111, 116, 118, 131, 135–136, 140–149, 151, 153, 156–157, 161–177, 179, 183, 186–189, 192, 197–202, 204–206, 208–209, 211–213, 216, 218–220, 224,
porters, ix, 44, 111, 128, 164
Potemkin village, xix, 85, 126
Preah Vihear, 43, 68, 87, 99, 108, 113, 128, 152, 160–161, 163, 167, 194, 208, 217, 219
Prey Veng, 14, 43, 47, 68, 108
prison, xviii, 19, 38, 40–41, 52–53, 62, 67–68, 76, 86, 161, 176, 204
PRK (People's Republic of Kampuchea), xv–xvi, xviii, 6, 93, 96, 108, 116, 137, 140, 150, 194, 215, 225
propaganda, xxi, xxiv, 15, 31, 50, 52–54, 57–58, 83, 100, 110, 155–116, 125, 139, 219
property, 1, 7, 159, 165–167, 183–184
prosecution, 190, 198–199, 201, 205–206, 224
provinces, xvii, 2, 21–22, 29–30, 37, 40–43, 47, 53, 68, 70, 74, 76, 84, 87, 89, 109, 113, 124, 126, 128–129, 136, 154, 159, 161, 163, 176, 190, 193–195, 198, 212–213, 217–221
punji sticks/stakes, 36, 100, 104, 118, 155, 164
purges, xviii, xxii, 6, 8, 11, 19, 23, 39, 51, 53–54, 59–61, 63, 65–66, 68–69, 71, 74–76, 83, 86, 144, 154, 160, 185, 189, 193–194, 198, 200–201, 203–205, 208, 224
Pursat, 43, 68, 108, 113, 120–121, 126, 199, 204, 210, 221
Pyongyang, 85, 92, 99

quarantine, 83
Quinn, Kenneth, xii, 46–49, 52, 88, 203–204, 216,

RAK (Revolutionary Army of Kampuchea), xvi, 19, 64, 197
Ranariddh, xix, xxiii, 92, 154, 167, 170–173, 176
Ratanakiri, 30–31, 36–37, 40, 42–43, 68, 103–104, 108, 113, 159, 163, 187, 194, 217
RCAF (Royal Cambodian Air Force), 166, 189, 221
reeducation, 15, 38–39, 55, 59–61, 66, 106, 115, 126, 142, 156, 205–206
refugees, ix, xvi, xviii–xix, xxv–xxvi, 25, 49–50, 54, 80, 97, 99, 103, 105, 118–123, 124, 128–130, 134, 176, 186, 193–195, 198–200, 202–205, 208, 210, 213–214
resistance, xvi, 6, 22, 38, 48, 75, 80, 87, 89, 92, 96, 113–114, 119–123, 138, 153, 179, 182, 190–191, 210–211
revenue, 23, 146, 151, 156
revolution, 1, 4, 5, 8, 14–15, 28, 30–32, 34, 39, 53, 55–56, 58–59, 61–63, 65, 77, 85, 180–182, 185, 188, 197–198, 221
RGC (Royal Government of Cambodia), xvi, 170–174, 178
rice, 29, 32, 47, 49, 51, 70, 74, 88, 101, 106, 112, 115, 157, 159, 184
rights, 43, 94, 122–123, 222, 224
Roobaert, Nathalie, 160–161
Ros Nhim, xxii, 14, 22, 29, 32, 43, 73, 194, 200
Royalist, xv, xviii–xix, 6, 35, 52–53, 94, 96–97, 194
RTA (Royal Thai Army), xvi, 89, 97–98, 102, 125
rubies, 126, 146, 218
Russia, 1, 5, 35, 180–181

Saloth Sâr. *See* Pol Pot
Samlaut, xvii, 32, 42, 146, 166, 171–172, 184, 187, 194, 200

Sangkum Reastr Niyum, xvii, 30, 144, 200
sàntĭbal, 195
sàntĭsok, 195
scorched earth, vii, xix, xxiii–xxiv, 8, 46, 48, 152, 154, 157
secrecy, 10, 34, 38, 41, 61, 67, 74, 96, 98, 100, 125, 135, 139, 166, 179, 194–195
security, xxiii, 19, 25, 38, 40–41, 45, 49, 56, 61–62, 65–66, 75–76, 83, 86, 90, 97, 99–100, 116, 119, 123–124, 128, 133, 136–137, 144, 151, 179–180, 189, 195
Siem Reap, xiii, 43, 68, 73, 79, 90, 108, 113, 120–121, 124, 128, 148–150, 161, 163, 199, 204, 208–209, 212, 215, 217–221
Sihanouk, xvii, xix, xxiii, 6, 19, 24–25, 28–30, 32–39, 42, 52–53, 63, 79–80, 82, 91–92, 137, 143, 154–155, 167–168, 171, 194, 200
Sihanoukist(e), xv, 35, 52–55, 59, 92, 94, 122, 211
Sihanoukville, 33, 208, 212
Slator, Mark, 160–161
"smash," 41, 55, 166, 176, 184
So Phim, xxi, xxiii, 14, 19, 22, 43, 62–64, 69–70, 73–76, 86–87, 189, 193, 208
So Saroeun, xxiii, 17, 86–87, 142, 156, 161, 169, 173–176, 189, 222
SoC (State of Cambodia), xvi, xviii, 96, 140, 145, 149, 155, 186
socialism, vii, 5, 9, 59, 85, 93, 106, 179–183, 185, 187, 189, 191
Sok Sann, 97, 120–123, 195
Son Sann, xxiii, 92–93, 195, 211
Son Sen, ix, xii, xvii–xix, xxi, xxiii–xxiv, 3, 9, 11–12, 14, 16–21, 23, 25–26, 28–29, 36–37, 39–42, 44, 57, 59, 61–69, 73–77, 79–80, 83, 85–89, 91, 96, 99, 101–105, 107–110, 113, 116, 118, 122, 125, 128, 131–133, 136, 140–145, 147–148, 151–152, 154, 159, 163–166, 170–176, 179, 184–187, 192–193, 198, 200–201, 204, 207, 210–211, 224
Sou Met, 87–88, 189–190
Soviet, xviii–xix, 7, 36, 38, 59, 90, 139, 180–182
stabbing, 123, 131, 161, 191
stalemate, 165, 181
Stalin, Joseph, 7, 181, 223
starvation, 2, 10, 104–105, 184, 222

Steung Trâng (Stung Treng), 37, 40, 43, 53, 73, 159, 163, 188, 217
students, xv, 14, 19, 24, 60, 63, 77, 79, 100, 131–139, 183, 187
suffering, xi, 13, 23, 70, 77, 85, 99, 118, 123–124, 137, 140, 147, 161, 198
suicide, xxiii, 23, 73, 123
Suong Sikoeun, 38, 57, 61, 152, 201, 204–205, 207, 220
surrender, xxiii, 168, 170, 174
Svay Rieng, 43, 76, 108, 113, 204

Ta Khmau, 60, 88, 195
Ta Luan, 120–121, 126–127, 195
Ta Mok. *See* Mok
Takeo, xvii, 21–22, 29, 42–44, 68, 70–71, 73–74, 108, 113, 136, 142
tanks, 75, 124, 166
taxes, 98, 126, 146
telegraph/telegram, 37, 88, 165–166
temples, 18, 132, 152, 160–161, 164, 194
territory, 2–3, 23, 25, 31, 36, 44, 53–54, 76, 78, 83, 87, 89, 109, 119, 130, 143, 150, 163, 166, 171
terror, 51, 68, 116, 156, 199, 202, 204, 206–208, 210
TF (Task Force) 838, 96–99, 124–125, 134
Thai, xi–xii, xvi, xviii, xxv, 3, 21, 25, 80, 83–84, 89, 91–92, 94, 96–103, 105, 109, 112–113, 118–119, 122–123, 126, 128–131, 134, 141, 143, 146, 152–153, 156–157, 160, 163, 166, 170–171, 174–176, 179, 186, 193–194, 198–200, 202–204, 210–215
Thailand, 23, 43, 64, 68, 83, 87, 89, 96, 98–99, 101–102, 108–109, 111–113, 118–121, 124, 129, 134, 143–144, 165–166, 168–169, 175–176, 193, 212
Thayer, Nate, 24, 57, 133, 175–176, 199, 202, 204, 208, 210, 212, 218, 220–222
theft, 52, 58, 67, 102, 123, 159, 223
Thion, Serge, 86, 143, 210–211, 218
Thiounn Prasith, 43, 57, 61, 82, 205
timber, 21, 23, 36, 64, 98, 146–147, 156–157, 165, 168, 174
Tonlé Sap, 42, 68, 108, 113, 120–121, 159
torture, xxiii, 15, 19, 41, 44, 56, 59–62, 66–69, 73, 77, 79, 85, 135, 195, 224

INDEX 249

Tou Samouth, 79
trade, 5, 23, 51, 64, 98, 115, 126, 128, 130, 146–147, 157, 163–164, 166, 169, 174, 187, 224
traitors, 61, 66, 74, 76, 86, 160, 167, 212, 221
treason, 5, 73, 116
trials, xx, 14, 21, 58, 83, 104, 175, 190, 206, 222, 224
Trotsky, 1, 5, 197
Tuol Sleng, xviii, xxi, 19, 40, 56, 66–67, 77, 85, 101, 133, 135, 195

UNBRO (United Nations Border Relief Operation), xvi, 122–124, 127–128
UNCOHCHR (United Nations Cambodia Office of the High Commissioner for Human Rights), 198, 215–216, 218, 220–221
UNHCR (United Nations High Commissioner for Refugees), xvi, 119–121, 194
united front, ix, xv–xix, xxiii, 1, 3–6, 11–12, 14, 18, 20, 24–27, 33, 35–44, 48, 52–53, 55–57, 59, 61, 63, 79–82, 84, 88, 90–91, 93–96, 103, 105, 114, 116, 118, 120–121, 128, 130, 133, 136–137, 139–140, 146–147, 151, 154, 167, 186–187, 197, 210
United Nations, 93, 119–122, 128, 137, 149, 151, 154, 173, 219
United States, 23, 33–34, 45, 47, 54, 90, 181
UNTAC (United Nations Transitional Authority in Cambodia), xii, xvi, xix, xxiii, xxv, 92, 99, 134, 136–137, 140–141, 143, 147–151, 153–154, 212–213, 215, 217–220
USAID (US Agency for International Development), 46
USSR. *See* Soviet

Van. *See* Ieng Sary
veterans, 17, 65, 83, 111, 114, 128, 148, 170–171, 189
Vickery, Michael, 88, 203, 210
victims, 11, 24, 31, 61, 65–67, 85, 145, 162, 185, 187
victory, xix, 8, 23, 39, 55, 77, 86, 92, 96, 113, 137, 140, 150, 171, 179–180, 182, 184, 186
Vietminh, 21

Vietnam, xvi, xviii–xix, xxii, 6, 14, 18–19, 22, 25, 29–30, 33–34, 38, 40, 46, 49, 54, 68, 70, 73–74, 80, 83, 86, 89–90, 93, 96, 108–109, 113, 116, 134, 137, 142, 189, 193–194, 200
Vietnamese, xvi, xviii–xix, xxii–xxiii, 2–4, 6–7, 25, 27, 29–31, 33–37, 39, 44–45, 47–48, 54–55, 60–61, 66, 68, 73–75, 77, 80, 83–84, 86–89, 92, 99, 103, 106, 108–109, 111–112, 114–116, 118–125, 130, 132–134, 137, 139, 142–143, 149–150, 159, 162, 186, 191, 195, 199–200, 211, 213, 216, 225
villagers, ix, 41, 47, 53, 101, 112, 114–117, 149, 165, 191
villages, xix, 16, 18–19, 21, 30–31, 35, 37, 40–41, 44, 49–51, 53, 65, 71, 76, 85, 88, 101, 114–118, 126, 132, 136, 149, 156, 160, 165, 175, 179, 190–191, 194, 198, 202, 204, 206, 208, 213, 219–221
violence, 1, 4, 7, 11–12, 18, 24, 26, 32, 34, 45–46, 51–52, 56, 64, 123, 138, 140, 144, 148, 153, 159, 187, 198, 214
Vorn Vet (Von Veth), xxi–xxiii, 14, 40–41, 44, 61–62, 86, 208
voting, 33, 117, 119, 150–151
VWP (Vietnamese Workers' Party), xvi, 34

war, xxi, xxvi, 1, 12, 21, 23, 33, 39–40, 42, 47–48, 51, 55, 62, 71, 86, 90, 96, 100, 102–105, 107–108, 110, 114, 118, 123, 125, 131, 135, 137, 141, 147–150, 157, 162, 176, 181, 186, 193–194, 197–200, 207–211, 214
warehouses, 67, 98–99, 219
Washington, DC, xiii, xxv, 33, 45, 54, 128, 137, 198, 204, 214–215, 220
weapons, 2, 96, 109, 114, 116, 118, 125, 133, 156, 159
workers, xvi–xviii, 5–6, 30, 34, 76, 85, 124, 131, 160, 185, 225

Y Chhean, xxiv, 84, 142, 146, 164–168, 171–172, 189, 220, 224
Ya (Ney Saran), xxii, 40, 67, 73, 197
Yun Yat, xxi, xxiv, 17–18, 41, 61, 64, 67, 83, 174, 207
Yung Moeun, 187–189, 224
Yuon, xxi, 35, 76, 112, 133, 195

INDEX

Zhou Enlai, 9
Zhukov, Gyorgi, 9
Zones
  Central Zone, 73, 68, 224
  Eastern Zone, xxii–xxiii, 19, 22–23, 65,
    68–70, 74–76, 86–87, 149, 185, 189,
    208, 210
  Northeast Zone, xvii, 22, 37, 67–68, 73
  Northern Zone, xxii, 53, 68, 73–74,
    157, 188, 224
  Northwest Zone, xxii, 32, 40, 68,
    191, 224
  Southwest Zone, xviii, xxiii, 40, 42–44,
    53, 61, 66, 68–71, 73–74, 76, 88,
    206, 208
  Western Zone, 68, 74

www.ingramcontent.com/pod-product-compliance
Lightning Source LLC
Chambersburg PA
CBHW021852230426
43671CB00006B/359